D1528810

THE KGB
AGAINST THE
"MAIN ENEMY"

The KGB
Against the
"Main Enemy"

How the Soviet Intelligence Service
Operates against the United States

by

HERBERT ROMERSTEIN

STANISLAV LEVCHENKO

Lexington Books

D.C. Heath and Company · Lexington, Massachusetts · Toronto

Library of Congress Cataloging-in-Publication Data

Romerstein, Herbert.
The KGB against the "main enemy".

Includes index.
1. Espionage, Russian—United States—History—
20th century.   2. Soviet Union. Komitet gosudarstvennoĭ
bezopasnosti—History.   I. Levchenko, Stan.   II. Title.
UB271.R9R66   1989   327.1'2'0947   88–27358
ISBN 0–669–11228–3 (alk. paper)

Published simultaneously in Canada
Printed in the United States of America
International Standard Book Number: 0–669–11228–3
Library of Congress Catalog Card Number: 88–27358

The paper used in this publication meets
the minimum requirements of American National Standard
for Information Sciences—Permanence of Paper
for Printed Library Materials, ANSI Z39.48–1984.

Year and number of printing:
89 90 91 92 8 7 6 5 4 3 2 1

Contents

Acknowledgments

T HIS book is dedicated to Pat Romerstein, who not only did the
hard work of typing the manuscript but also provided the in-
spiration that made it possible.

The authors would also like to thank Dewitt Copp, Lawrence
Cott, Henry Durkin, John Dziak, Paul Joyal, Todd Leventhal, Ruth
Matthews, Raymond Rocca, and Michael Steinbeck, who provided
valuable advice and material. Any conclusions in this book are, of
course, the responsibility of the authors.

Introduction

T HE Soviet Intelligence Service has always considered the United States its ultimate *glavnyy vrag* (the main enemy). Even when the fledgling Soviet Union was encircled by its European enemies and the United States was a sleeping giant, Lenin considered the U.S. his eventual target.[1]

The Soviet Party/state rests on two foundations: the army and the intelligence service. But it is significant to note that the intelligence service was established first, in a decree dated December 20, 1917. The Red Army was established on January 28, 1918.[2] In 1957, then KGB head, Ivan Serov, pointed out that "the state security organs . . . are an armed detachment of the Communist Party of the Soviet Union."[3]

The KGB role today, in the era of *glasnost*, is more important than ever before. The Soviets want to use "political" rather than military methods to achieve their goals, according to Foreign Minister Edward Shevardnadze.[4] Intelligence collection, to understand the enemy, and "active measures," to influence the enemy's actions, are the responsibility of the KGB.

The KGB did not grow "full blown from the brow of Jove." It has been carefully built over seven decades. An understanding of this development will enable us to respond to the threat today. During the last few years the Soviet Union has revealed much that was hidden in its society. Even the KGB has had some of its secrets revealed. We have taken advantage of the recent revelations to reevaluate our understanding of the KGB. This book is the product of that reevaluation.

The Soviet Intelligence Service has been the cutting edge of operations against the main enemy. While in the early years the primary concern of the Soviets was defense against its hostile neighbors, since the end of World War II the main thrust of Soviet activities, overt and covert, has been against the United States.

The Soviet Intelligence Service has had many names. Today's KGB was yesterday's Cheka, GPU, OGPU, NKVD, MGB, and MVD. The Soviet Military Intelligence Service, now called the GRU, was once the Fourth Bureau of the general staff of the Red Army. The political action arm of the Soviet Communist Party, the International Department, has replaced the Communist International, or Comintern. The methods, however, remain the same. Recent cases bear a remarkable resemblance to cases over a half-century old.

In the seven decades since the November 1917 Bolshevik Revolution, the Soviet Union has evolved from a poor, backward country into a poor, backward country that is a major military and political power. The Soviet Intelligence Service has played an important role in that evolution.

The technology needed by the Soviet military to match, and even in some areas to surpass, the West, was provided in large part by Soviet intelligence. The substantial influence of the Soviet Union in the world is, in part, due to intelligence activities coordinated with other Soviet entities.

Operations against the main enemy range from classical espionage to active measures (influence operations). Some of these activities are coordinated with other elements of the Soviet apparatus. The KGB and GRU collaborate in classical espionage, technology transfer, and theft of military secrets. The KGB and the International Department collaborate in active measures. The KGB prepares forgeries and directs agents of influence, while the International Department directs the activities of communist parties and international Soviet fronts. All are carefully coordinated to influence specific targets.

In this book we tell the story of the development of what is now a highly skillful and coordinated apparatus. The current sophistication and coordination did not always exist. Methods and procedures were created as they were needed. Some activities that began under other parts of the apparatus fell under the jurisdiction of the intelligence service later.

A wide variety of people have served as officers, agents, and assets of the Soviet Intelligence Service. They have ranged from ideologues to mercenaries, from sensitive idealists to thugs. In Soviet intelligence operations against the United States there were brilliant, idealistic officers, willing to sacrifice everything for the Soviet cause, who ultimately fell victim to Stalin's purges. On the other hand, there were clumsy, stupid operatives who succeeded only in alerting American counterintelligence to their agents. Among the agents there were traitors willing to sell their country's secrets for a few dollars, and idealistic dupes who were embarrassed when their Soviet handlers presented them with gifts.

The Soviet Intelligence Service was shaped by its founder, Felix Dzerzhinsky, son of a well-to-do Polish family, who was appointed by Lenin to head the Cheka (the first Soviet secret police and intelligence service) on December 10, 1917. "Felix Edmundovich Dzerzhinsky, a prominent Party leader, and staunch Leninist who had gone through the grim school of underground activity, czarist jails, and penal servitude, a man infinitely devoted to the Revolution and ruthless toward its enemies." So said Yuri Andropov, then head of KGB, in a 1967 speech marking the 50th anniversary of the Soviet Intelligence Service.[5]

Dzerzhinsky was indeed ruthless, or in his own word, "merciless." On May 27, 1918, Dzerzhinsky wrote in a letter to his wife: "The ring of enemies is steadily closing in on us, approaching nearer to the heart. . . . Each day compels us to resort to ever more resolute measures. . . . My purpose compels me to be merciless and I am firmly resolved to pursue it to the end." Later in the same letter: "I am determined to fight and to look with open eyes at all the danger of the threatening situation, and I too must be merciless."[6]

By 1919 Dzerzhinsky wrote to his wife: "I know that for many there is no name more terrifying than mine."[7]

Dzerzhinsky was the kind of man Lenin needed—one who could take charge. As Lenin told a trade union meeting in 1920, "Dictatorial powers and one-man management are not contradictory to socialist democracy."[8] Only a man of passion, a man who knew how to hate, could carry out the tasks Lenin gave Dzerzhinsky. While Dzerzhinsky was a prisoner of the czar in 1902, his sister had suggested that he make his peace with the Catholic church and speak to a priest. His answer was a measure of the man:

I detest priests, I hate them. They have cloaked the whole world in their black soutanes in which is concentrated all evil—crime, filth and prostitution; they spread darkness and preach submission. I am engaged in a life and death struggle with them, and for this reason you must never write to me about religion, about catholicism because if you do all you will get from me is blasphemy.[9]

As head of the secret police he carried out the war against religion—indeed against every rival to Soviet power.

A Polish national, Dzerzhinsky was assigned by Lenin to play a major role in the abortive 1920 Soviet invasion of Poland. He served as a member of the five-man Provisional Revolutionary Committee, which Lenin hoped would become the puppet government of Poland.

Writing to his wife in August 1920, Dzerzhinsky described the military and political disaster. He wrote: "The fear that catastrophe would overtake us had long been troubling me. . . . We . . . learned of the scale of the defeat only when the whiteguard forces were within thirty kilometres of us, not from the west, but already from the south. . . . Things are in a bad way in Poland. The Party, apparently, has been smashed and has lost its bearings."[10]

Even under such circumstances Dzerzhinsky could find ways for Communism to benefit. He instructed his wife in the same letter: "The most important task for you in Moscow at the moment is work among the prisoners of war. They should be won over, won to our principles, so that they return to Poland convinced Communists."[11] This use of POWs was to become a major activity of the Soviet Intelligence Service during World War II and afterward.

In 1920 Lenin complained at a meeting of Communist Party activists in Moscow that, "our intelligence service in the Cheka, although splendidly organized, unfortunately does not yet extend to the United States of America."[12]

Dzerzhinsky did not take long to accomplish Lenin's goal. In December 1924 he reported to the Soviet Council of People's Commissars that:

The OGPU not only works energetically by paralyzing the espionage of foreign citizens in the U.S.S.R., but it has also succeeded in creating a network of information intelligence agencies in all other large centers of Europe and North America. Responsible workers of the OGPU are detailed to all the diplomatic and trade missions of the

U.S.S.R. abroad. The total strength of the Foreign Department of the OGPU is 1,300 including the employees in the foreign section in Moscow. The OGPU has reportedly rendered service to the Commissariat of Foreign Affairs and the staff of the Red Army in supplying secret information both of a political and military nature.[13]

Although the Soviet Intelligence Service has both internal and external functions, this book will deal primarily with its external operations, particularly those against the United States. Lenin, however, drew few distinctions between internal and external enemies. Indeed, in a letter to D. I. Kursky, people's commissar for justice, Lenin suggested a criminal code that would provide the death penalty for "Propaganda or agitation that objectively serves . . . the international bourgeoisie."[14] He was not suggesting death only for those actually working for the external enemy, but for those whose actions could be viewed by the Bolsheviks as aiding the enemy.

Lenin and Dzerzhinsky created a shield to protect the Soviet Party/state and a sword to use against its enemies. In 1983 a Soviet journalist graphically described both the internal and external functioning of the Soviet Intelligence Service. He wrote: "The first generation of Bolshevik Chekists forged our shield. But neither has our sword remained peacefully in its sheath. We are optimists, and we would like to beat all swords into plowshares. And we believe that this time will come. But, first of all, we have our shield. And then there is still—the sword."[15]

1

Early Days: Names, Aliases, and Associations

A LTHOUGH Lenin had complained to a December 6, 1920, Moscow meeting that the Soviet Intelligence Service was not yet functioning in the United States, parts of the apparatus had been put into place two years earlier when the Soviets established an office in New York that they called an "embassy." On January 2, 1919, Ludwig C. A. K. Martens was appointed Soviet representative to the United States. As the U.S. was not to recognize Soviet Russia until 1933, Martens, the pseudo ambassador, had no official standing. The "embassy" was opened in New York rather than in Washington, and Martens was a Russian-born Communist residing in the United States, rather than a representative sent from Russia.[1]

In testimony before the Senate Committee on Foreign Relations in 1920, Martens revealed that he was financed by cash carried to him by Soviet couriers whom he refused to identify.[2] The use of couriers to carry cash and instructions continues to be used by Soviet intelligence seven decades later.

The staff of his "embassy," Martens told the committee, were all members "of some Socialist party, or rather I would say that some of them are members of the Socialist Party, some of the Communist Party, and some of the Communist Labor Party." He explained that this was "because we have a Socialist Government and we prefer to employ socialists."[3]

One of those identified by Martens as belonging to the Socialist Party was Arthur Adams.[4] When Martens was deported from the United States in 1920, Adams went with him. But Adams was to

return to the United States many times in the next two and half
decades as a high-ranking Soviet espionage officer. His specialty was
the theft of American technology.[5]

According to Martens's testimony, Adams was the director of the
"embassy's" Technical Department. Adams was "Born in Russia.
Citizenship British. Graduate of School of Science, Kronstadt, and
of the University of Toronto, Canada."[6]

Another employee of Martens was Santeri Nuorteva, who served
as secretary to the pseudo embassy. Born in Finland in 1881, Nuorteva had Russian citizenship. From 1907 to 1911 he served in the
Finnish Parliament while Finland was part of the Russian empire.
He was appointed secretary by Martens on March 18, 1919. Prior
to that he had served as the representative in the United States of
the short-lived Finnish Communist Government.[7]

Martens maintained close contact with American Communist leaders. During his Senate testimony, he identified a poster of the Communist Labor Party announcing a November 7, 1919, meeting to
celebrate the second anniversary of the Russian revolution. Among
the speakers listed was "L. C. A. K. Martens, Soviet Ambassador
to United States" and Benjamin Gitlow, a high-ranking American
Communist official. The chairman of the meeting was Dr. Julius
Hammer.[8]

Years later Gitlow broke with the Communist movement, and
described his relationship with Martens in his book *I Confess*. He
wrote, "I conferred with him [Martens] often . . . and received
from him from time to time financial help for our organization and
its press." According to Gitlow, Martens had as one of his advisers
"Dr. Hammer, whose generous financial assistance made the establishment of the 'Embassy' possible."[9]

Gitlow and Hammer were both on the New York City Committee
of the Socialist Party Left Wing, which in 1919 became the Communist Labor Party.[10] Minutes of a meeting of the Left Wing dated
April 20, 1919, reveal that "a message sent to the gathering by Mr.
Ludwig C. A. K. Martens, who was unable to attend in person,
extending his allegiance and support to the Left Wing movement,
was delivered by Dr. Hammer."[11]

Martens became the subject of investigations by the New York
State Legislative Committee, the U.S. Senate Foreign Relations
Committee, and the Justice Department, which detained him while

his office was being searched. The Soviet response was contained in a report submitted by the People's Commissariat for Foreign Affairs to the Congress of Soviets. "On June 20th [1919] we sent a protest to the American Government on account of the arrest of comrade Martens, the Russian representative in America, threatening reprisals on American citizens in Russia." The Soviets soon learned that Martens had not been arrested but only detained for a few hours. On November 20, 1919, another protest note was sent by the Soviet government to the United States, when they learned that Martens had been rearrested. Again reprisals were threatened.[12]

On December 15, 1920, Martens was ordered deported by the United States secretary of labor as an alien affiliated with an organization "that teaches or advocates the overthrow by force and violence of the government of the United States."[13]

Lenin's dream for the Soviet Union was for it to serve as the base and instigator of the world revolution. As early as 1915 Lenin wrote:

> The victory of socialism is possible first in several or even in one capitalist country alone. After expropriating the capitalists and organizing their own socialist production, the victorious proletariat of that country will arise against the rest of the world—the capitalist world—attracting to its cause the oppressed classes of other countries, stirring uprisings in those countries against the capitalists, and in case of need using even armed force against the exploiting classes and their states.[14]

To carry out this work the Soviet government issued a decree, which was published in the *Gazette of the Temporary Workers and Peasants Government (IZVESTIA)*, December 13, 1917. The decree read:

> An Ordinance on assigning two million roubles for the needs of the revolutionary internationalist movement. Taking into consideration that Soviet authority stands on the ground of the principles of international solidarity of the proletariat and the brotherhood of the toilers of all countries, that the struggle against war and imperialism, only on an international scale, can lead to complete victory, the Soviet of Peoples commissaries, considers it necessary to come forth with all aid, including financial aid, to the assistance of the left, internationalist, wing of the workers movement of all countries, entirely re-

gardless whether these countries are at war with Russia, or in an alliance, or whether they retain their neutrality. With these aims the Soviet of Peoples Commissaries ordains: the assigning of two million roubles for the needs of the revolutionary internationalist movement, at the disposition of the foreign representatives of the Commissariat for Foreign Affairs.

President of the Soviet of Peoples Commissaries—VI. Oulianoff (Lenin).

Peoples Commissary for Foreign Affairs—L. Trotzky.

Manager of Affairs of the Soviet of Peoples Commissaries. VI. Bonch-Bruevich.

Secretary of the Soviet—N. Gorbounov. [spellings as in original][15]

The Communist International (Comintern) was established in 1919 in Moscow as the General Staff of the World Revolution. While the Red Army and the Soviet Intelligence Service defended the revolutionary base, i.e., the Soviet Union, the Comintern would carry out aggressive action to achieve the world revolution, if necessary aided by the intelligence service and the army.

Two American groups attempted to affiliate with the Comintern, the Communist Party and the Communist Labor Party. The former, in a report to the Comintern, explained, "The Communist Party realizes the immensity of its task; it realizes that the final struggle of the Communist proletariat will be waged in the United States, our conquest of power alone assuring the world Soviet Republic. Realizing all this, the Communist Party prepares for the struggle."[16]

On orders of the Comintern the two parties merged. As they described it in their newspaper, "Sometime recently, somewhere between the Atlantic and the Pacific, between the Gulf and the Great Lakes, two groups of elected delegates assembled as the unity conference of the Communist Party and the Communist Labor Party. Of the former, 32; of the later, 25, and one fraternal delegate; also a representative of the Executive Committee of the Communist International."[17] Due to government repression, the new party was born underground.

This was a party of Soviet patriots. They looked upon the Comintern as their guide. Even before the merger, the Communist Labor Party explained why its members resisted deportation to Soviet Russia:

[W]e hold it to be the duty of every Communist to help with the struggle as best he may where most needed. In Soviet Russia, Communism is now triumphant. The few hundred Comrades that the American Government is now proposing to deport would not be of any great help there. They are not now needed there, but during this present crisis their help is sorely needed here.

It is the duty of everyone to get out on bail as quickly as he can, and then to remain as long as he can in the ranks of the Communist Labor Party as an active worker to hasten the triumph of Communism in the United States.[18]

Despite its loyalty to the Soviet Union, the Communist Party in the 1920s was a small, ineffective sect enjoying little contact with the American people. During 1925, with a party membership just over 16,000, few more than 2,000 members were in English-speaking party branches. Over 6,400 members were in branches that spoke Finnish, almost 900 in Russian-speaking branches, 1,400 in Jewish (Yiddish-speaking) branches, and over 1,000 in Serbo-Croatian-speaking (South Slavic) branches.[19]

Not only did most members in the 1920s not speak English, but the Communist Party itself was underground, working through an aboveground front called the Workers Party. For a number of years after coming aboveground in 1924, the Communist Party used the name Workers (Communist) Party. Its views were expressed in 1928 by its frequent candidate for president of the United States, William Z. Foster, when he said in an election speech, "No Communist, no matter how many votes he should secure in a national election, could, even if he would, become president of the present government. When a Communist heads a government in the United States— and that day will come just as surely as the sun rises—that government will not be a capitalistic government but a Soviet government, and behind this government will stand the Red Army to enforce the Dictatorship of the Proletariat."[20]

Although the party itself had come out of the underground, an underground apparatus remained in place after 1924 and served as the main recruiting base for Soviet espionage. A number of leading Communist Party members worked with the Soviet Intelligence Service through this apparatus. One example was Nicholas Dozenberg.

Dozenberg was born in 1882 in Latvia, and came to the United States in 1904. He testified before the House Special Committee on Un-American Activities in 1940. He was serving a one-year jail sentence for passport fraud, to which he had pleaded guilty, when he was brought before the committee.

Dozenberg told the committee that he had become a member of the Socialist Party during the pre–World War I period when the Lettish (Latvian) Workman's Association affiliated with the Socialist Party. The LWA became the party's Lettish Federation, splitting in 1919 to help form the new Communist Party, becoming its Lettish Bureau.[21] In 1923 Dozenberg became the literature director for the Workers Party, the aboveground arm of the underground Communist Party.[22]

Questioned by J. B. Matthews, the House Committee's director of research and chief investigator, Dozenberg spoke openly about his Communist Party responsibilities. But when Matthews asked "it was at the end of 1927, was it not, that you enlisted in the work of the Soviet Military Intelligence?" Dozenberg answered, "I do not remember anything of the sort." The argument continued:

> Mr. Matthews: Well, what was it? Early in 1928?
> Mr. Dozenberg: I have never enlisted in the Soviet employ.
> Mr. Matthews: How do you describe your work under the Soviet Military Intelligence?
> Mr. Dozenberg: Mr. Chairman, may I address a request?
> The Chairman: Certainly.
> Mr. Dozenberg: If you wish me to make any statements along those lines at all, I would suggest an executive session. I am not going to make any public statements, and I want you to understand that, irrespective of what the committee might decide to do with me; because I figure that a question of my welfare is at stake.

Dozenberg had been a dedicated soldier of Communism. But now he feared that his life was threatened by his former comrades. After extracting a promise from Dozenberg that he would testify truthfully, Congressman Martin Dies, the committee chairman, ordered the committee to proceed in executive, or secret, session.[23] The hearing room was cleared, and the secret session began. In the secret session Dozenberg spoke freely about his Soviet espionage work, but tried to shield his associates in the U.S. Communist Party. He admitted that he had been recruited by Alfred Tilton, then head of Soviet Military Intelligence for the United States. When J. B. Matthews suggested to him that his service with the Soviets began in late 1927 or early 1928, Dozenberg answered, "I can swear I don't remember the exact date," but he would not dispute it.[24] Other evidence indicates, however, that Dozenberg actually dropped out of the open Communist Party in January 1927. The minutes of the Communist Party Political Committee for January 14, 1927, reveal that a letter had been received from the Lettish Bureau "advising of the resignation of Comrade Dozenberg as a member of the Bureau." The motion to accept the resignation was adopted unanimously.[25] The minutes of the meeting were secret and were marked "read and destroy."

When questioned whether his closest friend, Jay Lovestone, then a Party leader, knew that he had dropped out to go to work for the Soviets, Dozenberg stumbled around in his answer. He testified, "Attorney-counsel, I could not say for sure. I surmise what could have happened was this: That someone else informed Lovestone that I wanted a different position or a different job altogether and thus Lovestone was informed that I was going to quit."[26] The secret minutes cited above reveal that Lovestone, who had attended most of the Political Committee meetings, was not at this one.[27]

Gitlow, Lovestone's closest associate, knew Dozenberg well. Testifying before Congress in 1939 Gitlow identified Dozenberg as a Soviet intelligence operative. Gitlow was somewhat imprecise in testifying that Dozenberg worked for "Ogpu" (pronounced as a word; OGPU was the Soviet internal and external intelligence service) when in fact he worked for Soviet Military Intelligence, and that his work started at the end of 1927. Gitlow nevertheless provided some valuable insights into Soviet operations and financial support for the American Communists. According to Gitlow, "at the end of 1927, the secretariat of the Communist Party took one of its leading people out of the national office, the organizational department of the party, and assigned him to the Ogpu to become an agent of the Ogpu, and to serve as liaison officer between the Ogpu and the secretariat of the American Party. This comrade was known by the name of Nick Dozenberg." He went on to say, "Nick Dozenberg was a steady visitor to the national office, and met continuously with us on confidential Ogpu matters, turning over work to the party, and was also a source of income for the party because whenever he was required to get certain contacts or certain information from the party, the party was always paid for that information."

According to Gitlow, after Dozenberg was assigned to Soviet intelligence, "He never attended party meetings, and he never attended the branch meetings. He actually dropped out of the party. That was done as a precaution so that party members should not come in contact with him, except only a few top leaders of the organization."[28]

It appears that Gitlow used the term "Ogpu" to designate a number of different clandestine Soviet entities. While he knew the difference between the OGPU, the Soviet internal and external intelligence service; the Fourth Bureau of the Red Army (Soviet Military Intelligence); and OMS, the organizational apparatus of the Comintern, in his testimony he referred to all of them as "Ogpu."

The use of a common term for all three entities may be explained by the close association they had with one another. The Comintern had its own intelligence gathering apparatus as part of OMS. Called the Information Department, it was headed by Joseph Pogany, who also served as Comintern representative in the United States under the name John Pepper.

At a meeting of the Information Department held in Moscow on April 6, 1925, Pepper complained that although the department had "been in existence [for] some time," it was not yet functioning properly. The meeting decided that the Central Committee of each Communist Party would appoint a "reporter" who would be responsible for sending Moscow economic and political reports.

A "net of contacts in the factory nuclei" of the parties would supply the information. Among the main targets of the intelligence gathering were Social Democratic politicians, who were looked upon by the Communists as dangerous enemies in non-Communist countries.

Lovestone served on the Information Department under the pseudonym "Powers."[29] This close association with intelligence gathering may explain why most of the American Communists who later served Soviet intelligence came from the Lovestone faction of the party rather than the rival Foster faction.

Dozenberg provided the U.S. government with significant information on Soviet intelligence operations. He identified Alfred Tilton as the head of Soviet Military Intelligence in the United States.

Tilton had lived in New York with forged Canadian papers in the name of Joseph Paquett. One of Tilton's successes was to photograph a complete set of plans of the British warship *Royal Oak*. The plans had been intercepted by a Soviet agent on their way to Washington, D.C.

Dozenberg traveled between the United States and the Soviet Union and received directions for setting up cover operations in the U. S. for Soviet intelligence gathering in France and Rumania. During one Moscow visit Tilton introduced Dozenberg to General Berzin, the head of the Fourth Bureau of the Red Army.[30] According to Dozenberg, Tilton returned to the Soviet Union in early 1929 and shortly thereafter was replaced by Mark Zilbert.

While Dozenberg spoke freely to the government about his Soviet contacts, he was much more reluctant to discuss what he knew about the American Communists with whom he had worked closely. The American Communist Party had been torn by factional struggle for many years. Dozenberg was a member of the Charles Ruthenberg/ Lovestone faction, which fought against the group headed by William Z. Foster. Ruthenberg headed the party for most of its early years. After his death in 1927, Lovestone led the party and the faction. In a party of immigrants, most of whom did not speak English, the leadership of the Lovestone faction produced a remarkable group of younger intellectual leaders. Among them were Bertram Wolfe, later a distinguished historian, Will Herberg, the philosopher and theologian, Ben Mandel (Bert Miller), later the research director of the Senate Subcommittee on Internal Security, and a host of labor leaders. These men became hardline anti-communists in their later days, but during the 1920s they led American communism.

Benjamin Gitlow, a fiery orator, was the party's first martyr. He served a jail sentence after the culmination of a sedition case that made legal history. The Supreme Court case *Gitlow v. New York* is a standard in the study of the American Constitution. But Gitlow's greatest source of pride was the statement of the prosecutor in the case: "He [Gitlow] would make America a Red Ruby in the Red Treasure Chest of the Red Terror." This quotation was used on the cover of the pamphlet version of Gitlow's address to the jury.[31]

The Lovestoneites led a party of Soviet patriots; nevertheless they were honest enough to find defects in Stalin's methods. Lovestone had been elected a member, and Gitlow a candidate or alternate

member, of the Executive Committee of the Comintern at the Sixth
World Congress held in Moscow in 1928.[32] In May of the following
year, they were recalled to Moscow to answer charges of deviation
from the party line.

The charges were brought by Stalin, who delivered speeches
against the pair at two meetings at the Presidium of the Executive
Committee of the Comintern and one meeting of the Comintern's
American Commission. Stalin accused them of factionalism (actually
refusing to obey orders) and ordered them to submit to the discipline
of the Comintern Presidium. They refused. As Stalin explained it
in his speech to the Presidium of the Comintern on May 14, 1929,
"Comrades, Gitlow and Lovestone announced here with aplomb
that their conscience and convictions do not permit them to submit
to the decisions of the Presidium and carry them into effect." Stalin
ranted, "Members of the American delegation, do you think that
the conscience and convictions of Comrade Gitlow are above the
conscience and convictions of the overwhelming majority of the
Presidium of the E.C.C.I. [Executive Committee of the Communist
International]? Do you begin to understand that if each of us starts
to act according to his own will without reckoning with the will of
the collective, we shall never come to any decision; we shall never
have any collective will nor any leadership?" He went on to call the
pair "strike-breakers."[33]

Stalin had suggested a week earlier that, "it would be better both
for the Communist Party of America and for the Comintern if Comrades Lovestone and Bittleman were kept in Moscow for a time."
Alexander Bittleman, a member of the Foster faction, agreed, but
Lovestone protested that he wished to return to the United States.
Stalin, in a fit of modesty, explained, "I said that although this was
my opinion, I agreed to submit the proposal of Comrade Lovestone
to the consideration of the Russian comrades." The Russian comrades, of course, agreed with the opinion of Comrade Stalin, that
Lovestone should remain in Moscow.[34]

The Comintern representative to the American Communist Party
had sided with the Lovestone faction. Joseph Pogany, called John
Pepper by the American Communists, was a legendary Hungarian
Communist who had served in the leadership of Bela Kun's abortive
Hungarian Soviet Republic. After the defeat of the Hungarian Rev-
olution in 1919, Pogany/Pepper engaged in work for the Comintern,

much of it in the United States. He too was punished for his deviation. The Comintern ordered Pepper removed from the American Communist Party and decided "to turn over Comrade Pepper's case to the International Control Commission for consideration." Pepper disappeared in the Soviet Gulag. Another decision of the Comintern was the ratification of Stalin's "suggestions" that "Comrades Lovestone and Bittelman [sic], as extreme factionalists of the Majority and Minority . . . be removed for a time from work in the American Communist Party."[35]

Bittleman remained in Moscow, but Lovestone was in a panic. He could not be sure that he would survive the stay. Lovestone tried to get permission to visit the United States before he began his stay in Moscow. On May 31, 1929, the Secretariat of the Executive Committee of the Comintern cabled the American Party:

> Lovestone requests permission to go to America for personal affairs for two weeks in America beginning June 12th after which he consents to remain at the disposal of the ECCI for work in the CI. . . . The Political Secretariat permitted him to go for two weeks but date departure will be fixed if you don't object to his going America now. Communicate your opinion immediately.

On June 4, Lovestone's American comrades betrayed him. They sent Moscow a cable saying that the Party "doubts the validity of the alleged personal reasons for Lovestone's voyage." They suggested that he be kept in Moscow until, "after the completion of the Enlightenment Campaign."[36] The purpose of that campaign was to convince the membership to repudiate Lovestone and Gitlow.

Lovestone's eventual exit from Russia was assisted by Nick Dozenberg, who intervened with Soviet officials to return Lovestone's passport. Lovestone was able to avoid surveillance by taking a plane out of Moscow instead of the train, which was watched.[37] Dozenberg subsequently denied his role in order to protect his friends still in the Communist movement. During his congressional testimony, Dozenberg and J. B. Matthews had the following exchange:

> Matthews: You can understand that Lovestone was in some jeopardy, having broken completely with the organization in Moscow. But nevertheless he is still in Moscow—he does not have his passport; that is taken up. You understand that. Now, the question in Love-

stone's mind is how is he going to get out of Russia; is he going to
get out of Russia. Now, didn't Lovestone come to you and appeal
to you on the basis of your past friendship to assist him in every
possible way to get out of Russia?

Dozenberg: I swear as a matter of fact there was no such a request
necessary from what I learned to appreciate, to my own satisfaction.
The passport was given back to him and he came out of the country
as regularly as any one else would have come out, so there was no
such a need at all for him to come and ask me. And what is more
there was no reason for him to come and ask me because I couldn't
have done one iota for him.

Matthews: Mr. Chairman, as a matter of fact the record shows that
is not correct as stated by Mr. Dozenberg. He did not come out
with his own passport and he did come out surreptitiously. Now
Mr. Lovestone himself, Mr. Dozenberg, states that you responded
to his personal appeal to you to use your good offices with Rudsutak
[a Soviet official] to help him get out.

Dozenberg: Why, God bless him. Lovestone believed I am dead.
That is one of the things put on me. Never anything of the sort,
absolutely not—never. [38]

Lovestone and his coworkers were to pay Dozenberg back for his
help. They played an important role in one of Dozenberg's most
disastrous projects, and provided an early example of Soviet intelligence using dissident Communists as agents. Dozenberg had been
ordered by Moscow to launder counterfeit U.S. money produced in
the U.S.S.R. It was to be used to finance Soviet operations in this
country and Rumania. To pass the counterfeit money and convert
it to real U.S. currency, Dozenberg enlisted the help of a member
of the Lovestone group, William Gregory Burtan (also known as
Valentine Burtan). As a result, Burtan was convicted of passing
counterfeit bills and, in 1934, sentenced to fifteen years in prison.
He served ten of those years.

Burtan was born in Russia in 1900 and was brought to the United
States in 1907. In 1921 he was naturalized as a U.S. citizen and two
years later graduated from medical school. While practicing medi-
cine Burtan was an active member of the Communist Party. He was
expelled with the Lovestone group in 1929. While the entire Lovestone group contended that they were still loyal to Moscow and
advocated reentry into the Communist movement, Burtan was one
of the most vociferous supporters of that view. [39]

Burtan also collaborated with Dozenberg in the establishment of the American-Rumanian Film Corporation, which was one of Dozenberg's covers for intelligence operations in Rumania. Burtan was to testify in 1949 that he knew of Dozenberg's espionage activity. He explained what he planned to do with the real U.S. money that he was to obtain for the counterfeit: "I was going to turn [the money] over to Dozenberg, who had financed himself, his enterprises, and part of it was to go to the Lovestone group."[40] The last allegation is not corroborated by any other source.

While Lovestone and most of the other members of the group were staunch anti-communists by 1950, Burtan appears not to have followed the same path. Burtan died in 1985. He spent the last decade of his life closely associated with the American Communist Party, working at one of their enterprises and attending their meetings. Lovestone, Gitlow, and their supporters had publicly spoken out in defense of Burtan. They helped him get a job when he finished his prison term. His open adherence to the Communist Party, decades after he had left prison, shocked his former friends. They might not have been so shocked had they been familiar with the testimony of Communist Party functionary, Max Bedacht, before the House of Representatives on October 16, 1939. Bedacht admitted to having transmitted funds to Mrs. Burtan while Burtan was in jail. Bedacht denied receiving the funds from any agent of the OGPU and insisted that he had raised it five dollars at a time. When asked why he did so, he answered, "Because, besides being a vigorous man, I am also soft-hearted. I saw a woman with a baby needing help."[41]

Bedacht, who was one of the instigators of the cable to Moscow urging the retention of Lovestone, was not always so kind. His big heart did not extend to his former comrade, Gitlow. Before going to confront Stalin, Gitlow had left in the Communist Party National Office a trunk containing a suit, an overcoat, and some of his son's clothes. Upon his return he asked Bedacht for the trunk, as he needed the clothes. Bedacht refused and claimed that Gitlow owed the party money that he had collected in Moscow as Communist Party dues from Dr. Julius Hammer. Gitlow insisted that the money had been spent on official Communist activity. After weeks of procrastination, Gitlow was informed that the trunk would be returned. When his wife went to party headquarters to obtain it, she found the trunk broken open and the clothing missing.[42]

Bedacht served as the party's acting executive secretary after the removal of Lovestone, as a reward for his repudiation of his former factional leader. After being relieved of that assignment, Bedacht served as the liaison between the open Communist Party and the underground, which was run by the Soviet Intelligence Service. It was Max Bedacht who in 1932 recruited Whittaker Chambers into Soviet espionage (see chapter 6).

A few years later Bedacht was put out to pasture and made the general secretary of the Communist Party's front organization for nationality groups, the International Workers Order.[43] He was able to obtain identification documents from the foreign-born members of the organization to assist Soviet intelligence obtain American passports. In 1948 Bedacht was expelled from the Communist Party for criticizing the party leadership, or as they phrased it, "vicious and slanderous attacks against the Party and its leadership."[44] Despite his expulsion from the party, Bedacht remained a dedicated communist until his death some years later.

The desire of the Lovestoneites to return to the Communist movement led them into contact with one of the most remarkable men in the history of Soviet intelligence. His real name was Moishe Stern, but he was known in America as Mark Zilbert, replacement for Alfred Tilton as head of Soviet Military Intelligence in North America.

In 1931 Lovestone met with a representative of the Communist International to discuss reentry of his group into the World Communist movement. This meeting was reported in a pamphlet by Benjamin Gitlow.[45] When Lovestone was asked about the pamphlet during his congressional testimony, he answered, "To the best of my recollection, this pamphlet essentially deals with the unity negotiations as conducted between General Klaber [sic] and myself." He was asked by J.B. Matthews, "Was this the General Klaber who for a time was held as the great hero of the Spanish Civil War?" Lovestone answered, "Yes, this is the same Klaber who saved Madrid from the Fascist bandits."[46]

Moishe Stern, who served as chief of Soviet Military Intelligence in North America as Mark Zilbert, and as chief of the International Brigades in Spain as General Kleber, was born in Austria-Hungary. While serving in World War I he was captured by the Russians and converted to Bolshevism after the 1917 Revolution. *Inprecorr*, the Comintern weekly, provided a biographical sketch of his career.

General Kleber, who is responsible to the Republican General Staff for the whole Northern Madrid front, is the Commander-in-Chief of the International Column. General Kleber is a man of few words, but an excellent linguist. He is a born general with long experience of wars and civil wars. When he was a prisoner of war in Russia he was released by the revolution and offered his services to the Soviet government. While in command of important units he first became well known for his victories over Kolchak and the French general Janin. After having participated in the organisation of the Hamburg Insurrection he became one of the military leaders of the anti-imperalist struggle in China.[47]

Shortly after this was written Stern was recalled to Moscow and killed in Stalin's purges. As indicated in the article, Stern had played an important role in the abortive Communist uprising in Hamburg, Germany, in 1923 and in Soviet operations in China in the late 1920s. He was then assigned to the United States and Canada as chief of Soviet Military Intelligence.

When Lovestone was asked during his congressional testimony about his discussions with General Kleber, he answered, "Well, we discussed the situation in the Russian Communist Party, in the Communist International, the relations between the American Communist Party and the Communist International, and the possibilities of reunification of our organization with the parent organization." Lovestone went on to say, "I can safely say that now, because General Klaber does not exist anymore." J. B. Matthews asked, "Has Klaber been liquidated?" Lovestone answered, ironically, "He has been liquidated a little, which means finished for good."[48]

In 1956, when the East Germans issued a commemorative pamphlet on the International Brigades, they neglected to mention Stern, although they listed every other commander and political commissar who had served.[49] Ten years later the Austrian Communists, in their commemorative pamphlet on the Spanish Civil War, proudly identified "General Kleber (Stern), Austrian born, Commandant of the Brigade."[50] In 1975, a Soviet book on the International Brigades stated: "The first commander of the 11th International Brigade, General Kleber (Manfred Stern), who played a prominent part in organizing the defense of Madrid in autumn 1936, was also born and brought up in Austria."[51] Stern had been rehabilitated as had most of the other Soviet military and intelligence people who had been executed in the Soviet Union after serving in Spain.

While Mark Zilbert (Moishe Stern) operated in the United States as head of Soviet Military Intelligence, his assistant was Boris Devyatkin, who used the alias Dick Murzin. Devyatkin had been born in Russia in 1888 and entered the United States in 1923. In 1929, when he was assigned to assist Zilbert, he obtained United States citizenship and established himself in New York in the real estate and insurance business. In 1947 he was identified as still operating in the United States, as an employee of the Soviet Purchasing Commission.[52]

In 1931 Stern made contact with William Disch, who was employed as a draftsman by the Arma Engineering Company in New York, which was manufacturing confidential mechanisms for the U.S. Navy. Stern, using the alias "Mr. Herb" told Disch that he was willing to pay fifteen hundred or two thousand dollars a year, a considerable sum in those days, to obtain classified information including plans for a fire control apparatus that the Navy had developed. The device stabilized naval guns while they were being fired. Stern pretended that he was purchasing the information for a competitive firm in England. Because of his accent, Disch thought Stern was a German agent. He was later told by the FBI that "Mr. Herb" was a Soviet agent.

After agreeing to meet "Mr. Herb" again, Disch revealed to the president of his firm what had happened. They contacted the Navy Department, and Naval Intelligence arranged for a surveillance of the meeting between Disch and Stern. Disch produced no information at this meeting but Stern gave him a one hundred dollar bill as evidence of good faith. During subsequent meetings Disch provided Stern with carefully doctored information that had been provided by the naval authorities.

Stern was followed to the offices of the Soviet trading corporation, Amtorg, where he apparently photographed the documents, which he returned to Disch the next day. After many months Stern became suspicious of Disch and broke contact.[53]

During the same year Stern contacted another American, Robert Gordon Switz, this time using the alias Kotasky. Switz became involved in Soviet espionage as a result of his desire to go to the Soviet

Union as an aviation instructor. During 1931 and 1932, he was trained as an expert photographer under Stern's direction and photographed copies of classified U.S. military documents that Stern had obtained from other agents.

Switz made two trips to the Panama Canal Zone to provide instructions to U.S. Army corporal Robert Osman on the transmission of military information concerning the Canal Zone to the Soviet apparatus in New York. In 1933 Osman was court-martialed and convicted of illegal possession of secret documents relating to the national defense, and of attempting to transmit those documents to a person identified as Herman Meyers in Brooklyn, New York. The address used was known to be one of the residences of Moishe Stern. Osman was sentenced to two years in jail. On appeal he was found "not guilty" but was discharged from the Army.

Stern's courier, Switz, went to France in 1933 where he served Soviet intelligence for a short time until arrested by the French police. After turning state's evidence against his French associates, he returned to the United States and had no further contact with Soviet intelligence.[54]

The United States did not recognize Soviet Russia until 1933. As a result, before that time the Soviets had no opportunity to provide diplomatic cover for their intelligence officers. To some extent that lack was filled by the Soviet trading corporation, Amtorg, established in 1924.

The role of Amtorg in Soviet intelligence operations was revealed in 1929 by the first senior Soviet intelligence officer to defect to the west. Using the name Georges Agabekov, he had served as chief of the Eastern Section and head of the OGPU *Rezidentura* in Constantinople. Two years after his defection he wrote a book about his experiences. In it he revealed:

> The first Resident of Ogpu in America was Tschatzky, who lived there until 1928; he then returned to Moscow where right now he directs the Anglo-American sector of the Foreign Section. As there is no Soviet diplomatic representative in America, Tschatzky was known in America as a collaborator of Amtorg. . . . Ogpu was looking for a successor to Tschatzky in the post of secret Resident in America, but at the time of my leaving [October, 1929] had not yet found the man.[55]

The OGPU, the predecessor of the present KGB, served as both the apparatus for internal repression and the foreign intelligence service for the Soviet Union. In the early years it was junior to the Fourth Bureau of the Red Army, the predecessor of the present GRU. It is interesting to note, however, that knowledgeable people in the Communist movement, such as Ben Gitlow, used the generic term "Ogpu" to refer to all of the Soviet clandestine services. According to Agabekov, the foreign intelligence apparatus was originally the Fourteenth Special Sub-Division of the Cheka. As its importance increased, it became the foreign section of the OGPU. The chief of this apparatus, in both the Cheka and OGPU days, was Mikhail Abramovitch Trilisser.[56]

In 1924 Trilisser had sent Agabekov to Afghanistan to serve as OGPU *rezident*. Agabekov's training in agent handling was similar to present-day KGB practices. Each agent was given a number and a pseudonym. Each month the *rezident* sent Moscow a report on the activities and character of the agent. Where feasible, he enclosed photographs. The true names were transmitted separately to Moscow by code.[57] The recruiting of agents in mid-1920s Afghanistan was done through local members of the Communist Party.[58]

Agabekov revealed that this was because "until 1926 the relations between Ogpu and the Third International were very intimate, because of the friendship between Trilisser, Chief of the Foreign Section of Ogpu, and Piatnitzky, Chief of International Relations of Komintern (Executive Committee of the Third International)."[59]

Despite the poor translation of Agabekov's book, it is possible to identify the phrase "International Relations of Komintern" as the unit headed for so many years by Osip Piatnitsky. This was the Comintern's Department for International Liaison, which was known by its Russian initials OMS. For years Trilisser had played a dual role, combining his OGPU functions with Comintern organizational work. As a result, he used OMS to spot and assess Communist Party members throughout the world for OGPU recruitment.

Trilisser served on the Mandate Commission of the 5th Congress of the Comintern in 1924, and on the Enlarged Plenum of the Executive Committee of the Comintern in 1925.[60] In 1935 Trilisser replaced Piatnitsky as head of OMS. Piatnitsky subsequently died in Stalin's purges. At the 1935 Congress of the Comintern, Piatnitsky's name was dropped from the list of members of the Executive

Committee and replaced by the previously unknown M. A. Moskvin. It was only in 1971 that the Soviets revealed in a book on Comintern history that Moskvin was in fact Trilisser. He too fell victim to Stalin's purges.[61]

Stalin's hand reached past the Soviet borders. The defector Agabekov was murdered in Bucharest by a Soviet intelligence officer named Sanakoyev in the summer of 1939. Ilya Dzhirkvelov, a former KGB officer who defected in 1980, had learned about the murder during his training lectures. The KGB wants its officers to remember the fate of those who defect. Dzhirkvelov later had the opportunity to examine the case reports on the Agabekov murder when he worked in the archives department of the KGB's First Chief Directorate.[62]

Despite Agabekov's revelations, the U.S. government knew little about Amtorg and even less about Soviet espionage activity in the United States in the late 1920s. The Department of Justice had ceased its investigation of communist activities after a raid on the underground Communist Party convention held in Bridgeman, Michigan, in 1923. J. Edgar Hoover, testifying before a congressional investigating committee on June 9, 1930, revealed that "since 1924 to date there has been no investigation conducted by the Department of Justice of communistic activities."[63] Only later, when American citizens such as William Disch provided them with evidence of Soviet espionage, did government officials begin to pay attention.

On November 25, 1930, Basil W. Delgass testified before a congressional committee. He was a former vice president of the Amtorg Corporation and shocked the committee by revealing that Amtorg was involved in Soviet espionage. He said, "Now I have some information; I have mentioned about this before and I do not know whether the Committee wants to hear it or not. It is about the military espionage conducted by employees of Amtorg." The chairman, Congressman Hamilton Fish, responded, "If you have any facts, we would be very glad to hear them."

Delgass revealed that Amtorg was deeply involved in the theft of militarily useful technology. He testified, "Very shortly after I was elected vice president of the Amtorg Trading Corporation—as far as I remember, this was in May or June, 1927—I was called by Mr. Bron, then chairman of the board of directors of Amtorg, and asked by him whether I would undertake the supervision of the automotive and aviation department of Amtorg . . . and the buying of Liberty engines, which were at that time prohibited to be exported." The Soviets bought Liberty engines through Americans, who purchased them from the War Department as if for use in this country. They also obtained drawings from the War Department on the latest modifications of the engines.

Delgass identified another Soviet agent involved with Amtorg as Andrew V. Petroff, alias Sergueev. According to Delgass, "While in the United States, Mr. Petroff (Sergueev) was busily engaged in studying military activities in the United States. During the summer of 1929, he undertook an automobile trip across the United States to inspect military airdromes and naval bases on the Pacific coast. During this trip, he was accompanied by his wife, his secretary, one of his assistants and several men, whose names I do not know, who came from Russia especially for this trip. . . . While on the Pacific coast he was particularly interested in airplane carriers, ships similar to the *Saratoga*."

Petroff made a second trip early in 1930 with a Mr. Baranoff, who came directly from Moscow. He was the chief of the Soviet military air forces. When he was obtaining his visa from the American consul in Berlin, he claimed that he was in charge of commercial aviation. Another intelligence officer was Khalepsky, chief of the technical department of the general staff of the Soviet Army. He visited the U.S. twice, the first time in October 1928, when he came under the pretense of signing contracts with the Ford Motor Company. He spent about six months visiting arsenals and the Aberdeen Proving Ground. Khalepsky was accompanied to the Aberdeen Proving Ground by Berkhaloff, chief of the Leningrad artillery proving ground, and his assistant Leonoff. They came to the United States for the specific purpose of visiting the Aberdeen Proving Ground. At that time they made complete sketches of a 75mm, quick-firing gun, which was exhibited in the proving ground.[64]

Delgass's testimony was corroborated by a former OGPU officer named Michael Hendler, who, in a letter sent to the committee, identified the head of the OGPU as Menjinsky (Vyacheslav Menzhinskiy) and the chief of the foreign division as Trilisser. Hendler described himself as one who had been "employed for several years as a responsible agent of military espionage division and also of foreign division of O.G.P.U. and therefore I have thorough knowledge of their organization work and methods."

Hendler went on to report:

Paying daily visits to the foreign department of the O.G.P.U., before leaving Moscow, I was once requested by Trilisser to recommend to him an experienced trustworthy man, to whom he could entrust the organization of undercover connections between Amtorg in New York and Hamburg Nuclei of Berlin branch of O.G.P.U.

I have presented to him a man, whom I knew under the name Mikhail. This man received instruction and departed to New York, where he arrived illegally. . . .

Before my last departure from Moscow in November, 1926, I attended a secret meeting of the officials of foreign departments of O.G.P.U., where it was decided to send to Amtorg three employees—Checkists [sic, Chekists, i.e., intelligence officers] who would fill official posts in Amtorg, but who would actually work under orders of O.G.P.U., military espionage division of the Red Army and Comintern.

A secret connection between Mikhail and these men was arranged. Mikhail arrived in New York illegally in 1926 with help of Soviet embassy in Mexico where a special organization for such purposes existed.[65]

The use of Mexico as a base against the U.S. by Soviet intelligence continues to this day. They refer to this as a "third country operation."

2

Influence Operations

T HE Soviet Intelligence Service has two major functions in target countries. One is classical espionage—the theft of technology and secrets. The other is what are now called active measures. These are "influence operations," designed to cause the target to take an action beneficial to the Soviet Union. In the early days influence operations were organized not by the intelligence service but by other Soviet entities, such as the Comintern and the Soviet Communist Party. Nevertheless, the methodology developed years ago by the Comintern serves the KGB in its operations today.

Armand Hammer

What appears to be the earliest influence operation conducted by the Soviet Communist Party was organized by Ludwig C. A. K. Martens, the Soviet pseudo ambassador, after he was deported from the United States. His instrument was a man sympathetic to the Soviet Union, the young son of Dr. Julius Hammer, Armand Hammer.

In 1921 Julius Hammer, a medical doctor, was in an American jail for having bungled an abortion in which the patient died.[1] His son, Armand, was in Russia. On October 14, 1921, Lenin wrote a letter to all members of the Central Committee of the Communist Party:

Reinstein informed me yesterday that the American millionaire Hammer, who is Russian-born (is in prison on a charge of illegally procuring an abortion; actually, it is said, in revenge for his communism), is prepared to give the Urals workers 1,000,000 poods of grain on very easy terms (5 per cent) and to take Urals valuables on commission for sale in America.

This Hammer's son (and partner), a doctor, is in Russia, and has brought Semashko $60,000 worth of surgical instruments as a gift. The son has visited the Urals with Martens and has decided to help rehabilitate the Urals industry.

An official report will soon be made by Martens.[2]

With the Soviet economy in collapse Lenin had to attract Western capital. He needed to persuade the Western capitalists that it was possible to do business with Russia. Armand Hammer, an American "capitalist," could set an example. Lenin wrote to Martens on October 19, 1921:

> If Hammer is in earnest about his plans to supply 1 million poods of grain to the Urals (and it is my impression from your letter that your written confirmation of Reinstein's words makes one believe that he is, and that the plan is not just so much hot air), you must try and give the whole matter the precise juridical form of a contract or concessions.
>
> Let it be a concession, even if a fictitious one (asbestos or any other Urals valuable or what have you). What we want to show and have in print (later, when performance begins) is that the Americans have gone in for concessions. This is important politically. Let me have your reply.
>
> With communist greetings,[3]

Lenin's vision was "to build communism with the hands of noncommunists."[4] As he explained in a letter to Soviet Foreign Minister Chicherin, "Agreements and concessions with the *Americans* are of *exceptional importance* to us."[5] (Italics in original.)

To an official of the People's Commissariat for Foreign Trade, Lenin wrote, "Comrade Martens has sent me the contract with the American company (Hammer and Mishell) signed by you. I believe this contract to be of enormous importance as marking the beginning of trade." Lenin ordered that reports be sent to him on this business arrangement two or three times a month.[6]

On May 11, 1921, Lenin wrote in English to Armand Hammer:

Dear Comrade Hammer:

Excuse me please; I have been ill; now I am much, much better.

Many thanks for Your present—a very kind letter from American comrades and friends who are in prison. I enclose for You my letter to Comrade Zinoviev or for other comrades in Petrograd if Zinoviev has left Petrograd.

My best wishes for the full success of Your first concession: such success would be of great importance also for trade relations between our Republic & United States.

Thanking You once more. I beg to apologise for my bad English. Please address letters & telegrams to my secretary (Fotieva or Smolianinoff). I shall instruct them.

Yours truly,
Lenin

Three other documents appeared in Soviet files attached to the letter to Armand Hammer. The first to Lydia Fotieva, Lenin's secretary, and another Soviet official, V.A. Smolyaninov, read, "Have this translated for you both, read it; make note of Armand Hammer and *in every way help* him on my behalf if he applies. ll/V. Lenin"

The second document was a letter to Grigory Zinoviev, a member of the Politburo of the Soviet Communist Party and chairman of the Communist International, indicating that Hammer was a "Comrade." It read:

I beg You to help the comrade Armand Hammer, it is extremely important for us that his first concession would be a full success.

Yours,
Lenin

I beg you to give every assistance to the bearer, Comrade Armand Hammer, an American comrade who has taken out the *first concession*. It is extremely, extremely important that his whole undertaking should be a complete *success*.

With communist greetings,
V. Ulyanov (Lenin)

[emphases in original; the first half of the document was written in English]

In addition, Lenin sent a telephone message to Zinoviev:

Today I wrote a letter of reference to you and your deputy for the American Comrade Armand Hammer. His father is a millionaire and a Communist (he is in *prison* in America). He has taken out our first *concession*, which is very advantageous for us. He is going to Petrograd to be present at the discharge of the first wheat ship and to arrange for the receipt of machinery for his concession (asbestos mines).

It is my earnest request that you issue orders at once to see that there is no red tape and that reliable comrades should personally keep an eye on the progress and speed of all operations for this concession. This is of the utmost importance. Armand Hammer is traveling with the director of his company, Mr. Mishell.[7]

Lenin used the Hammer deal as a path to entice American business to the Soviet Union. In a letter to Stalin dated May 24, 1922, he wrote:

To Comrade Stalin with a request to circulate all Politbureau members (being sure to include Comrade Zinoviev)

On the strength of this information from Comrade Reinstein, I am giving both Armand Hammer and B. Mishell a special recommendation on my own behalf and request all C.C. members to give these persons and their enterprise *particular* support. This is a small path leading to the American "business" world, and this path should be made use of *in every way*. If there are any objections, please telephone them to my secretary (Fotieva or Lepeshinskaya), to enable me to clear up the matter (and take a final decision through the Politbureau) before I leave, that is, within the next few days.

24/V. Lenin[8] [emphases in original]

Hammer soon returned to the United States. But in an interview with the *New York Times* he refrained from identifying himself as a sympathizer of the Soviet regime trying to bring American business to support the Soviet economy. Instead the *Times* of June 14, 1922, quoted him:

When I conferred with officials of the Government I told them I was a capitalist; that I was out to make money but entertained no idea of grabbing their land or their empire. They said in effect, "We understand you did not come here for love. As long as you do not mix in our politics we will give you our help." And that is the basis on which I conducted negotiations.

Lenin had long been seeking such a "conduit" to the American capitalists. In a 1920 interview with Lincoln Eire, correspondent of the *New York World,* Lenin claimed, "Some American manufacturers appear to have begun to realize that making money in Russia is wiser than making war against Russia, which is a good sign."[9] Actually the American capitalists had no such ideas. Through his use of Hammer Lenin hoped to convince them that it was possible to deal profitably with the Bolsheviks. In later years the job of such influence operations was given to the intelligence service.

Over two decades later, when Hammer was in the liquor business, a puff piece was written about him in the trade organ *Spirits* for August 1945. According to this article:

So efficiently did his company perform its functions that when Amtorg—official Russian export-import company—was organized by the Soviet, and it was necessary to cancel the concession for Hammer's company in 1925, the Russian government compensated for the cancellation by giving Hammer the concession to build and operate a Moscow pencil factory. His success at this chore can be judged by the fact that from a pencilless nation, Russia became a pencil-exporting nation in a few short years.

In 1930, Hammer sold his pencil factory to the Soviet at a good price payable in U.S.A. dollars. For years, he had been investing his profits (yes!) in Russian art treasures and jewels because while money could not be taken out of the country without a lot of red tape, things could be exported more easily and at a handsome profit.

Armand's brother, Victor, who had studied art at Princeton, organized the Hammer Galleries on New York's Fifth Avenue, and the carefully chosen Hammer art and jewel treasures now flowed across the ocean to Manhattan, to be disposed of there.

The czar's treasures were very profitable for Hammer. The *Washington Post* reported on February 13, 1932:

The largest collection of Czarist treasures which has left the soviet Russian frontiers is in Chicago today. Jeweled objets d'art of the autocrats are in it—dazzling pieces set with diamonds, rubies, sapphires, emeralds. Imperial silverware from the palaces, porcelain, glassware, liquor accouterments of the regal "little fathers" are here. There are brocades, brilliant with threads of gold and silver, copes and chasubles of cut velvets, and icon dating from Ivan the Terrible.

> The collection—valued at $500,000 and including 1,500 separate pieces—is to be put on display in the interior decorating galleries of Marshall Field & Co. next week by Dr. Armand Hammer and his brother, Victor J. Hammer, both of New York, who went to Russia in 1921 and collected the treasures in the course of nine years of residence in the land of Lenin and Stalin.

Hammer continues today to be a friend of the Soviet Union. He has traveled there many times and has the opportunity to meet with the top leadership. On February 27, 1980, Radio Moscow's Domestic Service reported on a meeting between Leonid Brezhnev and Hammer. Brezhnev complained about the deterioration of American-Soviet relations. He was particularly concerned about the American perception of the Soviet intervention in Afghanistan. A few hours later Moscow broadcast in its English-language World Service a recording of an interview with Hammer. Brezhnev, according to Hammer, "explained to me why the Soviet Union had moved into Afghanistan: that it was at the request of the government—three governments of Afghanistan had requested it."

This was a bizarre version of recent Soviet-Afghan history. The Communist government that allegedly invited the Soviets was overthrown by the Soviet army and its leader killed. The Soviets then installed a different Communist faction as the government. Hammer went on to say, "If the United States and the neighbors of Iran [*sic;* Afghanistan] would guarantee that there would be no interference with the internal affairs of Afghanistan and the people of Afghanistan, Russia would remove her troops, since the cause for which they went there would be removed."

Hammer's next moves were described by Edward Jay Epstein in an article in the *New York Times Magazine* of November 29, 1981. Epstein had interviewed Hammer extensively and had heard the story from his own lips. After meeting with Brezhnev, Hammer flew to Pakistan and met with President Mohammad Zia ul-Haq. The Pakistanis, according to the Soviets, were the main supporters of the anti-communist rebels in Afghanistan. Hammer asked President Zia to withdraw that support in exchange for which Hammer's company, Occidental Petroleum, would redrill shallow offshore oil fields and build a new oil refinery in Pakistan, potentially very profitable ventures. According to Hammer, as told to Epstein, "General Zia showed considerable interest in the idea but he was reluctant to commit himself on Afghanistan." Hammer later tried to get Senator Charles Percy, then chairman of the Senate Foreign Relations Committee, to apply pressure. When President Reagan, for other reasons, ended the embargo on grain to the Soviet Union, which had been imposed after the Afghan invasion, Hammer abandoned his campaign.

Every time a new leader emerges in the Soviet Union, Hammer makes public statements about the new opportunity for peace now available because of the new leader. Armand Hammer is special. His contacts are in the open, and since the earliest years he has dealt with the highest levels of Soviet leadership. No one else deals with the Soviet Union at that level.

TRUST

Despite the Bolsheviks' concern about foreign enemies, the internal enemy was of primary importance. The Cheka was originally designed to cope with that problem. However, as internal enemies fled abroad and joined with foreign enemies in conspiratorial planning to overthrow the Soviet government, the Cheka developed external operations aimed at them as well.

One technique used by the Cheka against its Russian internal and external foes was "provocations," a method learned from the czarist secret police. The creation of notional organizations—that is, organizations that did not really exist but could be used to deceive the enemies of the Bolsheviks—was a particularly effective weapon. In addition the Cheka infiltrated and captured real opposition organizations and turned them against their organizers. The Cheka was later to use similar operations against their foreign enemies including the United States.

The most famous of the notional organizations was the case of the *TRUST*. It grew out of the capture of a real monarchist group. In early 1922, Felix Dzerzhinsky, head of the Cheka, decided to penetrate and take control of an underground monarchist organization operating in the Soviet Union. Called the Monarchist Organization of Central Russia, it had branches in several cities.[10] Its capture made possible the creation of a major deception, *TRUST*, which convinced the émigré conspirators and foreign governments that they were dealing with a powerful anti-Soviet group in Russia that could take power.

The man chosen by Dzerzhinsky to run the *TRUST* operation was the chief of counterintelligence, Artur K. Artuzov. Although born in Russia, Artuzov's father was a Swiss of Italian origin named Khristian Frauchi. Artuzov, fluent in a number of languages, joined the Bolshevik Party in 1917. He became a staff member of the Cheka and then chief of the counterintelligence department when Soviet intelligence changed its name to OGPU.[11]

Artuzov's two major targets were Boris Savinkov and Sydney Reilly. Savinkov was a leader of the Social Revolutionary Party of Russia, which had fought violently against the czar but had broken with the Bolsheviks. He was deeply involved with the British in conspiracies against the Soviet government. Savinkov cooperated with monarchist groups, but he was a populist who believed in the establishment of a new Russia, where, for once, the ruling power would be in the hands of the peasants.

Reilly, a Russian-born Jew whose real name was Rosenblum, had worked for many years before World War I as a British agent. On behalf of the British, he worked closely with Savinkov as well as with the monarchists. Reilly had been involved in plots against Soviet rule from the earliest days of Lenin's regime. The Cheka plan was to bring these two enemies of Bolshevism into the Soviet Union where they could be dealt with.

In an operation similar to *TRUST*, Savinkov was lured into Russia by a supposed social revolutionary group called the Liberal Democrats.[12] Savinkov was captured in August 1924. Accompanied by two associates, Savinkov's mistress and her husband, as well as two Cheka provocateurs sent from Moscow to entice them in, Savinkov penetrated the Soviet border with Poland. They were met on the Soviet side of the border by other Cheka agents who were supposedly anti-Bolshevik activists and taken to Minsk. The next morning Red Army soldiers burst into the room where they were having breakfast and arrested them. Savinkov was placed on trial and confessed to all of the charges against him. His death sentence was commuted to ten years in prison because of his confession. In May 1925 the Soviets announced Savinkov's death. They claimed he had committed suicide. His friends in the West insisted that he had been murdered.

Before leaving for Russia, Savinkov had discussed the matter with Sydney Reilly. He explained to Reilly that his chief associate inside Russia had written to him telling him that a revolution was imminent and that Savinkov had to come back to lead it. Two men had brought the letter to Savinkov in Paris. One of them had been known to him earlier, the other was a stranger. Reilly's response was, "Don't go."[13]

Despite the good advice he gave Savinkov, a year later, in September 1925, Reilly himself was convinced that the *TRUST* was an authentic anti-Soviet organization operating within the Soviet Union and its members needed his presence to assist them in their work. On September 25 Reilly wrote to his wife: "[I]t is absolutely necessary that I should go for three days to Petrograd and Moscow. I am leaving tonight and will be back here on Tuesday morning." "Here" was Finland. Reilly crossed the Finnish border into the Soviet Union and was taken to Moscow by members of *TRUST*.

Arriving in Moscow on the evening of September 26, 1925, Reilly was met at the railroad station by a group of Cheka officers playing the part of counterrevolutionaries. They took him to a cottage in the suburbs of Moscow where a meeting was supposedly taking place of the political council of the anti-Soviet organization. An elaborate charade took place. Cheka officers, playing the part of counterrevolutionaries, reported on the activities of their various "anti-Soviet" cells to Reilly. He in turn laid out a program of sabotage against the Soviet Union. After the meeting Reilly was to be taken back to Moscow, to be put on a train to Leningrad. In fact he was driven into the courtyard of Lubianka Prison where he was arrested.[14]

Reilly's confession was published by the Comintern in their publication *International Press Correspondence* in 1927. In it he supposedly said, "I entered Soviet Russia upon my own initiative because I heard of the existence of apparently serious anti-Soviet groups in the Soviet Union." In a comment on the Reilly "confession" the Soviets claimed that he admitted that "the excellent British espionage work in the Baltic states makes it possible for the British Secret Service not merely to utilize the reports compiled with the friendly assistance of the various general staffs [of countries bordering on the Soviet Union], for the purposes of Great Britain, but also to share them with the less intelligent American Secret Service." Reilly also supposedly corroborated that "the British Secret Service hands over everything from the material at its disposal which might be of interest to America, to the American Secret Service."[15]

The American Secret Service then (as now) was a section of the Treasury Department and had as one of its functions the physical protection of the president. It did not (and does not) collect foreign intelligence. In fact, there was little American intelligence activity of any kind during the mid-1920s. It can only be conjecture what Reilly meant in his confession, if indeed he made the confession at all. There is also much confusion as to when Reilly died. One story indicates that he was executed shortly after his capture, but others claim he was alive much later.

Artur Artuzov, the godfather of the *TRUST*, fell victim to Stalin. On May 13, 1937, Artuzov was arrested. He had failed to take action against others that Stalin wished to victimize. Artuzov has been rehabilitated, like numerous others killed during the purges.[16]

TRUST-type operations, the creation of an ostensibly anti-Soviet internal organization to confuse anti-Soviet émigrés and Western governments, has continued to be used as a Soviet intelligence method. We will see other examples of this kind of activity in later chapters.

Willi Muenzenberg

Before it was "dissolved" in 1943 the Comintern played a major role in influence operations. Using the Communist parties, it established an entire network of front organizations for the purpose of influencing non-Communists to engage in activities in the interest of the Soviet Union.

Comintern official Otto Kuusinen told the 1926 Plenum of the Executive Committee of the Comintern:

> The first part of our task is to build up not only Communist organizations, but other organizations as well, above all mass organizations sympathizing with our aims, and able to aid us for special purposes. . . . We must create a whole solar system of organizations and smaller committees around the Communist Party, so to speak, smaller organizations working actually under the influence of our Party (not under mechanical leadership).[17]

Some of the organizations already existed. Kuusinen listed the International Red Aid and Workers International Relief as examples. The latter had been formed by the man who was to become the Comintern's impressario of international Soviet fronts, Willi Muenzenberg. An organizer of the pre–World War I Socialist international youth movement, Muenzenberg was a close friend and ally of Lenin.[18]

Although Muenzenberg was the expert and main practitioner of the front tactic, he did not enjoy engaging in these activities. At a secret meeting of the Workers International Relief, he revealed the real purpose of these groups. He said:

> Now we must get hold of other groups under other names. The question of clubs for New Russia is particularly important. Personally, these do not interest me very much, and it is not really interesting to form these "Innocents" Clubs. We must not indulge in any illusions as to the significance of these clubs. We must penetrate every conceivable milieu, get hold of artists and professors, make use of theatres and cinemas, and spread abroad the doctrine that Russia is prepared to sacrifice everything to keep the world at peace.[19]

Muenzenberg was involved in a wide variety of activities in support of Comintern programs. One of those activities in 1928 was to organize support for the Nicaraguan revolutionary movement led by Sandino, whose brother was in the United States. When Muenzenberg needed the brother, Socrates Sandino, a member of the American Communist Party, to make a propaganda tour of Europe, he addressed the request to the American Communists. The minutes of the Communist Party Political Committee for June 15, 1928, reveal:

> Comrade Gomez reported on the request of Munzenberg [sic] to have Socrates Sandino make a tour of the European cities, and recommended that: permission be granted provided that the fare would be paid.
> Motion by Gomez:
> That the Polcom approve the sending of S. Sandino to Europe provided he received his fare.
> Voting: Carried unanimously[20]

Muenzenberg also organized the Comintern's penetration of the film industry. At a time when movies were still silent, he promoted a decision by the Comintern to order all Communist parties to use film as a significant propaganda weapon, and wrote a pamphlet to explain the idea.[21]

Muenzenberg was expelled from the German Communist Party and the Comintern in 1939.[22] He was mysteriously murdered in 1940.[23] But during the 1930s Muenzenberg used the front apparatus that he had created during the 1920s to influence millions of people to support Soviet programs.

3

Forgeries

F ORGERIES are a favorite device of the Soviet Intelligence Service to influence a target audience; but the Communists hardly invented the technique. Political forgeries have been known in history from time immemorial. They were particularly effective when used by the czarist government in Russia.

The most famous, or infamous, of the czarist forgeries was the *Protocols of the Elders of Zion,* a forgery properly designated as a "warrant for genocide." Supposedly minutes of a secret meeting of Jewish leaders, the *Protocols* described a plot to take over the world. Pogroms in Russia in the early part of the century and anti-Semitic violence in other parts of the world can be traced directly back to the distribution of this forgery. The Nazis used it as an excuse for their program of annihilating European Jewry.[1] Anti-Semitic groups keep it in print even now. In 1987 a Soviet organization called Pamyat promoted this forgery as an explanation of the "Jewish plot" against the Soviet Union. Pamyat, although criticized in the Soviet media, is led by members of the Communist Party of the Soviet Union.[2]

The Bolshevik-German Connection

One of the earliest Soviet forgery operations was directed against the United States. Six months after the Bolshevik seizure of power, American representatives in Russia presented to President Woodrow Wilson a collection of documents that purported to show that the German government was financing the Bolsheviks and had done so prior to the Revolution. This thesis was not outlandish. Lenin himself had been sent back into Russia by the German government in a sealed railway car. The documents, however, have been subject to considerable criticism since their release in 1918. The President had them on May 9, 1918, and they were released to the press on September 15. The *New York Times* of September 16 featured a headline that read "Documents Prove Lenine and Trotzky Hired by Germans [spellings in the original]." The documents had been released by an official U.S. agency, the Committee on Public Information, headed by George Creel. They had been obtained in Russia by Edgar Sisson, the Creel Committee's representative in Russia. The Creel Committee was the predecessor of the United States Information Agency.

The *New York Evening Post* challenged the authenticity of the documents the day after they were released. On September 21, 1918, the paper published a statement by Santeri Nuorteva, who was described as the head of the Finnish Information Bureau of New York. The paper did not say that Nuorteva was in fact a notorious Soviet propagandist. He was later to be publicly identified as an employee of the Soviet pseudo ambassador, Martens.

The *New York Evening Post* headline read "Calls Sisson Papers 'Brazen Forgeries'—S. Nuorteva Says They Will Prove False—Creel Committee's Russian Revelations He Asserts Were Revived After Inquiry and Rejection." According to Nuorteva the documents had first been delivered to Raymond Robins, the Red Cross administrator in Russia, and Robins and his associates had investigated the truth of the statements in the documents and decided that they were forgeries. Robins, in fact, was an active Bolshevik sympathizer and, according to the U.S. ambassador, was on very intimate terms with Lenin and Trotsky and was a "courier for the Soviet Government."[3] For decades later Robins was actively engaged in propaganda on behalf of the Soviet Union.

Sisson met with Nuorteva in Washington on September 23. According to Sisson, Nuorteva admitted he had no personal knowledge on which to base his accusations. Creel decided to place the issue in the hands of scholars, and he requested the National Board for Historical Service to investigate the documents. A committee was established headed by Professor Samuel N. Harper of the University of Chicago, an expert on the Russian language and history. J. Franklin Jameson, the managing editor of *The American Historical Review*, also served on the committee.[4]

The experts divided the collection of documents into three groups. One group consisted of Russian originals or photographs. There were fifty-three of those. Two documents were available in the original German. The final group of documents, for which no originals or photographs existed, were available in mimeographed text in Russian with an English translation. There were thirteen such documents. The experts' conclusion concerning the documents in the first category was: "[W]e have no hesitation in declaring that we see no reason to doubt the genuineness or authenticity of these 53 documents." The two documents in German, however, were challenged. According to the experts, "The errors of typography, of spelling, and even of grammar, in these German circulars, make it impossible to accept them as original prints of the General Staffs named." The experts could not determine whether the mimeographed documents, which were translations from German into Russian, were authentic.[5]

As late as 1928 the well-known Bolshevik sympathizer, Frederick L. Schuman, of the University of Chicago, wrote of the documents in a book published by the American Communist Party: "While perhaps not entirely spurious, they show many evidences of crude fabrications and their genuineness is most questionable." He went on to argue that the impression given by the documents that the rulers of Russia were "wholly dishonest cat's paws of Germany" was "not in accordance with the facts."[6]

Alexander Kerensky headed the democratic government of Russia that had replaced the autocratic rule of the czar. In November 1917 he was overthrown in the Bolshevik Revolution. Kerensky's view was that the Bolsheviks were in fact assisted by the Germans in achieving power. Although his memoirs make no reference to the Sisson documents, Kerensky did discuss Lenin's relationship to the Germans. According to Kerensky, "Lenin's treason to Russia, committed in the very heat of the war, is an historically unquestionable and undeniable fact. Of course, Lenin was no common agent of Germany in the ordinary sense of the word." Kerensky argued that Lenin's defeatist theory allowed him to receive German support.[7]

When the German Foreign Office archives were captured by the British in World War II, a significant document was found dated December 3, 1917. The document was written by Baron R. von Kuhlmann, the German World War I minister of foreign affairs. It was addressed to an official who was to communicate the information to the kaiser. An attached document indicated that the kaiser was aware of and in agreement with the communication. Von Kuhlmann wrote:

> Russia appeared to be the weakest link in the enemy's chain. The task therefore was to loosen it and, when possible, to remove it. This was the purpose of the subversive activity we caused to be carried out in Russia behind the front—in the first place promotion of separatist tendencies and support of the Bolsheviki. It was not until the Bolsheviki had received from us a steady flow of funds through various channels and under varying labels that they were in a position to be able to build up their main organ, *Pravda* to conduct energetic propaganda and appreciably to extend the originally narrow basis of their party.

The German official went on to point out that now that the Bolsheviks were in power they desired peace in order to strengthen their own position. He suggested that "we should exploit the period while they are in power, which may be a short one, in order to attain firstly an armistice and then, if possible, peace."[8]

The evidence that the Germans provided substantial support to the Bolsheviks raises the question of whether the Bolsheviks did not mix forgeries and authentic documents and release them through one of their sympathizers, Colonel Robins, in order to defuse the true accusations that the Bolsheviks were receiving German money. The United States government, which released the documents, was the first victim of Soviet forgeries.

In 1956, George F. Kennan wrote a lengthy critique of the Sisson documents, concluding that they were all forgeries.[9] However, there has been no proper investigation of the origin of the documents or of the possibility that any or all were forgeries done by the Bolsheviks themselves, as they were the ultimate beneficiaries of the forgeries.

The Zinoviev Letter

On October 25, 1924, the British Foreign Office provided to the press a document that purported to be a letter signed by Grigory Zinoviev, the head of the Communist International, ordering the British Communist Party to carry out activities against the Labour government and to organize communist cells in the British Army.

Along with the document, the Foreign Office released the text of an official note to the Soviet government protesting the fact that instructions were being given to the British Communist Party. It is common belief that the release of those documents resulted in such strong anti-communist feelings in England that the Labour Party lost the elections that took place a few days later. Although the Zinoviev letter ordered the British Communists to operate against the British government, conservative papers such as the *London Daily Mail* accused the government of being naive for trying to lend Russia money while these activities were taking place.

The letter was immediately branded a forgery by the Soviet government, and the debates that have taken place over the many years since the release of the documents indicate that most scholars accept that characterization. However, the question of who forged the letter and why continues to be a matter of speculation, and there are those who believe that the forgery, if it was a forgery, was of Soviet origin.

The October 25, 1924, issue of the *London Daily Mail* headlined:

Civil War Plot by Socialists' Masters—Moscow Order to Our Reds— Great Plot Disclosed Yesterday—Paralize the Army and Navy—and Mr. MacDonald Would Lend Russia Our Money—Document Issued by Foreign Office—After *Daily Mail* Had Spread the News.[10]

The accepted version of the origin of the Zinoviev letter may be found in the book *The Zinoviev Letter* by Chester, Faye, and Young, published in 1968. The authors had interviewed Mme Irina Bellegarde, the widow of Alexis Bellegarde, a prominent White Russian émigré who was active in Berlin in the 1920s. According to Mme Bellegarde the forgery was organized by her husband and another former White Russian officer named Gumansky. She claimed that while the actual drafting of the letter was done by these two, they did not have available a Communist International letterhead. They contacted another White Russian, named Druzhelovsky, who had been involved in a number of previous forgeries. Druzhelovsky succeeded in obtaining one sheet of Communist International letterhead, which he had allegedly stolen from the Soviet Embassy in Berlin. It is unclear why the embassy would have a blank sheet of Communist International letterhead. Mme Bellegarde claimed that the actual signature of Zinoviev was forged by another anti-communist, a Latvian named Edward Friede.[11]

This detailed story is the widely accepted version of the origin of the Zinoviev letter. There is a significant problem with the story, however. In 1960 a collection of classified State Department documents stored at the National Archives were declassified. These reports include an actual copy of the Zinoviev letter that had been obtained, apparently, from the same source used by British Intelligence. The Zinoviev letter is not typed, nor does it appear on letterhead. It is completely handwritten in Russian and contains not the signatures but simply the names of Zinoviev and two other officials of the Communist International.[12] Whatever Zinoviev letter may or may not have been forged by the White Russians in Berlin, it was not the Zinoviev letter that was distributed by the British Foreign Office.

An examination of the text of the letter reveals that it is quite consistent with decisions made at the Fifth World Congress of the Communist International, which took place in Moscow during the summer of 1924. The forger may very well have seen the resolutions on the British Labour Government and on the Young Communist International which contained many of the concepts found in the Zinoviev letter. The resolutions in question had been printed in the September 5, 1924, issue of the Comintern's publication, *International Press Correspondence*. The German- and English-language editions of this publication were printed in Vienna and would have been available in Berlin within a few days. Thus the forgers could have had enough time to concoct the letter. They did not need a letterhead or an authentic signature to copy, as they simply wrote the Zinoviev letter in Russian, on blank sheets of paper. The forgery carried the date September 15, 1924.

Zinoviev denied authorship and claimed that on September 15 he was on holiday and could not have signed any official letter. In addition he challenged the concepts in the text, even those that were consistent with the Comintern decisions made a few months earlier.[13]

The Foreign Office's protest letter to the Soviet government was dated October 24, 1924, the day before the text was released to the British press. It was answered the next day by Rakovsky, the Soviet chargé d'affaires in Great Britain. Rakovsky, of course, denounced the letter as a forgery and claimed:

The whole of the contents of the documents are, moreover, from the Communist point of view, a tissue of absurdities, intended simply to arouse British opinion against the Soviet Union, and to frustrate the efforts being made by both countries to establish durable and friendly relations.[14]

Some interesting insights into the origin of the Zinoviev letter are provided by two women who had served the Comintern for many years and later broke with it, Ruth Fischer and Aino Kuusinen. Ruth Fischer had been a German delegate to the Fifth Congress of the Communist International, where she had been elected an alternate member of the Executive Committee of the Comintern.[15] Fischer, in her monumental history of the German Communist Party, revealed that Zinoviev had told her the letter was, of course, a forgery but may have been produced by the Soviet Intelligence Service (then called the GPU [State Political Directorate]) to discredit him. Zinoviev, however, admitted that he could not prove this.[16]

The Zinoviev letter in the possession of the British government contained two names in addition to that of Zinoviev. They were Arthur MacManus, the British member of the Executive Committee of the Communist International, and Otto Kuusinen. Although much was made of the fact that MacManus's name was spelled wrong in the document issued by the British government, where it appeared as "McManus," in the Russian-language original found in the National Archives his name is spelled correctly—MacManus. Otto Kuusinen, a Finnish member of the Executive Committee and of the Secretariat of the Comintern, was always known as O. W. Kuusinen and not as O. Kuusinen as his name appeared in the forgery.

Additional information on the document was provided by Kuusinen's former wife Aino, who had worked at the Comintern during the 1920s and 1930s. According to her, after the Fifth Comintern Congress instructions had been sent to the British Communist Party that included orders to set up cells in the British Army. Some of these instructions had leaked and, as a result, the Zinoviev letter was concocted. Moscow was extremely upset that their secret letters to the British Communists were not kept secure. When the British Trade Union Congress sent a delegation to Moscow to examine the files and to determine whether the Zinoviev letter was authentic, they were given the opportunity. However, for three days Comintern officials went through the files, removing compromising documents, particularly those related to the actual secret instructions given to the British Communist Party. The daily entries of incoming and outgoing correspondence were rewritten so that some of these documents were not listed. The Trade Union delegation concluded that not only was the Zinoviev letter a forgery, but that no similar document had been sent by the Comintern. According to Mrs. Kuusinen, "[E]veryone had a good laugh over the fact that they had been able to pull the wool so easily over the Englishmen's eyes."[17]

The Zinoviev letter remains controversial. It was clearly a forgery, but there is at least as much evidence that it was a Soviet forgery as that it was an anti-Soviet forgery. The evidence of Fischer indicates that the Soviets had need for such a forgery. Kuusinen reveals a Comintern cover-up that may show guilty knowledge. If in fact Druzhelovsky was involved in its production, then it was probably a Soviet forgery.

Other Forgeries

The man listed by Mme Bellegarde as having obtained the Comintern letterhead, Druzhelovsky, played a major part in a number of other forged documents. There is good reason to believe he was a Soviet agent provocateur. An account of his background was provided by the Soviet government in a 1926 report on anti-Soviet forgeries. According to the Soviet booklet, *Anti-Soviet Forgeries,* "Druzhelovsky was a native of Mogilev province in Russia, the son of an official in the police services. During the great war he was an officer in the Russian air service. Subsequently he worked for the Polish general staff, under Captain Bratkovsky." In 1922 or 1923 he was convicted of "treasonable practices" by the Poles and deported to Danzig from which he went to Berlin at the end of 1923.[18]

The Soviet booklet attributed a number of forgeries to Druzhelovsky. Among them was a document from the Communist International instructing the Communist Party of Bulgaria to commit terrorist acts to start an insurrection, beginning April 15, 1924. The forgery, which appeared in full and facsimile in the Bulgarian newspapers of April 4 was quickly exposed.

Although the document clearly was a crude forgery, on April 15 General K. Gheorghieff was murdered. The next day at a memorial service in the Sofia Cathedral, a bomb was exploded. More than two hundred people were killed, and five hundred were injured. The Communist International claimed, "It is not the work of a party. The whole population is conducting the struggle against the bloody reaction."[19]

The head of the Bulgarian Communist Party was George Dimitrov, later to become the general secretary of the Communist International. He had organized an insurrection in the summer of 1923 that had been brutally suppressed by the Bulgarian government. Dimitrov fled to the Soviet Union where he headed the Balkan Communist Federation and the West European Bureau of the Communist International.[20]

In 1934 Dimitrov was in the hands of the Nazi government of Germany, accused of setting fire to the Reichstag as a signal to the German Communists to start their insurrection. Dimitrov denied responsibility. However, during his trial he said:

> I would also remind you of the outrage in Sofia Cathedral. This incident was not organized by the Bulgarian Communist Party, but the Bulgarian Communist Party was persecuted on account of it. Under this false accusation two thousand Bulgarian Communists, workmen, peasants and intellectuals were murdered. That act of provocation, the blowing up of Sofia Cathedral, was actually organized by the Bulgarian police.[21]

By 1948 Dimitrov, then Communist dictator of Bulgaria, had forgotten that fourteen years earlier he denied the Bulgarian Communist Party was responsible for the bombing of the Sofia Cathedral. Reporting to the Fifth Congress of the Bulgarian Communist Party, which took place in December 1948, Dimitrov outlined the history of the party. Describing the period of 1925, he said:

> The fascist government continued with even greater fierceness its terroristic course. Exploiting *the desperate acts of the leaders of the Party's military organizations culminating in the attempt at the Sofia Cathedral*, it started a mass slaughter of active Communists, worker and peasant activists. The terror following the attempt in the Sofia

Cathedral on April 16, 1925, dealt a very serious blow to the Party. Its leadership was disorganized [emphasis added].[22]

If the letter that appeared in the Bulgarian press in 1925, almost two weeks before the attempted Communist insurrection, was forged by White Russian émigrés, how would they know the exact date that the Bulgarian Communists would murder a general? The Soviets attributed the forgery, probably correctly, to Druzhelovsky. The question has been raised as to whether Druzhelovsky was actually an agent of the Soviet Intelligence Service.

On July 9, 1926, *IZVESTIA* reported that Druzhelovsky had been captured crossing into the Soviet Union. The Russian-language Soviet booklet containing many of Druzhelovsky's forgeries was in the hands of the U.S. State Department on August 13, 1926, only a month later. Many of the forgeries shown in the book attributed to Druzhelovsky had never surfaced anywhere before. This would indicate that either he brought them with him into the Soviet Union when he was captured, or more likely, that he had been an agent from the beginning and had done the forgeries on behalf of the Soviets. In the case of the Bulgarian forgery, its exposure prior to the insurrection might very well have been to convince the Bulgarian government that no insurrection would take place on April 15, since presumably a White Russian forger, not the Communists, had set the date. Druzhelovsky supposedly was tried in the Soviet Union where he confessed to all of his forgeries and was sentenced to death.[23] He remains a man of mystery, and the question of whether he was actually a Soviet agent has never been resolved. His alleged execution in 1927 was announced by the Soviets, but there is no independent confirmation.

The leftist American journalist, George Seldes, wrote in 1929 that he had bought some documents from Druzhelovsky after the latter had been recommended by the American consulate as a legitimate source. Seldes wrote:

One was a letter about $25,000 sent by the Third International for Bolshevik work in Buenos Aires. The man who sold me this document confessed forgery (according to the Moscow press), but American newspapermen in Russia say Drushilowsky [sic] always was and is now a secret agent of the Chekah [sic]. I suppose the documents were his forgeries but I cannot understand the excitement in the radical press about them because in open sessions of the Third International Congress of 1922 I heard announcements about the sending of money for Bolshevik enterprises in South America. The document may have been a forgery, the forged words, however, relate historic facts. [24]

Here as in the Sisson documents, alleged forgeries were used to "disprove" the truth. As we shall see in later chapters, forgeries became a major Soviet technique in influence operations during the post–World War II period.

4

The Whalen and Tanaka Forgeries

W HILE the Zinoviev and Sisson documents have attracted considerable scholarly analysis over the years, one set of forgeries that surfaced in the United States in 1930 have received no analysis. These are the Whalen documents, presented by then New York City police commissioner Grover Whalen to the press on May 2, 1930. The documents, which were clearly forgeries, purported to prove that the Soviet trading organization Amtorg was involved in Communist propaganda in the United States. As Amtorg was deeply involved in Soviet espionage, the accusation of involvement in propaganda was similar to accusing a felon of a misdemeanor. Examination of the evidence leads to the conclusion that these documents were Soviet forgeries, designed to mislead and discredit American officials.

The Whalen Documents

There were six Whalen documents, all in Russian. Five were printed on purported letterhead of the Communist International, the other on what was supposed to be an Amtorg letterhead. Only photostatic copies of the Communist International documents have survived; the Amtorg document cannot be located.[1] Translations of all the documents, however, are available in a congressional publication.[2]

An examination of the alleged Communist International documents brands them an obvious forgery. The letterhead, instead of saying Executive Committee, Communist International, has the

Russian words *Ispolkom Kominterna*, the Russian contraction for Execom Comintern. Organizations, of course, print their full names on their letterhead, not their nicknames.

In October 1925 the British government had obtained a number of authentic Comintern documents at the time of the arrest of some leaders of the British Communist Party, including a complete letterhead. This letterhead, printed by the British government in an official report, read in Russian, German, French, and English, "Secretary of the Executive Committee of the Communist International."[3]

Numerous other inaccuracies appeared in the Whalen documents, including misuse of Russian words and misspellings of names of Soviet officials. Amtorg prepared an extensive analysis of the documents, which showed them to be forgeries. However, the one point not made in the Amtorg analysis was that the letterhead was clearly a forgery because of the use of the nickname of the Communist International. This may have been because Amtorg did not want to produce a copy of a genuine Comintern letterhead to protect against anyone creating an authentic-looking forgery. All but one of the printed Comintern letterhead documents obtained by the British in their 1925 raid had been mutilated by the Communists before filing for security reasons. Portions of the letterhead and the signatures had been torn off.[4]

The Whalen documents were first reported in the afternoon newspapers of May 2, 1930. That was a Friday. The next day John L. Spivak was asked by the editor of the *New York Evening Graphic* to investigate the authenticity of the documents.[5] Spivak claimed that he visited type foundries to obtain the names of printers who had ordered Russian-language type. He finally found the printer, Max Wagner, who admitted printing the letterhead.[6] According to Spivak, he reported to his editor, Swain, on the evening of Thursday, May 8, that he had identified the printer. Swain then sent Spivak to Washington.[7] Spivak contacted Congressman Fiorello La Guardia, who agreed to expose the documents. He also agreed to wait until Monday, May 12, so that the *Graphic* could have the scoop. La Guardia exposed the forgeries in a speech to the House of Representatives. Whalen and his charges against Amtorg were discredited.[8]

There is something seriously wrong with Spivak's story, however. When we examine the dates, they don't match. Spivak claimed to have learned about the existence of the documents on the morning of May 3, which was a Saturday. He did not report discovering the identity of the printer until Thursday, May 8. His reason for the four days' interval was that he was investigating type foundries and the Underwood Company, which produced the typewriter used. However, when the printer, Max Wagner, testified before the House Committee to Investigate Communist Propaganda on July 24, 1930, he indicated that Spivak had been in to see him on Saturday, May 3. This was the same day that Spivak learned of the existence of the documents, and before he could possibly have done the investigation that he claimed. Wagner testified in broken English:

> I saw in *Vorwarts*, a newspaper, published it on the front page. I recognized those documents and I started to look around to see all that was printed in it in typewritten form. I did not know of it. The first man came in and I said, "I find some documents, and the letterhead I printed." There was some documents printed. [He] said, "I will see what I can do to help you out." I said, "What will you do?" He took away newspapers and in ten minutes Mr. Spivak was in my store and he said, "Have you any of those documents or copies?" I said, "There are some there. If you give me time, I will look them up."[9]

The date of Wagner's meeting with Spivak can easily be determined by the date of the newspaper in question. *The Jewish Daily Forward*, known in Yiddish as the *Vorwarts*, printed copies of the documents on the front page on May 3, 1930, Saturday. That was the day Spivak began his investigation.

Wagner testified further, "Mr. Spivak asked me sign an affidavit that this document was printed. I signed the affidavit, and then he took away those two documents with him." The documents in question were proof copies of the letterhead that Wagner had printed.

During his speech Congressman La Guardia quoted the affidavit signed by Wagner as follows: "I printed this about 4 months ago and submitted two copies as a proof, but the man did not come back for the order. Signed, M. Wagner, printer." The next day the Communist Party newspaper in New York, the *Daily Worker*, carried a facsimile of some of the documents and of the handwritten Wagner affidavit. In the affidavit facsimile, however, the "two" was given as a number, not a word, and instead of the word "printer" after M. Wagner, there appeared the date May 8, 1930. It was apparent that the supposed affidavit of Wagner printed in the *Daily Worker* was not the same as the original affidavit quoted by Congressman La Guardia. It may be that the date was added to explain why Spivak had not immediately reported his conversation with Wagner to his editor.

The New York City Police Department was completely taken in by the forgery. Commissioner Whalen, testifying before the congressional committee, insisted that the documents had been provided to the department by undercover agents who would be made available to the committee. There is no indication they ever were. Whalen provided a ridiculous explanation of why he had only photostats, not the originals: "The original documents, according to the information we have here—these are the original photostats from the Amtorg Co., made by them. The originals, of a criminal nature, are all forwarded back to Russia according to the information which our undercover men are prepared to give you."[10] Why they would bother to photostat them instead of keeping the originals and why it was necessary to send the originals back to Russia, where presumably they had originated, was not explained by Whalen.

Who was John L. Spivak? Spivak was a longtime newspaper man who had written for a number of non-Communist publications. However, in 1945, fifteen years after the surfacing of the Whalen documents, Elizabeth Bentley identified Spivak as a member of the Soviet spy ring for which she worked as a courier. Bentley told the FBI that although she had not met Spivak, she had been told by Jacob Golos, the head of the ring, that Golos had paid expenses and compensation for "considerable investigating" Spivak had done on behalf of the Soviets. According to Bentley, she had seen receipts signed by Spivak, and after the death of Golos the Soviet official who took over the spy ring discussed Spivak with her and mentioned that he had some material to return to him.[11]

When Spivak testified before the congressional committee in 1930 his attorney was identified only as Mr. Antonio. In his autobiography Spivak identified the attorney as Vito Marcantonio. According to Spivak, Congressman La Guardia had recommended Marcantonio to him.[12] La Guardia, of course, later became the famous mayor of New York City, while Marcantonio went on to become a member of the United States Congress. Although Marcantonio was a well-known leftist and a joiner of a number of communist fronts, he spent many years in Congress. Finally, after losing his seat, he served as an attorney for the Communist Party USA in their proceedings before the Subversive Activities Control Board where the party was charged with being under Soviet control.

In 1952 Marcantonio cross-examined a government witness named John Lautner, who had been the head of the New York State Control Commission of the Communist Party, that is, the party's own internal investigative arm. Marcantonio asked why Lautner had allowed an FBI spy to get into the office of the Communist Party's Defense Committee. Lautner answered that he did not have responsibility for that office, that it was run by the National Control Commission rather than the state party. He testified, "In that Defense Office you had John L. Spivak in charge of security; you had Leon Josephson in charge of another phase of security. . . ."[13] (Josephson's involvement with Soviet intelligence is discussed in chapter 8.)

Spivak was a reporter for the *Daily Worker* during the 1930s and the author of numerous booklets published by Communist Party publishing houses in the 1930s and 1940s. His last pamphlet was *The Save the Country Racket*, published by New Century Publishers, the official Communist Party publishing house, in November 1948. In May 1942 an official report of the Justice Department signed by Attorney General Francis Biddle identified Spivak as a "well known Communist."[14]

There are the obvious questions: Who benefited from the Whalen forgeries? In what way did they benefit? The answers: The Soviets and the American Communist Party benefited. Months before the surfacing of these forgeries the Congress of the United States was discussing establishing a committee to investigate the Communist Party and Soviet propaganda. The forgeries were used to discredit that effort.

In April 1931 Earl Browder, then head of the American Communist Party, spoke at a meeting of the Executive Committee of the Communist International held in Moscow. According to Browder, "the notorious forged 'Whalen documents,' produced by the Czarist 'General' Djamgaroff, became the occasion for the U.S. Congress to set up the Fish Committee to investigate Communist activities in the U.S."[15] The Fish Committee, chaired by Congressman Hamilton Fish of New York, was officially called the Special Committee to Investigate Communist Activities in the United States.

Spivak claimed in his testimony before the Fish Committee that a Russian anti-communist in New York, named George Djamgaroff, was involved in giving the documents to Whalen. Djamgaroff denied the accusation.[16]

The Fish Committee did indeed take testimony concerning the Whalen documents, but it did so at the request of Amtorg and did not authenticate the documents. In the original resolution to establish the committee, Amtorg was not even mentioned.[17] During the congressional debate on establishing the committee, Congressman Bertrand Snell of New York, a supporter of the committee, said:

> At first I was very much opposed to putting into the resolution the name of the Amtorg Trading Corporation. I knew they were buying a great many of our manufactured products. But after the exposé in New York City I was told by men who knew the direct representatives of this corporation that they wanted an opportunity to clear themselves and show themselves absolutely clean, so far as these accusations are concerned, and that this was the only forum before which they could present their evidence.[18]

Max Bedacht, the editor of the Communist Party's theoretical organ, *The Communist,* and interim party leader before the assumption of power by Browder, wrote:

> Representative Hamilton Fish, Jr., is a blunderer and a bungler. He made a mess out of the job he undertook. Instead of keeping his eyes on the aims which the capitalist government in Washington desired to achieve, he kept his eyes on some clumsy forgeries in the circulation of which he himself had been instrumental even before the commission went into session. Thus instead of accomplishing the job that was assigned to him, Mr. Fish tried to use his committee to stamp as genuine some clumsy forgery that not even the most loyal capitalist protagonist could accept as genuine."[19]

The Soviets attempted to get a small additional benefit from the production of the forgeries in an article in *International Press Correspondence,* the official organ of the Communist International. Datelined London, this article claimed that the documents made reference to "the Lovestone renegade group (apparently in order to give local colour to the affair), which is alleged to have stolen the papers from the headquarters of the CP."[20] The Lovestone group had been expelled from the Communist Party the year before, in 1929, but was still working to get back in. Not only did the Lovestoneites not have any involvement with the documents, they had publicly denounced them. In a statement in their newspaper they said:

> For years we have been working as an integral part and as the leaders of the Communist International organization of the United States. We know its workings and methods thoroughly. Therefore, we are in a position to declare categorically that these "documents" and the "information" given out in reference to so-called Soviet agents are a stupid concoction from beginning to end. . . . the product of a fantastic fraud which could be manufactured only by cheap forgers and ambitious politicians like Grover A. Whalen.[21]

The exposure of the forgery by Spivak, an identified Soviet agent, who apparently was aware of the print shop used only one day after the forgeries were released, indicates that these were similar to the forgeries used in Europe to discredit the Soviet's gullible political enemies.

The Tanaka Memorial

In 1929 a new kind of forgery surfaced. This was not a collection of forged Soviet documents meant to discredit enemies foolish enough to accept their authenticity, but a single document purported to be a secret Japanese plan to conquer the world. The Tanaka Memorial appeared to be a memorandum from General Baron Tanaka, prime minister of Japan from 1927 to 1929, to the emperor. It was widely used in the United States to create anti-Japanese sentiment during the 1930s.

After first surfacing the forgery in China, the Comintern published it in the December 30, 1931, issue of its theoretical organ, *Communist International*. It was then published in pamphlet form by the communists in a number of editions. Non-Communist publishers also issued copies of the forgery, including the American Harper & Brothers, which published a 1942 edition edited by the non-Communist pro-Chinese author Carl Crow.[22]

An introduction to a version of the Tanaka Memorial published by the American Communist Party in December 1941 gives the following history:

> The Tanaka Memorial . . . was written in 1927 as a confidential document. It first came to light in 1929 after it had been purchased from a Japanese by Chang Hsueh-liang, then the young Marshall of Manchuria. It was published in English by the China Council of the Institute of Pacific Relations and shortly thereafter printed in a Shanghai English-language newspaper. It was later reprinted in quantities throughout the world.[23]

Chang was a Manchurian warlord who had an on-again, off-again friendly relationship with the Chinese Communist Party. In December 1936 he kidnapped Chiang Kai-shek to force him to form an alliance with the Communists for a united front against the Japanese invaders. Official Chinese Communist Party statements praised the "patriotic sincerity and zeal" of the young marshall who committed the kidnapping.[24]

The Tanaka Memorial contained innumerable inaccuracies, including wrong dates and incorrect explanations of incidents relating to the life of Tanaka. The American Communists, in attempting to explain the contradictions, wrote:

> Certain internal inconsistencies, of an extremely minor nature, one or two incorrect dates, and the misspelling of a number of place names, doubtless the result of translation, have been cited as evidence of the non-authenticity of the document. The Japanese took pains to point out that from the nature of the memorandum, that is, the directness and informality of the style, the document was plainly not a Memorial to the Emperor. This evidence may be dismissed as trival. The text of the memorandum itself states that it results from a special conference called "in order that we may lay plans for the colonization of the Far East and the development of our new continental empire" which met from June 27 to July 7, 1927. The Tanaka Memorial is clearly the secret report of that conference, the official program of the confidential information of the fascist cabal that enslaves the Japanese nation. Its authenticity is evidenced by the subsequent detailed carrying out of its plans. The Tanaka Memorial is today the clearest, most authentic revelation of the adventurist Japanese plan for world conquest.[25]

The classic Soviet work, *Militarism and Fascism in Japan*, published in 1934 by the two Soviet experts, O. Tanin and E. Yohan, treated the memorial as authentic.[26] A Communist Party USA pamphlet published in 1935 and aimed at American Negroes quoted extensively from the forged document and pretended that it was authentic.[27]

Its internal evidence makes it clear that the Tanaka Memorial is clearly a forgery. But the evidence that it was a Soviet forgery came from an unusual source. In 1940 Leon Trotsky wrote an article attempting to prove that the Tanaka Memorial was an authentic document. He succeeded in providing the evidence that it was a Soviet forgery. The article, which was not complete at the time of Trotsky's assassination by the Soviet Intelligence Service in 1940, was published in the official Trotskyite magazine, *Fourth International*, in June 1941.[28]

Trotsky claimed that "the 'Tanaka Memorial' was first photographed in Tokyo in the Ministry of Naval Affairs and brought to Moscow as an undeveloped film. I was perhaps the very first person to become acquainted with the document in English and Russian translations of the Japanese text." The document had been made available to him in 1925 by Felix Dzerzhinsky, the chief of the Soviet Intelligence Service. Trotsky did not explain how a document dated 1927 was shown to him in 1925. The answer obviously is that if a document was stolen by a Soviet spy in Japan, it was not the Tanaka Memorial but a document used later by the Soviet Intelligence Service to create the forged Tanaka Memorial. Nevertheless what Trotsky said about the document and about the Soviet Intelligence Service at the time is of some interest. He wrote:

The Military Intelligence Service was under a two-fold jurisdiction: subject on the one hand to the War Department and on the other to the GPU. The Foreign Department of the GPU was headed by an old Bolshevik, Trilisser, who was later removed and apparently liquidated along with many others. The Military Intelligence was headed by Berzin, an old Lettish Bolshevik. I was not closely acquainted with the organization of our agency in Japan, being little interested in the technical aspects of the matter. I handed this over to my aides, first Sklyansky, later Unschlicht and, to a certain extent, Rosenholtz. Permit me to recall that Sklyansky, one of the outstanding and most meritorious organizers of the Red Army, was drowned in 1924 or

1925 in America while taking a boat ride on a lake. Unschlicht disappeared, and was evidently liquidated. Rosenholtz was shot by verdict of the court.[29]

Trotsky boasted that Soviet intelligence was successful because:

The party had at its disposal not a few people who had passed through a serious conspiratorial school and who were well acquainted with all the methods and subterfuges of the police and counter-espionage. They brought into their work an international experience, many of them having been émigrés in various lands and possessing a broad political outlook. They had personal friends in many countries. Nor was there any lack of self-sacrificing support on the part of the revolutionary elements in different countries. In many government institutions of capitalist countries the lower functionaries were sympathetic to a considerable degree to the October revolution. Provided one knew how, their sympathy could be utilized in the interests of the Soviet power. It was so utilized. . . .

Dzerzhinsky was brought into the Political Bureau after Lenin's death. This step was taken by Stalin, Zinoviev and Kamenev in order to attract to their side the honest but vain-glorious Dzerzhinsky. They succeeded completely.

Dzerzhinsky was very talkative, very hot-tempered and explosive. This man of iron will who had served terms of hard penal labor possessed traits which were absolutely childlike. Once during a session of the Political Bureau he boasted of his hopes shortly to lure Boris Savinkov to Soviet soil and arrest him. My reaction to this was highly skeptical. But Dzerzhinsky proved right. Savinkov was lured by agents of the GPU to Soviet territory and arrested there. Shortly thereafter, Dzerzhinsky expressed his hopes of apprehending Wrangel in the same way. But this hope did not materialize because Wrangel proved more cautious.

Trotsky further wrote:

One day in 1925, in the summer or early autumn, Dzerzhinsky talked excitedly about his expectations of obtaining an extremely important document from Japan. He stated ecstatically that this document in and of itself could provoke international upheavals, events of vast importance, war between Japan and the United States, etc. I remained, as always in such cases, even more skeptical.

"Wars are not provoked by documents," I objected to Dzerzhinsky. But he insisted: "You have no conception of the importance of this document; it is the program of the ruling circles, approved by the Mikado himself; it embraces the seizure of China, the destruction of the United States, world domination."

"Mightn't your agent be duped?" I asked. "No one writes such documents as a rule. Why would such plans be put down on paper?"

Dzerzhinsky was himself not very sure on this point. He replied, as if to dispel the doubts in his own mind: "In their country they do everything in the name of the Emperor. In order to justify risky measures, risky politics, and vast army and naval expenditures the military men and the diplomats have been seeking to tempt the Mikado with a colossal perspective which is equally indispensable to themselves for the political adventures in which they are engaging. That is why Tanaka has written down the plans of the military circles in a special report to the Emperor, and this report has met with the Emperor's approval.[30] We will receive a photographic copy of the document directly from the archives of the Ministry of Foreign Affairs."

I remember that Dzerzhinsky mentioned a sum to be paid for the photographic copy. It was relatively modest, about three thousand American dollars.

According to Trotsky, Dzerzhinsky told him that the GPU enjoyed the services of a trusted Japanese functionary who had access to the secret archives of the Japanese Ministry of Foreign Affairs. For more than a year he had provided very valuable information. The spy wished to hand-copy the document but the GPU demanded photographic copies. A GPU technician had to teach the spy the art of photography. Several copies of each page were photographed, and the film was then forwarded by different routes. All the copies arrived safely in Moscow.

Trotsky described the scene in Moscow:

"The document has arrived!" Dzerzhinsky announced joyously. Where was it? It had arrived as a film which was being developed. The developing was coming out successfully and the document was being translated by our Japanese experts as it was developed. They were all staggered by the contents of the very first few pages. I would get my report from Trilisser. (It might have been Unschlicht.) . . .

The film was developed and the translation made at once in the offices of the Intelligence Service, and both were rushed immediately to the Kremlin. The photostats were still wet. . . .

[W]hen the Political Bureau met, all the members were acquainted with the document. Although personal relations were already very strained at that time, all the members of the Political Bureau seemed temporarily to draw closer together because of the document. In the preliminary discussion the main topic was naturally the voracity of the Japanese. The megalomania in which mysticism and cynicism remarkably supplemented each other was spoken of with astonishment tinged with grudging admiration.

"Isn't this perhaps a poem, a forgery?" asked Bukharin who with all his childlike gullibility loved, whenever a propitious occasion offered itself, to play the part of a cautious statesman. Dzerzhinsky exploded, as usual.

"I have already explained to you," he said, speaking with a Polish accent which always became thicker as he grew excited, "that this document is supplied by our agent who has proved his complete trustworthiness; and that this document was kept in the most secret section of the archives of the Naval Ministry. . . ."

Zinoviev suggested that the document be published in the periodical, *Communist International*. This was rejected. It had to appear elsewhere first. Trotsky offered a plan to publish the document abroad and avoid any link whatever between the document and Moscow.

I proposed that, after the document was translated into English, it should be transmitted to the press by a trustworthy and authoritative friend of the Soviet Republic in the United States. At that time the calling of a friend of the Soviet Union had not yet become a profession. The number of friends was not large; important and influential personalities were all too scarce. In any case the task turned out much more difficult than I had presumed. . . .

Any reference to the real source, i.e., the GPU, would arouse additional mistrust. In America the suspicion would naturally arise that the GPU itself had simply manufactured the document in order to poison relations between Japan and the United States.

The English translation was painstakingly made in Moscow. The photostats together with the English text were forwarded to New York, and in this way any trace of a connection between this document and Moscow was eliminated. . . .

In those years the Soviet republic did not as yet have its own diplomatic representative in the United States. At the head of the Amtorg was the engineer, Bogdanov. He and his colleagues, who are today better known and more influential, fulfilled all sorts of diplomatic missions. I cannot now recall just who among them was entrusted with the task of finding a competent person among the Americans and putting the document in circulation through him.

Trotsky was not ignorant of the 1927 date assigned by the communist distributors of the document. He wrote:

> According to indications the "Tanaka Memorial" was signed by the Mikado in July 1927. In that case it is quite obvious that the document was forwarded to Moscow prior to its being actually signed by the Mikado. . . . Tanaka became Premiere in April 1927. He might have well obtained the post of premiere precisely because of undertaking to win the Emperor's sanction for this program of the extreme wing of the militarists and imperialists.

Of course, Trotsky was wrong. The document was not signed by the Japanese emperor—the Mikado—it was supposedly signed by Baron Tanaka. In addition, in 1925, when Moscow allegedly had the document, Tanaka was not yet the prime minister.

It is interesting to note that Trotsky assigned to Bogdanov, the head of Amtorg in the United States, the role of finding the appropriate agent of influence to make the document available to the press. Trotsky appeared unaware that Bogdanov did not arrive in the United States until January 1930 to assume the job of director of Amtorg. It is possible that Trotsky's knowledge of Amtorg's role in the distribution of the Tanaka document came not from his own recollection but from information provided years later by his sympathizers who remained in the GPU. Still, the plan outlined by Trotsky to surface the document first elsewhere, then later in the *Communist International* magazine, was indeed followed.

The new style of forgery represented by the Tanaka Memorial— the creation of documents attributed to opponents of the Soviets— became the pattern for Soviet forgeries in future years. Since the 1940s forgeries have become part of the influence operations, or "active measures" of the KGB.[31]

5

On-the-Job Training
for Spies

C OMMUNIST Party training for underground activity provided
the basis for the espionage used by Americans on behalf of the
Soviets. In 1931 American and Canadian communists received mimeographed copies of a secret pamphlet issued by the Comintern.
Signed B. Vassiliev, the pamphlet provided instructions for underground work.

Vassiliev was an important functionary of the Comintern's Organizational Bureau. In 1931 he spoke at the 11th Plenum of the Executive Committee of the Comintern.[1] A former Comintern and
Communist Party USA functionary, Joe Zack Kornfeder, who was
in Moscow from 1927 to 1930, identified Vassiliev as the one who
assisted Piatnitsky, the head of the Organization Bureau.[2] As Trilisser
was Piatnitsky's assistant at that time, it is possible that he used the
Vassiliev name.

Eugene Victor Dennett, a former Communist Party USA functionary, testified before the House Un-American Activities Committee in 1955 that he had received the mimeographed Vassiliev
pamphlet from the Central Committee of the CPUSA, when he "was
an agitprop [agitation and propaganda] director."[3] Some of the methods taught in the Vassiliev pamphlet were identical to espionage
trade craft. It instructed the Communists in the use of codes and
ciphers. The code taught was simple word substitution, but the
ciphers were more sophisticated.

[B]esides a code . . . ciphers are used, illegal [secret] parts of letters
being put not only into code but also into cipher. There are many

different systems of cipher. The simplest and at the same time most reliable system of cipher is the system of cipher by the help of a book. Some book or other is agreed upon beforehand and then the cipher is made in this way: simple fractions or decimals are ciphered. The first figure of the first fraction shows the page of the book. Then further comes the actual cipher. For the numerator of the fraction we must take a line counting from above or below, for the denominator that counting from the left or from the right which it is necessary to put into cipher. For example, we need to put into cipher the letter "A". We look in the book and we see that this letter is in the third line from the top, the fourth letter from the left to the right. Then we cipher 3 over 4 (3/4), that is the third line from the top, fourth letter from left to right. You can agree also on this method: for example, counting the line not from above but from below, then the 3 will be not the third line from above but the third line from below. You can agree to count the letter in the line not from left to right but from right to left. Finally, for greater complexity in order to keep the sense from the police, you can also add to the fraction some figure or other. Let us say the numerator is increased by 3 and denominator by 4. In this case, in order to decipher, it will be necessary first to subtract in the numerator and denominator of every fraction. A whole number of similar complications can be thought out in order to complicate the cipher. The advantage of such a cipher is that it is not only very simple but also that each letter can be designated by a great number of difference signs and in such a way that the cipher designation of letters are not repeated. The book cipher can be used without a book. In place of a book some poem or other can be chosen, learned by heart and ciphering done according to it. When it is necessary to cipher or decipher, the poem must be written out in verses and then the ciphering or deciphering done and the poem destroyed.

Vassiliev also instructed the Communists in the use of invisible ink.[4] These methods are, of course, the traditional activities of espionage agents. The Communist Party underground workers who learned these methods were able to use them when the needs of the Soviet Intelligence Service required it.

In 1930 the Communist Party had issued an internal pamphlet on how to publish a "shop paper." An entire chapter was devoted to surreptitious distribution of the paper.[5] Contacts made through distribution of the papers could then be used by the Communist underground for more serious activity.

During 1934 J. Peters, who took over the leadership of underground activity from Max Bedacht, explained to party members the need to establish "safe houses" in underground work. According to Peters, in an article in a party magazine meant for members only, "Every comrade must have prepared already today a place where he or she can stay in case of any emergency; the home of a sympathizer who is not known by the police should be secured in advance so that when the terror breaks, the comrades can disappear from their home."[6] Peters's knowledge of espionage trade craft was particularly useful, as he was the liaison during most of the 1930s for Soviet espionage in the United States (see chapters 6 and 7).

When the Roosevelt administration recognized Russia in 1933, the Soviet government agreed to "restrain all persons directly or indirectly in the employ of the government, from carrying on propaganda for a change by force of the political or social system of the other country." These agreements or "undertakings" caused some confusion in the ranks of the American Communists, who had understood that they were under the instructions of the Soviet regime to overthrow the American government. The undertakings were explained in a document dated December 12, 1933, which was ordered to be read at all Communist Party units "at the earliest possible date." The explanation was:

> In connection with these undertakings, the important thing to bear in mind is that the CP [Communist Party] of the S. U. [Soviet Union] and the C. I. [Communist International] and the Soviet Government are not one and the same thing, and they have different functions to perform. The function of the CP on a national scale, and the CI on an international scale is to lead in the struggles of the masses and to organize them for the overthrow of capitalism, and after the overthrow of capitalism to guide in the most rapid transformation of the old order into the Socialist order. The function of the Soviet Government, which is the organ of the dictatorship of the proletariat, is to consolidate its power within the country, to proceed with the building of Socialism and to defend the country from Imperialist aggression. For this purpose it has to establish relations with the Capitalist countries, utilizing their needs for markets and their conflicting interests to

postpone the imperialist attack upon it as long as possible, in the meantime improving its own economy and means of defense, while at the same time the forces of the international revolution mature.[7]

Penetrating the Military

An important element of Communist Party work was penetration of the United States military, both to weaken its will to fight and to obtain information for the Soviets. Paul Crouch played a major role in this activity. In 1925 Crouch had been court-martialed for writing a letter to the Comintern offering to organize a communist unit in the U.S. Army in Hawaii. Crouch was not a Communist Party member at the time but joined after serving a prison sentence. At a meeting of the Communist Party Secretariat on September 21, 1927, Lovestone reported that Crouch was seeking admission to the Communist Party, asking that his membership be dated from May 1925, "immediately after his arrest when he first made application to join the Party." Approval was unanimous.[8]

At a meeting of the Political Committee of the Communist Party held November 2, 1927, Lovestone reported on the antimilitarist work of the party. It was decided that a meeting would be held with Crouch to look into how this work was going.[9]

At a Political Committee Meeting on October 12, the decision had been made to send Crouch to Moscow for the Soviet tenth anniversary celebration. The trip was at the invitation of Willi Muenzenberg.[10]

Crouch was apparently delayed, because it was not until December 1927 that he went to Moscow, where he remained approximately five months. During that time he was made a member of the Anti-Militarist Commission of the Young Communist International. According to Crouch, this apparatus "during the early part of 1928, drafted detailed plans for operational work in the armed forces of all countries." A photograph of Crouch in Red Army uniform was printed in the U.S. Communist Party newspaper *Daily Worker* of May 1, 1928.

At a meeting with Soviet Marshall Tukhachevsky and three other members of the Soviet general staff, Crouch was instructed to recruit communists to penetrate the U.S. Army in Panama and Hawaii. He was also instructed to send communist agents into the navy. The

USS *Oklahoma* was selected, and after Crouch's return from the Soviet Union a cell was organized on that ship.

Walter Trumbull, who had also served a jail sentence for communist work in the army, succeeded Crouch as head of the Communist Party's Anti-Militarist Department. Max Bedacht was assigned by the Central Committee to guide the work of Crouch and Trumbull. According to Crouch, Bedacht was responsible for the underground work of the party and instructed him on the operations in the army.

Crouch also knew Dozenberg. In 1929 Dozenberg took Crouch to an apartment on the West Side of New York City to meet with a man he described as the head of the OGPU in the United States. The man was a Russian who spoke broken English and was interested in placing young American Communists in the State Department or other government agencies. He also expressed an interest in obtaining blank American passports.[11] The man he met was probably Moishe Stern, the head of Soviet Military Intelligence in the United States and Canada.

The Communist Party issued a number of newspapers aimed at organizing members of the military or workers in factories producing military equipment. One of those papers aimed at the army was called the *Soldiers' Voice*. The issue for December 1933 carried an article explaining the difference between the U.S. and Soviet Army. Soldiers were urged to follow the Soviet path and overthrow the U.S. government. A similar paper, *Shipmates' Voice*, claimed to be issued "by and for sailors and marines." The first issue, dated April/May 1934, contained articles very similar to those in *Soldiers' Voice*; some were identical. In April 1934 the first issue of *Navy Yard Worker* was distributed to the employees of the Washington, D.C., Navy Yard. It was similar to the other two papers.

Dedicated Revolutionaries

The Communist Party was able to find people so dedicated that they would sacrifice anything for the Soviet Union. One such couple, Gene and Peggy Dennis, devoted their whole lives to the party, working both aboveground and underground. When Gene Dennis died in 1961 he was the general secretary of the Communist Party. Peggy left the party in 1976 but has remained a dedicated communist and Soviet patriot. Their story, told by Peggy in her autobiography,[12] typifies the life and dedication of a Communist apparatchik.

In September 1929 Gene Dennis (whose real name was Francis Waldron) with his pregnant girlfriend, Peggy, arrived in San Francisco to work on the magazine *Pan Pacific Monthly*. The magazine was published by the Pan Pacific Trade Union Secretariat of the Red International of Labor Unions, the Comintern's trade union front. In reality the secretariat was the cover operation for Comintern and Soviet intelligence work in Asia.

In 1931 the Dennises and their baby son, Timmy, were sent to Moscow. After some training, Gene was sent to do underground work in the Philippines, South Africa, and China. Peggy was left in Moscow. She was given a job as a research worker in the Red International of Labor Unions (Profintern). After a time she was enrolled in a one-year course at the Lenin School, an international communist school in Moscow that still exists to train foreign Communist cadre. It is also called the Higher Party School. After her training Peggy served as a Comintern courier, traveling throughout Europe. Her young son, Timmy, was placed in the Comintern's International Children's Home outside of Moscow. In 1934 Peggy was assigned to Shanghai, where she could again live with Gene. Timmy, however, stayed in the children's home. In early 1935, after serving as a Comintern courier in Turkey, Egypt, and Palestine, Peggy was ready to return to the United States with Gene.

Before leaving Moscow they met with top officials of the Comintern. One of them, Dimitri Manuilsky, told them that Timmy would not go back with them. The two dedicated Communists accepted this order and left their son behind.

In 1937 the Dennises returned to Moscow where Gene served as the American representative to the Comintern. Timmy was allowed to live with them, but a year later Gene and Peggy returned to the United States, again leaving Timmy behind.

In 1941 the Dennises returned again to Moscow on Comintern business, but when the Nazis attacked the Soviet Union they were sent home. Again Timmy remained in the Soviet Union. The Comintern's general secretary, George Dimitrov, said that perhaps he could be sent back to them after the war. He was not.

In October 1959 Khrushchev came to the United Nations. Among the Soviets accompanying him was the thirty-year-old son of Peggy and Gene Dennis. Peggy, in her autobiography, described their meeting at the Soviet Union mission. They were to meet with Khrushchev and Gromyko. Gromyko said jokingly to Peggy, "We are very proud of Tim. He is ours, you know. We have no intention of giving him back to you." At Khrushchev's suggestion Timmy served as translator for Khrushchev and his father.

Even though she has left the Communist Party, Peggy still visits Moscow to see her son and his family, and he now visits the United States. What she did not reveal in her autobiography was the name that her American-born son now uses. He is Timur Timofeyev, the director of the Institute of the International Labor Movement of the USSR Academy of Sciences.

Like Eugene Dennis, a number of other Americans served in China during the late 1920s and early 1930s. Some of them were assigned to the Comintern's Intelligence Division. Others worked for the Fourth Bureau of the Red Army (Soviet Military Intelligence). The links between the two intelligence elements were close, and Comintern cadre from various countries were often reassigned to the Fourth Bureau.[13]

Richard Sorge was a legendary Soviet intelligence officer who was finally captured in Japan during World War II. Sorge joined the German Communist Party on October 15, 1919. He held the low membership number 8678. By 1921 the party had increased to 360,000 members. Sorge was a delegate that year to the Party's Second Congress. In 1925 he went to Moscow where he was admitted to the Soviet Communist Party. The Soviet archives still retain the original questionnaire filled out by Sorge when he joined the Soviet Communist Party. Under occupation he listed "intelligence worker."[14]

For many years Sorge worked for the Comintern's intelligence service. However, he was subsequently reassigned to the Fourth Bureau of the Red Army. In Sorge's confession to the Japanese, he referred to the Comintern's intelligence division as "one of the three major departments which laid the groundwork for the concrete organizational and political decisions by means of which leadership was exerted over the international Communist party movement." He stated that he was a member of this organization as early as 1925 and assisted in the expansion of this apparatus, which was controlled by the Organizational Department of the Comintern, called by the initials OMS. According to Sorge:

> Only a party comrade with years of international experience—for example, Kuusinen and others who held the position for a time—could become the chief of the Intelligence Division. Under the chief, there was a secretariat headed by a chief secretary, under which the affairs of the various countries were controlled and grouped in the following manner: Europe, British Empire, North America, South America, and East Asia, including all the nations and parties in the southwest Pacific. These major classifications were further subdivided, the Europe group for example, being broken down into German-speaking nations and parties, Romance language nations and parties (France, Italy, Spain), Scandinavian parties, and Balkan nations. East Asians were divided into China, Japan, Korea, the Netherlands East Indies, and a single office lumping together all the other parties in the area."[15]

In 1929, after a number of operations in western Europe on behalf of the intelligence division of the Comintern, Sorge returned to Moscow where he was separated from the Comintern apparatus and assigned to the Fourth Bureau of the Red Army. He became a Soviet Military Intelligence officer. From January 1930 to December 1932 Sorge operated on behalf of Soviet Military Intelligence in China. He worked closely with Agnes Smedley, an American who, while probably not a member of the Communist Party of the United States, had a close association with it as well as with Soviet intelligence. Smedley collected information for Sorge's spy ring.

While in Shanghai Sorge had contact with a number of other Soviet intelligence groups. These included the Comintern group, which was headed by Gerhart Eisler, who later became the Comintern's secret representative in the United States, and the Frolich Group. Frolich, who also used the code name Theo, was described by Sorge as a major general in the Red Army and had the responsibility of collecting data for Soviet Military Intelligence on Chinese military activities.[16]

One of the members of Sorge's spy ring was Ruth Werner, a German Communist. In her memoirs, published in East Germany in 1977, she identified Frolich as Manfred Stern, alias General Kleber, who commanded the International Brigades at the Madrid front during the Spanish Civil War. According to Werner, who used the code name "Sonja," Stern was also known as "Fred." He had participated in Communist uprisings in Germany in 1921 and 1923 and in 1932 was chief military adviser to the Communist Party of China.[17] This, of course, was Moishe Stern, who operated in the United States as Mark Zilbert just before going to Shanghai.

The Comintern intelligence apparatus in Shanghai operated under the cover of the Pan Pacific Trade Union Secretariat of the Red International of Labor Unions, the Moscow-based international trade union front. Among the American Communists who participated in this apparatus were Gene Dennis, Margaret Undjus, Max Granich (the brother of the American Communist novelist, Mike Gold), and Earl Browder. Browder headed the group until 1930 when he returned to the United States to become head of the American Communist Party and was replaced by Gerhart Eisler.

Among the Germans in the Comintern group were Arthur Ewart, who used the name Harry Berger, and two Germans who dealt with both the Sorge ring and the Comintern apparatus, Otto Braun and his wife Olga Benario.[18]

Harrison George, a prominent member of the American Communist Party, ran the apparatus of the Pan Pacific Secretariat in San Francisco, which served as the political cover for the Comintern intelligence unit and provided instructions and funds where necessary. George also edited *Pan Pacific Monthly*. Prior to going to Moscow, Gene Dennis had worked as George's assistant.[19]

Dennis used the name Paul Eugene Walsh in Shanghai. The Shanghai Municipal Police file gives the following information about him:

> When and how Walsh arrived in Shanghai are unknown, as are his previous activities. From December 1, 1933, until June 1, 1934, he resided at Flat 6, Gresham Apartments, No. 1224 Avenue Joffre. On May 30, 1934, the lease of Flat 34D, Foncim Apartments, No. 643 Route Frelupt was transferred to his name from Harry Berger [Arthur Ewart], with whom he was obviously on terms of good friendship. Walsh resided at the latter address from June 1, 1934, until October 9, 1934 when he secretly left Shanghai for Trieste on SS *Sonte Verde*. It has been established that Walsh was one of the masterminds of the local machine of the Komintern, and as such was responsible for the

collation of many important documents relating to the propagation of Communist ideas in the Far East.

The file also shows that he held American passport number 331741, issued in Washington on December 12, 1930.[20]

Dennis apparently came to Shanghai to take over the Comintern apparatus when some of the group were forced to leave as a result of police raids. Margaret Undjus returned to the United States where, under the names Margaret Cowl and Margaret Krumbein, she served in leadership positions in the American Communist Party. In 1932 she wrote a pamphlet, *The Soviet Union, Your Questions Answered,* which she said was based on her experience answering questions about her years in the Soviet Union during a lecture tour of twenty American cities.

Agnes Smedley wrote a number of books on China and ultimately became one of the leading American propagandists for the People's Republic of China. Gene Dennis, after his return from China, held numerous posts in the Communist Party USA leadership, ultimately achieving the top post of general secretary. Ruth Werner, after serving as a Soviet agent in England for a number of years, returned to East Germany where she still resides. Otto Braun worked for a long time as an advisor to the Chinese Red Army and ultimately returned to Moscow. In 1949 he went to East Germany, where he lived until his death. Braun's wife, Olga Benario, left him to marry Luis Carlos Prestes, the head of the Communist Party of Brazil. Arthur Ewart was also reassigned to Brazil.

The Seventh World Congress of the Communist International took place in Moscow in July and August of 1935. During the 23d session on August 7, Wang Ming (real name Chen Shao-Yu) spoke on the national and colonial revolutions. He pointed to Brazil where a National Liberation Alliance was organized by the Communist Party and led by Prestes. Wang Ming ordered "all power to the National Liberation Alliance." This paraphrase of Lenin's slogan, "all power to the Soviets," was the instruction to the Brazilian Communists to organize an insurrection.[21]

A number of the Comintern apparatchiks who had served in China were sent to assist Prestes in this operation. These included the new wife of Prestes, Olga Benario, Arthur Ewart, and his wife, Maria. A young American, Victor Barron, represented the Young Communist International. Barron was the son of Harrison George, the Comintern's man in San Francisco.

The insurrection failed and the conspirators were captured. Benario and Maria Ewart were returned to Nazi Germany by the Brazilian police. They perished in the Ravensbrueck concentration camp. The East German government issued stamps in their honor in 1959.[22] The child of Benario and Prestes, born in prison, was taken away from Benario before she was sent back to Nazi Germany; she was raised in Brazil. Arthur Ewart was so badly tortured by the police that his mind snapped and he never again was able to work for the Comintern. After World War II he went to East Germany where he lived out the rest of his life. Young Victor Barron fell, or was pushed, out of a window at police headquarters. A worldwide campaign was conducted by the Comintern in support of Prestes and the demand for his release.[23]

In July 1936, the American Communist Party issued a pamphlet about Prestes. The introduction was written by Harrison George, who spoke about the death of his son, Victor Barron. In 1947, though no longer a member of the American Communist Party, Harrison George remained a dedicated communist. A booklet that he wrote at that time was dedicated, "In memory of my son Victor who died unyielding to fascist torture, March 6, 1936, at Rio de Janeiro."[24]

Richard Sorge went from China to Japan where he developed the most significant Soviet espionage operation directed against the Japanese. Sorge had been forbidden by Moscow to engage in "nonintelligence activity," which meant that he should not try to influence the political situation in Japan. Political influence operations, now called active measures by the Soviets, have a long tradition; but during the 1930s they were primarily the work of Comintern intelligence rather than military intelligence.

Sorge, who learned his trade in the Comintern, decided that there were many opportunities to influence Japanese elite opinion in a pro-Soviet direction. The opportunities were too good to miss. In 1941 he asked Moscow whether it would be permissible to have Ozaki, a member of his group with very high-level connections, promote the idea of a peace policy toward the Soviet Union. Ozaki, according to Sorge, "was confident that if he took a strong stance toward a Soviet-Japanese war in the Konoye Group, he could turn Japanese expansion policy southward" (i.e., against the United States).

Moscow's response was negative, saying that this was unnecessary. Sorge construed their response as not banning the activity. He therefore encouraged Ozaki to promote that line.[25]

Finally captured in 1941, Sorge wrote an extensive confession of his activities. In the 1960s the Soviets began a propaganda campaign eulogizing Richard Sorge. A stamp was issued in his honor and the Soviet magazine *New Times* wrote, "The remarkable life of Richard Sorge, staunch Communist and legendary Soviet intelligence agent, has lately received much attention in the Soviet Union. Under the Stalin personality cult his heroic work got no recognition. . . ."[26] A 1973 book on *Soviet Peace Efforts On The Eve Of World War II* carried a number of communications from Sorge to Soviet military intelligence headquarters. The communications themselves are relatively innocuous, but their publication by the Soviets is of some interest. Each of the cables was described as "telegram from a Soviet military intelligence officer in Japan to the General Staff of the Red Army." The telegrams were signed "Ramzai." The Soviets identified this code name as "R. Sorge."[27] In 1985 the East Germans printed photostats of two of Sorge's reports.[28]

In 1939 the U.S. State Department picked up the trail of the Comintern intelligence apparatus during an investigation of the illegal use of U.S. passports. They discovered that Arthur Ewart had traveled to China and then Brazil on a fraudulent passport under the name Harry Berger. The passport, which was issued in New York in 1932, indicated that the applicant had been born in New York on February 18, 1892. The passport was renewed at the U.S. Consulate General in Shanghai, China, on June 30, 1934. When Ewart was arrested in Brazil in December 1935 he was carrying the passport. Maria Ewart was also using a forged passport. Hers was in the name of Machla Lenczyski. This passport, too, was obtained in 1932 and was renewed at the American Consulate in Shanghai on July 1, 1934. Mrs. Ewart identified herself as a naturalized American citizen who had obtained citizenship in the Bronx, New York, in September 1928. The State Department investigation revealed that the passport had been obtained by using the legitimate identification papers of a naturalized citizen who had come to the United States in 1932 on a nonimmigrant visa and left with a fraudulent passport.[29]

Margaret Undjus used an authentic passport issued in her own name based on application she had made in 1927. In China she joined Charles Krumbein, an official of the American Communist Party, whom she identified as her husband. Krumbein was also in China as a Comintern representative. When he returned to the United States he served in numerous capacities in both the New York State and national organizations of the Communist Party. When he died in the 1940s he was national treasurer of the Communist Party. Krumbein had traveled on a fraudulent passport issued to an Albert E. Stuart. He had also used other names on other passports during his many years working for the Comintern.[30]

Upon her return to the United States in 1935, Undjus claimed to the State Department that her passport had been lost in a lake when her handbag fell out of a rowboat. State Department officials told her they did not believe her story, whereupon she mailed her passport to the department. She also sent an affidavit claiming that she had forgotten where she had lost her passport but that later her attorney, Mr. Joseph Brodsky, had found the passport in his safe. Joseph Brodsky, a charter member of the Communist Party, had also been involved in Communist underground activities. In 1927, when the British government raided Arcos, the Soviet purchasing agency in Britain, they found documents indicating that Brodsky maintained a mail drop on behalf of the Comintern intelligence network.[31]

The State Department's investigation uncovered an organization called World Tourists Incorporated. In the files of that organization investigators found two accounts, which paid for the overseas travel of Communist Party members. One account was in the name of George Primoff and the other A. Blake. The Primoff account paid for the trip to Brazil by Victor Barron that resulted in his death.[32] World Tourists Incorporated was run by Jacob Raisin, also known as Jacob Golos.[33] Golos was the spy master for whom courier Elizabeth Bentley later worked.

The 1930s provided new opportunities for Soviet intelligence working through the small band of Soviet patriots which now called themselves the Communist Party USA. The Great Depression, the liberal, Democratic president, Roosevelt, and the U.S. recognition of Soviet Russia, provided new situations that could be exploited both by the Soviet Intelligence Service and the American Communists.

Earl Browder, who headed the Communist Party in the 1930s, was to boast years later:

> Entering the 1930s as a small ultra-left sect of some 7,000 members, remnant of the fratricidal factional struggle of the 1920s that had wiped out the old "left wing" of American socialism, the CP rose to become a national political influence far beyond its numbers (at its height it never exceeded 100,000 members), on a scale never before reached by a socialist movement claiming the Marxist tradition. It became a practical power in organized labour, its influence became strong in some state organizations of the Democratic Party (even dominant in a few for some years), and even some Republicans solicited its support. It guided the anti-Hitler movement of the American League for Peace and Democracy that united a cross section of some five million organized Americans (a list of its sponsors and speakers would include almost a majority of Roosevelt's Cabinet, the most prominent intellectuals, judges of all grades up to State Supreme Courts, church leaders, labour leaders, etc.). Right-wing intellectuals complained that it exercised an effective veto in almost all publishing houses against their books, and it is at least certain that those right-wingers had extreme difficulty getting published. It displaced the old Socialist Party of Norman Thomas as the dominant influence on the left, and that party split up during the 1930s.[34]

The new opportunities did not change either the nature of the Communist movement or its world outlook. An America more open to communist activities was simply a softer target for Soviet intelligence.

6

The 1930s: Heyday for Soviet Espionage

Part 1: Whittaker Chambers

THE American people first learned during the late 1940s what the Soviets had been able to create a decade and a half earlier. The 1948 testimony of Whittaker Chambers and Elizabeth Bentley, who had worked in separate Soviet intelligence rings, shocked America. Key figures in the Roosevelt administration had secretly worked for the Soviet Union, America's secrets were known to Soviet intelligence, and policies were developed that aided the Soviet Union at American expense.

The story began when Earl Browder took over the leadership of the American Communist Party in 1930 while his predecessor, Max Bedacht, concentrated on building up the underground apparatus under the direction of Soviet intelligence officers. Max Bedacht had served as temporary American Communist Party leader as a reward from Stalin for having betrayed his factional colleagues Lovestone and Gitlow when they came under attack from Moscow. Bedacht was then relegated to the apparently unimportant job of running a front organization called the International Workers Order, which provided low-cost insurance for communists and communist sympathizers. However, this aided his second assignment: running the Communist Party's underground apparatus. This apparatus, directed by the Comintern's organizational bureau, or Orgburo, also known as OMS, served Comintern intelligence. However, when significant intelligence opportunities arose party members assigned to the Comintern apparatus were transferred to Soviet Military Intelligence.

In the spring of 1932 Bedacht telephoned the office of the communist magazine, *New Masses*, and spoke to the magazine's new editor, Whittaker Chambers. Chambers had joined the Communist Party in 1924 but left in 1929 with the Lovestoneites. He had recently returned and been given the *New Masses* assignment. Bedacht met with Chambers and advised him that he had been selected for underground work. He would have to leave the overt Communist Party and would be responsible directly to Bedacht. Chambers argued that this was a bad idea. He had only recently gone back into the party and separating himself so soon would look peculiar. In addition, his wife was opposed to the idea of him going into the underground. Bedacht would accept no excuses and told Chambers that he had to do what he was told. Bedacht then brought him to meet John Sherman, another former Lovestoneite who had remained in the party underground after being expelled from the party itself. Sherman and Chambers worked together for a number of years.[1] Chambers's job in the underground was courier, bringing material that had been collected to his Soviet contacts.

Who Was J. Peters?

In 1933 Bedacht told Chambers that he was going on a vacation or a mission (Chambers was unclear which) and would be away for some time. He left Chambers under the control of J. Peters. Chambers soon came to understand that Peters was the new head of the Communist underground. For some time Chambers met both with Bedacht and Peters, but soon Bedacht drifted away and Peters was his primary contact.[2] Peters, too, was a former Lovestone supporter who switched to the Foster group when Stalin transferred the American Communist leadership.[3] It appears that most of the American Communists involved in Soviet espionage came originally from the Lovestone faction. They worked for the Soviets even after the Lovestoneites were expelled from the party. The use of dissident communists for espionage began in the 1920s and has continued.

Ludwig Lore had been a leading member of the American Communist Party. In 1925 he was expelled. A bitter attack on him was written by Max Bedacht in a pamphlet titled, *The Menace of Op-*

portunism. Bedacht wrote, "A vicious American variety of opportunism presents itself to our party in the form of Loreism."[4] Ben Gitlow, who knew Lore well, wrote that:

> Lore, when a communist, did what was expected of him. He collaborated with the OGPU and served them in whatever capacity possible. . . . Lore, the split personality, became so involved with the OGPU that in spite of his expulsion from the Communist Party and the Comintern, he could not extricate himself from their clutches. The transformation of Lore, who was basically honest in his convictions, did not come on the moment of his expulsion. It took a long time, many years, during which he considered it an honor to serve the Soviet government with the result that, when he wanted to tear himself loose from the OGPU, he could not do so.[5]

Chambers broke with the Soviets in 1938. After ten years of unsuccessfully trying to alert American officials to the existence of a Soviet-directed underground in the American government, Chambers finally testified in public in 1948.[6] However, shortly after breaking with the underground, Chambers prepared a manuscript on Soviet espionage in the United States. Although never published, this document sheds new light on some of the people he worked with in the underground. In the manuscript he identified J. Peters only as "Sandor." Chambers wrote, "It is no pleasure to write about him, for he is one of the few American Communists who is at once decent and intelligent. 'Sandor' is the organizer of most of the illegal activities of the Communist Party in America." According to Chambers, Peters reported every day to Earl Browder, the head of the American Communist Party. His main function, however, was "organizing the Party 'underground' in what Communists call 'strategic places'." These included the Labor Department and "the Treasury Department (from which a well-placed comrade every week sends the Party a really useful digest of information). Little 'Sandor,' a former Austrian army officer illegally resident in the United States, sits, in the person of his underground Communists, in the councils of the American Government, is in a position to, and has, more than once influenced Government decisions."[7]

John Lautner, a Communist Party official until 1950, had known J. Peters since 1929. He testified before Congress in 1956 that Peters's real name was Sandor Goldberger. According to Lautner, a fellow Hungarian, Peters, "comes from Hungary. . . . He took some law courses in Budapest and during the war [World War I] he was a lieutenant in the Austro-Hungarian Army."[8]

In his 1948 testimony before Congress, Chambers said, "Peters told me at one time that he had been a petty officer in the Austrian Army during World War I. After the Bela Kun revolution in Hungary he was a member of the Soviet Government of Hungary, I think, in the agricultural commissariat."[9] During a later session Chambers recalled that Peters had told him of his experiences in the First World War, "first on the Serbian front and later on the Russian front and then on the Italian front." Chambers continued:

> He also told me that he was believed by the soldiers to bear a charmed life, so that during a heavy fire they would cluster around him, endangering themselves and him. I remember him telling me that toward the end of the war, when the Austrian armies were crumbling, the first soldiers of the Soviets were appearing, he was called up for some kind of insubordination, I believe, and took his medals and either handed them or tossed them at his superior officer.[10]

Louis Rethy Reed was a former Hungarian Communist who knew Peters well and had supervised his party work during the 1920s. Reed told quite a different story of Peters's experience. According to an affidavit by Reed:

> Alexander Goldberger [Peters's true name] was born at Munkacs in north Hungary in the year of 1897. He attended grammar school there. He finished high school at the Calvinist high school in the town of Sarospatak and entered the Calvinist College in the city of Debrecen, where he studied law. After less than a year of college he was drafted to the army, but by the time he came out of officers school with the rank of ensign, the war was over. He had no part whatsoever in the 1919 Communist uprising. He only began to give vague hints about his activities in Hungary after the actual participants like myself were gone. In fact Szanto and Lustig (two Hungarian-American Communist leaders) related to me some very tall stories he told to the gullible American Communists.

Reed left the Communist Party in 1929 with the Lovestone group but said that, "Peters, the opportunist, double-crossed his mentor

Lovestone and stayed on with the Foster group." In 1932 the Communist Party attempted to entice Reed back. At the suggestion of party leader Earl Browder he visited Moscow. Instructed to report to Clarence Hathaway, the American representative at Comintern headquarters, Reed was surprised to find that in Hathaway's absence his deputy was Peters, who greeted Reed in a friendly manner. Peters was living with a woman named Manya at the Hotel Lux where the Comintern housed foreign communists. Peters and Manya were attending the Lenin School, the Comintern's international training school, but Manya told Reed that, "it was only a cover for the espionage school they were really attending."[11]

In March 1932 Peters was signing documents as the "Acting Representative C.P., USA, E.C.C.I." The initials E.C.C.I. refer to the Executive Committee of the Communist International.[12] Peters was arrested in the United States on October 8, 1947, as an illegal alien. On April 12, 1949, a warrant was issued for his deportation. On May 3 he was granted voluntary departure and on May 6, 1949, he left the United States to return to Hungary.[13]

Whether Peters was a participant in the Bela Kun regime and a World War I hero as he told his American comrades, or a boastful fraud as claimed by his former associate Reed, Peters played a major role in Soviet espionage in the United States during the 1930s and 1940s. Both Peters and Bedacht were deeply involved in obtaining false passports for Soviet spies. Chambers's unpublished manuscript was primarily an account of this activity. He wrote it at the urging of his friend, Herbert Solow, an anti-communist writer whom Chambers had known since college. Solow had taken an interest in a sensational case that had broken in the American press in December of 1937.

The Soviet Passport Racket

The case began when American officials in Moscow learned that there was a frightened American woman in a room at the Hotel National not far from the American embassy. She was awaiting the return of her husband, who had been missing for a number of days. Loy Henderson, the chargé d'affaires, and Angus Ward, the second secretary, visited the young woman in her room. She identified herself as Mrs. Donald Louis Robinson, an American citizen. She stated that her husband, also an American citizen, was a writer. He had disappeared some days earlier but she was awaiting his return. The Americans returned to the embassy to check files. When they returned to the hotel a short time later, Mrs. Robinson also had disappeared. The management claimed that she had checked out leaving no forwarding address. When Henderson and Ward visited the room they found a new occupant, but porters were moving out the furniture that had been in the room. A check of State Department files turned up the Robinson passports and two other passports issued to the same people as Mr. and Mrs. Adolph Arnold Rubens.

Solow suspected that this case was related somehow to the purge trials that were being carried out in Russia. Under pseudonyms Solow wrote articles in the *New York Sun* and the *New Leader*. Some of the latter were signed "W. C. Hambers" and "Walter Hambers." These names were used deliberately in the hope that Chambers would see them and make contact with Solow, who had heard of Chambers's disillusionment with the communists. Although this ploy did not succeed, Chambers later did make contact with Solow and wrote the manuscript that provides considerable inside information on Soviet espionage and the use of false passports.

During his investigation Solow concluded that Robinson/Rubens was a GPU agent. Jay Lovestone, to whom Solow had gone for information and advice, insisted that he abandon the investigation. In a letter to Lovestone, Solow wrote, "I feel it my duty to continue my investigation and exposure."[14]

When Chambers contacted Solow, Solow revealed the story and, at his friend's urging, Chambers wrote the two-part manuscript under the general heading "The Faking of Americans." The first part was subtitled "The Soviet Passport Racket" and the second "Welcome, Soviet Spies." Chambers wanted the articles published, but they never were. In the manuscript Chambers identified Bedacht only as "Barber," in a reference to his former occupation. Chambers signed the articles "Karl," one of his underground names. Chambers wrote that this pseudonym would be recognized by his former Russian, Latvian, and American comrades, especially the military Communists. He warned them that if the usual campaign of slander and denial was started, he would reveal the identities of "Barber" [Bedacht] and "Sandor" [Peters].

According to Chambers, in Soviet intelligence circles fraudulent passports are called "boots." Chambers revealed that the manufacturing of "boots" is a major branch of Soviet espionage. Most of the Soviet Union's other espionage activities are dependent on false passports. Russia couldn't send out its agents in the guise of salesmen as other countries do as Soviet business is a monopoly of the government. Soviet agents at that time needed fraudulent papers.

Chambers described the most successful organizer of "this enterprise" as Robinson/Rubens, a Latvian who held Soviet citizenship. Rubens had been supplying the Soviets with at least one hundred fraudulent American passports every month. He was known in the Soviet intelligence service as "Ewald" and by his American Communist coworkers as "Richard." The Robinson and Rubens passports had not been applied for in person but had been obtained by a New York City politician as a favor. When the authorities investigated they were led from one person to another until they discovered Aaron Sharfin, a thirty-year-old "office boy" employed by the Royal Egyptian Consulate. Sharfin, who had been arrested twice during violent communist demonstrations, was believed by the authorities to have been the assistant to the chief of the passport ring.[15] Herbert Solow, in a 1939 article in the *American Mercury*, identified Sharfin as Arthur Sharfin, a member of the Communist Party, New York district, Section XV (mid-Bronx) who was assigned at one time to "unit 12" then to other units. He was for a time organizer of the Communist-controlled Unemployed Councils. Solow also identified Ewald's wife as an American woman named Ruth Marie Buerger who was also active in the Unemployed Councils.[16]

On March 29, 1938, a well-known Fifth Avenue photographer, Ossip Garber, was arrested as the photographer for Robinson/Rubens and for assisting in the creation of fraudulent passports used by the American Communist Party to send volunteers to Spain for the International Brigades. The Soviets, of course, were very interested in what the American government was learning about Soviet espionage through its investigation of the Robinson/Rubens case. According to Chambers, Soviet Military Intelligence provided the Soviet government with photographic copies of everything sent out on the Rubens case by the American embassy in Moscow to the State Department at Washington.[17]

In 1939 Chambers went to Adolf Berle, then assistant secretary of state, in an attempt to reach President Roosevelt with his information. In Berle's notes of the conversation, he wrote, "When Loy Henderson interviewed Mrs. Rubens his report immediately went back to Moscow. Who sent it? Such came from Washington." The answer to his question was undoubtedly found in the previous paragraph of his memo, where he listed Alger Hiss as a member of the ring.[18] During the 1949 trial of Hiss, a copy in Hiss's handwriting of Henderson's report was introduced as one of the exhibits. It had been saved by Chambers as one of the last batch of documents he had received as a courier, which he had failed to turn over to the Russians but kept as insurance to protect his life.[19]

According to Chambers, the American authorities demanded that the Soviets allow them to speak with Mrs. Rubens in accordance with their signed agreement that any American arrested could be interviewed by the American embassy. After much delay the embassy was finally permitted to send Loy Henderson to interview her at Butirki Prison.

However, Mrs. Rubens requested that the American government leave her to her fate. After a second visit, Henderson wrote a detailed confidential report of the interview to the State Department in which he expressed the opinion that Mrs. Rubens and her husband were agents of the Communist International caught in the Purge. He was wrong, as they were intelligence agents. But, the Soviet government concluded after reading Henderson's report that there would be passivity in the Rubens case in Washington.[20]

According to Chambers, Robinson had graduated from the position of technical worker, a low level in military intelligence, to a "chief" in charge of creating legends to obtain false American passports. When Robinson arrived in the United States in the early 1930s, after working for the Soviets in Germany, he found the passport apparatus in the hands of Max Bedacht, called by Chambers "Comrade Barber." Bedacht, as has been noted, was head of the International Workers Order, a Communist front that provided low-cost insurance to many foreign-born workers. As a considerable number of the order's members were naturalized American citizens, Bedacht had access to naturalization documents that could be used to obtain passports.[21]

Chambers revealed how the Soviets were able to secure the bogus passports through their possession of authentic documents—birth certificates and naturalization papers. According to Chambers, the Soviet agents obtained the naturalization papers of dead men and the birth certificates of dead children. Since the United States admits a large number of foreign-born persons to citizenship every year, their citizenship papers can be used. Of course, while most Russians cannot pass as native-born American citizens, they do not find it difficult to pass as naturalized Americans. Naturalization papers were much more important for Soviet espionage than birth certificates.[22] Bedacht, as the head of IWO, could procure such documents for Soviet intelligence.

Chambers used the Robinson/Rubens case to describe in detail how "Sandor" (J. Peters) developed false passports for use by Soviet intelligence. Chambers revealed that the real Donald Louis Robinson was born in Ridgewood, Queens, on March 25, 1905, and died March 21, 1909. The child was buried in the Calvary Cemetery in Queens.

Ruth Norma Birkland was the name on the birth certificate used by Mrs. Robinson to obtain her passport. The real Birkland was born on December 23, 1909, in Brooklyn, New York, and died November 19, 1915. She was buried in the Cemetery of the Evergreens in Brooklyn.

The Soviet ring obtained information from the Genealogy Division of the New York Public Library to secure real birth certificates for use in applying for passports. According to Chambers, the ring employed several quiet-looking women who spent their days making transcripts of records. First they would examine death records from the first decade of this century. Then they would correlate this with births. The birth certificates were taken by American Communists to the Passport Bureau, together with a witness to swear that he had known the applicant for five years. The passport obtained was part of the monthly consignment for Moscow.[23]

Whittaker Chambers

Whittaker Chambers was not only a Soviet spy, he was also a remarkable intellectual. In 1925 a friend from college days, Clifton

Fadiman, then employed by the publishing house of Simon and Schuster, got Chambers the job of translating Felix Salten's novel *Bambi* from German into English.[24] This beautiful translation is still in use today. Chambers did so well that Simon and Schuster also asked him to translate Salten's *Fifteen Rabbits*, published in 1930.

It is interesting that Chambers, an expert in the German language, should find himself in the Soviet intelligence apparatus, which frequently used German rather than Russian words in its trade craft. A meeting, for example, was called a *"treff."* Chambers pointed out that the word used for liaison man, the job he held, was the German *"Verbindungsmensch."*[25]

The use of German words in trade craft may have stemmed from the large number of Soviet intelligence officers who originated in the pre–World War I Austro-Hungarian Empire. Many of these were Jewish and spoke Yiddish, a German dialect. The purges of the 1930s wiped out most of the Jewish intelligence officers, and German words no longer appear in Soviet intelligence trade craft.

During the first month of Chambers's Soviet service, John Sherman introduced him to a man he knew as Ulrich or Walter. In 1949, when the FBI showed Chambers a series of photographs, he identified Ulrich as Alexander Petrovich Ulanovski. Ulrich, strangely enough, was not a Communist Party member but a Left Social-Revolutionary. Members of this political movement in Russia had cooperated with the Bolsheviks in the early days and had been rewarded with posts in the government and intelligence apparatus. Most had been removed and killed by the early 1930s, but Ulrich had survived. According to the stories Ulrich told Chambers, he knew Stalin well, having been in a Siberian penal colony with him on two occasions. As a result he detested Stalin. Ulrich had been a partisan leader in the Crimea and southern Russia during the civil war and had fought against the anarchist leader Machno. He had also done underground work in Argentina and in China prior to 1927. He had been accompanied in China by his wife, Elaine. They had to escape after the abortive 1927 communist insurrection in Canton.

Long after breaking with communism, while working for *Time* magazine in 1947, Chambers received greetings from an unknown woman in Moscow named Nadya. The greetings were sent in a letter from *Time*'s bureau chief in Moscow, Craig Thompson. When

Thompson returned to the United States, Chambers asked him about the mysterious Nadya. Thompson replied that she was a Russian woman employed by the *Time* bureau in Moscow to do translations from Russian. The description of the woman and her husband, provided by Thompson, convinced Chambers that they were Ulrich and Elaine. Nadya told Thompson that she knew Chambers personally but said nothing of the underground work. Thompson said that Ulrich and Elaine "had become bitterly anti-Soviet and lived in constant fear of being shot or sent to Siberia."[26]

Nadezhda (Nadya) Ulanovskaya, known to Chambers as Elaine, was found in Israel by Allen Weinstein while researching his book on the Alger Hiss case.[27] Ulrich is now dead, but Nadya and their daughter, Maya, have published a book about Nadya and Ulrich's experiences. Written in Israel and based on tape recordings that Nadya made in the Soviet Union, the book was published in Russian in New York in 1982.[28]

Nadya describes in the book the couple's arrival in America in 1931 on the maiden voyage of *The Bremen*. They traveled under the name of Hoffman as first-class passengers and stopped at the Pennsylvania Hotel in New York. While in America Ulrich met with Richard Sorge, with whom he had worked earlier in Shanghai. Sorge was on his way to Japan and was in very high spirits.

Ulrich and Nadya's first contact in America was Leon Minster, known to them as "Charlie." Minster went to Shanghai in 1934 as a member of a Soviet intelligence ring. According to the Shanghai police, Minster's wife was the sister of Molotov.[29] Chambers's impression, however, was that Minster was related to Molotov's wife.[30]

Minster put Ulrich and Elaine in touch with Dr. Philip Rosenbliett. According to Chambers, Rosenbliett, a dentist, played a major role in Soviet espionage. Rosenbliett told Chambers a great deal about the history of Soviet intelligence, some of which Chambers repeated to the FBI.

> In the course of these various conversations with Rosenbliett, he once told me how the Red Army came to be equipped with Christie tanks. He said that a representative of the underground of the Irish Republican Army in London had gotten together with Soviet agents in that city. The Irish agents had informed the Russians that they had

a contact in the United States War Department. I believe Dr. Rosenbliett stated that this contact was a General Miller. As a result, the Irish and the Russians made a deal whereby General Miller would provide material from the War Department files for a Soviet apparatus in the United States. In return, the Russians were to send two submarines loaded with machine guns and arms to the West Coast of Ireland for the Irish Republican Army. I have no direct knowledge but presume that this incident took place in the late 1920s.

General Miller was connected with the Soviet apparatus in the United States through the medium of an individual named Connie Neenan, who was a friend of Dr. Rosenbliett. Dr. Rosenbliett described Neenan as a sporting character or a politician in Queens. Neenan supposedly put the Soviet agents in contact with General Miller. Dr. Rosenbliett indicated that he, Dr. Rosenbliett, had a hand in this matter. However, General Miller reportedly stated that he would be "happy to supply War Department material to the Irish Republican Army but not for the G— D—— Russians." From Dr. Rosenbliett's tone, I gathered that General Miller's remarks implied the latter knew who he was dealing with.

According to Dr. Rosenbliett, General Miller eventually produced a great amount of material on Christie tanks, which supplied the designs for the then Russian Tank Corps. Dr. Rosenbliett also told me that General Miller was a man who loved his "liquor" and he was kept well supplied with it by Soviet agents. Dr. Rosenbliett said that the Russians never kept their part of this bargain in that no submarines ever brought arms to Ireland. Later, according to Dr. Rosenbliett, two representatives of the Irish Republican Army appeared at his [Rosenbliett's] office and threatened his life, but he was able to talk them out of any direct action. Rosenbliett explained that they had probably approached him because of his acquaintanceship with Connie Neenan.[31]

According to Chambers an apartment on Gay Street in New York's Greenwich Village was used by Ulrich, Elaine, and Charlie to process instruction messages from Moscow. Chambers told the FBI:

The Gay Street apartment was used primarily during the time that I visited there, as the base of operations for a communications system between the underground in the United States and Europe. This consisted of the receipt in the United States of communications carried by couriers who were seamen and stewards attached to the various ships of the North German Lloyd SS Line and Hamburg

American Line, and the forwarding of communications to Germany. These incoming communications consisted of microfilm and letters containing secret writing. However, the material delivered in the United States to these couriers for transmission to Germany took the form of microfilm only.

Chambers described two types of communications.

The first type was a letter, which was enclosed in an unaddressed sealed envelope. The letter itself contained a short innocuous family message in the German language, and was double- or triple-spaced and was typed. . . . There was only one sheet of paper in an envelope and only one envelope was delivered on each trip. . . . Upon receipt of this letter at the Gay Street address, it would be opened and processed by either Charlie or me. In processing this letter, the washbasin in the bathroom would be partially filled with lukewarm water and a small quantity of permanganate of potassium would be dissolved in the warm water after which the letter would be immersed in this solution, and after a short period of time the secret writing, which had a rusty red color, would appear. The secret writing was always in the Russian handwriting. . . .
     The second type of communication took the form of microfilm. At the same time that the envelope containing the single sheet of paper was delivered to the Gay Street address, a cheap ten-cent store pocket mirror would also be delivered by the same courier. . . . Charlie or I would take the backing off the mirror and in between it and the actual back of the mirror would be roughly six frames of 35 millimeter developed film. These frames had been cut apart and each individual frame was trimmed so that only the printing appeared thereon. These frames were placed one on top of the other and wrapped in thin tissue paper. These frames would then be enlarged, one frame to a standard piece of enlarging paper.

Chambers told the FBI about a man known to him as "Henry" who served as a "cut out" between the couriers and Chambers's group. He said:

Henry would meet the courier. These meetings would occur some-times in a cafeteria and sometimes at a designated meeting place on a street in New York City. . . . Henry, after meeting the courier, would travel about New York City in various types of public conveyances and eventually would arrive at a predesignated place, where Henry would be met by Charlie. Charlie would thereafter take a circuitous route from the meeting place to the Gay Street apartment. The method used by Henry and Charlie in eventually getting the mail to the Gay Street apartment was a more or less routine underground apparatus maneuver in order to elude any possible surveillance.

Sometime after I became associated with these operations, Ulrich suggested that, as an added security measure, the "chain" should be lengthened. When this plan was put into effect, I was introduced to Henry by Charlie and thereafter Henry would initially obtain the material from the courier, pass it on to me, and thereafter I would give it to Charlie, who would subsequently deliver it to the Gay Street address for processing.

I recall that on one occasion Henry and the courier failed to make contact when the ship arrived in the Port of New York. The courier, I learned, got in touch with George Mink, who was the Communist Party organizer on the New York waterfront, and gave the mirror and envelope to Mink. Subsequently, George Mink turned this material over to Max Bedacht who in turn gave it to me. I handed the mirror and envelope over to Ulrich. This incident occurred prior to the time that I was a part of this communications chain.

Before I went underground, I had seen George Mink occasionally in the *Daily Worker* office and once had to order him out of there for making a commotion. He was generally regarded as the "dregs of the Communist Party" but was said to be related to one of the Russian big shots, namely Lozovsky, who was in those days the head of the Profintern, or Red International of Labor Unions. Later, of course, I learned that George Mink had been arrested as a Soviet agent in Copenhagen and still later I heard that he had been active behind the Republican lines of Spain during the civil war. At that time, he was said to be employed as an executioner of Trotskyists and other elements that the Communists in Spain were interested in liquidating.

To the best of my recollection, the couriers usually arrived in the United States about once in every fortnight.

My connection with the communications chain embraced probably a little less than a year, and I would place the actual dates thereof as probably late in 1932 and continuing into 1933 when Hitler came into power. About two weeks after Hitler took over the Weimar Republic, we ceased to receive any communications from Europe. It was my understanding that Hitler had wiped out the courier system that was being utilized aboard vessels of German registry.[32]

At one point in 1933 another Russian appeared on the scene. Ulrich introduced the newcomer to Chambers as "Herman." It soon became clear that Herman was a rival of Ulrich and intended to take over the apparatus. He apparently reported to Moscow, complaining about Ulrich's leadership. Chambers was in contact with Herman for a relatively short time.

Herman suggested that the apparatus be used to gain control of an American newspaper. When Chambers asked why, Herman replied that a newspaper provided a good cover for sending people around to secure information. Chambers later learned from his friend Ludwig Lore that the newspaper that Herman contemplated taking over was the the New York German-language paper, *Volkszeitung*, which Lore edited. Lore was a former American Communist leader who had run afoul of the Communist Party in the 1920s but continued to work for Soviet intelligence. As they would later use the dissident Communists from the Lovestone group, Soviet intelligence during the 1920s used Lore despite his opposition to the American Communist Party.

Lore knew Herman under the name "Oscar." He told Chambers that Herman, who had a bad habit of flashing large amounts of money, had done so in a New York bar and had been beaten and robbed. He subsequently died of his injuries. After Chambers's 1938 break with the Soviets, he met with a high-level Soviet intelligence defector, Walter Krivitsky, who identified Herman as Valentine Markin. Krivitsky believed that Herman had been murdered on orders of the Soviet Intelligence Service.[33]

The American Communist who did the most to create a Soviet-directed underground movement in the American government was Harold Ware. The son of "Mother" Bloor,[34] an old and highly respected Communist apparatchik, Ware had spent considerable time in the Soviet Union. Chambers told the FBI:

Almost at the very beginning when J. Peters began directing operations, he began to tell me of the background of one Harold Ware. I do not believe I had ever heard of this individual previous to his being mentioned by Peters. This was probably due to the fact that

Ware had apparently been in Russia most of the time. According to Peters, Ware was a member of a group of Americans who had gone to form an agricultural cooperative in the Kuznetz Basin in Russia. This project later died and Harold Ware returned to the United States. I gathered from Peters' remarks that Ware was the "spark plug" of this movement.

Later either Peters or Ware himself told me that when he, Ware, returned to the United States from Russia, he was carrying about twenty thousand dollars in a money belt. These were funds for the United States Communist Party. He also told me that Harold Ware was the son of Mother Bloor.

Sometime in 1934, through Peters, I met with him and Ware in New York City. It was my understanding that Ware was the organizer of an underground Communist group which was operating in Washington, D.C., which I will refer to hereinafter as Apparatus A. I was to act as a courier between that group and J. Peters in New York City. I understood that most of the members of this group were employed in New Deal agencies. According to what Peters told me, it was his "dream" to penetrate the "old line agencies," such as the Navy, State . . . etc. I was to learn the setup and the personnel of the present apparatus and attempt to build up a parallel apparatus (which I will refer to as Apparatus B), using certain members of the Ware Group at first and then branching out. Consequently, about the end or in the fall of 1934, I made my first trip to Washington, D.C., where I met Harold Ware by prearrangement. Ware took me to the violin studio of his sister, Helen, which was located on Connecticut Avenue, near Dupont Circle.

It was my understanding that Harold Ware, upon his return to the United States from Russia, had gone to Washington for the purpose of seeing what type of work he could engage in, in the agricultural field, which would aid the Communist Party. He secured a job in the AAA (Agricultural Adjustment Administration) and there found a small group of Communist Party sympathizers. This group included Lee Pressman, Alger Hiss, Nathan Witt, and possibly Charles Krivitsky. Ware then quickly realized that the possibilities for the Communist Party far exceeded this little group in AAA. I believe that either Ware, or Ware and J. Peters, then began to organize Apparatus A. However, Harold Ware himself retained his interest in the general agricultural field and I believe he retained a small underground apparatus which dealt with agricultural activities. Webb Powell was the only member of this latter group that I knew. He worked closely with Harold Ware.

Shortly after my first visit to Washington, D.C., I was introduced to Henry Collins by Harold Ware in the former's apartment on St. Matthews Court. . . . On my first visit to Collins' apartment I was introduced to him under the name of Carl. I recall that at the time of my first visit to Collins' apartment, the leading group in Apparatus A had assembled to hold a meeting. I was introduced to the people at this meeting simply as Carl, and after some casual conversation with these individuals they went into another room in the house to hold a meeting in which I did not participate. The group at this meeting were the leading members in Apparatus A and were as follows: John Abt, Charles Krivitsky, Henry Hill Collins, Jr., Nathan Witt, Donald Hiss, Victor Perlo, Lee Pressman, Harold Ware.[35]

Ware's closest associate in the Communist Party was Lement Harris, who served the cause by working among American farmers. In 1978 Harris wrote a pamphlet for the Communist Party USA front, The American Institute for Marxist Studies, Inc. The pamphlet, entitled *Harold M. Ware (1890-1935) Agricultural Pioneer, U.S.A. and U.S.S.R.*, was issued as a limited edition. According to Harris, Ware decided in 1931 that he had done enough in the Soviet Union and it was time to return to the United States to work among American farmers. He established an organization in Washington called Farm Research, Inc., which Harris ran for many years after Ware's death in an auto accident in 1935.

Although Harris made no mention in his pamphlet of Ware's espionage activity, he repeated an interesting story that his friend had told him about an incident in the Soviet Union. When Ware arrived in Moscow in 1922, he discovered that carloads of tractors and supplies were scattered around different freight yards. Someone told him that this was due to "sabotage" by enemies of the regime and that it would take a month to assemble the equipment for shipment to where it was needed. Ware went to Felix Dzerzhinsky and explained the problem. Dzerzhinsky instructed his secretary to contact the station master in each yard where the freight cars were scattered and ordered them to be assembled within three days. This order from the head of the secret police was, of course, carried out.

Harris identified Ware as the author of the pamphlet, *The American Farmer*, credited to the pseudonym George Anstrom, published by the American Communist Party late in 1932.[36]

An examination of the advertisements published by the Communist Party before the pamphlet was released provides some interesting insights into Ware's close associates and collaborators. In 1931 and early 1932 the authors were listed in the advertisements as A. Bosse and Harrison George. George was a Comintern apparatchik who handled the American end of the Communist underground operations in the Far East.[37] Bosse was the pseudonym of Alfred J. Brooks, who worked in Moscow from 1927 to 1929 as the U.S. representative to the Information Department of the Communist International.[38] Later in 1932 the advertisements listed the authors as H. Ware and L. Harris. Still later in the year only Harold M. Ware was listed as the author of the forthcoming pamphlet. When it was issued at the end of 1932, it bore the name George Anstrom.[39]

When Chambers met Ware in Washington in 1934, he learned that a second underground apparatus was being established, designated Apparatus B. Chambers told the FBI:

> It was my understanding that at the time of my first going to Washington, Alger Hiss was separated from Apparatus A because of his just getting a new position with the Nye Committee. I had previously discussed Alger Hiss with J. Peters and Harold Ware. It had been decided that he should become the first member of the parallel Apparatus B. During the meeting with Alger, Harold Ware, Peters, and myself, it is my recollection that the nature of the new organization being developed was made known to him and he was perfectly agreeable to it.[40]

The Nye Committee was the Senate investigator of the munitions industry. This provided Hiss and the Soviets with considerable information on the weapons of the world powers.

Chambers went on to describe to the FBI details of his knowledge of the career of Alger Hiss and other members of the underground:

> I am unable to recall just how long Alger Hiss remained with the Nye Committee. However, after some time, Stanley Reed, Solicitor General of the United States, offered Alger a position in the Department of Justice as Assistant Solicitor General. Alger advised me

of this offer and I, in turn, brought it to the attention of J. Peters. Peters instructed that Hiss should take this position though there was no immediate purpose in view. I believe that Alger kept this position as Assistant Solicitor General for rather a short time.

He was then offered a position by Francis Sayre, the then Assistant Secretary of State in the State Department. This offer was likewise brought to my and J. Peters attention, and the latter again decided that Alger should take this new offer. I believe that Alger was somewhat hesitant about accepting this new position, inasmuch as his stay as Assistant Solicitor General had been of such short duration. Regardless of appearances in connection with his position in the Justice Department, Peters and I decided he should make this change.

In the meantime, while I was attempting to make other contacts for the apparatus, Harold Ware had introduced me to one Robert Coe, who was very close to Harry Dexter White of the Treasury Department.

Robert Coe, I believe, was a member of one of the cells of Apparatus A. I did not know what department of the Government he was employed in, if any. His older brother, Frank Coe, was at this time, I believe, an economics instructor at McGill University in Canada. On several occasions, from J. Peters, George Silverman, Harry Dexter White, and probably Harold Ware, I had heard mentioned plans to bring Frank Coe from Canada so that he could be placed in the Treasury Department by White. It was my understanding that Frank Coe, as well as his brother, Robert, was a member of the Communist Party.

Harry Dexter White was at that time (1935) the monetary expert in the Treasury Department. He was not then, so far as I knew, nor did he become a member of the Communist Party. However, he was known to Harold Ware and J. Peters as a strong sympathizer of the Communist Party. White's close tie with the Communist Party was through his friendship with George Silverman. . . .

It was also my impression from conversations with Ware and J. Peters that White had knowingly given positions in the Treasury Department to communists. I might mention in particular, Solomon Adler and Dr. Harold Glasser. . . . I do not know how White became so strong a supporter of the Communist Party but I presume his friendship with George Silverman had a great deal to do with it.

Ware was of the opinion that White could produce some very interesting and valuable material and that Robert Coe would be the person who would be able to obtain this information from White. I brought this matter to J. Peters' attention and he said that it was all right and to go ahead and approach White through Coe. On one occasion Coe did get some documents from Harry Dexter White.

I cannot remember exactly the contents. However, they may have been lists of Japanese agents and Chinese agents in Japanese employ, about which I will speak later. I photographed these in John Herrmann's apartment. In order to return these documents to Coe, I had arranged to meet him on a certain street in Washington, D.C., at a particular hour. However, Coe was one hour late for this appointment, which fact made me very angry and alarmed. I have never seen Coe since that time. The films of these documents, secured from Harry Dexter White, were turned over by me to J. Peters.

Just about this time (1935), J. Peters introduced me to David Carpenter in New York City. I was introduced to the latter under the name of Carl [Karl]. Peters indicated to me that Carpenter had been in some kind of underground work in Washington and was connected with some people who might possibly be brought into my new apparatus, which as I have stated I will hereinafter refer to as Apparatus B.

I subsequently met Carpenter on a number of occasions in Baltimore and Washington. We discussed his connections and he later introduced me to Julian Wadleigh, Ward and George Pigman and Victor Reno. I believe that I met these individuals in that order. It was my impression at the time that all of these individuals had been previous contacts of Carpenter and were members of some underground group of which he was the organizer or leader. Carpenter further definitely led me to believe that all those people were his contacts. At that time, however, I did not know of Eleanor Nelson. It was later my impression she was the actual leader and organizer of this underground group.[41]

In 1936 J. Peters introduced Chambers to another Russian. This one bore the pseudonym "Peter." Chambers later learned from Krivitsky that this was Boris Bykov, who from 1936 headed Soviet Military Intelligence in the United States. Bykov suggested to Chambers that the members of the underground should be offered money to "put them in a productive frame of mind." Chambers protested that they were loyal Communists and would be insulted by such an offer. Bykov then suggested that at least some of the best of them be given an expensive present. Chambers again objected, but Bykov prevailed. He gave Chambers one thousand dollars, a considerable amount of money at that time, to purchase four Bokhara rugs to be given to George Silverman, Harry Dexter White, Alger Hiss, and Henry Julian Wadleigh. Chambers was instructed to tell them that the rugs had been woven in Russia and "were being given to them as gifts from the Russian people in gratitude to their American comrades." Chambers later told the FBI, "I personally did not believe that the Communists in Washington would swallow this speech, but I informed each of the above-mentioned persons as I was instructed." Chambers bought the four rugs and distributed them as ordered. He was later instructed by Bykov to introduce the latter to some of the key members of the Washington apparatus. Alger Hiss traveled to New York in the spring of 1937 where he was introduced by Chambers to Bykov. The meeting was handled in a clandestine fashion, first in a movie theater in Brooklyn and then, after a subway ride, at a restaurant in New York's Chinatown. According to Chambers:

> I want to point out that at this time, Bykov could or would only speak a little English. He therefore spoke in German, which I interpreted for Alger Hiss.
>
> Bykov spent some time explaining to Alger the seriousness of Fascism and its danger to Russia and the necessity of aiding Russia in every way and the importance of intelligence work in such aid. In my opinion, this explanation on Bykov's part was somewhat similar to his previous offer to give money to Alger Hiss, and indicated his failure to grasp the fact that Hiss was a developed Communist who, as such, well knew that it was the function of every Communist to aid the Soviet Union in every way, including espionage. In general, Bykov underrated the Leninist development of American Communists.
>
> Bykov specifically discussed with Hiss the possibility of the latter's bringing out documents from the State Department which might be copied and the originals returned to the State Department. Bykov also inquired of Alger Hiss whether the latter's brother, Donald, could procure documents. Alger informed Bykov that he was not sure whether his brother was ready to do this. Bykov then told me in German, "Tell him perhaps he could persuade him." I specifically recall that the word "persuade" was used, inasmuch as I had trouble translating the word because of Bykov's pronunciation of it in German. As a result of this conversation, Alger agreed to bring out State Department documents. I recall that Bykov indicated that he was gen-

erally interested in anything concerning Germany and the Far East. At some later time, I believe that he was interested in any material concerning the anti-Comintern Pact.

It is my further recollection that it was understood that specific documents were not to be secured, nor were any secured, but rather Alger Hiss was to obtain any documents on the particular subjects mentioned, or any others that Hiss would think as being of interest and which in the normal course of State Department business would come into his hands.[42]

Chambers described how the documents stolen from the State Department were copied. He told the FBI that shortly after the New York meeting between Hiss and Bykov, Hiss began to supply the espionage ring with documents. According to Chambers:

The method of transmitting this material was as follows. Alger Hiss would bring home original documents from the State Department over night as "a matter of custom." On an agreed night, I would go to the 30th Street house and Alger would then turn over to me a zipper case containing these documents. I might state that it is also entirely possible that I brought a zipper case and placed the documents therein to avoid carrying or using Alger's case. I would then take these documents by train to an apartment which was located on the corner of Calvert and East Madison Streets in Baltimore, Maryland. . . . I believe that the apparatus paid a part or all the rent for this apartment.[43]

Chambers identified the occupants of the apartment as Mr. and Mrs. William Spiegel, who were friends of David Carpenter. Chambers brought to the apartment a Leica camera and other photographic equipment given to him by Bykov. In the beginning he did the photographic work himself, but later that job was given to another ring member named Felix Inslerman who had been set up in another apartment. David Carpenter was given the photographic equipment from the first apartment.[44] Over three decades later Carpenter reappeared as an official of the American Communist Party using the name Daniel Mason. His real name was David Zimmerman, which lent itself to the translations Carpenter and Mason.[45] He worked closely for many years with Jessica Smith, the editor of the communist magazine *New World Review*, previously called *So-*

viet Russia Today. Smith was the widow of Harold Ware. She later married another member of the ring, John Abt.[46]

Felix Inslerman admitted being a photographer for the Soviet espionage ring to a congressional committee in February 1954. He stated that he had not been a member of the Communist Party. He identified a number of his Soviet espionage contacts only by their first names but testified that he was able to recognize a man he had known only as "Bob," as Whittaker Chambers. During a 1935 trip to the Soviet Union, Inslerman was trained to operate a Leica camera and to use codes. Inslerman broke with the ring in 1939.[47] Carpenter never publicly admitted his role in the spy ring.

The transmission of the documents for photographing became more complex when Inslerman took over the work. Chambers told the FBI:

Felix owned a car, possibly a Chevrolet, and he would drive to Washington. There I would meet him by prearrangement and such meetings were very often in the general vicinity of Union Station. Shortly prior to this meeting with Felix, I would have visited Alger and secured the documents. I would then turn these documents over to Felix, who would return to Baltimore in his car. He would photograph the documents in his apartment and several hours later return them to me at another prearranged meeting place. Sometimes I believe Felix would return them to me in Baltimore and I would then travel by train to Washington and return the documents to Alger Hiss. On occasions, however, Felix would drive back to Washington and deliver the documents to me at a prearranged meeting place in that city. In further explanation of this operation, I might state that the first step in the transmission was the prearranging of the night on which Alger Hiss would see me. I would then arrange to see Felix on the same night. I have a recollection that I had Felix' telephone number and it is possible that I would call him and inform him of the date on which we were to meet. Those transmissions generally occurred once a week or once in every ten days. Of course, there may have been some weeks in which Alger Hiss, for some reason or other, would not deliver any documents. As an example, he did not deliver any documents during his summer vacations.

Documents obtained from other members of the ring such as Henry Julian Wadleigh of the State Department and Ward Pigman of the Bureau of Standards, as well as Harry Dexter White, were handled the same way.[48]

Harry Dexter White began supplying Treasury Department documents around 1935. He had not met Chambers at this time but supplied the documents through another ring member, Robert Coe. Subsequently Chambers was brought together with White by ring member George Silverman. They did not like each other, and Chambers had difficulty getting documents from White on a regular basis. In 1937 Chambers complained to J. Peters about his inability to deal with White. According to Peters, White was not a party member but was highly regarded as a communist sympathizer. He told Chambers that White had "stocked the Treasury Department with people who were either members of the Communist Party or sympathizers."

White again began supplying Chambers with documents in 1937, but these were in small quantities and came irregularly. Bykov expressed a desire to meet George Silverman and White. Silverman and Chambers met with Bykov in a prearranged place. After a lengthy discussion, while driving around in Silverman's car, the three went to a Washington restaurant for dinner. They later walked up Connecticut Avenue and met White at a prearranged place. They entered Rock Creek Park where Bykov and White engaged in an extensive conversation while Chambers and Silverman went off in another direction.

White then began providing more extensive information, including a list of Japanese agents and Chinese employed by the Japanese, as well as reports from the Office of Naval Intelligence. White also provided handwritten memoranda concerning political matters that he had learned about at the Treasury Department. Chambers told the FBI that he had continued to receive material from White until breaking with the spy ring in 1938.[49]

Alger Hiss also assisted Chambers in recruiting new people into the apparatus. Hiss and his wife began a series of social visits with four State Department employees that they considered likely recruits. With two of the employees the Hisses made no headway, and they were dropped. The other two, Lawrence Duggan and Noel Field, appeared to be good prospects. Duggan committed suicide in 1948 when his name became known, despite the fact that his relationship to the spy ring was peripheral. Field, however, was another matter.

Hiss had several discussions with Field and finally decided that the time was right to approach him to "help the Communist Party." Field responded that he was already attached to an underground apparatus. That group was a Comintern intelligence apparatus run by Hedda Massing. When Hiss reported this to Bykov he was told to stay away from Massing. He supposed this was because he was crossing the wires of a parallel apparatus. Chambers told Hiss to stay away from Field, but Hiss remained in casual contact and later learned that Field, on orders of the apparatus, had left the State Department to work for the International Labor Organization in Geneva. Chambers later learned from General Krivitsky that Field, while assigned to the Geneva post, worked for Krivitsky, then a leading official of Soviet intelligence in Western Europe.

The attempts to recruit Duggan were less successful. He turned down such an attempt by Henry Collins in 1937. J. Peters later introduced Chambers to Frederick Vanderbilt Field (no relation to Noel Field), a millionaire leftist who had been a Princeton classmate of Duggan's, to help in the effort to recruit him. Peters identified Field as a member of a Communist Party underground cell in New York. According to Peters, another member of this cell was the well-known newspaperman Joseph Barnes.[50]

Noel Field and his wife, Herta, had been recruited to the Soviet intelligence service by Hedda Massing. She had cultivated the Fields when she learned of their pro-communist proclivities. As Herta was a German, and the Fields were concerned about Nazism, Massing used that as the basis for their recruitment. The Fields had read and been impressed by a book written by Hedda's husband, Paul Massing. The book was called *Fatherland*, and was written under the pen name Carl Billinger. It was about Massing's experiences in the anti-Nazi underground in Germany.[51]

Using the cover of the Unitarian Service Committee, a charitable organization, Field served the Soviets during World War II. At the same time he was affiliated with the United States Office of Strategic Services (OSS) and in direct contact with its chief, Allen Dulles, in Bern. His loyalty, however, was to the Soviets, and he never betrayed their interests.[52] Field maintained contact with Communist underground operatives in Nazi-occupied Europe on behalf of Soviet intelligence.

Noel Field fled to communist Hungary when his espionage activities became known. Field's service to the Communists did not prevent them from arresting him in connection with a series of frame-ups against those communist leaders in Eastern Europe whom Stalin wanted to eliminate. Most of the victims were communists who had spent the war years in the underground fighting Hitler. They were being replaced by communists who had safely hidden in the Soviet Union during the war.

Field's contact with the underground communists was his undoing. He spent years in Hungarian prison cells and torture chambers. He nevertheless never lost his Communist beliefs. Writing in 1961 after being freed from prison at the time of the Hungarian uprising, Field repeated his thoughts during imprisonment. He pointed out that it was a hard road from the pacifist idealist he was to the militant communist he had become and remained. He professed innocence of the charges made by his comrades that he was an imperialist spy and a traitor. He expected that one day his name would be cleared by the Communists who kept him in solitary confinement. He said, plaintively, that his accusers have the same convictions that he has: "they hate the same things and the same people I hate." Since they believed him guilty, Fields "approve[d] their detestation."[53]

Anti-Nazism was the powerful tool used by the Soviets to convince Americans to help their cause. In 1936 Chambers needed a "clean" contact to serve as a "mail drop." He recruited a former college friend, David Zablodowsky, who had once expressed some communist sympathies but was in no way a communist. Chambers introduced him to J. Peters to help with "underground work against Germany, or against Hitler." Zablodowsky was given an envelope to transmit to a person who would call for it. The person did so, and Zablodowsky's work was finished.

The anti-fascist instincts of Zablodowsky put him in touch with a number of communists, but his aid to the apparatus consisted only of holding an envelope to be picked up. This act, insignificant to Zablodowsky, shows how Soviet intelligence could use innocent people in important work. In 1952 he testified before the United States Senate and revealed his activity on behalf of Chambers. During World War II he served in the OSS.[54]

After breaking with the Communist Party in 1938 Chambers tried to tell his story to the government. No one would listen. In August 1948 he finally told his story in public to the House Committee on

Un-American Activities. He told the committee that when he was
sent to Washington by J. Peters in 1934 he found an apparatus
already in place. Its leader was Nathan Witt and it consisted of a
committee of seven members, each of whom was head of an underground cell. The committee members he named were Alger Hiss,
Donald Hiss, Lee Pressman, Victor Perlo, Charles Kramer, John
Abt, and Henry Collins. The members of the cells had been recruited into Marxist study groups and then into the Communist
Party.[55] Harold Ware had set up this apparatus. The Committee in
its report listed the government employment records of the people
named.

Harold Ware (deceased), Department of Agriculture
John J. Abt, Department of Agriculture; Works Progress Adminis-
   tration; Senate Committee on Education and Labor; Justice
   Department
Nathan Witt, Department of Agriculture; National Labor Relations
   Board
Lee Pressman, Department of Agriculture; Works Progress
   Administration
Alger Hiss, Department of Agriculture; Special Senate Committee
   Investigation of the Munitions Industry; Justice Department; State
   Department
Donald Hiss, State Department; Labor Department
Henry H. Collins, National Recovery Administration; Department of
   Agriculture
Charles Kramer (Krevitsky), National Labor Relations Board; Office
   of Price Administration; Senate Subcommittee on War Mobilization
Victor Perlo, Office of Price Administration; War Production Board;
   Treasury Department[56]

While Alger Hiss directly challenged the testimony of Chambers
and denied being involved with a communist cell in the government,
most of the others named invoked the Fifth Amendment and refused
to answer questions. One of these, Lee Pressman, had been general
counsel of the Congress of Industrial Organizations and was a leading
figure in Henry Wallace's presidential campaign. While Pressman
refused to answer questions, he posed one for the committee, "Has
there been any charge made by any witness that has appeared before
this committee that I have participated in any espionage activity,

either while a member—or rather an employee—of the federal government, or thereafter?" The committee counsel responded, "No, there has not been."[57] In 1950 Pressman again appeared before the committee and admitted being a member of a secret communist group in the government, which consisted of a number of the people identified by Chambers, but claimed to have no knowledge of any activities of Alger Hiss. However, he denied having been involved in espionage.[58]

Chambers in his testimony had, in fact, not accused any members of the group of espionage. He was attempting to protect Alger Hiss and other members of the ring, whom he hoped had broken with the Soviets, as he had. Chambers said, "The purpose of this group at that time was not primarily espionage. Its original purpose was the Communist infiltration of the American government. But espionage was certainly one of its eventual objectives."[59]

Alger Hiss not only challenged the testimony of Chambers but demanded that he repeat them unprotected by congressional immunity so that he could be sued. Chambers agreed to appear on the radio program "Meet the Press," where a *Washington Post* reporter, Edward Folliard, challenged him to say that Alger Hiss was a communist. He answered, "Alger Hiss was a communist and may be now." When Folliard pressed him again and asked whether he was prepared to go into court and answer a suit for slander or libel, Chambers answered, "I do not think Mr. Hiss will sue me for slander or libel."

When another participant, Tom Reynolds of the *Chicago Sun Times,* asked whether Alger Hiss had done "anything that was treasonable or beyond the law of the United States," Chambers, still protecting Hiss, answered, "I am quite unprepared to say whether he did or did not. I am not familiar with the laws of treason." Reynolds pressed him to reveal any "overt acts" committed by Hiss. Chambers responded that the purpose of the group to which Hiss belonged was, "not, as I think is in the back of your mind, for the purpose of espionage, but for the purpose of infiltrating the government and influencing government policy by getting communists in key places."[60]

Alger Hiss brought suit. Chambers, looking for evidence to prove his case, remembered that he had left a package of material in the possession of a relative of his wife. This was the last batch of documents he had received as a courier. He had not delivered them but saved them as a "life preserver." When he got that material back it turned out to be documents and microfilm of documents, many typed on Alger Hiss's typewriter. Some had Hiss's handwritten notations. In addition, there were documents in the handwriting of Harry Dexter White. Those documents proved that Hiss had made copies of State Department materials that were supposed to be kept secret. The documents proved not only Chambers's contention that Hiss was a communist but that Hiss had committed espionage. The lawsuit died, but Hiss was indicted for perjury. The statute of limitations prevented an indictment for espionage.

After two trials, Hiss was convicted. His supporters continue to try to contradict the evidence. They have never succeeded in court.[61] In 1978 a book was published that finally put the case to rest. Allen Weinstein set out to write a defense of Alger Hiss. After extensive research and access to documents both in the possession of Hiss and of the government, Weinstein concluded that Hiss was guilty. His monumental work, *Perjury*, is a valuable contribution to our understanding of Soviet espionage against the United States in its heyday.[62]

Chambers alerted the American people to a shocking fact. During the 1930s Soviet intelligence was able to penetrate deep into the American government. The story of Elizabeth Bentley (told in the next chapter) showed a higher level of penetration than even Chambers knew.

7

The 1930s: Heyday for Soviet Espionage

Part 2: Elizabeth Bentley

THE same year that Whittaker Chambers left the Soviet service, Elizabeth Bentley joined. In the middle of October 1938, Elizabeth Bentley was introduced to Jacob Golos, a Soviet spy master. Bentley had been a Communist Party member since 1935, having joined because of her deep concern about the threat of fascism. She had visited Italy in 1933 and 1934 and was horrified at what she saw. She joined the American League Against War and Fascism, a Communist Party front, at Teachers College in New York and was soon brought into the party proper. Her interest in fighting Italian fascism brought her into contact with a fellow communist named Juliet Stuart Poyntz.

Bentley had the impression that Poyntz was trying to recruit her for underground work in Italy. Before anything materialized, however, Poyntz disappeared and the press carried stories that she had been kidnapped by the Soviet secret police. Golos later informed Bentley that her friend had been "liquidated" because she was a German agent. The accusation was untrue, but this didn't save the hapless woman who had devoted many years to the communist cause.

In 1938 Bentley penetrated the Italian Library of Information, a front for the fascist government. During this time her Communist Party contacts put her in touch with a man she knew as Mr. F. Brown. He was in fact Mario Alpi, a longtime Comintern agent.

Alpi introduced her to Golos. In 1945, after the death of Golos, who had become her lover, and she his courier, Bentley went to the FBI and told them her story. Bentley revealed, "During one of my first meetings with Golos he told me I should not attend any meetings or take part in the Communist Party activities, but that he would bring me literature to keep up my political education." In March 1939 she lost her job at the Italian Library because they suspected her of being an antifascist.[1]

Golos ran an organization called World Tourists, which handled travel to the Soviet Union. This enabled him to provide false documentation for Communist Party functionaries and Soviet agents when they traveled to Moscow. In 1939 World Tourists came under the scrutiny of a congressional committee and the Justice Department. Years later the United States Senate published the government's extensive documentation of the involvement of Golos in passport frauds.[2]

Late in 1940 Golos came to Bentley's apartment with a large package that he wished burned in her fireplace. Much of the material consisted of letters and pamphlets in the Russian language. In addition there were thirty to forty American passports. He also burned an identification folder that had his photograph and signature on one side. The other side had writing in Russian, including in large letters, "OGPU." Golos then explained to Bentley that there were three branches of Soviet intelligence abroad, "the Military-Naval, the political, and the general." He was apparently referring to the Fourth Bureau of the Red Army, Comintern intelligence, and the OGPU, which we now know as KGB.[3]

Naming Spies

In 1948 Bentley testified before the House Committee on Un-American Activities. She listed the members of two groups of government employees who had worked on behalf of the Soviets in the late 1930s and early 1940s. She had traveled between New York and Washington, D.C., as the courier for these groups. An official congressional report listed the persons identified by Bentley. They were:

Silvermaster Group

Nathan Gregory Silvermaster, Director of Labor Division, Farm Security Administration; detailed at one time to Board of Economic Warfare

Solomon Adler, Treasury Department

Norman Bursler, Department of Justice

Frank Coe, Assistant Director, Division of Monetary Research, Treasury; special assistant to United States Ambassador in London; assistant to the Executive Director, Board of Economic Warfare and successor agencies; Assistant Administrator, Foreign Economic Administration

Lauchlin Currie, administrative assistant to the President; Deputy Administrator of Foreign Economic Administration

Bela Gold (known to Miss Bentley as William Gold), assistant head of Division of Program Surveys, Bureau of Agricultural Economics, Agriculture Department; Senate Subcommittee on War Mobilization; Office of Economic Programs in Foreign Economic Administration

Mrs. Bela (Sonia) Gold, research assistant, House Select Committee on Interstate Migration; labor-market analyst, Bureau of Employment Security; Division of Monetary Research, Treasury

Abraham George Silverman, director, Bureau of Research and Information Services, United States Railroad Retirement Board; economic adviser and chief of analysis and plans, Assistant Chief of Air Staff, Materiel and Services

William Taylor, Treasury Department

William Ludwig Ullmann, Division of Monetary Research, Treasury; Materiel and Service Division, Air Corps Headquarters, Pentagon

Perlo Group

Victor Perlo, head of branch in Research Section, Office of Price Administration; War Production Board; Monetary Research, Treasury

Edward J. Fitzgerald, War Production Board

Harold Glasser, Treasury Department; loaned to Government of Ecuador; loaned to War Production Board; adviser on North African Affairs Committee in Algiers, North Africa

Charles Kramer (Krevitsky), National Labor Relations Board; Office of Price Administration; economist with Senate Subcommittee on War Mobilization

Solomon Leshinsky, United Nations Relief and Rehabilitation
    Administration
Harry Magdoff, Statistical Division of War Production Board and
    Office of Emergency Management; Bureau of Research and Sta-
    tistics, WPB; Tools Division, WPB; Bureau of Foreign and Do-
    mestic Commerce
Allan Rosenberg, Foreign Economic Administration
Donald Niven Wheeler, Office of Strategic Services

Miss Bentley also testified that Irving Kaplan, an employee of the
War Production Board at the time, was associated with both groups,
paying dues to the Perlo group and submitting information to the
Silvermaster group. She identified the late Harry Dexter White,
the wartime assistant secretary of the treasury, as another individual
who cooperated with the Silvermaster group.

Bentley also listed the following persons who were obtaining information for the Soviets from government files but who were not
affiliated with either of the two groups:

Michael Greenberg, Board of Economic Warfare; Foreign Economic
    Administration; specialist on China
Joseph Gregg, [Office of the] Coordinator of Inter-American Affairs,
    assistant in Research Division
Maurice Halperin, Office of Strategic Services; head of Latin Amer-
    ican Division in the Research and Analysis Branch; head of Latin
    American research and analysis, State Department
J. Julius Joseph, Office of Strategic Services, Japanese Division
Duncan Chaplin Lee, Office of Strategic Services, legal adviser to
    General William J. Donovan
Robert T. Miller, head of political research, Coordinator of Inter-
    American Affairs; member, Information Service Committee, Near
    Eastern Affairs, State Department; Assistant Chief, Division of
    Research and Publications, State Department
William Z. Park, Coordinator of Inter-American Affairs
Bernard Redmont, Coordinator of Inter-American Affairs
Helen Tenney, office of Strategic Services, Spanish Division[4]

While Bernard Redmont, in a letter to the committee, admitted
knowing Bentley, he pointed out that she never said he gave her
classified information. He had given her only press materials.[5] Red-

mont was being somewhat disingenuous. According to Bentley's 1945 confession to the FBI, Redmont was introduced to her by William Remington. When she told Golos about Redmont, he instructed her to have Remington solicit Redmont's assistance. When Redmont moved to New York, Bentley and Golos met him at the New York Public Library. Golos asked Redmont to provide any information that came into his possession, saying that this information would be given to Earl Browder, the head of the Communist Party. At the early stage of recruitment Golos often claimed that the information was for American Communist use rather than Soviet use, its real purpose.

When Golos received the information Redmont supplied, it was the kind of data that would be available in the press division of his agency. Golos felt this was not of much value. A press office would not normally handle the kind of classified information Golos wanted to supply to the Soviets.

Redmont went into the Marine Corps and Bentley lost contact with him. After he was discharged due to war wounds, Bentley met him in the summer of 1944. Later that year he phoned Bentley to say that he was returning to his old job at the Coordinator of Inter-American Affairs. In the spring of 1945 a Soviet superior told Bentley that they had no need for Redmont and had decided not to contact him further.[6]

William Remington was another Soviet agent identified by Elizabeth Bentley. Remington denied the charge. Bentley revealed that she was introduced to Remington by Golos in early 1942. During the next two years she met with him approximately fifteen times. She collected Communist Party dues from both Remington and his wife. At Remington's trial his former wife verified Bentley's charges. The evidence was overwhelming and he was convicted of perjury. Remington died at Lewisburg Penitentiary on November 24, 1954.[7]

Harry Dexter White, who was identified by Chambers as well as Bentley, denied knowing either. He died of a heart attack before Chambers produced the documents in White's own handwriting that proved he was a Soviet spy.

White was a tremendous influence on his boss, Secretary of the Treasury Henry Morgenthau, Jr. Some historians credit White with the idea of the so-called Morgenthau Plan, announced during World

War II, to turn postwar Germany into a pasture. It is argued that this threat prolonged the war with Germany long enough to guarantee the Soviet occupation of Eastern Europe.[8]

One of White's friends, a former Treasury Department colleague, Fred Smith, wrote an article that appeared in *United Nations World*, March 1947, in which he told the story of the Morgenthau Plan. According to Smith, a meeting was held on August 7, 1944, in southern England. General Dwight Eisenhower, Secretary of the Treasury Henry Morgenthau, and Morgenthau's two assistants, Harry Dexter White and Fred Smith, were there. White complained that the Allied troops were under orders to reestablish the German economy as they conquered parts of Nazi Germany. White thought this was wrong and that no help should be given to the local people. Eisenhower agreed and said he thought that the Germans needed punishment. He said, "I am not interested in the German economy and personally would not like to bolster it if that would make it any easier for the Germans." Eisenhower claimed that those who wanted to let Germany "off easy" really wanted to strengthen Germany as a potential bulwark against Russia. Eisenhower opposed that view of the future and suggested that it was necessary to be "good and hard" on the Germans and to take no step to help them. White responded, "We may want to quote you on the problem of handling the German people." Eisenhower agreed that they could quote him and said, "I will tell the President myself if necessary." According to Smith, "From that moment, Morgenthau's chief interest in life" was the creation of a plan, "that would forever prevent the German people from making war."[9]

Fred Smith sent a copy of his article to Harry Dexter White. It was clear that White played a major role in encouraging Morgenthau to develop a plan that terrified the Germans, and may very well have lengthened the war.

One of the most remarkable services performed by Harry White for the Soviets involved the occupation currency printed by the United States government for use in Germany. The U.S. decided in 1943 to print all the notes for the U.S., British, French, and Soviet zones. The Soviets insisted on being given the plates, the ink, and a sample of the paper so they could print their own notes. The Director of the Bureau of Printing and Engraving, A. W. Hall, protested, but White, a higher authority in the Treasury Department, overruled him. According to Hall, "to permit the Russian government to print a currency identical to that being printed in this country would make accountability impossible." But according to an official memorandum of a Treasury Department meeting held March 7, 1944, "Mr. White said that he had read with considerable interest the memorandum of March 3 from Mr. Hall . . . on this subject but that he was somewhat troubled with the views expressed therein, which indicated that we could not make these plates available to the Russians. Mr. White said that, in all probability, such an answer would be construed by the Russians as expressing a lack of trust and confidence in their handling of the plates." And further, "Mr. White reiterated . . . that Russia was one of the allies who must be trusted to the same degree and to the same extent as the other allies." A week later Secretary Morgenthau advised the Soviet Ambassador that the decision had been made to give them the plates. He turned them over at that time.[10]

To make it even more difficult to determine whether the Soviets were printing excessive numbers of occupation notes that the U.S. would have to redeem, they were given a numbering system that hopelessly confused the Soviet printed notes with replacements for damaged notes used in the American occupation zone.[11]

In 1953 a representative of the Department of the Army admitted at a Senate hearing that "there is no way of determining just to what extent the Russians did use these plates."[12] Some historians believe that the U.S. taxpayer paid millions of dollars to redeem notes printed by the Soviets. Harry Dexter White indeed performed a remarkable service for the Soviet Union.

Bentley told a Senate Committee in 1951 that among the avenues for planting agents in the U.S. government, "I would say that two of our best ones were Harry Dexter White and Lauchlin Currie. They had an immense amount of influence and knew people, and their word would be accepted when they recommended someone."[13]

Bentley told the FBI in her sworn statement that Lauchlin Currie supplied information to the Silvermaster ring. Although she had never met him, she knew of his role through two of the other members of the ring, Nathan Gregory Silvermaster and George Silverman, with whom he was friendly. Currie did not supply actual documents to the ring but would "inform Silverman orally on various matters. In an example of the information orally furnished Silverman, I recall one occasion when Currie informed him that the United States was on the verge of breaking the Soviet code."[14] Testifying before Congress, Bentley described the incident as: "Well, Mr. Silvermaster told me that one day Mr. Currie came dashing into Mr. Silverman's house, sort of out of breath, and told him that the Americans were on the verge of breaking the Soviet code. Mr. Silverman, of course, got immediately—in due course, got in touch with Mr. Silvermaster." Bentley got the information from Silvermaster and passed it on to the Soviets.[15]

While Currie denied any wrongdoing, he testified that he had met Anatole Gromov of the Soviet embassy and had been entertained at Gromov's home. Gromov had been identified by Bentley as the highest ranking Soviet intelligence officer she had met.[16]

The most shocking part of Bentley's story was that Currie had revealed that the U.S. had been on the verge of breaking the Soviet code. This was very closely held information, but it would have been known in the White House. In 1986, Robert Lamphere, a former official of the Federal Bureau of Investigation, was permitted by the government to reveal that in November 1944, William Donovan, then head of the Office of Strategic Services, had purchased 1,500 pages of code and cipher material, including a partially burned code book that the Finns had captured during their war with the Soviets. Because the United States and Russia were allies, then-secretary of state Edward Stettinius protested to the White House and forced the OSS to return the material to the Russians. Despite this, the United States had used the material to break the NKVD (People's Commissariat of Internal Affairs, the Soviet Intelligence Service) code. In May 1945 the NKVD suddenly changed their codes.[17]

Bentley's testimony about Currie was challenged by Congressman John Rankin. Throughout the hearings Rankin made it plain that he did not like Jews and believed that they were all communists. He also did not like the idea that the gentile, Lauchlin Currie, was being accused of Soviet espionage based on what was told to Bentley by persons who were Jews. The exchange was bitter, but Bentley made her point.

> Rankin: Now, the thing that disturbs me is that you take the testimony, the statement of two men, Silverman and Silvermaster, relayed from one to the other, about what this Scotchman in the

White House, Mr. Currie, said about communism. Did you ever investigate to find out whether or not Silverman or Silvermaster were telling the truth?

Bentley: Well, for one thing, in espionage rings you cannot investigate. They are built up on this particular type of flimsy connection.

Rankin: Well, here we have gone on all day—here is what is disturbing me . . . we have put in the whole day accepting from an ex-Communist, which you admit you are, testimony relayed through two Communists as to what this man, Currie, in the White House is supposed to have said. . . .

But here we put in a whole day, a whole day, smearing Currie by remote control through two Communists, either one of whom you admit would swear to a lie just as soon as he would swear to the truth if it suited his purposes, and relayed to you, who at that time was a member of the Communist Party. We have come in here and put in a whole day with that kind of testimony about a man who happened to occupy a rather responsible position in the White House.

Bentley: Might I say just one thing in that respect? It is quite true that communists lie to the outside world. It is not true that they lie within the party, particularly to the person whom they regard as their superior. They do not do that. That was what was told me by Mr. Silvermaster. I have every reason to believe that he was telling me the truth. I have no desire to smear anyone. I have simply told the facts as they were told to me. It is up to the committee to decide whether or not that is credible or not.

Rankin: You certainly have an unlimited credibility. If you would take the word of any Communist, Silverman or Silvermaster, or both of them, and I believe you named another one, whom you relayed it through, who was also a Communist, if you take that testimony as to what this man Currie, as I said, a Scotchman, has said about the Communists—it just looks to me as if we have gone pretty far afield here to smear this man by remote control, instead of getting someone who heard him or who knew that he had made any statement.[18]

To Rankin a statement from Jews against a Scotsman was not to be believed. The fact that the Jews were communists and the Scotsman held high government office made it worse.

Currie denied Bentley's charges, but the details he provided about his relationship with members of the ring were identical with those provided by Bentley. Congressman Karl Mundt was unsure of who was telling the truth. He wanted to believe Currie, but Bentley's details were rather shocking. Mundt said:

> Without in any way casting any reflections on the testimony of Mr. Currie, it is interesting to me how thoroughly this whole chain of events corroborates the testimony of Miss Bentley. Somehow or other, she knew who Mr. Currie knew, she knew about the fact that Silvermaster and Silverman had ingratiated themselves into the confidence of Mr. Currie, she knew of the relationship of Mr. Currie to the information in the civil services files, she knew he had called them at one time to the attention of Judge Patterson, she knew that Judge Patterson had sent back a letter saying that in his opinion the person in question was not guilty of the charges. That doesn't reflect on the testimony at all of Mr. Currie, but it certainly does corroborate the fact that Miss Bentley had an uncanny access to official information in the government, which I am prepared to believe she did not get from Mr. Currie but she got from the direct contacts, probably without any knowledge—I think without any knowledge of Mr. Currie at all; they were using him as they would use anybody to further their own nefarious purposes.[19]

Lauchlin Currie had denied Bentley's charge but left the United States immediately after the congressional hearings of 1948. He never returned, and he has never had to face charges.

Writers for the Cause

Bentley revealed to the FBI that a British Intelligence officer operating in the United States was really working for the Soviets. Although she had never met the man, he had been identified to her by Golos as Cedric Belfrage. The British writer, Cedric Belfrage, was serving at that time as the chief of the Political Warfare Section for Sir William Stephenson's British Intelligence Unit working in New York City.[20] Stephenson's unit, which existed prior to the U.S. entry into World War II, continued to operate and assisted the United States in establishing the wartime OSS.[21]
Bentley told the FBI:

> Sometime toward the latter part of 1942 or in early 1943 I learned that one Cedric Belfrage was contacting Golos and turning over to

him certain information. I learned through Golos that Belfrage was connected with British Intelligence in the United States and operated out of a "cover" office someplace in the Rockefeller Center. I also recall that Belfrage was introduced to Golos by either Earl Browder or V. J. Jerome. During the course of my connection with Golos, I found out that Belfrage had supplied Golos with a report apparently emanating from Scotland Yard, which was more or less of a treatise on espionage agents. This work dealt with the type of people who might be employed for this sort of work, the precautions that should be taken to allude or identify whether or not a person was being followed. I also recall that in this article was a contribution by some prominent burglars in England, who apparently made the following information available as a patriotic gesture. This contribution concerned the technique of surreptitiously opening safes, doors, locks, and gaining admittance to most any type of building or office equipment. This document was a carbon copy and was apparently extracted by Belfrage from some British file. Belfrage also contributed information regarding British policy as it concerned the Middle East and Russia, and other information that apparently emanated from his connection with, probably, high-ranking British officials in the United States.

V. J. Jerome was the cultural commissar for the American Communist Party and was a close associate of Browder. After the death of Golos, Bentley's Soviet case officers asked her to make contact with Belfrage through Browder. But Browder responded, "He is out of the racket now, let him stay out of it." However, in the spring of 1945 Bentley met Jerome on the street. He asked if she was still interested in contacting Belfrage. When she was noncommittal, Jerome suggested that she should be interested, as Belfrage, "was back with British Intelligence."[22]

Actually by late 1944 Belfrage was in Europe working as an intelligence officer in the "denazification" of Germany. His book describing that experience was published in 1954 under the title *Seeds of Destruction*.[23]

Based in part on Bentley's evidence, after a lengthy procedure, Belfrage was deported from the United States in August 1955. At no time, either in court or before congressional committees, did Belfrage take the opportunity to deny Bentley's information. Indeed, in a book published in 1973, Belfrage implied that he had been deported because he was a journalist.[24]

In 1957 Belfrage wrote an article for the Soviet magazine *New Times*, which appears weekly in a number of languages.[25] *New Times* is closely associated with the KGB. One of the authors of this book (Levchenko) was a KGB officer under cover as a *New Times* correspondent in Japan when he defected in 1979. At that time, of the twelve *New Times* correspondents around the world, ten were KGB officers, and only two were "clean."

Another writer identified as a Soviet agent by Bentley was Albert Kahn. He was later to be the publisher of Belfrage's 1954 book. Bentley told the FBI:

> In January 1942, to the best of my recollection, I was taken by Golos to the home of Albert Kahn, on East 9th Street between Fifth Avenue and University Place, New York City. I recall having heard his name previously, but had never met him before nor did I know a great deal about him. I learned that he was a dues-paying Communist Party member at the time I met him and in fact on a couple of occasions I collected his party dues from him although he was working with a Jewish bureau of the party in New York.

The fact that Bentley collected dues from Kahn even though he was active in a Communist Party unit and paid his dues there indicates that he was also paying dues to the underground apparatus. The Soviets insisted that their ideological agents must either take money, as do their mercenaries, or they must pay dues to the apparatus. The act of passing money or "presents" ties the agent to the apparatus.

According to Bentley, Kahn was publishing a newsletter called *The Hour*. A brochure advertising *The Hour* described it as follows:

> *The Hour* is a weekly confidential news-bulletin devoted to exposing and publicizing the activities of Fifth Column groups and individuals in the United States. It is published primarily for the use of professionals in publication and radio fields.

Bentley reported that Kahn provided Golos with "miscellaneous information taken by him from the files of the Anti-Defamation League, and also information concerning the Ukrainian Nationalist Movement. It was my impression that this later data interested Golos the most. . . ." Bentley said that her association with Kahn terminated in the spring of 1943 when he began to devote himself to writing books."[26]

The May 20, 1943, issue of *The Hour* contained the following notice:

> With this issue, *The Hour* is suspending publication. Other writing commitments, and particularly the fact that the editor of *The Hour* is working on a new book with Michael Sayers, make it necessary for the editor to discontinue this newsletter at this time. (Regular subscribers will be advised in the near future regarding the issues still due on their subscriptions.)
>
> The first issue of *The Hour* appeared in April 1939, as the official publication of the American Council Against Nazi Propaganda, of which the late William E. Dodd, former Ambassador to Germany, was chairman, and for the past four years *The Hour* has devoted itself to exposing fifth-column organizations and individuals operating in the United States. In a number of cases, government action has followed the disclosures which have appeared in this newsletter.

Kahn's claims that *The Hour* was an influential publication were probably true. The Sayers and Kahn books were very influential, widely distributed, and endorsed by prominent persons and government officials.[27]

Actually the first book written by Sayers and Kahn had already been published in late 1942. Titled *Sabotage! The Secret War Against America*, the book accused numerous individuals and groups of engaging in sabotage against American war industry. A particular target of Sayers and Kahn were Ukrainian-Americans who opposed the Soviet occupation of their homeland, Western Ukraine, which had been ruled by Poland from 1920 to 1939 and was turned over to the Soviet Union as part of the Stalin-Hitler Pact.

According to the acknowledgments in the book, "Much of the material for this book has come from the files of *The Hour* and from special reports prepared by our own investigators. We have also drawn heavily upon the public records of the Department of Justice, the State Department and various Congressional Committees." The authors also said, "We wish to express our appreciation to the Anti-Defamation league of B'nai B'rith for having generously placed at our disposal the contents of its splendid files."[28] The Anti-Defamation League, of course, did not know that Kahn was using their files not only for his writing but also, as Bentley revealed, to supply information to Soviet intelligence.

The second book by Sayers and Kahn, *The Plot Against The Peace*, appeared in 1945. Its theme was that Nazi Germany had a secret conspiracy to "split the United Nations" and start World War III.[29]

The most significant of the Sayers and Kahn books was called *The Great Conspiracy*, subtitled *The Secret War Against Soviet Russia*. It was published in hardcover early in 1946, and a magazine-size paperback edition appeared in June of that year under the title *The Great Conspiracy Against Russia*.[30] This was the most flagrant Soviet propaganda book issued by the pair. Any criticism of the Soviet Union was treated as evidence of participation in the "Conspiracy." The Soviet purge trials were treated as proof that Trotsky and most of the early Bolsheviks were Nazi agents conspiring to destroy the Soviet Union.

On April 7, 1952, a former Soviet official, Igor Bogolepov, testified before a Senate committee that he was familiar with the book of Kahn and Sayers. He testified, "The largest part of this book which is known to me was written by a certain Veinberg, who was a vice chief of the south-western division of the Foreign Office in Moscow. . . . I saw myself the Russian manuscript before it was sent to New York to be there." In answer to the question of whether the manuscript was identical with the book he had read, Bogolepov answered, "Yes, it was. They rearranged it, perhaps, but the facts and the ideas are the same."[31]

In 1958 Kahn testified before the same committee and claimed that the book "was written in English . . . by me. . . ."[32] Kahn's claim of sole authorship is challenged by a document written by Cedric Belfrage. In a letter to Kahn on May 31, 1946, Belfrage wrote:

Dear Albert

This is my formal confirmation, for the benefit of whom it may concern, that I have received from you and Michael Sayers a cash settlement in lieu of royalties payable to me on *The Great Conspiracy*, and have no further claim on the earnings of any American editions of this book.

Yours sincerely
Cedric Belfrage

The Communist Party conducted a major campaign to publicize and circulate the book. Communist Party official Fred Blair, reviewing the book in the April 1946 issue of the party's theoretical organ, *Political Affairs,* wrote:

> This book is a real weapon against the anti-Soviet prejudices that have been inculcated in the minds of the masses by press, radio, pulpit, and cinema. It has mass appeal. It is, above all, useful at this crucial moment, as an instrument for exposing the plot of American and British imperialism to drag the peoples into a new anti-Soviet war.

On May 8, 1946, William Z. Foster, chairman of the Communist Party, wrote a letter to all state and district secretaries of the party advising them that the one-dollar edition of *The Great Conspiracy* would be available in early June. Although the book was being issued by a publishing house not publicly identified with the communists, the party's publishing house, New Century Publishers, had made arrangements to handle the distribution to party members. Foster wrote:

> Because of its timeliness and importance, New Century Publishers has made special arrangements to handle the national distribution to our organizations. The important thing is to discuss the ways and means of really getting behind this book and ensuring that it receives the widest mass sale possible under the circumstances. Every Party member should understand the vital necessity of actively helping to popularize *The Great Conspiracy* and seeing to it that it gets read, particularly among the trade unionists. Also, it is a book which should provide valuable educational material for every branch. Please discuss this matter and let us know how many copies you can sell in your district, as the aim is for a really big circulation of this book.

A letter from the California state literature director of the Communist Party, George Walker, dated June 10, 1946, and addressed to "All County Committees" and "All Education and Literature Directors" advised the communists:

> With Comrade Foster giving us this perspective on the book, we intend to distribute a minimum of 5,000 copies in California, and in order to guarantee this, we are sending along some ideas and pro-

posals to help organize this campaign. First of all, since the one dollar
edition is being published by Boni & Gaer, a commercial publishing
house in New York, and will have a special introduction by Senator
Claude Pepper of Florida, it will be possible to approach wide sections
of the people with the book, particularly the conservative trade unionists who need very much to have this information.

In 1947 a pocket-size paperback edition of the book was published.
Eugene Dennis, then national secretary of the Communist Party,
wrote in a letter to all state and district secretaries:

> The 25 cent price of this new pocket-book size edition makes it pos-
> sible to reach an audience of literally hundreds of thousands with the
> vitally important information contained in this book. Today it is more
> urgent than ever to get this material before the widest possible sec-
> tions of the American people.

The California Communist Party instructed its members, in a
mimeographed plan for selling the book, on how to carry out the
assignment:

> Comrades [will] be responsible for selling the book to friends on job,
> in neighborhood, and in mass organizations. Comrades who have few
> contacts (e.g., mothers with small children, comrades living in iso-
> lated parts of the state, etc.) [are] to phone and write friends and
> select names regarding book. Branches [are] to organize sales of book
> at busy street corners, in precincts and at factory gates, especially of
> concentration industries. Youth and student branches to organize
> sales at college entrances (Sale to be preceded by distribution of leaflet
> advertising the book and announcing sale).

Max Bedacht, as general secretary of the communist front International Workers Order, circulated a memo of quotations praising
the book to IWO officials who could use the material "in letters to
your lodges and in articles for your press."[33]

Raymond Robins, the American Red Cross official who had supported the Soviet cause at the time of the Russian Revolution, was
a great fan of the book, buying copies and sending them to friends
and acquaintances. His mind-set can be found in a July 1946 letter.
Robins wrote:

The line-up against the Soviet Union is practically complete. The monopoly capitalists, Imperialists, Landlord and Empire exploiters, plus the Roman Catholic hierarchy and the Jesuit "machine" are marching in all lands for the overthrow of the Soviet Revolution and the Soviet Government.[34]

After World War II, Kahn served for many years as an official of the international Soviet front World Peace Council.[35] In May 1977 that organization held its World Peace Conference in Warsaw, Poland. A month earlier Kahn invited Jim Jones, the leader of the bizarre cult that committed mass suicide in Guyana the next year, to attend the conference. Documents found in Jonestown after the tragedy told the story. One of the documents written by a Jones associate, dated April 17, contained the following information:

Romesh Chandra suggested that Jim go to Warsaw with the Guyanese delegation. (He is Secretary-General of World Peace Council.)

Albert Kahn felt that he should NOT go with the Guyanese delegation; but should come to New York to fly out with the US guests. He stresses that if Jim went with American guests, he would be much more comfortable, would get to meet "top" people, and would in general get decent treatment. Kahn mentioned that often at these kinds of conferences, there is danger of people having to go through a lot of hassles. Kahn would want to shepherd Jim through, he would want to insure that his visa were appropriately cleared with Russian embassies in San Francisco and Washington (Dobrynin). He would also make it possible for Jim to visit in the USSR. The plan will be for them to fly on May 1st to Moscow direct. Spend a day in Moscow, then fly to Warsaw (one hour). The conference begins on May 5th. When it is over, Kahn suggests that Jim go to Moscow and he will be able to arrange for him to travel wherever he wants in the USSR with a car, driver, interpreter, the works. This he (Kahn) can arrange.

In speaking earlier with Marceiline, Albert said he would speak forthrightly about Jim's work in Warsaw to the assembled delegation, and that his work would thereby get international recognition.

Kahn thought it would be critical for Jim to be identified with U.S. delegation, so world would hear of his work in USA—his contribution in American peace movement would be crucial for the international community to hear about. This would be obscured if he were to come with another nation's delegation. Note: Officially, Jim would be coming as a "guest" invited specially by Romesh Chandra. However,

Kahn was a LOT influence at this meeting—he is one of most principle
dignitaries there.
(grammar and spelling in original)

Albert Kahn died on September 15, 1979, when he lost control
of his car and struck a utility pole. A police officer who saw the
accident reported that he was traveling between sixty and seventy
miles per hour.[36]

David Karr was only twenty years old when he went to work for
Kahn as a reporter for the newsletter *The Hour* in 1938. He was
also writing freelance articles for the *New York Daily Mirror*. At
that time he met a young woman working in the office of the United
States Attorney who supplied him with information about an investigation that was under way concerning Nazi espionage in the United
States. The *New York Daily Mirror* was not interested, so Karr
wrote his articles for the *Daily Worker*, the Communist Party newspaper. He also assisted another *Daily Worker* writer, Lowell Wakefield, to write about the subject in the *Daily Worker* and in a pamphlet
called *Hitler's Spy Plot in the U.S.A.*

In one of Karr's articles for the *Daily Worker* he attacked Richard
Krebs as a Nazi agent. Actually Krebs had broken with Communists
and, after falling into Nazi hands, was able to escape by agreeing to
work for them. He did not do so, however, and once in the free
world wrote a book, *Out of the Night*, under the pen name Jan
Valtin. He exposed both the Nazis and the Communists. Karr was
a participant in the communist campaign to have Krebs deported
(see chapter 8). Karr admitted working for the *Daily Worker* and
The Hour during closed-door testimony before the Dies Committee
in 1943. At that time Karr was employed by the Office of War
Information as a "senior liaison officer working with other Federal
agencies." He testified that he obtained the job on the recommendation of a man he had known about three years, Alan Cranston.[37]
Alan Cranston is now a U.S. senator from California. There is no
evidence he understood that he was being used by Karr.

After World War II Karr became a major wheeler-dealer in Soviet
trade. *Business Week* reported on May 19, 1975, that Karr had
arranged a 250 million dollar credit for the Soviet Foreign Trade
Bank. According to the magazine, "Among the bankers and businessmen in Europe who have cultivated contacts in the Soviet gov-

ernment, Karr is probably near the head of the pack." He was a partner of the prestigious French bank Lazard Freres et Cie. The magazine identified Karr's main contact in Moscow as Jermen Gvishiani, deputy chairman of the Soviet State Committee for Science and Technology. Not coincidentally Gvishiani was the son-in-law of then Soviet premier Aleksey Kosygin.[38]

On July 7, 1979, Karr died in Paris after a visit to Moscow. *Fortune* magazine, reporting on his death said:

> Whispers of a KGB connection followed Karr everywhere, once he started commuting to Moscow in 1972. However, in his bargaining with the Russians, just as in his wheeling-dealing with everyone else, it was always difficult to be sure whose side Karr was on.

Karr's longtime friend, Senator Alan Cranston, said of him, "He had a strong social conscience that made him an intense promoter of detente." But others who knew him said his only interest was money. Karr bragged that he had privately advised presidents Ford and Carter on how to deal with the Soviet Union. Karr, who was sixty, died of a heart attack, but his thirty-year-old widow insisted that he was a victim of foul play. The evidence did not sustain that conclusion. One of Karr's last deals was the sale of Soviet gold Olympic coins. One of Karr's firms got 40 percent of the take, half of that going to Karr. Armand Hammer's Occidental Petroleum got 33 percent.[39]

8

The Spanish Civil War

THE Spanish Civil War began in July 1936 when the military revolted against the elected left of center government. The Nationalist forces, led by General Francisco Franco, received the assistance of Germany and Italy. The Republican Government received the support of the Soviet Union and the international Communist movement. While communist influence in Spain was insignificant when the war broke out, the external support gave the Communists significantly more influence as the war went on.

Stalin's message to the Spanish Communist Party in 1936 boasted:

> The toilers of the Soviet Union are only fulfilling their duty by rendering every assistance within their power to the revolutionary masses of Spain. They realize that the liberation of Spain from the oppression of the fascist reactionaries is not the private affair of the Spaniards, but the common cause of all advanced and progressive mankind.[1]

That slogan became the communist rallying cry for the rest of the war. The Comintern sent a large portion of its cadre to Spain. "The International Brigades are selected units formed of anti-fascist volunteers from all over the world in reply to the call of the Communist International. . . ." boasted German Communist functionary Fritz Dahlem.[2]

The American volunteers were organized into the Lincoln Battalion. The head of the Communist Party USA, Earl Browder, revealed in a report to the Central Committee on June 17, 1937, that 60 percent of the Lincoln Battalion members were members of the Communist Party.[3]

The Soviet Intelligence Service too played a major role in Spain. Some of that story has been told by two of the most active participants, Walter Krivitsky, who served as a high-ranking official of Soviet Military Intelligence in Western Europe, and Alexander Orlov, head of the OGPU in Spain. Both of these men broke with Stalin and tried to tell their stories to the West. Both were ignored by the governments that needed to understand their information.

Krivitsky, who defected in 1937, published a book about his experiences in 1939. He was found dead under mysterious circumstances in a Washington hotel room in February 1941. Orlov survived the purges and escaped to the United States, but at least a decade went by before the Western governments would bother to interview him properly. His book, *The Secret History of Stalin's Crimes*, was not published until after the dictator's death in 1953.

According to Krivitsky, on September 14, 1936, a meeting was held at OGPU headquarters in the Lubianka, Moscow. The meeting, called by Yagoda, the head of OGPU, included Frinovsky, who at that time commanded the military forces of the OGPU (he was later commissar of the navy but was purged in 1939); Sloutski, chief of the Foreign Division of OGPU; and General Uritsky of the Red Army general staff. Krivitsky learned from Sloutski that a veteran intelligence officer had been detailed to establish the OGPU in Spain. Krivitsky identified the officer as Nikolsky, a man of many aliases, including "Orlov." According to Krivitsky:

> This Lubianka conference also placed the Soviet secret police in charge of Comintern operations in Spain. It decided to "co-ordinate" the activities of the Spanish Communist Party with those of the Ogpu. Another decision of this conference was to have the movement of volunteers to Spain from every country secretly policed by the Ogpu. There is in the central committee of every Communist Party in the world one member who holds a secret commission from the Ogpu and it was through him that this would be accomplished.[4]

By early November the first International Brigade contingents had arrived in Spain, led by the legendary General Kleber. He was, of course, the old Soviet Military Intelligence officer Moishe Stern (see chapter 1). Krivitsky reported that Stern, whom he knew personally, had graduated from the Red Army's Frunze Military Academy in 1924. For a while the two worked together in the intelligence department of the general staff.[5] Stern, who had served the Soviet Union in dangerous assignments in Germany, China, and the United States, died at the hands of Stalin's executioners, probably in 1940.

The International Brigadiers were idealistic and naive. The mentality of these young fanatics can be judged from a collection of letters, published in the Soviet Union, written by John Cornford, one of the early British casualties. Cornford, writing about breaking up with his girlfriend, expressed his innermost feelings: "I am very sorry in one way, though I am always glad of any break with the past that reflects my own position from a new angle. If one's ready to kill and be killed for the revolution, this kind of break shouldn't make too much difference, Heil, Rot Front!"[6] The cynical apparatchiks of Soviet intelligence used such young idealists in the most brutal way.

American Brigadiers

The first volunteer from the United States to appear in Spain was Humberto Galleani. *Newsweek* magazine carried his photograph on July 4, 1937, identifying him as "Major Galleani, first United States volunteer." A World War I veteran of the Italian army, Galleani joined the American Communist Party in 1934 or 1935. He had left Italy in 1924 to escape Mussolini's fascism. Testifying before a congressional committee April 12, 1940, Galleani described how one American volunteer, using the pseudonym Paul White, had tried to leave Spain. Apparently White's real name was John Quincy Adams and he was descended from the two presidents Adams.

According to Galleani, "He was arrested on the Pyrenees while he was trying to get out of Spain. There was, of course, a mock trial, you know—it was very easy to make mock trial in the International Brigade, and after a couple of days this rather ironical communication was made to the battalion that for unanimous decision of the battalion the volunteer Paul White had been executed." He referred to the communication as ironical because this was the first time that the members of the battalion knew that they had made this unanimous decision.

Galleani identified the American volunteer who ran the International Brigade prison at Castle de Fells near Barcelona as Tony De Maio. He described meeting De Maio at a railroad station about fifteen kilometers from Barcelona. De Maio was with a group of between 180 and 200 prisoners. Galleani spoke to some of the Italians in the group who, he said, "complained to me about the brutal treatment that De Maio was giving to the prisoners."[7]

William C. McCuistion was another volunteer. A seaman by profession, he told of meeting Tony De Maio and George Mink. According to the testimony of McCuistion, "I saw George Mink and Tony De Maio and Captain Cohn on May 2, 1938, in a little cafe— one of the nicer but small cafes on the Rambla de Catalonia. I saw Tony De Maio kill two men in that cafe." He said the shootings were "an everyday occurrence with other groups." However, "It hadn't been so frequent with the American groups, but the American that was killed at that time was going under the name of Matthews. He had a State Department passport issued under the name of Aronofski—I think that was his correct name, but he was using the name 'Matthews' over there, and he was shot through the side— through the temple, right in here (indicating). The other fellow wasn't quite dead. His name was Moran an Englishman. He was taken away to the hospital. Whether he died or not, I don't know." In answer to a committee question, he said, "Tony De Maio shot them." "Why?" he was asked. The answer: "Because they were stragglers." He apparently meant they were absent without leave.

When asked about Albert Wallach, a volunteer who was missing, McCuistion answered: "Albert Wallach was stowed away on board the American steamship *Oregon* with the assistance of several members of the crew. I think one of them was named Samuel Singer [*sic;* Sam Usinger]. He is at present a member of the sailors' union of the Pacific coast and is in San Francisco at this time. He [Wallach] was aboard the ship for ten days. He got careless and he came out and was taken off the ship by Tony De Maio and others, and placed in prison in Barcelona." Asked by committee research director J. B. Matthews, "In what prison?" McCuistion answered, "He was placed in the military prison, either at Karl Marx Barracks or up on the hill or at San Sebastian. I don't know which one he was placed in."[8]

Albert Wallach's father told the congressional committee that his twenty-three-year-old son had gone to fight in Spain. Wallach had attempted through the State Department to secure his son's return. On March 6, 1938, he received a telegram from the State Department which read, "Your son has been discharged and released and is being sent out of Spain." But young Wallach never appeared.

The father contacted a number of returned volunteers who had known his son in Spain. Based on their information Wallach charged that his son had been murdered. He testified:

> This happened in a so-called prison camp or jail known as Castle de Fells, which I understand is about twenty-five kilometers south of the city of Barcelona, and that it was done under the supervision of the officer known as Captain Gates, and that the man in charge of this prison was a fellow by the name of Tony De Maio, who I understand was the actual killer, not only of my boy but of six other American boys, whose remains to this very moments are in the courtyard of this prison camp, Castle de Fells.

Wallach attributed the murder to the fact that he was trying to get his son released.[9] There is no way to know if his conclusion was correct or if the killers had a different motive.

Anthony De Maio testified before congress on the same day as the other witnesses. He denied knowing anything about Albert Wallach or George Mink. He also denied being in charge of the prison at Castle de Fells. He did, however, admit knowing William McCuistion.[10]

In 1954, hearings were held before the Subversive Activities Control Board, concerning an organization called "The Veterans of the Abraham Lincoln Brigade." The government was attempting to prove that the organization was a front for the Communist Party. The organization cross-examined witnesses against it and presented its own witnesses.

Edward Horan, a former member of the American Communist Party, had served as a volunteer in Spain. While there he became a member of the Spanish Communist Party. After his return to the U.S. he was active in the Veterans of the Abraham Lincoln Brigade. His testimony before the Subversive Activities Control Board was summarized in the recommended decision of board member Kathryn McHale:

> Horan was imprisoned at Castillo De Fels, an International Brigades prison at Castells, Spain, where he met a number of other Americans, including Frank Cone, Lewis Oliver, and Albert Wallach. Wallach,

while in Barcelona with the ALB, had contacted the CNT (Anarchist labor union organization) and had been given a commission as a colonel in a division commanded by CNT personnel. While working in the CNT offices at Barcelona, he was picked up by several plainclothesmen and accused of being an American spy. Horan last saw Wallach when he was taken from the hole, which they shared, in the middle of the night and Wallach indicated that he wouldn't be back. Shortly thereafter, machine gun fire was heard and Wallach has never been seen since. His chief accuser and interrogator had been Tony De Maio.

At Pozorubio, an International Brigades training base, two Czechs, during a party, made critical remarks about the Communists in Spain. The following morning these men were missing and troops were told that they had been disciplined for their remarks the night before.

The Petitioner's witnesses establish that Paul White, formerly a Political Commissar of the ALB, was executed by a firing squad consisting of ALB members near Marsa, Spain, in or about May of 1938, for political reasons, not having committed any military offense and not having been tried by a military court.

William Herrick, a former member of the Young Communist League and a volunteer in Spain, also testified before the Board. His testimony was summarized by Kathryn McHale:

Marvin Stern, who had been a political commissar, succeeding Phil Bard (both established as Party members), was removed as such and disciplined (assigned to a penal battalion and then disappeared) for criticizing the political and military leadership.

In August of 1937, when a committee from the FALB, (Friends of the Abraham Lincoln Brigade) including Max Bedacht, a member of the Party's National Committee, and Phil Bard, former ALB Political Commissar, toured Spain, Herrick inquired of Bard on the basis of friendship as to the whereabouts and welfare of Marvin Stern, whereupon he was told "Communist Party discipline is higher than all friendship, and if I were you I would not discuss this matter any further."

In May of 1937, three high-ranking CPUSA members, namely, Harry Haywood, Bill Lawrence, and Steve Nelson, visited the ALB. When questioned concerning the whereabouts of various persons, including Marvin Stern, Nelson indicated that Marvin Stern should be forgotten and not inquired after in the future.

Robert Gladnick was a member of the Young Communist League and operated for the Communist Party on New York's waterfront before going to Spain. His testimony before the board as summarized by McHale:

> Gladnick was also told in Spain by John Gates, high Party functionary and a Brigade Political Commissar, that one Harry Perchick, a mutual acquaintance from the Young Communist League in New York, had been executed because he was criticizing the Party and the Communist movement. When asked by Gladnick how he could take care of such a matter when he had eaten in Perchick's home and knew him so well, Gates replied to the effect: "You have to be a Bolshevik, and a Bolshevik would take care of his own mother. We have to introduce discipline."[11]

John Gates, after his break with the Communist Party, spoke to one of the authors of this book. He denied knowing anything about Wallach and that anyone had been executed in Spain. Before his break Gates had been a National Committee member of the Communist Party and the editor of the *Daily Worker*. In 1987 one of the authors spoke to Robert Gladnick. We believe that he is a more credible witness. Gladnick was under oath when he testified. Gates, in private conversation, was not.

Mink and Josephson

George Mink had a long record in the Communist movement before going to Spain. A book published in 1939 by an anti-communist group of maritime workers provided some of Mink's background:

> George Mink, said to have been a taxi driver in Philadelphia prior to 1926–27, was the National Chairman of the Marine Workers' Industrial Union. He is also secret agent for the OGPU (now the NKVD) and carries credentials as such. Prior to the formation of the MWIU he was active in forming and propagating the International Seamen's Club, Marine Workers Educational, Progressive, and Marine Workers' Leagues. He went to Latin America and Europe in 1928–29 and –30 where he attended various Red conventions and congresses in Hamburg, Germany and other points, always returning to the U.S. via Russia. In Copenhagen, Denmark, on July 30, 1935, George Mink

and Nicholas Sherman were sentenced to eighteen months imprisonment, guilty of espionage against a neighboring country (Germany). They were also charged with having forged passports."[12]

William McCuistion, testifying before Congress in 1939, stated, "I first personally became acquainted with George Mink at the convention of the Marine Workers League in New York in April 1930." The organization was a front for the Communist Party. Mink made frequent trips to the Soviet Union and according to McCuistion claimed to have been a brother-in-law of Losovsky, head of the Red International of Labor Unions. McCuistion testified:

Mink had served under some name—I think it was the name of Hertz, but it might have been under his right name—in the United States Navy. He bragged that he had been in about seven different armies and had deserted. He was officially known as a member of the military intelligence and the GPU of the Soviet Union. He paid particular attention to getting photographs, various things like that. For instance, if a guy was working regularly, steady on the ship, Mink even went to the extent of buying him cameras as a present at various times.

McCuistion testified further that about 1934

[Mink] was arrested with an American lawyer who also is in the Soviet Military Intelligence, Leon Josephson . . . . They were arrested together with quite a group of people in Denmark. They were accused of trying to jeopardize the international relations between Denmark and Germany, that they were at the head of the communications system that was maintaining and supporting the then illegal Communist movement in Germany, and they were accused of plotting the assassination of Hitler. Some of them were arrested in Germany and Mink and a group of them got across to Denmark. I think they were sentenced to eighteen months and those that were foreign born were to be deported.

McCuistion claimed that Mink was responsible for the ring being captured, as he had gotten, "mixed up with a woman Gestapo agent who turned over the whole bunch to the Danish and German authorities."[13]

The State Department reports about the incident make interesting reading. One of them entered into the record of a congressional hearing of 1947 reads:

> Leon Josephson, a naturalized citizen, was arrested in Denmark in February 1935, charged with espionage. About the same time two of his associates, George Mink and a man who had an American passport in the name of Nicholas Sherman, were also arrested. Four American passports were found in Mink's possession, one in his own name, one in the name of Al Gotlieb, which bore Mink's photograph, and the others in the name of Abraham Wexler and Harry Herman Kaplan. In addition to the American passport, Sherman also had a Canadian passport in the name of Abraham Goldman and a German passport in the name of Willy Carl Herman Breitschneider.
>
> When first questioned, the persons arrested intimated that they were members of a Jewish organization planning the assassination of Hitler, that Josephson was the head of the organization in Europe, that Mink had been acting as treasurer and that Sherman was to attempt the actual assassination. Subsequent investigation did not verify this claim but established that the organization was part of an extensive espionage system on behalf of a foreign government. It was ascertained that one of the persons arrested had in his possession detailed plans for the installation and operation of a secret radio station in Denmark. Another had in his possession detailed information regarding German naval plans. It was also found that the three men had contacts in practically all countries in Europe, as well as the United States, and that they were directing the operation of a courier system which carried messages in secret code between Copenhagen, Antwerp, the British Isles, and New York.
>
> The three were brought to trial on May 11, 1935, after they had been in prison for four months. Josephson was acquitted and the other two men convicted. Josephson was permitted to return to the United States. Mink and Sherman were each sentenced to eighteen months imprisonment and subsequently deported from Denmark. They were released in the early summer of 1936 before serving the full term and traveled to the Soviet Union with travel documents supplied by the Soviet authorities in Sweden.

Lester Maynard, American consul general in Copenhagen, Denmark, made a report to the secretary of state on May 16, 1935. He wrote:

Shortly before the trial I had a further interview with Josephson and he spoke rather frankly of his communistic activities and his association with the other men under arrest.

He came to the Consulate General on Tuesday, May 14th, having been released from prison on Monday, and then enlarged considerably on the information which he had previously given. He stated that as long as he had been acquainted he did not mind telling me about his association with the communist party in the United States and his activities abroad. He stated that to him communism is more than a political theory or belief and is a religion. He stated that he is an atheist and a member of the active Communist Party in America and in its inner circle.

He admitted long association with the man known as Sherman and stated that one of the many mistakes he had made was to directly secure letters for Sherman from American concerns so that Sherman might appear to be a commercial representative and thus more freely move about Europe. . . . He believes that Sherman entered over the Canadian border, without papers, but he had no definite knowledge on the subject. When discussing Mink he stated that Mink's activities in the seamen's union had brought him into bad repute and that it was only after he had lost his influence there that he joined the communist organization and was sent by them to Copenhagen to act as the center for their courier service. . . . He bitterly reproached Mink for carelessness and stupidity and predicted that if Mink should return to the United States he would pay heavily to the Communist Party for his indiscretions. He enumerated the latter and stressed the folly of Mink in securing four passports, two with his own photographs, and pointed out that this might mean five years in the penitentiary if Mink goes to the United States. He added that Sherman's activities were of such a nature as to terminate his usefulness to the Communist Party in any country but Russia and that Sherman would attempt to go there, but even in regard to Russia he expressed some doubt, as he stated, that the Russian Government did not like to receive a communist who had been in the hands of the police charged with espionage.[14]

An FBI report on Philip Levy, an associate of Josephson, was stolen by Judith Coplon, an employee of the Justice Department, and provided to the Soviet intelligence officer, Valentine A. Gubitchev, in 1949. The report included a summary of an interview Josephson gave the State Department in 1943. Josephson admitted that Levy had provided him with credentials indicating that Josephson was employed by one of Levy's companies. Josephson used the credentials in his espionage work, which he referred to as "working with the underground anti-Nazi movement in Germany." He claimed that Levy was unaware of his purpose. However, he mentioned that "Mr. Levy asked me about the whereabouts of Messrs. Sherman and Mink. About five years ago [apparently 1938] I received letters from them from Moscow and that was the last I heard from either of them, directly or indirectly."

The FBI report showed that the records of World Tourists, which was headed by the Soviet espionage agent Golos, reflected that the transportation of Josephson from New York to Copenhagen was charged to the American Communist Party.

The FBI report also revealed that a confidential source had gained access to the possessions of Levy and had found a file that belonged to Leon Josephson. This file included correspondence of Jack Stachel, a National Committee member of the Communist Party, correspondence of John Spivak, and a file of material that had belonged to Jay Lovestone. The FBI identified the material as that which Lovestone had testified was stolen from his home in 1938.[15]

Lovestone testified before the Dies Committee:

In July 1938, in the height of the fight against Communist Party domination of the United Automobile Workers, C.I.O., an attempt was made to get me. The attempt was made on a Sunday, because generally I would be staying home on Sundays to work, but that Sunday I happened not to be at home. I was not gotten, but my home was rifled and confidential documents of all sorts and sundry were stolen. I immediately knew that that could be performed by only one of two agencies, either the Gestapo, because of my vigorous fight against the Nazis, and because of my visiting Germany and organizing the underground revolutionary movements in Germany after Hitler took power, or by the GPU.

I must confess I was wrong in thinking it was more likely the Gestapo, because a couple of weeks after that the *Daily Worker* came out with full photostatic copies of quite a number of documents rifled from my home, documents pertaining to the struggle against the Communist Party manipulation and domination in the United Automobile Workers. When I saw that I knew it was a GPU job. Through our own channels we began to investigate and we learned that it was a GPU job, directed by a GPU agent in this country by the name of

Mr. Leon Josephson. I issued a statement to the press, and notified the New York police authorities and tried to press the case, but since the GPU robbers were not caught on the spot, nothing very much was done by the New York authorities, and at this time, while I am not minus my life, I am minus my papers.[16]

The discovery of papers stolen from Lovestone in 1938 in the files of Josephson in 1944 proved that Lovestone was correct in his guess as to which GPU agent had done the burglary. It is also interesting that Josephson's file contained material belonging to Spivak, who also has been identified as a member of a Soviet ring.

Liston M. Oak was a member of the Communist Party from 1927 to 1935. He edited a number of communist magazines and shared an apartment with a party functionary named Herbert Goldfrank. Frequent visitors to that apartment included Leon Josephson and George Mink. In congressional testimony in 1947, Oak identified Mink as a "goon"—which he defined as "a tough guy, a gangster"—in the Maritime Union. Describing Mink and those like him, Oak said:

[T]hey were all doing what was in the party called special work. In other words, they were serving as agents of the Comintern, and especially of the NKVD. I heard of Mink from time to time, from that time on, and finally I met him in a hotel in Barcelona in April 1937. He didn't know that I had become disillusioned and had resigned from the Communist Party and greeted me very cordially and invited me to his room, where he got drunk and boasted about his NKVD work, and he urged me to accept an assignment in this passport racket, and I told him that the doctor had told me that I would have to leave Spain on account of my health, whereupon he said, "That is all right, you can work in France and England and the United States."

So I told him I would think it over, and left. Incidentally, he was very sore at the time at Josephson, because Josephson, being a lawyer, had managed to finagle himself out of a jail sentence in Copenhagen and Mink had had to take the rap.

Oak further testified:

A few days after that I went to see Adris [*sic;* Andreas] Nin, the leader of the POUM—which means Partido Obrero Unification Marxista

[Workers Party for Marxist Unification]. It had broken from the Communist Party and for a time was Trotskyist in trend, and then broke with Trotskyism and became a sort of left wing Socialist Party, to the left of the Socialist Party of Spain, and was headed by Andris Nin. I went to him and warned him that Mink had boasted to me that the Communists were about to provoke POUM, the CNT [Confederacion Nacional Del Trabajo; National Confederation of Labor], and the Left Republicans and the others in the coalition government in Catalonia, into a revolt on May 1, and Andris Nin boasted to me that they were supported by all the workers and he wasn't afraid of what the Communists might do. And very soon after that he was killed.

The day following that a man named Albert Edwards, who was an American, the representative of the American Communist Party in Barcelona, a mechanic from Detroit, called me to his hotel and told me that I had been seen leaving the office of the POUM, and wanted to know about it. I told him that I went there as a newspaperman to interview Andris Nin, but I knew that for my own safety I had better get out of Spain, which I did in company with John Dos Passos.[17]

In 1937 Oak had written in a socialist party paper about his meeting in Spain with Mink. He wrote:

I met George Mink, American Communist, who boasted about his part in organizing the Spanish GPU and offered me a job—to put the finger on "untrustworthy" comrades entering Spain to fight against fascism, such as the members of the British Independent Labor Party and the American Socialist Party.[18]

Andreas Nin was murdered by the GPU. Communist troops forced the POUM and the anarchist trade unionists into combat during the first week in May 1937. The non-Communists were defeated, and the GPU used the excuse of the supposed uprising in Barcelona to arrest and kill anarchists and POUMists.[19]

Richard Krebs was a functionary of the German Communist Party. His autobiography, *Out of the Night*, written under the name Jan Valtin, was a best-seller in 1941. In May 1941 he testified before a congressional committee. Krebs identified a photograph of George Mink taken at a 1930 conference of the International Seamen and Harbor Workers held in Moscow. The ISHW was the maritime section of the Red International of Labor Unions. According to Krebs, who knew Mink well, Mink was a former taxi driver who began organizing communist groups among seamen on the East Coast. Krebs testified that "Mink was not subjected to orders from the American Party leaders. He had his own budget—that is his own subsidy from Moscow and operated directly under Moscow's orders."

Krebs was asked if he knew of specific instances in which money was transmitted from Moscow to American Communists for use in the maritime industry. His answer provided a link to the transmission apparatus used by Soviet intelligence and described by Whittaker Chambers—couriers on the Hamburg-American Line. Krebs testified:

> In 1930 the sum of forty thousand dollars was relayed through the ISHW offices in Hamburg to George Mink in New York, to the address 140 Broad Street, for an extension of the network of International Seamen's Clubs and also for an enlargement and increase of circulation of the Communist maritime newspaper, *The Marine Workers Voice*, at that time. The money was shipped in cash by a Communist courier serving aboard the Hamburg-American Line, (ship) Albert Balin [*sic;* Ballin].

Mink was the leader of the Marine Workers Industrial Union, the American section of the International Seamen and Harbor Workers Union. Krebs testified, "George was the head of the Marine Workers Industrial Union until 1932, but he had entered the GPU service already in 1930, but was taken altogether out of the Marine Workers Industrial Union in 1932 to do full-time GPU work."

According to Krebs's testimony:

> As long as I was active in Communist organizations, the rule was it was mandatory that every Communist fraction, every Communist organization operating in the maritime industry, also every Communist Party itself, should send once a month a detailed report on the past month's activities and results obtained, plus a plan for the next month's work, to international headquarters. . . . All reports arriving at headquarters were analyzed first by the maritime division and then they were handed over to the local GPU office. They were studied there and then the reports were given to the couriers serving as seamen aboard a Soviet ship. It must be noticed that wherever a Communist headquarters is located it is always a harbor which has regular contact with Soviet shipping, Russian shipping. These ships

are the last link of all material which comes in which is sifted first in Copenhagen and then put aboard a Soviet ship and forwarded to Moscow.[20]

Instead of appreciating the valuable evidence provided by Richard Krebs, the United States government in 1942, bowing to Communist pressure, attempted to deport him.[21] Despite strenuous efforts, the attempt failed. Had it succeeded it might have discouraged many of the valuable postwar defectors from the Soviet Intelligence Service. The charges against Krebs related to lack of good moral character as a result of his admissions of activity on behalf of the Soviet service.

Guerrilla Operations in Spain

Three American volunteers in Spain received guerrilla warfare training and participated in behind-the-lines hit-and-run raids with a Spanish unit, the 14th Corps. They were identified by the American scholar, Barton Whaley, as William Aalto, Irving Goff, and Alex Kunslich. The latter was killed in Spain, but Goff and Aalto went on to serve together during World War II as officers of the American intelligence service, the OSS, in the Mediterranean Theater. After the war Aalto worked as an organizer for a communist controlled union, the United Electrical and Machine Workers. Goff became chairman of the Communist Party of Louisiana.[22]

In 1941 Aalto and Goff wrote of their experiences in Spain for the American communist magazine *Soviet Russia Today*. The magazine was edited by Jessica Smith, who had been married to the late Harold Ware, founder of the Soviet espionage network in the U.S. government. After Ware's death she married John Abt, a member of the ring. Goff and Aalto wrote:

> Our Soviet advisers . . . not only put at our disposal their experience, but also practical aid. In our guerrilla schools, lessons from the Red Army's experience were taught to us, verbally and through Spanish translations of Red Army manuals. The mines and the trick apparatus we used in Spain were constructed from patterns given to us by our Soviet advisers. . . . The whole Spanish army and especially the guerrillas were reminded of the support of the Soviet Union every time they loaded a gun—for the bullets so often were Soviet.[23]

The man in charge of propaganda work behind the enemy lines in Spain was one of the most sinister of the Comintern apparatchiks. In Spain he was called Carlos Contreras. His picture appeared over that name in the June 1, 1937, issue of *Volunteer For Liberty,* the newspaper of the American brigadiers. His real name was Vittorio Vidali, but he was known by many other names. Born in Trieste in 1900, he became a member of the Italian Communist Party in 1921. He fled Italy in 1923 to come to the United States. As a member of the American Communist Party, he was deported in 1927. He then went to work for the Comintern and became a member of the Soviet Communist Party. He admitted this in his 1974 book, *Diary of the Twentieth Congress of the Communist Party of the Soviet Union.* In this book he denied taking part in the murder of Leon Trotsky but stated that the murder was based on "a plan worked out in detail in Moscow probably by Stalin himself." Interestingly, Vidali admitted knowing George Mink and listed him in a group that he said were "all arrested, found guilty and now dead" during the Soviet purges of the late 1930s.[24] As Mink never appeared elsewhere, this may well have been his fate.

On January 11, 1943, Carlo Tresca, an Italian-American editor and opponent of both fascism and communism, was shot to death on the street corner of 15th Street and Fifth Avenue in New York City. A commemorative pamphlet published by his friends in October 1945 revealed that

> when Tresca went before a federal grand jury to accuse one of their number in connection with the disappearance of Juliet Stuart Poyntz, ex-secret agent for Soviet Russia, the party press had assailed him as a Fascist spy. It was pointed out, too, that on May 14, 1942, he published a front-page attack in *Il Martello* on Carlos Contreras, also known as Enea Sormenti and as Vittorio Vidali, charging him with being "a commandant of spies, thieves, and assassins," and with being one of a band of killers who committed horrible crimes in Spain in the interest of Stalin.
>
> Two hours after Carlo's death, the District Attorney's office was informed that two or three weeks earlier he had told various friends that he had lately seen Contreras-Sormenti-Vidali in New York City and that Tresca had said to them then: "Where he is, I smell murder. I wonder who will be the next victim." The authorities also were told soon after the slaying that two Philadelphia anti-Fascists had reported

seeing Sormenti lately on a farm near Landisville, N.J., a few miles from Camden.

At one time Sormenti and Tresca had been friendly. Sormenti, at odds with Mussolini, came here from Italy in 1923 and joined up with the Communists, serving as secretary of the Italian Federation within that party. Four years later, he was ordered deported for illegal entry. In those days, before Tresca had become disillusioned about the Communists, he gave whole-hearted support to Sormenti in his fight against deportation, contending that the man would be shot if sent back to Italy, as so many anti-Fascists had been. Finally, Sormenti was permitted to go to Russia, where (according to the *Herald Tribune*) he attended a GPU school and learned "terrorist methods."

For some eight years before his death Tresca had been an implacable enemy of the Stalinists. In speeches and writings he charged the GPU with the murders of Camillo Berneri, Anarchist leader, in Barcelona; of Rudolph Klement, a lieutenant of Leon Trotsky, in Paris; of Andreas Nin, in the Spanish Civil War; of Trotsky himself, in Mexico; of Ignatz Reiss, a former GPU agent who had made a political break with the Stalinists; and of others struck down in Spain and France.

In *Il Martello*, in May, 1942, Carlo accused Sormenti of moving against the Mazzini Society by order of Stalin. "The method is the same," he wrote. "If you don't want unity with us, you are agents of Hitler and Mussolini." And there were veiled threats. The GPU is not to be taken lightly. When the GPU, through Sormenti, says, "Then let's fight," the meaning of the threat is clear.

While Tresca's widow and friends accused the communists of murdering him because of his refusal to enter into a united front with them, a U.S. government official made the opposite claim. On January 18, 1943, Alan Cranston, chief of the Foreign Language Division of the Office of War Information, announced that, "Tresca was not opposed to participation of Communists in the Victory Council, because he felt that all anti-Fascists should unite until fascism is defeated." Tresca's friends challenged the assertions and pointed out that he had fought to keep the communists out of the Victory Council.[25]

Thomas Black was a member of the American Communist Party who was recruited by Soviet intelligence to penetrate the Trotskyite movement. At one point he asked his Soviet intelligence control officer, whom he knew as Jack Katz, about Carlo Tresca. According to Black, Katz answered that "Tresca was an enemy of the working class and that, as such, he had received a fair trial in Moscow. . . . He had been tried in Moscow in absentia, and this was not a murder, it was an execution."[26]

No one was ever arrested for the murder of Carlo Tresca. Vidali became head of the Communist Party in postwar Trieste. Previously independent, the Communist Party of Trieste became part of the Italian Communist Party in 1958. Vidali became a member of the Central Committee.

Because the Spanish Civil War coincided with the new wave of Stalin purges, which included assassinations of dissidents who had fled abroad, Americans who participated in Soviet intelligence activities began to be used even in murder.

Influence Operations

Willi Muenzenberg's apparatus also had a role to play in Spain. After the Nazi takeover in Germany, Muenzenberg had moved his publishing and organizational apparatus to Paris. Anti-Nazism was its theme and Muenzenberg was able to recruit many important figures who were willing to lend their names to his front organizations. In addition to his overt operations, Muenzenberg was engaged in many covert ones.

One of his covert operations involved the dissident Nazi, Otto Strasser. An early follower of Hitler, Strasser broke with him in 1930 and after the seizure of power escaped from Germany. Although still a Nazi, albeit anti-Hitler, Strasser was useful to Muenzenberg who distributed Strasser's pamphlets and his magazine *Die Deutsche Revolution* (The German Revolution), published in Prague. Strasser and his organization, The Black Front, provided inside information on Nazi crimes and intrigues. Despite Strasser's claimed anti-communism, he was a tool of Muenzenberg.

A 1939, *On Guard Notice,* issued by the Communist Party USA to warn its members against Muenzenberg's American representative, Andrew Kertesz, revealed that Kertesz "has become distributing agent for *Die Schwartze Fronte* of Otto Strasser, exiled 'left wing' Nazi" and that he still "maintained contact with Willy Muenzenberg," despite Muenzenberg's expulsion from the German Communist Party.[27]

His secret work promoting Strasser was consistent with Muenzenberg's overt anti-Nazi activity. In 1933 he published the famous
Brown Book of the Hitler Terror, which contained an introduction
by Lord Marley, chairman of one of Muenzenberg's fronts,[28] The
World Committee for the Victims of German Fascism. The book
itself was unsigned but had been written by one of Muenzenberg's
closest collaborators, Otto Katz. Under the name Andre Simone,
Katz was to perish as one of the victims in the Prague Communist
purge trial of 1952. Most of the victims, including Katz and the main
defendant, Rudolf Slansky, were Jews.[29]

In 1935 Muenzenberg published another unsigned book written
by Katz, *Das Braune Netz* (The Brown Network), which exposed
Nazi agents around the world. Printed in German by Muenzenberg's
Paris publishing house, Editions du Carrefour, it carried an introduction by Lord Listowel. An American edition was published the
next year.[30]

Otto Katz edited another unsigned book in 1937. Designed to
support the Spanish Republicans, it was titled *The Nazi Conspiracy
in Spain*, credited to the editor of *The Brown Book of the Hitler
Terror*. Arthur Koestler was one of Katz's coworkers. He described
in his autobiography how the Spanish foreign minister, Del Vayo,
had met with him and Katz in Paris. He wrote:

> Otto was at that time the unofficial chief of the Spanish government's
> propaganda campaign in Western Europe, and had large funds (partly
> of Spanish, partly of Comintern origin) at his disposal. These funds
> played a considerable part in securing the sympathy of influential
> French journalists, and of entire newspapers for the Loyalist cause.
> In fact, Otto was the gray eminence of the propaganda war, and was
> treated as such by everybody in the Spanish Embassy, including Del
> Vayo himself.[31]

Koestler described a meeting he had with Muenzenberg. Like
Otto Katz, he was writing a propaganda book for Muenzenberg.
Koestler revealed:

> Willy was impatient to get the books out. He would burst into my
> flat—a thing which he never used to do before—to see how mine
> was getting on. The Spanish War had become a personal obsession
> with him as with the rest of us. He would pick up a few sheets of

the typescript, scan through them, and shout at me: "Too weak. Too objective. Hit them! Hit them hard! Tell the world how they run over the prisoners with tanks, how they pour petrol over them and burn them alive. Make the world gasp with horror. Hammer it into their heads. Make them wake up. . . ." He was hammering on the table with his fists. I had never seen Willy in a similar state. He believed in atrocity propaganda. The first *Brown Book* had created a world sensation through the horrors that it disclosed, and he wanted me to use the same formula. I argued with him, pointing out that Hitler's was a one-sided terror, whereas in a war the atrocity stories of both sides cancel each other out. But it was difficult to argue with Willy. He insisted on adding to the book a supplement of horror-photographs on glossy paper.[32]

Another of Muenzenberg and Katz's propaganda specialists was Claud Cockburn, who wrote for the *London Daily Worker* as Frank Pitcairn. He also edited a newsletter called *The Week,* which was used to influence British politicians. Cockburn entered Spain in the summer of 1936, operating mainly behind enemy lines. He described his activity as "a mixed job of propaganda and espionage." Back behind Loyalist lines he joined the Fifth Regiment, which was organized by the Spanish Communist Party, and spent a few weeks at the front. He was recalled to Britain, Cockburn admitted, "to take a hand in the campaign to influence the policies of the Labour Party and Trade Union Congress against nonintervention." The Communist argument was that since Germany and Italy were intervening on the side of Franco, Britain and France should give up their policy of nonintervention. He appeared as the featured speaker at a giant rally but felt that he did not go over well, because, he said, "I am one of the worse public speakers who ever bored and exasperated an audience."

Cockburn was grateful when he was summoned to Communist Party headquarters by the party leader, Harry Pollitt, who ordered him to write a book about the Spanish Civil War. The problem was that it had to be done by the end of the week. Cockburn claimed that he was locked in a room in a nursing home and told not to come out until the book was done. The book, *Reporter in Spain,* was published in London in 1936 and in an English edition in Moscow in 1937. It was filled with atrocity stories that Cockburn could not possibly have witnessed.[33]

Upon returning to France, Cockburn met with Otto Katz, "a propagandist of genius." During one meeting Katz advised Cockburn, "You are the first eyewitness of the revolt at Tetuan" (in Nationalist-held Spanish Morocco). Cockburn protested that he had "never been in Tetuan in my life." To Katz this didn't matter. The important thing was that a shipment of artillery was being held up in France that was vitally needed in Spain. But Leon Blum, the Socialist premier of France who had sometimes allowed arm shipments to go through, was not helping this time. The next day, a group of communists and left-wing socialists were to meet with Blum to urge the release of the guns. If Blum could be convinced by a newspaper story that Franco's forces were crumbling, he would allow the shipment. Katz said, "Believe me, the psychological effect upon Blum of a rising against Franco in Morocco would be absolutely immense. And that is why you arrive here, so providentially, as the first eyewitness of the great revolt in Tetuan."

Cockburn wrote the article based on guidebooks to the town, describing in detail combat that never took place. He included names of officers made up on the spot. The article appeared in the next day's newspapers, and Blum discussed it with the visiting delegation. When they requested that he allow the arms shipment, he did so. Cockburn believed that the artillery he helped get into Spain was of major importance in winning the first battle of Teruel, a significant Republican victory.[34]

Agents of influence could and did influence government leaders during the Spanish Civil War. Agents in the media could and did distort the news for political purposes. They were used with great efficiency by the Soviets. The Soviet Intelligence Service and the Comintern played important roles in converting the Spanish Republican government into one influenced by the Soviet Union. After the defeat of the Spanish Republic, the Soviets were able to use their experienced cadre in other violent activities.

9

The Murder of
Leon Trotsky

L EON Trotsky was born Lev Davidovich Bronstein in 1879 in
the Ukraine. He became a revolutionary as a teenager, and by
the time he was eighteen had founded a socialist group. He soon
became a major figure in the Russian revolutionary movement. After
years of revolutionary organizing and time spent in prison, he came
to New York in January 1917. In February 1917 he was working as
an editor for a Russian-language socialist publication, *Novyi Mir*,
when word reached him that the czar had been overthrown. He
returned to Russia, arriving in Petrograd on May 4. While Trotsky
had often had disagreements with Lenin, he joined the Bolshevik
Party in July 1917. He was arrested that month, by the provisional
government. His influence was so great that he was elected in absentia to the Bolshevik Central Committee in August. Released on
September 4, he became one of the two principal leaders of the
Bolshevik Party and was elected chairman of the Petrograd Soviet.

As chief of the Revolutionary Military Committee, Trotsky directed the coup that brought the Bolsheviks to power on November
7, 1917. He first became people's commissar for foreign affairs and
then commissar for war. In the latter capacity he is credited with
organizing the Red Army.[1]

Trotsky and Lenin

Trotsky and Lenin disagreed on many issues. But on important
things they agreed; neither was a democrat. Years later, writing

about the revolution, Trotsky boasted that the Bolsheviks remained a minority, even after the revolution. He wrote:

> The Social Revolutionists were the party of the greatest numbers in the Russian revolution. In the first period, everyone who was not either a conscious bourgeois or a conscious worker voted for them. Even in the Constituent Assembly, that is, after the October revolution, the Social Revolutionists formed the majority. They therefore considered themselves a great national party. They turned out to be a great national zero.

Trotsky's explanation for why the Bolsheviks won: "[O]n the scales of the revolutionary struggle, a thousand workers in one big factory represent a force a hundred times greater than a thousand petty officials, clerks, their wives and their mothers-in-law."[2]

Some actual statistics were given by Lenin in a 1919 pamphlet. In the elections to the Constituent Assembly held immediately after the Bolsheviks took power, of over 36 million votes the Social Revolutionaries obtained 20.9 million or 58 percent. The Bolsheviks polled only a little over 9 million votes or 25 percent.[3] Other parties divided the remaining votes.

Lenin also believed that "dictatorial power and single man management are not inconsistent with socialistic democratism."[4]

Not everyone thought this way, even in the Bolshevik Party. Factions demanding democracy developed in the party. One group, The Workers' Opposition, demanded that the Communist Party:

(1) Return to its principle of election all along the line with elimination of bureaucracy, by making all responsible officials answerable to the masses.

(2) Introduction of wide publicity within the party both concerning general questions, and where individuals are involved; paying more attention to the voice of the rank and file (wide discussion of all questions by the rank and file, and their summarizing by the leaders; admission of any member to the meetings of party centres, save when problems discussed require particular secrecy); establishment of freedom of opinion and expression (giving the right not only to criticize freely during discussions, but to use funds for publication and literature proposed by different party factions).

(3) Making the party more of a workers' party with limitations imposed on those who fill offices both in the party and the soviet institutions at the same time."[5]

Lenin could not tolerate this expression of democracy. With the support of Trotsky, at the Tenth Party Congress he insisted that, "the views of the Workers' Opposition and of like-minded elements are not only wrong in theory, but are an expression of petty-bourgeois and anarchist wavering in practice, and actually weaken the consistency of the leading line of the Communist Party and help the class enemies of the proletarian revolution." He demanded that "the propaganda of these ideas [be declared] incompatible with membership of the R.C.P. [Russian Communist Party]."[6] At Lenin's demand the Congress passed a resolution which read in part:

The Congress, therefore, hereby declares dissolved and orders the immediate dissolution of all groups without exception formed on the basis of one platform or another (such as the Workers' Opposition group, the Democratic Centralism group, etc.). Nonobservance of this decision of the Congress shall entail unconditional and instant expulsion from the Party.[7]

Others were also demanding democracy. Just before the Tenth Communist Party Congress, the sailors at Kronstadt rose in rebellion. Their demands included:

(1) In view of the fact that the present Soviets do not express the will of the workers and peasants, immediately to hold new elections by secret ballot, the pre-election campaign to have full freedom of agitation among the workers and peasants;
(2) To establish freedom of speech and press for workers and peasants, for Anarchists and left Socialist parties;
(3) To secure freedom of assembly for labor unions and peasant organisations;
(4) To call a non-artisan conference of the workers, Red Army soldiers and sailors of Petrograd, Kronstadt, and of Petrograd Province, no later than March 10, 1921;
(5) To liberate all political prisoners of Socialist parties, as well as all workers, peasants, soldiers, and sailors imprisoned in connection with the labor and peasant movements;

(6) To elect a Commission to review the cases of those held in prisons and concentration camps;

(7) To abolish all *politotdeli* (political bureaus) because no party should be given special privileges in the propagation of its ideas or receive the financial support of the Government for such purposes. Instead there should be established educationals and cultural commissions, locally elected and financed by the Government. . . .[8]

The Bolsheviks were taken by surprise. On March 5, three days after the start of the insurrection, Trotsky arrived in Petrograd, accompanied by Kamenev, Lebedev, and Tukhachevsky, who was appointed by Trotsky to command the troops against Kronstadt. Trotsky ordered him to suppress the rebellion. The first attempt failed. On March 16, the Bolsheviks attacked with new units. Three hundred and twenty delegates from the Congress participated in the combat. On March 18 the insurgents were defeated.[9]

Lenin believed, "the terror and Cheka are absolutely indispensable."[10] Trotsky agreed. Writing in 1922:

A victorious war, generally speaking, destroys only an insignificant part of the conquered army, intimidating the remainder and breaking their will. The revolution works in the same way: it kills individuals, and intimidates thousands. In this sense, the Red Terror is not distinguishable from the armed insurrection, the direct continuation of which it represents. The State terror of a revolutionary class can be condemned "morally" only by a man who, as a principle, rejects (in words) every form of violence whatsoever—consequently, every war and every rising. For this one has to be merely and simply a hypocritical Quaker.

But, in that case, in what do your tactics differ from the tactics of Tsarism? we are asked, by the high priests of Liberalism and Kautskianism. [Karl Kautsky was a German socialist who advocated democracy and a peaceful path to socialism.]

You do not understand this, holy men? We shall explain to you. The terror of Tsarism was directed against the proletariat. The gendarmerie of Tsarism throttled the workers who were fighting for the Socialist order. Our Extraordinary Commissions shoot landlords, capitalists, and generals who are striving to restore the capitalist order. Do you grasp this . . . distinction? Yes? For us Communists it is quite sufficient.[11]

Trotsky supported Lenin's dictatorship, the suppression of factions in the party, and the use of terror outside the party. But in 1923, when he led a faction in the party, he did not like the suggestion, supported by Lenin, that the secret police should be advised about factional activity. In a letter to the Central Committee of the party dated October 8, 1923, Trotsky complained that, "One of the proposals of Comrade Dzerzhinsky's commission declares that we must make it obligatory for Party members knowing about groupings in the Party to communicate the fact to the GPU, the Central Committee and the Central Control Commission."[12] The former was the new name of the Cheka, now the KGB. The latter two were leadership organs of the Communist Party.

An attempt had been made on the life of Lenin by a Social Revolutionist. Lenin survived but was seriously weakened and ill until his death on January 21, 1924. Stalin, as general secretary of the party, took the opportunity to increase his power. The Thirteenth Congress of the Russian Communist Party took place from May 23 to 31, 1924. Lenin's widow, Krupskaya, transmitted to the Congress letters that Lenin had written during December 1922 and January 1923. These letters were designed to undermine the power of Stalin. Lenin wrote:

Com. Stalin, having become General Secretary, has concentrated boundless authority in his hands, and I am not sure whether he will always be capable of using the authority with sufficient caution. Com. Trotsky, on the other hand, as his struggle against the CC [Central Committee] on the question of the People's Commissariat for Railways, has already proved, is distinguished not only by outstanding ability. Personally he is perhaps the most capable man in the present CC, but he has too enterprising self-assurance and excessive enthusiasm for the purely administrative side of the work. These two qualities of the two prominent leaders of the present CC can accidently lead to a split, and if our Party does not take steps to prevent this, the split may take place unexpectedly. I shall not give an appraisal of any other members of the CC according to their personal qualities. I shall just recall that the October episode of Zinoviev and Kamenev was not, of course, a coincidence, but neither can it be laid down to their personal fault any more than non-Bolshevism to Trotsky. Among the young members of the CC, I wish to say a few words about Bukharin. . . . [He is], in my opinion, [one of] the most outstanding figures among the youngest ones, and the following must be borne in mind in respect [to him]: Bukharin is not only a most valuable and major theoretician of the Party, rightfully considered as the favourite of the whole Party; but his theoretical views can be classified as fully Marxist only with great reserve, for there is something of the scholastic about him (he never studied, and, I think, never fully understood dialectics).[13]

The Congress decided not to publish Lenin's letters. They were leaked, however, to the American communist sympathizer, Max Eastman, who published the documents as part of his book, *Since Lenin Died*.

The Communists were scandalized. Krupskaya issued a statement attacking Eastman and calling his book, "a collection of petty gossip." She was particularly incensed that Eastman had revealed Lenin's letters, which he referred to as "testaments." She complained that to call them this showed that "Eastman fails absolutely to understand the spirit of our Party. . . . To call them 'testaments' is folly."[14]

Although the testament favored Trotsky over Stalin, Trotsky also repudiated the documents. Trotsky did not reveal, of course, that it was he who leaked the "testament" to Eastman.[15] In a statement dated July 1, 1925, Trotsky wrote, "Comrade Lenin has not left any 'will'; the character of his relations to the Party, and the character of the Party itself, exclude the possibility of such a 'will'." Denying Eastman's claim that Lenin's letters to the Party had been suppressed, Trotsky accused Eastman of "pure slander against the Central Committee of our Party."[16]

Having announced to the world in 1925 that there was no will and that Lenin's letters to the party had not been suppressed, Trotsky, in 1928, published the testament in his book, *The Real Situation in Russia*. In 1935 Trotsky published a pamphlet called *The Suppressed Testament of Lenin*.[17]

Lenin's testament remained concealed by the Soviet Union until Khrushchev delivered his secret speech on Stalin at the Twentieth Congress of the Communist Party of the Soviet Union. At that time a set of the documents were made available in secret form to the delegates and were distributed to Communist Party organizations as a supplement to Khrushchev's secret speech. The State Department obtained both the speech and the supplement from a confidential source and released the speech on June 4, 1956, and the Lenin documents on June 30, 1956.[18]

The Soviets released only the Lenin testament and documents, but not the Khrushchev speech, shortly afterward, in a pamphlet with the unattractive title, *Letter to the Congress—The Attribution of Legislative Functions to the State Planning Commission—The Question of Nationalities or of "Autonomization"*. A few years later the materials were released again under the equally uninteresting title, *Problems of Building Socialism and Communism in the U.S.S.R.*

Trotsky did not object when the powers of the Soviet Intelligence Service were used to persecute political opponents of the Communists, only when this force was used against him and his followers. When the "Organs of State Security" organized a frame-up trial against Russian Mensheviks, who were members of the Labour and Socialist International, Trotsky was silent. The trial, which took place in 1931, was organized by the OGPU in an incredibly inept manner. Leon Blum, later to become the Socialist Premiere of France, wrote in 1931:

> The terrorism of Stalin rests upon a universal system of spies and informers. The Moscow trial shows us what it has made of justice. Sometimes its place is taken by summary death sentences, sometimes—which is worse—it works behind an apparent correctness, but its verdicts, concocted beforehand, are the outcome of false witness and *false confession*. This last point is worth dwelling upon. Nothing is more significant nor more abominable. The accused of Moscow *confessed* the crimes charged against them which they had not committed. They formally acknowledged the truth of facts proved to be substantially false. . . . The base of the whole edifice constructed by the Ogpu is the collusion between the accused and the Executive of the Menshevik Party. To establish this, the essential facts put forward by the prosecution are a secret journey made by Abramovitch to Russia, his interviews with the accused, and the instructions which he is alleged to have conveyed to them. Now *this journey never took place*. Raphael Abramovitch, a Menshevik leader, has proved this conclusively by an alibi precluding any possible argument. (emphasis in original)

Abramovitch was able to prove that on the very date he was supposed to have been in Moscow, he was in attendance at the

International Socialist Congress in Brussels. He had a picture taken with the delegates who had come from all over the world to attend the congress.[19]

The Campaign against Trotsky

The Trotskyites soon became a major target of Soviet intelligence. Indeed from the late 1920s until the mid-1940s, Soviet intelligence devoted a considerable amount of valuable time and cadres to operations against the Trotskyites instead of against the real dangers to Soviet security, the rise of Nazism and the threat of war.

Trotsky described a 1927 incident in which a supposed former czarist officer collaborated with the Trotskyite opposition. Trotsky wrote: "[In] 1927 the GPU sent one of its official agents who had formerly fought in the Wrangel army to a young man, unknown to everybody, who was distributing the documents of the Opposition. And then the GPU accused the entire Opposition of maintaining relations . . . not with the GPU agent, but with a 'Wrangel officer.' Hired journalists immediately transmitted this amalgam to the Western press."[20]

Stalin, in a speech to the Communist Party Central Committee on October 23, 1927, boasted of how the OGPU had linked the Trotskyite opposition to former officers who had served under the czarist generals, Wrangel and Kolchak. Stalin said:

> There is talk about a former Wrangel officer who is helping the OGPU to unmask counter-revolutionary organisations. The opposition leaps and dances and makes a great fuss about the fact that the former Wrangel officer to whom the opposition's allies, all these Shcherbakovs and Tverskoys, applied for assistance, proved to be an agent of the OGPU. But is there anything wrong in this former Wrangel officer helping the Soviet authorities to unmask counter-revolutionary conspiracies? Who can deny the right of the Soviet authorities to win former officers to their side in order to employ them for the purpose of unmasking counter-revolutionary organisations?
>
> Shchberbakov and Tverskoy addressed themselves to this former Wrangel officer not because he was an agent of the OGPU, but because he was a former Wrangel officer, and they did so in order to employ him *against* the Party and *against* the Soviet Government. That is the point, and that is the misfortune of our opposition. And

when, following up these clues, the OGPU quite unexpectedly came across the Trotskyists' illegal, anti-Party printing press, it found that, while arranging a bloc with the opposition, Messieurs the Shcherbakovs, Tverskoys and Bolshakovs were already in a bloc with counterrevolutionaries, with former Kolchak officers like Kostrov and Novikov, as Comrade Menzhinsky reported to you today.[21]

In fact, the whole incident was an OGPU concoction. In 1953 Alexander Orlov, who in 1927 had been a high-ranking official of OGPU, revealed a conversation between Stalin and Genrikh Yagoda, then deputy chairman of the OGPU. Orlov wrote:

In 1927, Yagoda reported to Stalin that the OGPU had uncovered and confiscated a hectograph on which a group of young Trotskyites printed anti-Stalinist leaflets. That hectograph had been uncovered with the help of a certain Stroilov, an agent provocateur of the OGPU, who promised the unsuspecting adherents of Trotsky to obtain for them a supply of paper and things needed for the hectograph. "Good!" Stalin said to Yagoda. "Now promote your secret agent to the rank of an officer of General Wrangel and indicate in your report that the Trotskyites collaborated with the Wrangelian White Guardist."[22]

The supposed czarist officers were not the only provocateurs thrown at the Trotskyites. In 1931 two brothers appeared as loyal followers of Trotsky. They quickly rose high in the ranks. For the next few decades they were major figures in Soviet intelligence operations against Trotsky and his followers. They were born in Lithuania as Ruvelis Leiba Sobolevicius, born 1900, and Abromas Sobolevicius, born 1903.[23]

Ruvelis was known to Trotsky under the pseudonym "Well." Abromas was known to him as "Senin" (sometimes spelled Senine). They were later to operate in the United States as major Soviet intelligence ring leaders under the names Robert Soblen and Jack Soble. It is unknown whether Trotsky knew that the pair were brothers. They played a major role for the Soviet Intelligence Service in spying on Trotsky and disrupting his movement.

In 1957 Jack Soble wrote a series of articles for the *New York Journal-American* describing his activities in Soviet intelligence. Soble wrote:

My services for the Soviet secret police went back to 1931. I was recruited in Berlin where I had completed my college education, under a "take it or else" edict—"Work for us," a Soviet secret agent there warned, "or you will never see your wife again.'" The job was to spy on Leon Trotsky for Josef Stalin, who was obsessed with the idea of knowing everything his hated rival was doing and thinking even in exile. I was selected for this task for two reasons—first, I was one of Trotsky's most trusted followers, and second, the Russians held my wife Myra as a hostage in Moscow when she returned there from Berlin to visit relatives. For two years, in 1931 and 1932, I spied on Trotsky and the men around him. Trotsky, suspecting nothing, invited me to his heavily guarded home at Prinkipo, Turkey. I duly reported back to the Kremlin everything Trotsky told me in confidence, including his pungent remarks about Stalin.[24]

The pressure on Jack Soble does not explain the role of his brother or their later work for the KGB after Soble's wife left the Soviet Union. It is possible that they were GPU agents even earlier than Soble indicated.

Well and Senin were in the leadership of Trotsky's international movement as well as the very important German section. Well succeeded in pitting Trotsky against the most efficient leader of the German group, Kurt Landau. With the help of Senin, who spread rumors and created antagonisms, Landau was driven out of the movement.[25]

On December 2, 1932, Trotsky was in Copenhagen where he met with Senin. Trotsky's son, Leon Sedov, described the last meeting that Trotsky had with Senin.

It has been possible to establish that Trotsky received only one Russian-speaking person in Copenhagen. This is a certain Abraham Senin (Sobolevich) [Sobolevicius], who was then a Lithuanian citizen and a member of the Berlin organization of the Opposition. He came to see Cde. Trotsky on the last day of his stay in Copenhagen (at the same time as E. Bauer) and spoke no more than one hour with Trotsky, under conditions of extreme haste before the sudden departure. Senin's trip to Copenhagen was made at the insistence of some of Trotsky's Berlin friends; they had wanted to make a last effort to save Senin from capitulation to the Stalinists, to whom he was drawing nearer and nearer. The attempt was not crowned with success; a few weeks later, Senin, with three or four friends went over to the Stalinists. This event was reported in both the Stalinist and Oppositionist press.[26]

According to Soble, it was at this meeting that Trotsky told him that he believed him to be a Stalinist spy. Well continued to serve on Trotsky's International Secretariat even after his brother had left. Minutes of the International Secretariat for December 15, 1932, show him continuing to cause friction among Trotsky's supporters.[27]

On December 1, 1934, Sergei Kirov, the leader of the Leningrad Communist Party and member of the Politburo, was murdered by a young communist. An American Communist Party pamphlet, published two months later, provided the party line on the assassination. Signed with the name M. Katz, it said:

> The Assassin later confessed that he was a member of a terrorist organization composed of the remnants of the former Zinoviev-Trotsky opposition at Leningrad. The dregs of this opposition, which has lost all contact with the masses, linked itself with various White-Guard elements and representatives of foreign governments for the purpose of overthrowing the Communist leadership and the Soviet government and of putting in their place men like Zinoviev and Trotsky by means of terroristic acts. The murder of Comrade Kirov was organized and directed by counter-revolutionists and White-Guardists, enemies of the working class, who parade under various guises in order to undermine the workers' State and its foremost leaders.
>
> As an answer to the murderous shot, the Soviet government arrested a number of persons connected with White-Guard terrorist organizations. In addition, it had under arrest quite a number of White-Guard terrorists who had been seized previously as they crossed the frontier from Finland, Poland, Rumania, and Latvia, carrying hand grenades and other concealed weapons for the purpose of murdering leaders of the Soviet government and the Communist Party, of setting fire to industrial plants, of blowing up bridges and disrupting transport.
>
> Due to the gravity of the crime committed on December 1, which showed that the White-Guardists aim their weapons at the very heart of the revolution, all these prisoners were, by decree of the Central Executive Committee of the Soviet Union, turned over to the Extraordinary Supreme Court of the Republic. The prisoners were tried on the basis of the material evidence discovered at the time of their

capture. One hundred and three terrorists, members of White-Guard organizations who had entered the Soviet Union from foreign countries with forged passports and armed, were sentenced to death and executed.[28]

Trotsky immediately responded, pointing out that on one hand the assassin was alleged to be connected with a terrorist group of white émigrés based *outside* the country who had crossed the borders of the Soviet Union, while on the other hand he was supposed to be connected with the *internal* communist opposition group of Zinoviev.

On December 28, 1934, the French Communist Party newspaper, *L'Humanité*, carried extracts from the indictment of Nikolayev, the actual assassin. He had confessed that he was in contact with a consul of a foreign power, who gave him five thousand rubles for expenses. In addition, the diplomat told the assassin that he (the diplomat) could establish contact with Trotsky if Nikolayev could provide a letter from the opposition group. Trotsky concluded from this that the GPU itself, "through the medium of an actual or fake consul," was financing the assassin and attempting to link him with Trotsky. According to Trotsky this showed that the GPU had the assassin under surveillance before the murder.[29]

The *New York Times* of January 24, 1935, reported from Moscow, that it had been officially announced that twelve GPU officials, including F. D. Medved, chief of the Leningrad GPU, had been found guilty of negligence in the Kirov case. Possibly confirming Trotsky's conclusion, the Soviet report said that they had failed to expose and end the activities of the terrorist group and the assassin of Kirov "although they were in a position to do so."

Many of the oppositionists arrested by the GPU, as well as those who were to perish during the purges of the next five years, were Jewish. Indeed, many of the victims who were not oppositionists but had been supporters of Stalin were also Jewish. There is good reason to believe that Stalin was strongly anti-Semitic. In 1907 Stalin was a delegate to the Fifth Congress of the Russian Social Democratic Labor Party, which took place in London. This was the congress at which the Bolsheviks split from the more moderate Mensheviks. Stalin, in an article on the congress, reported on a "jest" by one of the Bolsheviks, who pointed out that since most of the Mensheviks were Jews, while most of the Bolsheviks were Russians, "the Mensheviks constituted a Jewish group while the Bolsheviks constituted a true-Russian group and, therefore, it wouldn't be a bad idea for us Bolsheviks to organize a pogrom in the Party."[30] As Russian Jews had been killed, maimed, and raped, in past pogroms, this "joke" was not terribly funny.

Purges

The murder of Kirov set in motion five years of purge trials, executions, and slave-labor camp sentences for millions. The Soviet military and intelligence services provided a substantial number of purge victims. Even the party's top leadership suffered severe losses. As Khrushchev pointed out in his secret speech in 1956, "of the 139 members and candidates of the Party's Central Committee who were elected at the Seventeenth Congress [1934], 98 persons, i.e., 70 percent, were arrested and shot." Khrushchev admitted that the charges against the victims were frame-ups.[31]

Stalin explained the purpose of the purges in a speech to the Communist Party Central Committee in March 1937. The English-language edition of the speech, published in the Soviet Union in 1937, bore the remarkable title, *Defects in Party Work and Measures for Liquidating Trotskyite and Other Double-Dealers*. Stalin said:

> The necessary measures must be taken to enable our comrades, both party and non-Party Bolsheviks, to become familiar with the aims and objects, with the practice and technique of the wrecking, diversionist, and espionage work of the foreign intelligence services. It must be explained to our Party comrades that the Trotskyites, who are the active elements in the diversionist, wrecking and espionage work of the foreign intelligence services, have long ceased to be a political trend in the working class, that they have long ceased to serve any ideal compatible with the interest of the working class, that they have become a gang of wreckers, diversionists, spies, assassins, without principles and ideals, working in the pay of foreign intelligence services.[32]

The Soviet Intelligence Service was not spared. In September 1988, the then head of KGB, V.M. Chebrikov, estimated that twenty thousand intelligence officers fell victim to Stalin's purges.[33]

Perhaps because the purges wiped out some of their best cadre, the GPU did not handle the trials very efficiently, although the poorly handled Menshevik trial in 1931 was before the GPU ranks suffered the purge.

Friedrick Adler, the Secretary of the Labor and Socialist International, wrote a pamphlet in 1936 exposing the first purge trial. He pointed out that one of the defendants, Holtzman, had confessed that he had met with Trotsky and Sedov (Trotsky's son) in Copenhagen in 1932 where he received orders from Trotsky to organize terrorist acts in the Soviet Union. He said, according to the official trial transcript, "I arranged with Sedov to be in Copenhagen within two or three days, to put up at the Hotel Bristol and meet him there. I went to the hotel straight from the station and in the lounge met Sedov. About 10 A.M. we went to Trotsky."[34] Adler pointed out that the Hotel Bristol existed in Copenhagen before World War I but had been pulled down in 1917. Adler compared this blunder of the GPU with the one made during the Menshevik Trial, when they compelled a defendant to confess that he met with Abramovitch in Russia at the same time photographic evidence proved him to be in Brussels.[35]

Trotsky demanded that an impartial commission of inquiry be established to examine the charges against him and his followers. He offered to make available any "documents, facts, and testimonies" to establish the truth. He said, "I declare: if this commission decides that I am guilty in the slightest degree of the crimes which Stalin imputes to me, I pledge in advance to place myself voluntarily in the hands of the executioners of the GPU."[36]

The Commission of Inquiry into the Charges Made Against Leon Trotsky in the Moscow Trials was established, headed by John Dewey. After extensive hearings and examination of documents, the commission reached the only possible conclusion, Trotsky and the defendants were not guilty.[37] The Soviet Union, since the 1956 Khrushchev Secret Speech, has rehabilitated most of the purge victims, with the exception of Trotsky.

Although Trotsky understood that Stalin wanted him dead, he could not grasp the extent of the Soviet Intelligence Service operations against him. In his closing speech to the Dewey Commission, Trotsky naively remarked, "The GPU knew about me only that which was published in the papers."[38] He did not understand that the GPU, in the form of the Sobolevicius brothers, had penetrated his inner circle, and that after they left an even deeper penetration had been organized.

Trotsky in Exile

When the first Moscow trial began in 1936 Trotsky had been in Norway for over a year. The Norwegian government had granted him political asylum. But Trygve Lie, the minister of justice, who would become secretary general of the United Nations after World War II, was pressuring Trotsky to leave. Lie demanded that Trotsky submit his writings to censorship. Trotsky refused, as this would prevent him from replying to the Moscow frame-ups. Lie then demanded that Trotsky voluntarily accept police control of his mail and visitors. Trotsky refused, asking, "If you want to arrest me, why do you need my consent?" Lie responded, "There is an intermediate status between arrest and full freedom." Trotsky replied, "That may be a trap. I prefer an outright arrest." Lie did just that, interning Trotsky and deporting two of his secretaries. Shortly thereafter Trotsky was expelled from Norway on orders of Trygve Lie.[39]

Trotsky left Norway on December 19, 1936. The Mexican government had offered him asylum. He arrived in Mexico January 9, 1937.[40] Mexico was a better environment for the GPU to murder Trotsky than any West European country. Trotsky continued his campaign to expose the Moscow Trials and to answer Stalin's attacks. On October 12, 1939, Trotsky received a telegram inviting him to appear before the Special Committee on Un-American Activities (the Dies Committee) to provide "a complete record on the history of Stalinism." The cable was sent by J. B. Matthews, the committee's chief investigator. Matthews's invitation read:

> Dies Committee of the United States House of Representatives invites you to appear as witness before it in the city of Austin Texas a city designated with a view to your personal convenience stop Date of your appearance to be approximately four weeks from now stop Dies Committee agrees to arrange for your entry into the United States for the purpose of testifying before it stop Will also arrange for proper protection stop The Committee desires to have a complete record on the history of Stalinism and invites you to answer questions which can be submitted to you in advance if you so desire stop Your

name has been mentioned frequently by such witnesses as Browder
and Foster stop This Committee will accord you opportunity to answer their charges stop You will please treat this invitation as not for
publicity for the present.

Trotsky responded to Matthews on the same day he received the
telegram:

> I accept your invitation as a political duty stop I will undertake nec-
> essary measures in order to overcome practical difficulties stop Please
> arrange under the same conditions entry for my wife stop She is
> indispensable for the purpose of locating the necessary documents
> quotations dates in my files stop Necessary to have your questions
> as soon as possible in order to select the necessary documents stop
> Also desire exact quotations from depositions of Foster and Browder
> concerning me personally.[41]

Trotsky never testified before the committee. J. B. Matthews
explained to one of the authors, years later, that the State Department prevented Trotsky from getting a visa. State Department records on this matter were still classified in 1988.

Despite Trotsky's failure to testify before the United States Congress, Stalin could not let him live. On May 24, 1940, a gang of men
dressed in Mexican Army and police uniforms attacked Trotsky's
home. After tying up the Mexican police who were on guard, the
gang fired machine guns into the house. Trotsky, his wife, and his
grandson survived the bullets that had penetrated the bedroom, but
the grandson had a bullet graze his toe. One of Trotsky's American
bodyguards, Robert Sheldon Harte, was kidnapped and murdered
by the gang.

When the Mexican police arrested the members of the gang they
found that the leader was the well-known Mexican painter, David
Alfaro Siqueiros, who had served as a colonel in the International
Brigades in Spain. Siqueiros later claimed that the attack on Trotsky's
home was only to get evidence of his counterrevolutionary activities.[42] Siqueiros had denied any involvement by the Communist
Party or the GPU in the murder attempt. However, when he was
arrested on another charge in 1960, his supporters pointed out that,
"Recently he was elected president of the Communist Party of Mexico."[43] In the twenty years between the murder attempt and the

"election" of Siqueiros to Communist Party president, he was active in the arts and had achieved a substantial reputation.

Trotsky's response to the murder attempt was to provide considerable information about the activities of the GPU to the world. On June 1, 1940, Trotsky wrote a letter to the attorney general of Mexico, the chief of the Federal Police, and the foreign minister. Trotsky discussed the attempt to assassinate him the previous week. He wrote:

> It is first of all necessary to affirm that the attempted assassination could only be instigated by the Kremlin; by Stalin through the agency of the GPU abroad. During the last few years, Stalin has shot hundreds of real or supposed friends of mine. He actually exterminated my entire family, except me, my wife and one of my grandchildren. Through his agents abroad he assassinated one of the old leaders of the GPU, Ignace Reiss, who had publicly declared himself a partisan of mine. . . . On the night of November 7, 1936, GPU agents broke into the Scientific Institute of Paris and stole part of my archives. Two of my secretaries, Erwin Wolff and Rudolf Klement, were assassinated by the GPU; the first in Spain, the second in Paris. All the theatrical Moscow trials during 1936–1937 had as their aim to get me into the hands of the GPU.

Trotsky went on to describe how the GPU functioned abroad. He wrote:

> The general scheme of the GPU organization abroad is the following: *in the Central Committee of each section of the Comintern there is placed a responsible director of the GPU for that country.* His status is known only to the secretary of the party and one or two trustworthy members. The other members of the Central Committee have but a slight inkling of the special status of this member. . . . As a member of the Central Committee, the country's GPU representative has the possibility of approaching with full legality all members of the Party, study their characters, intrust them with commissions, and little by little draw them into the work of espionage and terrorism, sometimes calling on their sense of Party loyalty, but as often making use of bribery.[44]

Trotsky also finished a lengthy article on the GPU, titled *The Comintern and the GPU,* a few days before he was murdered.

In the article Trotsky released the texts of affidavits from Benjamin Gitlow and General Krivitsky that had been made available for use in the Mexican court. Gitlow wrote in his:

> When I was a member of the Presidium and Executive Committee of the Communist International, I helped direct the affairs of the Communist International and was intimately acquainted with the way in which the organization functioned as an agency of the GPU.
>
> Every representative of the Communist International sent out of Russia to foreign countries always carried special GPU instructions and, if not directly an agent of the GPU, worked under the direction of a GPU agent.
>
> The special department of the Communist International in Moscow which took charge of passports, visas, and the financial subsidies to Communist parties and to Communist newspapers outside of Russia, was in charge of the GPU and its director was an employee directly responsible to this organization.
>
> It was common knowledge to me that the financial affairs of the Communist International were in the hands of the GPU.[45]

General Krivitsky's affidavit discussed the GPU under its new title, the GUGB (Chief Directorate for State Security) of the NKVD (People's Commissariat of Internal Affairs). The name of the GPU was changed in 1934. The popular name used for the Soviet Intelligence Service was NKVD, rather than GUGB. Krivitsky wrote:

> In the agencies abroad the G.U.G.B. has its representatives.
>
> Officially they occupy some diplomatic post. Under their direction is the surveillance of all the official Soviet organs in the respective country.
>
> All the work of the Comintern abroad is carried on through the Section of International Relations, the OMS [Organizational Department of the Comintern]. The entire apparatus of the OMS in Moscow and abroad since the years 1936–37 has been integrated through agents of the GUGB and all the activity of OMS is under its control. In all the countries where the Communist Party is legal, there is a representative of the OMS of Moscow. Formerly, he occupied some secondary post in the diplomatic corps. Lately, these representatives have gone underground. Their functions are: the control over the activity and the financial situation of the Communist Party, the transmission of instructions and economic subsidies proceeding from Mos-

cow. The Soviet government subsidizes not only the official Communist Party and its press, but also the pro-Stalinist journals which do not belong to the party. For example: the journal *Ce Soir* of Paris. All the work of the Comintern in Latin America is concentrated in the United States, where the principal representative of the OMS is found, including the Latin American countries. His aides are found in various countries. The instructions and the economic subsidies are received principally through the Embassy at Washington. Aside from this main center, the OMS has at its disposition an illegal interlocking apparatus, with different sections for Europe, Asia, and America. This has been organized and is destined for a case of war or of rupture in diplomatic relations with any country.

The GUGB organizes terrorist acts abroad. In virtue of the risks and diplomatic difficulties which carrying out orders represents, they are given personally by the chief of the GUGB, National Commissar of Internal Relations, through the sanction of Stalin. The organizers of these terrorist acts are responsible agents of the GUGB abroad. The killers are always foreigners in the service of the GUGB. They are well tested militants of the Communist parties. Some of them because of considerations of a conspirative character, do not officially belong to the party.[46]

The Death of Trotsky

On August 20, 1940, an assassin killed Trotsky with a pick ax blow to the head. Captured on the spot by Trotsky's bodyguards and turned over to the Mexican police, the murderer was found to have in his pocket a letter explaining his act. He claimed that Trotsky had ordered him to go to Russia to kill Stalin. In addition, Trotsky prevented him from marrying the girl he loved. As a result he was forced to murder Trotsky, although he wrote, "I was a devoted disciple of L. T. and I would have given the last drop of my blood for the needs of the cause."

In a statement to the Mexican police, the murderer claimed that Trotsky was sending him into Russia with other agents:

Our mission was to bring demoralization to the Red Army, commit different acts of sabotage in armaments plants and other factories. He spoke to me of his plan only in generalities, and when I asked him if I could take Sylvia with me, he told me in a firm tone: "It is not possible, because Sylvia is with the Minority!" For me this was total destruction. Trotsky crushed me in his hands as if I had been paper. It was then that there was born in my brain the idea to kill him. I thought for a week, and came to the conclusion that no other remedy remained than to kill him and then commit suicide.[47]

The assassin had called himself Jacson but told the police his name was Jacques Mornard. His true identity was not learned for many years. The American writer and journalist, Isaac Don Levine, identified Jacson in a 1959 book as Ramon Mercader, a Spanish communist. Levine identified the GPU officer in charge of the murder as Leonid Eitingon, an experienced intelligence veteran who was also the lover of Jacson's mother, Caridad Mercader, a Spanish Communist Party member and operative for the Communist International.

Levine revealed that Eitingon had operated for the GPU in Spain under the name General Kotov. He had been involved in the kidnapping of a White Russian officer in Paris in 1930.[48] The GPU defector, Agabekov, identified Eitingon as the GPU *rezident* in Harbin in 1929, when he was transferred to be GPU *rezident* in Constantinople.[49] After a long career in the Soviet Intelligence Service, Eitingon was arrested after Stalin died.[50]

Trotsky's murderer had entered Mexico on an altered Canadian passport, which had been issued to a man named Tony Babich, who had been killed while serving as a volunteer in the International Brigades in Spain. Babich's photograph had been replaced by Jacson's.[51]

The communist authorities in the International Brigades confiscated thousands of passports from the volunteers. Some of those passports turned up later in the hands of the Soviet Intelligence Service. A passport similar to Jacson's was used by Tito when he reentered Yugoslavia after Comintern service during the Spanish Civil War and a stay in Moscow.[52]

Hundreds of United States passports fell into Soviet hands the same way. When General Krivitsky defected he warned the U.S. State Department about this. As a result, according to Ashley Nicholas of the State Department Passport Legal Division, the U.S. government, "put on a very expensive program of replacing all passports of that type, which had red covers on them, with green-covered passports. We replaced every outstanding passport in the world with a new passport at government expense, primarily due to these passports which were taken from Spain to Moscow." Nicholas claimed that these measures were effective and the Soviets were denied the use of the American passports.[53] The Canadians had not taken such precautions, and their passports were very useful to Soviet intelligence.

Jacson's entrée to the Trotsky home was through Sylvia Ageloff, a follower of Trotsky, whom Jacson claimed to love. How the Soviet Intelligence Service brought the lovers together was told by Louis Budenz, who broke with the Communist Party in 1945 while he was the editor of its newspaper, *The Daily Worker*. Budenz, in an affidavit dated November 11, 1950, revealed that about December 1936, early in his Communist Party career, he was called to the ninth floor of the Communist Party headquarters in New York City. Jack Stachel, a member of the political bureau, had telephoned that he wished to see him.

In the office with Stachel was Jacob Golos, then chairman of the Control Commission of the Communist Party, who was conducting Soviet espionage activities under cover of World Tourists, Inc.

Stachel sent Budenz with Golos "to meet some friends of importance, from abroad."

At a restaurant facing Union Square Budenz was introduced to a man sitting in one of the cubicles, who gave the name of Richard or Richards. "It was clear that this was a fictitious name and his Russian accent emphasized that fact." Budenz revealed years later:

> During the course of my ten years in the party, particularly as I came to be a member of the national or central committee, and a constant attendant on political bureau meetings, I met many other Soviet agents going under such first names or adaptations of first names.
>
> Richards advised me that he wanted my cooperation in getting information in regard to the Trotskyites and their movements, in order to offset any plots against the life of Stalin and against the Soviet Union that might be planned. This was the period of the great purge trials, and I agreed to help.

After that Budenz met with Richards in various restaurants in New York, on the average of several times a week. He provided lists of Trotskyites and also information in regard to the Norman Thomas wing of the Socialist Party.

In the spring of 1937 Richards introduced Budenz to another member of the Soviet secret police, whose name was said to be Michaels or Michael. Both Richards and Michaels claimed that their purpose was to halt Trotskyite plottings against Stalin. Budenz revealed:

> I therefore collected and took them all the available information I could obtain in regard to the movings of secret Trotskyites, Trotskyite couriers, and their relations to the left-wing Socialists. At that time, I had a number of agents for the Stalinist group planted in the Trotskyite camp, that being one of my first assignments with the Communist Party and from them I obtained this information. Prominent among these concealed Stalinists acting as Trotskyites was Bill Reich, who later openly announced his Communist Party affiliations.

In 1937, Budenz's handlers introduced him to another, clearly more important agent, who went by the name of Robert or Roberts. Budenz reported:

> This man was a very intelligent person, fatherly in his manner, and immediately proceeded to organize new activity on my part. He instructed me to introduce to him various Stalinists who were penetrating the Trotskyites or might be useful along that line because of their work or associations.
>
> I should state here that after five years' investigation on my part, and after examining hundreds of photographs of men connected with Soviet espionage in one form or another, or with the conspiracy as a whole, I now know that this man Roberts was in reality Dr. Gregory Rabinowitz, or Rabinowitch, head of the Russian Red Cross in the United States. He was a physician and also a surgeon. . . .
>
> Among those whom I introduced to Roberts was Ruby Weil, whom I had known as a member of the Conference for Progressive Labor Action, of which I had been national secretary prior to becoming a Communist. Miss Weil had secretly joined the Communist Party shortly after I had entered it openly, and had been assigned to a secret training school or unit for infiltration. This assignment had been given her by Comrade Chester, whose correct name was Bernard Schuster or Zuster, the notorious underground agent who directed infiltration of the National Guard and other organizations in the New York and New England areas for the Soviet fifth column.
>
> In addition to her knowledge of infiltration methods, Miss Weil had been on very friendly terms with Hilda Ageloff, sister of Leon

Trotsky's secretary, Ruth Ageloff. Hilda was also sister to Sylvia Ageloff, a Brooklyn social worker who devoted vacation periods and other free time to Trotskyite courier work.

Roberts and I agreed that he should be known as "John Rich" to Miss Weil, and as such I introduced him to her. Before I had introduced him to her, Roberts had given me a considerable sum of money in cash to present to Miss Weil for expenses. This was for the specific purpose of enabling her to be dressed well, and to keep up telephone and other connections. She was reluctant to take the money, but upon learning its purposes, agreed to do so.

Weil and Ageloff visited Paris during the 1938 Trotskyite International Congress held there.

According to Budenz:

After her return from Paris, though I did not see her then, Roberts told me that she had done a splendid piece of work for the Soviet secret police there.

After the assassination of Leon Trotsky, in 1940, Miss Weil came to me in great distress to tell me of her part in this act. . . .

As Miss Weil filled out the story of her Paris visit to me, it ran as follows: Before going to Europe, Roberts had sent her to see a member of the Communist conspiratorial apparatus residing in Greenwich Village and known by the name of Comrade Gertrude. As Roberts had on one or two occasions mentioned this Gertrude to me, I knew that she existed. The plan was that Gertrude would be in Paris at a certain address when Ruby arrived there and that she would give Miss Weil the instructions which she should follow, and also introduce her to the persons (Stalinist agents) whom she should introduce to Miss Ageloff.

In this manner, Miss Weil was introduced to the man Jacson, who eventually killed Trotsky. In turn, Jacson was introduced to Sylvia Ageloff, and immediately Jacson instituted a whirlwind courtship. Representing himself to be a Jacques Mornard, a descent [sic] of Belgian counts, he won Miss Ageloff's favor and she smuggled him into Mexico and into the Trotsky household.

Weil asked Budenz to arrange her reentry into the Communist Party. He brought up the question with Jacob Golos. Golos stated that he would first have to consult the Soviet consulate officials, or MVD agents located in the consulate. After conferring with them he reported that Miss Weil could not have a Communist Party card and she was forbidden to go near the party headquarters or to visit Budenz's home. He conveyed this information to her, and she was gravely disappointed.[54]

Sylvia Ageloff testified before Congress in December 1950. She described her relationship with Ruby Weil. They had known each other, Sylvia testified, in the 1930s in a leftist organization called The American Workers Party (actually the group was called The Conference for Progressive Labor Action). The CPLA had merged with the Trotskyites but Ruby didn't join the new merged group, called The American Workers Party. There were rumors, Sylvia said, that she was interested in joining the Communist Party. Budenz, too, had come out of CPLA and had joined the Communist Party rather than merge with the Trotskyites.

Sylvia planned to go to Europe in the summer of 1938, when she received a call from Ruby who said that she too intended to go to Europe with money sent by a sister in England named Corinne. Ruby suggested they go together. They met Ruby's sister in England and then went on to France. Ruby now announced that she had a second sister named Gertrude who had lived in France and had been friendly with a young student who had visited her house in Paris. Ruby got in touch with the young student and introduced him to Sylvia Ageloff. She became enamored of him and stayed with the young man from June 1938 to January or February 1939. He told her his name was Jacques Mornard.

Sylvia returned to New York and, in September 1939, Mornard arrived. Sylvia testified:

> He came with a forged passport as Frank Jacson. The reason he gave for using a forged passport was that he was in the Belgian Army and would not have been permitted to leave the country. Mornard claimed that he was going to Mexico to meet a man "through his mother's connections" who would employ him.

In January 1940 Sylvia went down to Mexico to join her boyfriend. Jacson used his relationship with Sylvia Ageloff to meet Trotsky and at an opportune moment, when he got Trotsky alone, murdered him.

Ageloff testified that Ruby Weil was not known to her as a member of the Communist Party, but that she did work for a pro-communist news service called *Federated Press*. The last time Sylvia saw Ruby was in June 1938, when she was introduced to Frank Jacson.[55]

Ruby Weil testified before Congress on the same day in December 1950. She identified herself as an editor for Associated Press in New York City. Ruby admitted being acquainted with Sylvia Ageloff but claimed that while they traveled to Europe on the same boat, they did not make the trip together. Ruby admitted joining the Communist Party in 1936 and claimed she dropped out sometime in 1937. Although she could not remember the names of anyone in the Communist Party, when asked about Louis Budenz she admitted she knew he was a member as "He joined very publicly."

When asked about Mornard, Ruby admitted meeting him in Paris through a woman she had known in New York who was a friend of his. The woman's name was Gertrude. Ruby could not remember the last name of the woman she had identified to Sylvia as her sister. She also claimed that she did not know Gertrude to be a member of the Communist Party. Her testimony was very vague, and while she challenged some of the statements of Budenz, she provided no details to refute the allegations.[56]

The murder of Trotsky did not end Stalin's vendetta against the Trotskyites. Some of that work was done by a spy ring that was remarkable for its versatility and variety of its targets.

10

The Classic Soviet
Espionage Ring

A SOVIET spy ring operated in the United States in the 1940s and
1950s that performed a wide range of functions. It spied on
American political groups as well as the government. During World
War II it penetrated the OSS. This ring grew out of the GPU operations against the Trotskyites.

Stalinist Spies versus the Trotskyites

Louis Budenz, in his affidavit to Congress (see chapter 9), identified
another young woman in addition to Ruby Weil, whom he had
provided to Soviet intelligence to work on the Trotskyites. Budenz
introduced his Soviet contact Roberts to Sylvia Franklin also known
as Sylvia Caldwell. Her maiden name was Sylvia Callen.
  According to Budenz:

> When I went to Chicago, under Roberts' instructions I got in touch
> with Jack Kling, head of the Young Communist League in that area.
> The purpose of this consultation was, in the name of the National
> Committee of which I was a member, to get hold of some Stalinist
> agent infiltrating the Trotskyites, who could be moved to New York
> and put into the Trotskyite national office.
>   Jack Kling introduced me to Sylvia Franklin, a Chicago social worker
> who was successfully infiltrating the Trotskyites. Her husband, Irving
> Franklin, had been in Spain working in secret work and had then
> been sent into Canada to aid in espionage activities there.

Roberts gave Sylvia Franklin three hundred dollars to make the trip to New York, where he had arranged her employment with a woman doctor who was connected with the Soviet secret police.

He also arranged that her husband, Irving, who had returned from his espionage work in Canada, be located in an apartment in the Bronx, so that Sylvia could visit him. She represented herself to the Trotskyites as unmarried and was set up in an apartment in Manhattan.

By volunteering to do secretarial work in the national offices of the Trotskyites in New York, Franklin, under the direction of Roberts/Rabinowitz, gradually made herself indispensable to James Cannon, the Trotskyite leader. She soon became his secretary. Roberts/Rabinowitz advised Budenz that she had proved to be invaluable, bringing copies of all of Trotsky's mail and other Trotskyite communications to him.

"As to Roberts/Rabinowitz," Budenz said "I bade farewell to him in 1939—after Miss Weil's trip to Paris but before the actual Trotsky assassination. He got in touch with me (as usual) through Jacob Golos and asked me to meet him at the Bronx apartment of Irving Franklin. There he told me he was leaving for the Soviet Union."[1]

Sylvia Callen, now remarried and named Sylvia Doxsee, testified before a grand jury on October 7, 1954. She admitted to having been married from 1935 to about 1943 to Zalmond David Franklin. However, she only remembered that when her recollection was refreshed by being shown a copy of her marriage license. She could not remember the answers for most other questions and for the few she could she invoked the Fifth Amendment.

On June 18, 1958, she reappeared before the grand jury. She remembered a lot more during her reappearance. She testified that she had been a member of the Young Communist League and admitted that she was planted by the Communist Party in the "Socialist Movement." (From 1936 to 1938 the Trotskyites held membership in the Socialist Party and its youth organization, The Young People's Socialist League.) She described how she had volunteered to work in the office of the Socialist Workers Party, the name adopted by the Trotskyite party when they set up their own organization in 1938. She soon became secretary to the leader, James Cannon.

When asked whether she discussed the things that she learned in Cannon's office with anyone else, she responded that she used to provide the information to a man called Jack, whom she would meet in the apartment of her then husband, Zalmond. The man she knew as Jack was Dr. Gregory Rabinowitz (Roberts). She reported giving Jack copies of minutes of the Trotskyite Political Committee as well as other documents. Jack responded by giving her money. Jack had been introduced to her in Chicago by Louis Budenz. Soon Jack was replaced by another man whose name she remembered as Sam. He turned out to be Jack Soble, who a decade earlier had been Senin, an infiltrator into the Trotsky camp—real name Sobolevicius. With his brother, who had been called Well, now known as Robert Soblen, Jack Soble ran a Soviet spy ring.[2]

Soble and Soblen were no longer mere agents penetrating the Trotskyite movement. Now they were principal agents running an entire network. The Soble spy ring had a variety of targets, ranging from the U.S. intelligence service to a variety of American political organizations. When the spy ring was broken, and its members indicted, those who spied on the government were charged with espionage. Those who merely spied on other Americans were listed as unindicted coconspirators. Sylvia Franklin (Caldwell, Callen) was an unindicted coconspirator.

Sylvia was a highly regarded member of the Socialist Workers Party. As secretary to the leader, James P. Cannon, she had access to all internal documents, including correspondence with Trotsky. After she was exposed, and even after her admissions to the grand jury were released, the American Trotskyites refused to believe that Sylvia was a GPU spy in their movement.[3]

In one incident, Franklin aided the Trotskyites in doing something that provided a valuable weapon for the Stalinists to attack them. In the winter of 1942, James Cannon was asked by the party school to give a series of lectures on Socialist Workers Party history. The twelve lectures were not written but spoken from notes. On her own initiative, Sylvia took down the lectures in shorthand. She typed her notes, possibly more for the Soviets than for the Trotskyites.

During one lecture Cannon told the story of the period from 1936 to 1938, when the Trotskyites worked inside the Socialist Party. They were thrown out and established the Socialist Workers Party. Cannon claimed that as a result, the Socialist Party, "has progressively disintegrated until it has virtually lost any semblance of influence. . . . Our work . . . contributed to that." Cannon quoted

Trotsky as commenting that the "pitiful state" of the Socialist Party justified the Trotskyite penetration of the organization, even if the SWP hadn't gained a single new member.[4] In November 1943, when Cannon was getting ready to go to prison for Smith Act violation (advocating the overthrow of the government by force and violence), the suggestion was made that his lectures be published in book form. Franklin's notes made this possible. Cannon had only enough time to correct some of the grammatical mistakes before he went off to jail.[5] If he had had more time, he might have deleted this story, which showed the Trotskyites as disruptive wreckers. The book was published by the Trotskyites, and the Communists found a use for the story. A 1947 pamphlet by Communist Party member Herb Tank, which was used in the fight within the National Maritime Union, quoted Cannon. The Trotskyites were supporting the non-Communist faction in the Union.[6]

In 1955 Herb Tank admitted in congressional testimony that he was employed by Albert Kahn as a bodyguard for an ex-communist who had returned to the fold and was writing a book.[7] Kahn had been identified by Elizabeth Bentley as a member of her spy ring.

Another member of the Soble ring, targeted against the Trotskyites, was Thomas L. Black. He had joined the Communist Party in 1931 but dropped out a few years later, intending to go to the Soviet Union to work. He contacted Amtorg, the Soviet trading organization, and met Gaik Ovakimian. This was Black's introduction to the Soviet Intelligence Service. Ovakimian was a veteran Soviet intelligence officer who operated under the cover of Amtorg. He ran a large number of agents in the United States and Canada and was in close contact with Jacob Golos, another Soviet spy master. One of the agents working for Ovakimian was an employee of the United States Department of Justice. This individual provided information from FBI files to the Soviets during 1937 and 1938. He was suspended and permitted to resign in 1941. Ovakimian was arrested by the FBI in 1941 for violation of the Foreign Agents Registration Act. He left the United States on a Soviet ship in July 1941 as part of a deal whereby six Americans or spouses of Americans were permitted to leave the Soviet Union.[8]

Black was told by Ovakimian that he had to supply technical information that would be of use to the Soviet Union. He prepared some reports on textile production but was told that this was not particularly valuable. Black was turned over to another Soviet who used the name "Paul Peterson" to be trained in espionage tradecraft. He was taught how to avoid surveillance, collect information, write reports, and use microfilm. Black performed a very valuable service to the Soviets by introducing them to Harry Gold, who was later to participate in the Rosenberg spy ring that provided America's atomic secrets to the Soviets.

Peterson instructed Black to join the Trotskyite movement in 1937. At that time the Trotskyites were still part of the Socialist Party. In 1938 Peterson turned Black over to another Soviet called "George." This was Semyon Semenov of Amtorg. Black was soon handed over to another Soviet called "Dr. Schwartz." This was Dr. Gregory Rabinowitz, who operated under cover of the Soviet Red Cross. Rabinowitz directed Black to go to Mexico to work in the Trotsky household. He was told that other Soviet agents were already in place and that he would meet them there and be told what to do. He later learned that the project was the assassination of Trotsky. Black used personal reasons to delay his trip, and after the murder of Trotsky he no longer saw Rabinowitz. His final Soviet handler was known to him as Jack Katz.[9]

The Soble Spy Ring

The Rabinowitz apparatus was taken over by Jack Soble when he arrived in the U.S. in 1941.[10] Soble inherited a number of agents who were already in place. The most interesting member of the Soble spy ring was the courier Boris Morros, a flamboyant Hollywood producer. Boris Morros was born in Russia in 1891 and came to the United States in 1922. He was the producer of such films as *Flying Deuces* with Laurel and Hardy and *Carnegie Hall*.[11]

In 1936 a man calling himself Edward Herbert contacted Morros. He identified himself as associated with Amtorg and assisted Morros in shipping packages to his parents in the Soviet Union. Morros later learned that this man was Vassili Zubilin, a veteran Soviet intelligence officer.[12] The FBI established that Vassili Zubilin had lived in New York City under the name Joseph Herbert. He was in the United States as a Soviet "illegal," that is, a Soviet intelligence officer using a false identity and apparently unconnected with the official Soviet establishments. Zubilin was in possession of a false

United States passport in the name of Edward Joseph Herbert.[13] He used the passport for a number of visits to the United States between 1934 and 1937.[14]

One afternoon Zubilin, still calling himself Edward Herbert, visited Boris Morros. He asked whether Morros was against the Nazis. The answer was yes, of course. Zubilin said that he lived in Germany and was organizing underground anti-Nazi work there for the Soviet government. Morros suggested that this sounded dangerous. Zubilin answered that Morros could help make it less dangerous by providing him with a letter certifying that "Edward Herbert" was authorized to act in Germany as a talent scout for Paramount Pictures, where Morros was employed. Morros was to write to him in Germany, since the letters would improve his cover. Some time later one of Zubilin's associates visited Morros to complain that he was not writing often enough, thus endangering Herbert's life. Morros did not see Herbert again until he reappeared under the name Zubilin in 1942.[15]

Zubilin had reentered the United States on December 25, 1941, as a Soviet diplomat. Accompanying him were his wife, Helen, and his son Peter.[16] Zubilin contacted Morros in 1942 and offered to assist him in bringing his father into the United States. In return for the favor Morros would have to work as an agent for the Soviets.[17] Boris Morros's father, Michael, arrived in the United States January 20, 1943.[18]

In the spring of 1943 Zubilin was under surveillance by the FBI and was observed in contact with Boris Morros. After extensive investigation of the activities of Morros, the FBI interviewed him in July 1947. Morros admitted that he was working for Soviet intelligence and that Zubilin had recruited him. He agreed to operate as a double agent of the FBI against the Soviets. Morros was eventually responsible for the FBI rolling up the Soble spy ring, almost ten years after he began his double agent activity. In 1944 Soble had participated with Morros in the operation of the Boris Morros Music Company, with offices in New York and Los Angeles, which was a cover for Soviet intelligence operations.[19]

The most significant member of the Soble ring in the operations against the Trotskyites was Mark Zborowski. His most successful operations, however, were in Europe, before he joined the Soble group in the United States. Zborowski had penetrated the Trotskyite apparatus at a very high level and was involved in the murder of Trotsky's son, Leon Sedov.

Zborowski was born in 1907 in Russia and was taken by his parents to Poland after the Russian Revolution. He became a communist in Lodz and was arrested in 1930 but jumped bail and went to France. Here he became involved in Soviet intelligence work. His first assignment was with the Union of Returnees, a Soviet-financed group working among czarist émigrés, to convince them to return to Russia. The Union was also involved in kidnapping and murder.

In 1935 Zborowski was ordered to contact Trotsky's son. As a Russian speaker he quickly worked his way through the French Trotskyite group and became a close friend of Sedov.[20] He became a coeditor with Sedov and Lilia Estrine (later Dallin) of Trotsky's major publication, *The Bulletin of the Opposition*. In 1938 Zborowski received an important assignment. It resulted in the death of his "friend," Leon Sedov. According to Zborowski, "the idea was, to lure him to a place where he and me together would be kidnapped and brought to Soviet Russia." When Sedov took sick, Zborowski got him to a hospital. The operation for appendicitis was successful, but the patient died.[21] Instead of a kidnapping the GPU committed a murder.

Trotsky wrote of his son:

> The first and natural supposition is that he was poisoned. It presented no serious difficulty for the agents of Stalin to gain access to Leon, his clothing, his food. Are judicial experts, even if untrammeled by "diplomatic" considerations, capable of arriving at a definitive conclusion on this point? In connection with war chemistry the art of poisoning has nowadays attained an extraordinary development. To be sure the secrets of this art are inaccessible to common mortals. But the poisoners of the GPU have access to everything. It is entirely feasible to conceive of a poison which cannot be detected after death, even with the most careful analysis. And who will guarantee such care?

Trotsky was as heartbroken about the slanders against his son as he was about the murder. Trotsky wrote, "Before they killed him they did everything in their power to slander and blacken our son in the eyes of contemporaries and of posterity. Cain Djugashvili and his henchmen tried to depict Leon as an agent of Fascism, a secret partisan of capitalist restoration in the U.S.S.R., the organizer of railway wrecks and murders of workers."[22] Djugashvilli was Stalin's real name, and Cain, of course, was the biblical murderer of his brother.

Zborowski was exposed by one of the most important defectors from the Soviet Intelligence Service. Alexander Orlov was the chief of Soviet intelligence in Spain when he defected in 1938. He was born Leon Feldbin to Jewish parents in Russia in 1895. Orlov joined the Bolshevik Party in May 1917 and in September 1920 was with the 12th Red Army on the Polish front, in charge of guerrilla activity and counterintelligence. Here he came to the attention of Felix Dzerzhinsky, head of the Cheka. Under the alias Leon Nikolayev, he operated in Paris as chief of the GPU *Rezidentura*. In 1928 he was transferred to Berlin under the cover of a trade delegation. During 1932 he visited the United States on an espionage mission. In September 1936 Orlov was sent to Spain, where he served as the Soviet liaison for intelligence matters to the Republican government.[23]

While Orlov was stationed in Spain he visited Paris, where his close friend, Nikolai Smirnov, was the *rezident*. One of Smirnov's officers, Alexeev, was known to Orlov from earlier assignments. In 1937 Alexeev, to impress Orlov, told him about an agent he was running who had gained the trust of Trotsky's son and who could be used in setting up the murders of Trotsky and Sedov. The agent was named Mark, but in the Trotskyite movement he wrote under the pen name, Etienne. Mark worked at an institute run by the Menshevik, Boris Nikolayevsky. It was at this institute that some of Trotsky's archives were stored. Mark organized the theft of these archives. Orlov actually watched on one occasion when Alexeev met with the agent.[24]

After Orlov's defection he wrote a letter to warn Trotsky of the agent in his camp. As an experienced conspirator, Orlov concealed his identity in the letter. He pretended to be the uncle of General Lushkov, a Soviet general and old GPU officer, who had defected to the Japanese in 1938. Orlov claimed to have gotten his information about the agent from Lushkov. Orlov wrote in his December 27, 1938, letter:

> Lushkov gave me detailed information about this agent provocateur with the understanding that no one, even you yourself, should know

that this information came from him. In spite of the fact that Lushkov forgot the last name of the provocateur, he supplied enough details to enable you to establish without any error who that man is. This agent provocateur had for a long time assisted your son L. Sedov in editing your Russian *Bulletin of Opposition*, in Paris, and collaborated with him until the very death of Sedov.

Lushkov is almost sure that the provocateur's name is "Mark." He was literally the shadow of L. Sedov; he informed the Cheka about every step of Sedov, about his activities and personal correspondence with you which the provocateur read with the knowledge of L. Sedov. This provocateur wormed himself into the complete confidence of your son and knew as much about the activities of your organization as Sedov himself. Thanks to this provocateur, several officers of the Cheka have received decorations.

This provocateur worked till 1938 at the Archive or Institute of the well-known Menshevik, Nikolayevsky, in Paris, and, may be, still works there. It was this Mark who stole a part of your archive (documents) from Nikolayevsky's establishment (he did it twice if I am not mistaken). These documents were delivered to Lushkov in Moscow and he read them.

This agent provocateur is about 32–35 years old. He is a Jew, originates from the Russian part of Poland, writes well in Russian. Lushkov had seen his photograph. This provocateur wears glasses. He is married and has a baby.

What surprises me more than anything else is the gullibility of your comrades. This man had no revolutionary past whatsoever. In spite of the fact that he is a Jew, he was about four years ago a member of the Society for Repatriation to Russia (this is a society of former czarist officers, in Paris). According to Lushkov, this was well known in Paris even to members of your organization. In that society he acted already as a Bolshevist agent provocateur. After that the Cheka assigned him to your organization, where for some reason, he was trusted. . . .

Lushkov expressed apprehension that now the assassination of Trotsky was on the agenda and that Moscow would try to plant assassins with the help of this agent provocateur or through agent provocateurs from Spain under the guise of Spanish Trotskyites.

Orlov had known Mrs. Mercador, whose son was to murder Trotsky, so he actually knew that Spanish Communists would be involved in that operation. He warned Trotsky, "The main thing: be on your guard. Do not trust any person, man or woman, who may come to you with recommendations from this provocateur." He suggested that when Trotsky received the letter he should put a notice in the Trotskyite newspaper in New York, *Socialist Appeal*, saying that the editorial office had received the letter from "Stein."[25]

The notice appeared in the newspaper, telling "Stein" to go to the editorial office and talk to Comrade Martin. Orlov went to the office but did not like the looks of Martin and left without identifying himself. He tried to telephone Trotsky but did not succeed in getting him to the phone.

In 1954 Orlov received a letter from David Dallin. The author of a number of books, Dallin was working on his major project, a book on Soviet espionage. Orlov agreed to meet him. Dallin was a Menshevik; his wife, Lilia, had worked with Sedov and Zborowski in Paris. Orlov told Dallin about an "agent provocateur" named Mark. Dallin asked if he knew the last name. When Orlov answered "no," Dallin asked if the name Zborowski meant anything to him. Orlov had never heard that name but asked where Mark might be now. Dallin answered he didn't know.

Orlov and Dallin arranged for a second meeting. As Orlov described the incident:

> I asked him where we should meet. He said: Well, if you could come to my apartment. I said, I would. "You probably won't like to have my wife present." A strange remark from a husband. I said, on the contrary I will take my wife and I will be glad to meet Mrs. Dallin too. We went to their apartment. And then Mrs. Dallin during the conversation about Mark suddenly remarked, "You know, Dallin and I were instrumental in bringing Mark into the United States." I said: "What? Is he the United States?" "Yes, indeed. He came here in 1941. He is already an American citizen." And she said she met him at the pier. That was a big surprise to me because had Mr. Dallin told me that Mark was here in this country, I would immediately have exposed him. I wish to emphasize here that as soon as I came into the open, while talking with the FBI officials and naming a number of spies and talking about the NKVD work, I mentioned to them Mark, but I didn't know his name was Zborowski and they probably put it in the index under the name of Mark.
>
> They asked me where he might be. I said if he was alive, he must be somewhere in Poland. But when I learned that from Dallin's wife, I immediately took steps—that was the 25th of December, that was

Christmas. Two days later I went to the U.S. attorney's office at Foley Square to one of the assistants whom I knew and told him immediately about the story that Mark Zborowski, an agent provocateur, is now a naturalized citizen and is now here in the United States.

Now returning to that visit to Dallin's apartment: Mrs. Dallin told me "You know your letter that you wrote to Trotsky arrived there when I was in Trotsky's household in Mexico. When I learned later that you were the author of that letter and what you were telling about Mark Zborowski, I told them this is not true."

Surely I was nettled. How come? Why should I, immediately after I received word about myself from Stalin's assistant and came to America, write a letter to Trotsky in Mexico and warn him against them? I gave the facts where he lived, that he had a baby, that he was recently married, that he worked at Nikolayevsky's Institute, that he wrote under the name of Etienne in the Trotsky's Bulletin.

She said, that was also strange to me. There were two Etiennes writing. I became incensed. It is a little magazine and there was only one Etienne. I said: no, there was only one Etienne. She wanted to contradict, but David Dallin motioned to her to become calm and said there was one Etienne.[26]

Orlov's report on Zborowski was sent to the FBI. They interviewed Zborowski. After some attempts at evasion, Zborowski made significant admissions about his activities in Europe. He made the same admissions when called to a Senate hearing in February and March 1956. Zborowski revealed that he had worked for Soviet intelligence. He identified the man who recruited him as Afanasyeff. He admitted that he was assigned to spy on the Trotskyites and eventually to make contact with Sedov. He denied knowing that the plan was to kill Sedov, and insisted that it was only to kidnap him and take him to Russia. Zborowski also admitted that he was involved in spying on the defector from Soviet intelligence, General Krivitsky. Sedov had assigned him as bodyguard to Krivitsky, not knowing, of course, that he was a Soviet agent. When asked about his FBI interview and whether he denied having been an NKVD agent, Zborowski responded "I did not deny, exactly, I told them my activities with the Trotskyites, but I did not state openly that I was an NKVD agent."

During his second session with the Senate committee, Zborowski told how Lilia Dallin assisted him in getting into the United States in 1941. He evaded questions about activities in the United States, but admitted that in 1944 he was contacted by a Soviet agent who tried to give him an assignment to report on the defector Victor Kravchenko. Zborowski claimed that he refused.[27]

Despite Zborowski's evasions, he had said enough to worry his KGB[28] handler, Jack Soble. In a letter to KGB Headquarters in Moscow (called the Centre), Soble explained his concerns. He reminded Moscow of Zborowski's services, "his old activities among the Trotskyites . . . his big and active work among the Mensheviks and deserters from the U.S.S.R. . . . the running of Kravchenko in the 1940s; the close "friendship" with the Dallins. . . ." Soble was particularly concerned because he had been introduced to Zborowski by the Soviet intelligence officer, Chaliapin, and Zborowski knew Soble's real name. Soble complained, "Since 1954, the FBI have been working on Zborowski. . . . To confess, I expected to be arrested at any moment because Zborowski knows me well by name. . . . Probably Zborowski has been silent about me the same way he was silent about the names of other people." Soble asked the Moscow Centre to consider the problem and "take the most urgent measures." He presumably meant to "exfiltrate" him from the United States.

Soble gave the letter to his courier, Boris Morros. As a result, the FBI read the letter before Moscow did.[29]

Some months later Jack Soble was arrested by the FBI. Charged and convicted of espionage, he identified his brother, Robert Soblen, and the other members of the ring. In August 1957 he confronted Zborowski, who admitted that Soble was his espionage superior. Zborowski was indicted for perjury. After one conviction was overturned, he was convicted again and served a jail sentence.[30]

After Soble's Arrest

Although Zborowski claimed to the Senate that he turned down the assignment against Kravchenko, in fact he spied on him extensively, as Soble reported in his letter to Moscow. During Soble's testimony in Zborowski's perjury trial, he revealed that Zborowski had learned about Victor Kravchenko a few weeks before the Soviet official's defection in 1944. He had learned the story, but not the name of the potential defector, from the Dallins. He had actually seen the defector on his way to the Dallin apartment, as Zborowski lived in

Dallin's building and had been asked directions by a visitor with a Russian accent. Soble reported Zborowski's information about a potential defector to Chaliapin. Soble suddenly got a phone call from Zubilin, who said he was coming over immediately. When he arrived he demanded to know everything about this man who wanted to defect. Soble said that Zborowski had identified the defector as an "old member of the Party." Zubilin then discounted the story, as he considered old members to mean someone who had been a party member before 1917. Kravchenko had actually joined the party in 1921. He was an old enough member for most people, but not for a Bolshevik purist like Zubilin. As a result, Zborowski's accurate information was discounted.

After Kravchenko's defection Zborowski made friends with him, and even assisted in the writing of his book, *I Chose Freedom*. Sections of the manuscript given to Zborowski were turned over to Soble. Chaliapin made photostats and Soble returned the originals to Zborowski.[31] During his first perjury trial, Zborowski admitted that Mrs. Dallin had introduced him to Kravchenko, who had asked for his help in writing the book.[32]

Kravchenko, in his second book, described some of the activities engaged in by the Soviet Intelligence Service to terrorize him after his defection. One day while he was visiting with a friend in Hollywood, the friend was called on the telephone and told, "I believe you have a small daughter? . . . There's a foreigner living at your home. If you're fond of your daughter—get rid of him. Otherwise something might happen to her—or to your whole family." When Kravchenko returned to New York he learned that three men had attempted to enter his apartment. When neighbors confronted them they said they were looking for Victor Kravchenko. He was not using that name at that address and believed no one knew he was living there. When Kravchenko wrote about the incident, he did not realize that Zborowski knew where he lived. Of course, at that time he did not know that Zborowski was an agent. An even more frightening incident occurred when Kravchenko noticed an odd object on a table in his home. It was a bullet, and had not been there earlier. He was concerned that someone had access to his home despite the triple locks on his door.

When Kravchenko was preparing to go to France to testify in a libel suit against a French Communist newspaper, a letter arrived for him at his publisher's office. The writer of the letter, mailed in

France and written in French, identified himself as an NKVD agent who claimed to be sympathetic to Kravchenko. He cited details and personal facts known only to Kravchenko's personal friends. He then warned Kravchenko not to go to Europe, and reminded him "Remember the incident of the bullet. . . ."[33]

The day after Kravchenko's press conference on April 3, 1944, announcing his defection the Communist Party newspaper in New York, *Daily Worker*, carried an article by Joseph Starobin, listing Kravchenko together with Trotsky, Bukharin, Krivitsky, and Barmine. The first three had been killed. The article said, "Kravchenko has evidently been living on borrowed time." Describing the fate of defectors, Starobin wrote: "[T]he vigilant and avenging hand of forward-moving humanity catches up with them and finally erases them." A similar threat had been directed against General Krivitsky before his death, in the Communist Party magazine, *New Masses*, of May 9, 1939. To prove their knowledge, the magazine wrote on behalf of the Soviets, " 'General Krivitsky,' you are Shmelka Ginsberg." In identifying his real name, the threat also made the point that he was Jewish.

In a piece of brazenness unusual even for the Soviets, two embassy officials tried to pressure the State Department to deport Kravchenko. When they were told that people are not deported from this country unless they have committed some crime, the embassy officials backed down. The officials were Vladimir I. Bazykin, first secretary of the Soviet embassy, and Vasily M. Zubilin, second secretary of the Soviet embassy.[34] Zubilin, was of course, the Soviet intelligence officer who failed to identify Kravchenko before the defection, even though he was warned by Zborowski through Soble.

Before his exposure Zborowski had coauthored a book titled *Life is With People*, about the small Jewish towns in Eastern Europe. The foreword was by the well-known sociologist, Margaret Mead. When Zborowski was arrested, Mead spoke out in his defense. After returning from prison, Zborowski wrote *People in Pain*, a study of how people of different cultures respond to pain—a fascinating study, indeed, for a GPU agent who participated in the inflicting of so much pain. Again Margaret Mead wrote the foreword to the book, published in 1969. That same year Zborowski was a visiting lecturer at the University of California at Berkeley.

A member of the Soble spy ring who was listed as an unindicted coconspirator was Esther Rand. Her target was the Zionists. In

Zubilin's first briefing to Soble, Zubilin reported that Russia regarded Judaism as an enemy of communism that needed to be fought. Two dedicated communists, a man and a woman (Esther Rand), were planted in the offices of the United Jewish Appeal. Through them Soble obtained copies of correspondence between the Jewish groups and the State Department regarding attempts to rescue Europe's Jews, who were in the hands of the Nazis. At meetings with his agents, which took place in the Times Square area, he also received information about other Zionist groups.[35]

Testifying in the case against his brother, Robert Soblen, Soble said that his agent among the Zionists was Esther Rand. He had not recruited her, he said, "She was an old agent from the Russians." He testified that he was introduced to her by the Soviet intelligence officer Chaliapin.[36]

Esther Rand was born around 1907 in Russia and had been brought by her parents to the United States shortly thereafter. On August 29, 1964, the *New York Journal-American* reported that Esther Rand was active in organizing rent strikes on the lower east side of Manhattan and had received support from the federally funded poverty program, Mobilization for Youth. Rand admitted to the newspaper that she was the same person who was named as a coconspirator in the Soblen case. As she was only spying on other Americans, and not the government, she could not be tried for espionage.

Alfred and Martha Stern

A husband-and-wife team who were indicted for espionage were the most socially prominent members of the spy ring. They were Alfred Kaufman Stern and his wife, Martha Dodd Stern. Alfred, born in 1897, was a graduate of Phillips Exeter Academy and also attended Harvard University. He left college to serve in the United States Army during World War I. His marriage to Marian Rosenwald, daughter of the head of Sears Roebuck, brought him into social prominence and considerable wealth. He served for ten years as director of the Rosenwald Foundation. Stern's marriage to Marian Rosenwald ended in divorce. The FBI files show that Stern attended meetings of the New York State Committee of the Communist Party in the 1940s and was relied upon to raise considerable amounts of money for the party.[37]

Martha Dodd Stern was born in 1908, the daughter of William E. Dodd, who from 1933 to 1937 was U.S. ambassador to Germany. A product of a finishing school in Washington, D.C., Martha attended the University of Chicago for three years and then spent one year at the Sorbonne, in Paris.[38]

The FBI reported that it was Zubilin who brought the Sterns together with Boris Morros and that Stern knew Zubilin as a Soviet intelligence officer. According to the FBI, Martha Dodd Stern had a special avenue of communication with the Soviets and was highly thought of by Soble's superiors in the Soviet Intelligence Service.[39]

Soble revealed that Martha Dodd admitted to him that she had served as a Soviet spy in the American embassy in Berlin when she lived there with her father. She told Soble that she had a love affair with an NKVD officer working undercover at the Soviet embassy, and that at his request she had stolen secret files from the embassy for the Soviets.[40]

In January 1957, when members of the spy ring were called before the grand jury, the Sterns were in Mexico. On February 12 subpoenas were served on the Sterns at their home in Mexico by embassy officers. Upon receiving these subpoenas to appear before the New York federal grand jury as witnesses in the case of Jack and Myra Soble and Jacob Albam, the Sterns immediately engaged the services of former U.S. ambassador to Mexico, William O'Dwyer. A half-hour after the subpoenas were served, O'Dwyer called to complain that the subpoenas were poorly drawn. They were served again on February 27, and the Sterns accepted 468 dollars each for expenses to return to New York and stated that they had to communicate with their lawyer, Bill O'Dwyer. But they did not return to the United States. After their continued refusal to appear, they were fined 25,000 dollars each for contempt of court.

According to a secret report from the U.S. embassy in Mexico to the State Department, dated August 9, 1957:

On June 7, 1957, in an endeavor to have the Sterns returned to the United States by Mexico, Ambassador White delivered personally to President Ruiz Cortines a verbal message from President Eisenhower, requesting cooperation in this matter of importance to our national security by sending the Sterns back to the United States. On June 24, Ambassador White again spoke to President Ruiz Cortines about the matter. . . . On June 26, the Ambassador spoke with the Minister of Gobernacion, Angel Carvajal and Finance Minister Antonio Carrillo Flores, both of whom promised to look into the matter, but nothing further was heard from them.

The report, declassified under the Freedom of Information Act, revealed:

Alfred Kaufman and Martha Dodd Stern, wanted by U.S. authorities for contempt of court in their failure to appear before a federal grand jury in answer to subpoena, departed from Mexico City at 1:00 A.M. July 12 via KLM for Montreal en route to Amsterdam with a continuing reservation for Switzerland. They were accompanied by their minor son, Robert.

O'Dwyer departed for a vacation in Ireland a few days before the Sterns left Mexico.

The report gave additional information about the Sterns:

After an exploratory visit by Alfred Stern in 1953 he, his wife Martha, and their adopted son Robert then seven years old, came to Mexico on December 17, 1953. At the border they presented to Mexican officials birth certificates and a marriage certificate and promised in writing to present valid American documentation within thirty days. Neither has a valid U.S. passport and they have not yet presented this documentation promised. Ambassador White in his conversation with President Ruiz Cortines stressed the fact that Sterns were in Mexico illegally.

After their arrival in 1953 the Sterns paid bribes to Mexican officials on varying levels in order to establish themselves in Mexico. . . .

The Sterns immediately established themselves in business and, although not shown as the principal stockholders, advanced the money for two companies, Compania Mercantil Latino Americano, S.A. and Negociadores, S.A. with Alfred as a director in the first and Martha as manager of the second. Offices for these businesses and the Sterns other investments are on the fifth floor of Reforma 104, Mexico City. Recently Stern sold stocks valued at $15,000,000 U.S. currency through a Mexican brokage company. It has not been possible to date to learn what he did with the money.[41]

The Sterns renounced their American citizenship and claimed to have become citizens of Paraguay. They traveled on their new Paraguayan passports to Prague, Czechoslovakia.[42] On September 6, they met with the Czech press. Western newspapers were barred. They claimed, according to the Czech newspapers of September 7, that they became Paraguayan citizens and fled to Europe because they were in danger from the FBI and State Department both in the U.S. and in Mexico. After the press conference, they accidentally met journalists from Reuters and Agence France-Presse. They refused to be interviewed and insisted they were tourists. They then drove away in an official car.[43]

On October 8, 1957, the government of Paraguay issued a statement concerning:

> The administrative proceedings instituted against Luis F. Garcete, Ex-Secretary of the National Embassy and Charge of the Paraguayan Consulate in Mexico, D.F. . . . from the investigations made and from the evidence accumulated to date, it appears clearly and convincingly that Passports Numbers 30 and 31 issued in the month of July of the current year by the then Secretary of the National Embassy and Charge of the Consulate General in Mexico, D.F., in the name of Alfred Kaufmann [sic] Stern and Martha Dodd Stern, were issued without meeting the legal requirements for so doing; . . . therefore the Minister of Foreign Relations resolves: Declare void and without any value Passports No. 30 and 31, issued . . . in the name of Alfred Kaufmann Stern and Martha Dodd Stern.[44]

Again, the wealth of the Sterns had been very useful to them, enabling them to "buy" passports.

The Sterns were indicted on September 9, 1957. The first count of the indictment contained the following charge:

> United States of America v. Alfred K. Stern and Martha Dodd Stern, defendants. The Grand Jury charges: Count One that from in or about January 1940 and continuously thereafter up to and including the date of the filing of this indictment . . . Alfred K. Stern and Martha Dodd Stern, the defendants herein, unlawfully, willfully, and knowingly did conspire and agree with each other and with Jack Soble, Myra Soble, Jacob Albam, George Zlatovski, also known as "George Michael," also known as "Rector," and Jane Foster Zlatovski, also known as "Slang," Petr Vassilievich Fedotov, Alexander Mikhailovich Korotkov, Vassili M. Zubilin, also known as "Edward Herbert," Elizabeth Zubilin, also known as "Lisa," Mikhail Chaliapin, Stepan N.

Choundenko, also known as "The Professor," Anatole B. Gromov, Leonid Dmitrievich Petrov, Vitaly Genadievich Tcherniawski, Afanasi Ivanovitch Yefimov, Christopher Georgievich Petrosian, Igor Vassilievitch Sokolov, Vladimir Alexandrovich, also known as "Volodia," whose full and complete name is otherwise unknown to the Grand Jury, and Vassili Mikhailovich Molev, coconspirators but not defendants herein, and with divers other persons to the Grand Jury unknown, to violate subsection (a) of Section 794, Title 18, United States Code, in that they did unlawfully, willfully and knowingly conspire and agree to communicate, deliver, and transmit to a foreign government, to wit, the Union of Soviet Socialist Republics and representatives and agents thereof, directly and indirectly, documents, writings, photographs, photographic negatives, notes, and information relating to the national defense of the United States of America and particularly information relating to intelligence and counterintelligence activities of the United States Government, and relating to the personnel, arms, and equipment of the United States armed forces, with intent and reason to believe that the said documents, writings, photographs, photographic negatives, notes, and information would be used to the advantage of a foreign nation, to wit, the Union of Soviet Socialist Republics.[45]

Martha Dodd Stern has written extensively. In 1941, together with her brother, William E. Dodd, Jr., she edited her father's diary, which described his service as U.S. ambassador to Germany. Her own book, *Through Embassy Eyes*, was published in 1939. Naturally she did not mention that she had been recruited as a Soviet agent during her stay in the American embassy in Berlin. A somewhat revised paperback version of her book appeared as *Aus dem Fenster der Botschaft* (Through the Window of the Embassy), published by the Soviet military government in Germany in 1947. She has had other books printed in East Germany since that time.

On June 30, 1977, Congressman Don Edwards of California began a correspondence with the Carter administration Justice Department and White House to secure the cancellation of the indictments against the Sterns. His first letter was to the attorney general asking what the intentions of the U.S. government would be if the Sterns returned to this country. In a letter dated July 18, 1977, Robert L. Keuch, deputy assistant attorney general, tried to convince Congressman Edwards that since the Sterns had attorneys representing them that it would be inappropriate for the Justice Department to discuss their case with anyone else.

On December 20, 1977, Congressman Edwards wrote to Robert J. Lipshutz, counsel to President Carter. He suggested that "the generous thing to do would be to quash the indictments and allow them to spend their last few years at home." On March 3, 1978, Edwards wrote to Attorney General Griffin Bell complaining that "Justice is 'going by the book,' and that would include these old sick folks returning, being interviewed by the FBI, court proceedings, etc." Benjamin Civiletti, then assistant attorney general, responded that the Sterns's attorneys had been offered a proposal that would have resulted in the dismissal of the indictments. The attorneys broke off the discussion without explanation. Civiletti again offered to continue the discussion with the attorneys for the Sterns.

On June 12, 1978, Congressman Edwards wrote again, this time to Anne Wexler, assistant to President Carter, urging her to assist by pressuring the Justice Department. On January 9, 1979, Edwards wrote another letter to the Justice Department, this time to Assistant Attorney General Phillip Heymann, again urging that the indictment be dropped.

Congressman Edwards's persistent badgering of the Carter administration paid off. On March 20, 1979, Deputy Assistant Attorney General Irvin B. Nathan wrote to Edwards:

> In accordance with my conversation last week with a member of your staff, this is to advise you that, at the request of United States Attorney Robert Fiske, Assistant Attorney General Heymann signed a motion to dismiss the prosecution which had been pending against Alfred and Martha Stern. The motion will now be signed by Mr. Fiske and filed in the U.S. District Court for the Southern District of New York.[46]

The *Washington Post* of March 23, 1979, reported that the indictment had been dropped, and pointed out that the FBI wanted the opportunity to interrogate the Sterns about their espionage activities in exchange for dropping the indictment. The Carter administration, nevertheless, dropped it without any reciprocity. The *Post* reported that "Sylvia Crane, of New York City, a family friend of the Sterns who interested Edwards in their case, said last night that she had just talked to the couple in Prague. 'They are overjoyed, of course,' she said."

The report filed in 1979 of his campaign contributions by Congressman Don Edwards revealed an October 24, 1979, contribution of five hundred dollars from Alfred Stern, Jinonicka 18, Prague, Czechoslovakia. He listed his occupation as retired. The Sterns never returned to the United States, despite the indictment being dropped. In 1986, Alfred Stern died in Prague.[47]

Others in the Soble Spy Ring

Perhaps the most valuable husband-and-wife team in the spy ring were Jane Foster Zlatovski and her husband, George. They penetrated U.S. intelligence for the Soviets. Jane was born in California in 1912. In 1942 she went to work for the Board of Economic Warfare as a junior analyst. On December 27, 1943, she transferred to the Office of Strategic Services, the forerunner of the CIA. She remained in that job until January 1946. From September 1947 to August 1948 she worked for the U.S. Armed Forces in Austria, at European American Command Headquarters in Salzburg. Army records show that she spoke French, Malay, Dutch, and German. Her husband, George, was born in Russia in 1913 and came to the United States with his parents in 1922. George Zlatovski entered the army in November 1942 as a private and left as first lieutenant in February 1948. Army records show that he spoke Russian, German, French, and Spanish. In an interview with the *Duluth Herald and Tribune* published September 3, 1938, George Zlatovski said that he was a member of the Abraham Lincoln Brigade fighting in Spain.[48]

According to FBI files, Jane was reported to have joined the Communist Party in the 1930s while living in the Dutch East Indies. George was identified as conducting Communist Party meetings in Duluth, Minnesota, in the early 1930s.

An investigation of the records of the United States Civil Service Commission by the FBI revealed that Jane Foster stated in an application for federal employment, "[F]rom 1936 until the spring of 1940 I lived in the Netherlands East Indies. During this period I traveled or lived in Java, Bali, Sumatra, Borneo, Malaya, Thailand, Indo China, the Philippines, Japan, and China."

The FBI files also show that:

The personnel records of the Office of Strategic Services reflect that
Jane Foster, while employed by the Office of Strategic Services, was
transferred from the United States to Kandy, Ceylon, July 1, 1944,
arriving there July 13, 1944. She was transferred from Kandy to
Calcutta, India, arriving in Calcutta on March 3, 1945. She departed
from Calcutta on September 9, 1945, for temporary duty in Rangoon,
Burma, Bangkok, Siam, Sumatra and Java. Foster returned to Calcutta and departed for the United States on November 5, 1945, arriving in Washington, D.C., on December 11, 1945.

George Zlatovski attended the U.S. Army Intelligence School in
1946 and then served as an interrogations officer in the Military
Intelligence Section of the U.S. forces in Austria.[49]

The indictment of the Zlatovskis included the same basic charges
as the indictment of the Sterns.

Among the specific counts of the indictment was one that charged
that Jane Zlatovski met with Jack Soble and provided to him, for
transmittal to the Soviet Union, a report on Indonesia, based on
information that she had obtained as an employee of OSS.[50]

An FBI report on Soviet espionage, given to the U.S. Senate in
1960, revealed:

In a report intercepted by Boris Morros, Jane Zlatovski claimed that
while employed by the U.S. Army in Austria in 1947 to 1948, she
obtained through her Army employment names, photographs, and
biographies of agents of the Counter Intelligence Corps. and the
Central Intelligence Agency, similar information concerning their
"native agents" and "practically every scheme they hatched." Only
disruption of contact with her superiors prevented successful delivery
of such information to the Soviet Intelligence Service.

The Zlatovskis could not be arrested, since they resided in France,
and efforts to force their return were not successful.[51]

It is interesting to note that the U.S. embassy in Paris reported
to the State Department in a confidential cable dated January 29,
1957, that the FBI had learned through contact with French intelligence that the Zlatovskis, under questioning by the French, were
providing information on espionage in France that was of great value,
and therefore the French government was reluctant to release them
to the United States.[52]

Another member of the ring was Johanna Koenen Beker, the daughter of a top-level East German Communist, Wilhelm Koenen. Johanna's brother, Heinrich, worked for Soviet intelligence during World War II, in the famous Rote Kapelle spy network.

In 1949 Johanna's former husband, Lorenz Harry Wagner, provided information to U.S. Army intelligence. He reported that he and Johanna had fled to Moscow when the Nazis came to power in Germany. After getting caught in currency manipulations, Wagner was blackmailed by the NKVD (later called KGB) to serve as an agent. He told army intelligence that he was arrested during the 1937 purge, and while under interrogation, was told that his wife was also working for NKVD.

In 1938 Johanna obtained a visa to the United States, while Wagner was released from prison and returned to Germany during the Soviet-Nazi pact. He was jailed by the Gestapo but survived the war and broke with communism. When Johanna was interviewed by the FBI in 1952 she denied working for NKVD. When Wagner was reinterviewed by the U.S. Army he retreated from the allegation.[53]

When the members of the Soble ring were arrested, Johanna began to talk. She revealed that during World War II she had obtained information from German refugees working for the OSS, which she provided to the spy ring. One of the sources she named was Dr. Hans E. Hirschfeld, who had worked as a consultant to OSS during the war. William Reuben, writing in the leftist *National Guardian* of October 30, 1961, reported on Johanna's testimony in the Soble trial, where she identified Hirschfeld. Reuben, a prolific writer of books defending such Soviet spies as Alger Hiss and the Rosenbergs, revealed that two prominent Americans had defended Hirschfeld against the allegations. They were H. Stuart Hughes, professor of history at Harvard, and Herbert Marcuse, professor of politics and philosophy at Brandeis. Marcuse claimed that Hirschfeld was an anti-communist and prominent Social Democrat, whom he had known since the days of pre-Hitler Germany. He denied that his friend could possibly have spied for the Soviets.[54]

Recently released, formerly secret State Department reports prove the opposite. A November 4, 1959, report from Berlin to the State Department for transmittal to the Justice Department and marked "Eyes Only" revealed that:

> Hirschfeld admits extended illegal activity and contacts with Com-
> munist agents in Europe prior to 1940. Also admits similar activity
> prior to 1940 on part of associates who were with him in United States
> prior to 1946. . . . However, he continues to deny allegations made
> by Johanna Koenen Beker.

By this time Hirschfeld was the press chief for then mayor of West
Berlin, Willi Brandt. When interviewed by a Justice Department
representative on November 28, 1959, and asked to appear in New
York before a grand jury, Hirschfeld demanded he be provided with
an official statement that he would not be prosecuted by the U.S.
government if he agreed to return. Two days later he suggested to
the Justice Department representative that he needed the permission of Willi Brandt to come to the United States. In addition, since
his wife was very worried, to reassure her he wanted the statement
that he would not be prosecuted in writing. On December 2, U.S.
officials briefed Brandt, who revealed that the day before Hirschfeld
had submitted a request for retirement. Brandt said he felt sorry
for Hirschfeld and believed his denial of the Beker allegations, but
had told him that if he refused to go to New York, Brandt would
understand.[55] Hirschfeld retired, but did not return to the United
States.

Jack Soble's brother, known in the United States as Dr. Robert
Soblen, had entered the U.S. on October 20, 1941. In addition to
his work as a Soviet intelligence officer, Dr. Soblen practiced med-
icine in New York City.[56]

Dr. Soblen was convicted of conspiracy to commit espionage. The
main witness against him was his brother, Jack Soble. Soblen was
sentenced to life imprisonment but released on bail pending appeal.[57] He fled the country and succeeded in making his way to
Israel. He claimed that as a Jew he had the right of citizenship and
could not be deported to the United States. The Israeli government
did not agree, and on July 1, 1962, placed him on an El Al flight to
Athens in the custody of a U.S. marshall. The plan was that another
El Al flight, scheduled for New York via London, would make an
unscheduled stop in Athens for "technical reasons" and Soblen, the
U.S. marshall, and a doctor would switch planes. In this way the
government of Israel would not be in a position of appearing to have
deported him to life imprisonment in the United States.

The switch took place on schedule and Soblen left Athens on the way to London. When the plane was about a half hour out of London, Soblen, using a knife that he had hidden during dinner, slashed his left wrist and stabbed himself in the abdomen. When the plane landed he was taken to a hospital under close police guard. His condition was poor and an operation was performed.[58]

Soblen demanded political asylum in England. His supporters in the United States demanded that he be given sanctuary. An ad was placed in the leftist New York newspaper, *National Guardian*, of July 16, 1962, as well as in newspapers in England and other countries. The ad declared that "the people of England must grant him sanctuary. The right of sanctuary of a political fugitive, such Dr. Soblen most certainly is, has historically been one of the basic rights of man."

On August 2, the British home secretary, Brooke, announced that there was no ground for granting Dr. Soblen political asylum. He was not in danger of persecution in his own country for his political opinions or on racial grounds. Dr. Soblen was a convicted spy, a fugitive from sentence imposed on him by the courts of a country whose life is based on democratic institutions and constitutional guarantees. The home secretary concluded that his proper course was to reestablish the situation in which Dr. Soblen would have found himself on his arrival in England but for his self-inflicted wounds. In that situation he would undoubtedly and properly have been refused leave to land, and the airline would have been required to remove him at once on the plane on which he arrived, which was bound for the United States. The home secretary revealed that Soblen had asked to go to Czechoslovakia, "or some other country willing to receive him."[59]

On September 11, 1962, Soblen died in the hospital. Two days later the Soviet government newspaper, *IZVESTIA*, carried a lengthy article entitled "Robert Soblen's Tragic Death—American Secret Police Hounds Innocent Man to Death."[60]

The Soviets considered the Soble ring very important. They used it for espionage against the United States government as well as to collect information on their political enemies, such as the Trotskyites and the Zionists. At one point, Soble had at his disposal Soviet funds amounting to three and a half million dollars.[61]

The ring was controlled by the highest ranking Soviet intelligence officer operating in the United States, Vassili Mikhailovich Zubilin. According to the information supplied by the Soviet government to the State Department, Zubilin was born January 20, 1900, in Moscow. He served as attaché in the Soviet embassy in China in 1941, and that year was reassigned to the United States. What the Soviets did not advise the State Department was that Zubilin had operated as an "illegal" in the United States and in Germany in the 1930s, or that his real name was Zarubin. He arrived in San Francisco December 25, 1941, accompanied by his wife, who was identified as Elizabeth, and his son, Peter, nine years old.

The FBI identified Mrs. Zubilin as Liza Rosenberg. She had previously been the wife of another Soviet intelligence officer who died in the 1920s. Elizabeth had accompanied Zubilin when he was operating as an "illegal" in the United States and had applied for a U.S. passport under the name Sara Herbert. The FBI report says, "In her youth Liza was a very beautiful girl."[62]

Liza had shown her courage during the 1930s when she and her husband, Zubilin, operated illegally in Nazi Germany. As a Jew she was in particular danger.

Boris Morros was impressed by her "aristocratic manner." He described her as "a frail, pretty, middle-aged woman." Based on his conversations with other members of the ring, Morros believed that Liza (sometimes spelled Lisa) was the brains behind Zubilin. Her code name was Helen, and Morros reported that in discussions in the ring decisions were often made based on what Helen said.[63]

Liza Zubilin performed many services for Stalin. The most dramatic was in 1929, when she betrayed her lover, Jacob Blumkin, to Stalin's executioners. At that time she was known as Lisa Gorskaia. Gorsky was the name of her late husband.

Georges Agabekov, the OGPU chief in Constantinople, who defected in 1930, had known Blumkin (which he spelled Blumkine) as an intelligence officer in Turkey. In August, 1929, Agabekov was in Moscow for meetings with M. A. Trilisser, the head of the OGPU Foreign Department. Agabekov revealed in his autobiography:

> I was in the waiting room outside Trillisser's [sic] office, when a woman-collaborator of the section of Foreign Affairs,[64] Lisa Gorskaia, entered and insisted that Trillisser admit her at once to speak to him of an urgent matter. She remained in the office about an hour. The

next day a collaborator of the Eastern Section, Minsky, informed me, as a secret, that Blumkine had been arrested during the night by order of the Executive Committee headed by Kutchareff, Treasurer of the Section of Foreign Affairs. The cause of the arrest was unknown to my informer.

Much interested, I applied for information to Gorb, Trillisser's assistant, who informed me as follows:

Blumkine, during his residence at Constantinople, had made common cause with Trotzky, who thanks to Blumkine's cooperation, was able to send letters to his partisans in the U.S.S.R. by the Ogpu secret channels. Before returning to the U.S.S.R., Blumkine had agreed to enter into conversation as Trotzky's representative with Karl Radek and other Trotzkyites. Blumkine revealed all that to Gorskaia, a woman-collaborator of Foreign Affairs with whom he was intimate, and he tried to enroll her as a Trotzkyite. She pretended to consent but revealed all to Trillisser.

Kutchareff told me later the circumstances of Blumkine's arrest. The officers sent by the Executive Committee arrived in an auto before Blumkine's apartment about one o-clock in the morning just as Blumkine, accompanied by the Gorskaia, was entering an auto. Smelling a rat, Blumkine ordered his chauffeur to drive full speed. The other auto pursued and its occupants fired several shots. Of a sudden Blumkine ordered his chauffeur to stop and, turning to his companion, he said: "Lisa, you have betrayed me." Thereupon he stepped out on the street and called to the officers in the other auto, which was near: "Don't fire, I surrender." He was taken to the Ogpu prison, and the Secret Section took charge of his case.

Agabekov reported that as Blumkin was an OGPU officer, there was no need for a trial. A resolution of the OGPU Council was sufficient. When this leading body of the intelligence service discussed the issue, Yagoda urged the death penalty. Trilisser was opposed. Menzhinsky was undecided. Finally the Politburo, that is, Stalin, ended the deadlock. "The Central Committee of the Party approved the death sentence, and Blumkine was liquidated. He died young; at thirty."[65]

Alexander Orlov, the GPU chief in Spain who defected in 1938, also knew the Zubilins. He identified Lisa as "an intelligence officer in her own right, and she worked in my department." He knew that the Zubilins had worked underground in Germany on false passports. Orlov also knew the story of Lisa's betrayal of Blumkin. Orlov told the U.S. Senate that when Blumkin was only seventeen years old (he actually may have been nineteen) he was a member of the Social Revolutionary Party which was allied with the Bolsheviks. The party had supplied a considerable group to the Cheka, including Blumkin. The Social Revolutionaries disagreed with the Bolsheviks on signing the Brest-Litovsk Treaty with Germany. Because of this, Blumkin shot and killed the German ambassador to Russia, Mirbach. According to Orlov:

> The Politburo wanted to shoot him, but Trotsky became interested in that fellow, seventeen years old, and had a talk with him. Blumkin said: "I know you will shoot me, but if you will spare my life I will serve the revolution well." And Trotsky liked him, defended him, and made him chief of his bodyguard and of his military train. That was why later, in 1929, Blumkin, when he was abroad went to see Trotsky, which was his undoing.[66]

In 1937, when Hede Massing was becoming disillusioned with the Soviet Union, her GPU control officer told her that he was going to introduce her to a "very intelligent, very responsible comrade." She was brought together with a woman called Helen, whom she later realized was Lisa Zubilin. Massing described "Helen" as a person with "strange beautiful eyes," a face with small delicate features and a warm engaging smile. Her posture was poor, however, and Massing described Lisa's hands as "ugly." Lisa pressured Massing and her husband, Paul, to keep following the Soviet line. Finally they agreed to make a trip to the Soviet Union. Here they were interrogated by a man identified as Peter. He turned out to be Lisa's husband, Vassili Zubilin. Finally it was decided that they would be permitted to go home, with the understanding that they would continue to work for Soviet intelligence. This they did not intend to do.

In the summer of 1940 Lisa contacted Hede again, in an attempt to pressure her to continue to work for the Soviets. Massing was frightened of Lisa but nevertheless stood her ground. In 1943 Hede was contacted by Vassili Zubilin. His pressure, too, was unsuccessful. Hede and Paul Massing had broken with GPU for good. They were unaware during the 1943 meeting that Zubilin was in the United States under diplomatic cover.[67]

Vassili Zubilin, with his wife and son, departed the United States August 27, 1944, on an airplane bound for the Soviet Union.[68] On his return to the Centre, Zubilin assumed his real name, Vassili Mikhailovich Zarubin, and was assigned as a deputy assistant chief of the NKVD. From 1947, he served as a deputy chief and head of the Illegals Department, which directs Soviet intelligence officers abroad who operate without any obvious Soviet connection. He held the rank of general.[69] He was the recipient of Jack Soble's letter expressing his concerns about Zborowski.

11

World War II:
Spying on the Allies

D URING the heyday of Soviet espionage in the 1930s, the most
powerful inducement the Soviets could use to get Americans
to spy was anti-fascism. The Soviet Union portrayed itself as the
leader in the fight against Nazi Germany. In August 1939 the Soviets
deliberately threw away that inducement. They did it for more important political reasons, but nevertheless many of those who had
flocked to their banner fell away. On the other hand, few of those
involved in espionage, even though they had been recruited on the
basis of anti-fascism, were lost.

The Soviet-Nazi Pact

On August 23, 1939, Nazi Germany and Soviet Russia signed a pact
that shocked the world. The two governments agreed that neither
would make war on the other, or join with anyone else in making
war on the other. After almost a decade of anti-Nazi propaganda,
the Soviet Union had signed a nonaggression pact with Hitler. What
was not announced at that time but became apparent very soon,
was that there was an additional secret protocol to the pact that
allowed Nazi Germany and Soviet Russia to divide Poland when the
Nazis attacked. Later secret agreements provided for the Soviet
annexation of Latvia, Lithuania, and Estonia.[1]

The pact was announced on the same day in the Soviet Union
and Nazi Germany, August 31. Speaking to the Supreme Soviet,
Molotov said:

The chief importance of the Soviet-German Non-Aggression Pact lies in the fact that the two largest states of Europe have agreed to put an end to the enmity between them, to eliminate the menace of war and live at peace with one another, making narrower thereby the zone of possible military conflicts in Europe.

He went on to refer to Stalin's speech at the Eighteenth Congress of the Communist Party of the Soviet Union several months earlier. In a clear reference to England and France, Molotov said:

We find fresh corroboration of Stalin's warning that we must be particularly cautious with warmongers who are accustomed to have others pull their chestnuts out of the fire for them. We must be on guard against those who see an advantage to themselves in bad relations between the U.S.S.R. and Germany, in enmity between them, and who do not want peace and good neighborly relations between Germany and the Soviet Union.[2]

In a speech in the Reichstag on the same day, Hitler said, "I am happy to be able to announce to you here an event of an especial moment. . . .", and he announced the pact with Soviet Russia. As Hitler's speech took place a few hours after Molotov's, he said, "This pact was greeted with exactly the same enthusiasm in Moscow as you are showing for it here. I can only underline every word of Foreign Commisar Molotov's speech." Hitler went on to announce that the war had broken out against Poland, and he said, "I have ordered my air force to confine its attacks to military objectives. If the enemy believes, however, that this gives them a free hand to fight with other methods, then he will receive an answer that will knock him out." Hitler claimed that the Poles had fired on German territory. This, of course, was untrue, but Hitler went on to say, "From 5:45 this morning this fire has been returned and from now on bomb will be repaid with bomb; poison gas will be fought with poison gas." These threats, of course, were to force Poland into submission.[3]

On the evening of September 3, the Nazi foreign minister, Von Ribbentrop, sent a very urgent, strictly secret message to the German ambassador in Moscow. The ambassador was ordered to decode the message himself and to pass the information on to Molotov. The Nazi foreign minister said:

We definitely expect to have beaten the Polish Army decisively in a few weeks. . . . Please discuss this at once with Molotov and see if the Soviet Union does not consider it desirable for Russian forces to move at the proper time against Polish forces in the Russian sphere of interest and, for their part, to occupy this territory. In our estimation this would be not only a relief for us, but also, in the sense of the Moscow agreement, in the Soviet interest as well.[4]

Molotov responded the next day that the Soviets agreed they would move at a suitable time, but they did not think this was the proper time, as "we might injure our cause and promote unity among our opponents."[5]

On September 10 the German ambassador reported to the Foreign Office about a conference with Molotov that took place on that day. The ambassador said Molotov had reported:

The Soviet government was taken completely by surprise by the unexpectedly rapid German military successes. In accordance with our first communication, the Red Army had counted on several weeks, which had now shrunk to a few days. The Soviet military authorities were therefore in a difficult situation, since, in view of conditions here, they required possibly two or three weeks more for their preparations. Over three million men were already mobilized. I explained emphatically to Molotov how crucial speedy action of the Red Army was at this juncture. . . . Then Molotov came to the political side of the matter and stated that the Soviet Government had intended to take the occasion of the further advance of German troops to declare that Poland was falling apart and that it was necessary for the Soviet Union, in consequence, to come to the aid of the Ukrainians and White Russians "threatened" by Germany. This argument was to make the intervention of the Soviet Union plausible to the masses and at the same time avoid giving the Soviet Union the appearance of an aggressor.[6]

On September 14, Molotov told the Nazi ambassador that, in fact, the Soviet Union was ready to move and would do so as soon as Warsaw fell.[7] On September 17 Soviet troops crossed the Polish border. On September 19 Hitler spoke at a meeting in Danzig. This was the city deep in Polish territory, populated by Germans, that Hitler supposedly had gone to war to protect. In reality he had gone to war to take half of Poland. Hitler's public speech exposed the false excuse used by the Soviet Union for its invasion. He told the assembled Nazis:

> In the meantime Russia has on her part found it necessary to march into Poland to safeguard the interest of the White Russian and Ukrainian minorities there. We are now experiencing the phenomenon that England and France look upon this co-operation between Germany and Russia as a monstrous crime, one Englishman actually described it as perfidy—after all they ought to know. I suppose England considers this action perfidious because democratic England's attempt to co-operate with Bolshevist Russia failed, where as the attempt of National-Socialist Germany to co-operate with Bolshevist Russia has now succeeded.[8]

On October 31, 1939, in a report to the Supreme Soviet, Molotov, too, dropped all pretenses as to the Soviet role in the aggression against Poland. He said, "one swift blow to Poland, first by the German army and then by the Red Army, and nothing was left of this ugly offspring of the Versailles Treaty. . . ." He went on to say, "One may accept or reject the ideology of Hitlerism as well as any other ideological system; that is a matter of political views."[9]

Orders from Moscow

Britain and France had gone to war against Nazi Germany in response to the aggression against Poland. The initial reaction of the communist parties of those countries was to support their own governments in the fight against Nazism. The British Communist Party, in a manifesto issued September 2, said, "We are in support of all necessary measures to secure the victory of democracy over fascism."[10] However, they were soon to learn that this was not Moscow's view, and for Communists it was Moscow's view that counted. A written communication was sent to them from the Communist International, which laid out the line they were to take. It read in part:

> The present war is an imperialist and unjust war for which the bourgeoisie of all the belligerent states bear equal responsibility. In no country can the working class or the Communist Parties support the war. . . . The international working class may under no condi-

tions defend fascist Poland. . . . The division of states into fascist and democratic States has now lost its former sense. From this point of view the tactics must be changed. The tactics of the Communist Parties in the belligerent countries in this first stage of the war is to operate against the war, to unmask its imperialist character . . . . Where Communist Parties have representatives in Parliament these must vote against the war credits . . . . The Communist Parties which acted contrary to these tactics must now immediately correct their policy."[11]

The British Communists reversed their line and opposed the war effort.

The French Communists, also following Soviet orders, worked for the defeat of their own government in the face of the Nazi threat. The Communist Party members in the French Parliament were arrested and placed on trial. At their trial they responded:

We have been arrested and are being prosecuted because we are Communists, because we have remained Communists in spite of all solicitations, threats, and repressions. We are being prosecuted because we have opposed, and are opposing to the last ounce of our strength, the imperialist war which has afflicted our country. . . ."[12]

When France fell to the Nazis in June 1940, the Communist Party of France issued a declaration, which said, "A foreign army has burst into France. The French imperialists . . . unleashed the war. . . ."[13] The rest of France knew that the Nazis had started the war.

The American ambassador to France, William Bullitt, came home to report on the fall of France to the American people. He said:

In France much of the most terrible and traitorous work was done was by the Fascists and Communists working together. Many honest French democrats and liberals had been snared by Communist propaganda and argued that, because the Communists called themselves a political party and pretended at the time to be in favor of democracy, it would be undemocratic to deny the Communists the rights of any other political party. The honest French patriots and democrats who protected the Communists did not discover until too late that the Communists were acting as spies and agents of the dictators, that the Communist Party was merely camouflaged as a political party and was in reality a conspiracy to commit partricide [sic] at the direction of a foreign dictator. They discovered too late that the Communists were traitors who were claiming the protection of the state which they intended to destroy only in order to better prepare for its destruction. When the German invasion began to sweep into Belgium and France, there were Communist and Nazi agents of Germany in each town and village who produced panic among the civilian populations by spreading fantastic tales of murdering by the German troops of men, women and children. By this means ten million civilians were harried in fear from their homes and clogged all the roads, so that the French, British, and Belgian armies could not maneuver, so the transport of supplies became almost impossible, and a magnificent fighting force became a clotted mass of men and material, a perfect target for bombing and machine-gunning from the air. At the most crucial moment of the fighting in Belgium, other German agents, this time Communist railway men, stopped all traffic on the Belgium railways so that there was no transport by train for the French, British, and Belgian armies. Throughout France, especially in Paris, there were hundreds of Communist and Nazi agents of the dictators with extremely short-wave portable radio transmitting sets in their hiding-places. They kept the Germans fully informed of the movements of the French army and of the intentions of the French government.[14]

On December 1, 1939, the Communist Party USA newspaper, *Daily Worker*, headlined, "Red Army Hurls Back Invading Finnish Troops, Crosses Frontier." This bizarre headline was the paper's announcement that the Soviet Union had invaded Finland. An explanation for this invasion was given by the Communist International, which said:

> It was England, primarily, that spurred the reactionary Finnish bourgeoisie to reject the peace offer of the Soviet Union. . . . [T]hey are using every method to keep the Soviet Union "preoccupied" in a military way; to organize a number of military ventures against it. Thereby, they hope to make it difficult for the Soviet Union to supply Germany with the necessary war materials.[15]

Stalin, too, explained who was the warmonger and who was the fighter for peace. In November 1939 Stalin made a statement to *Pravda*, in which he said:

It was not Germany that attacked France and England, but France
and England that attacked Germany, thereby assuming responsibility
for the present war; after hostilities had broken out, Germany made
overtures of peace to France and England, and the Soviet Union
openly supported Germany's peace overtures. . . . The ruling circles of England and France rudely rejected both Germany's peace
overtures and the attempts of the Soviet Union to secure the earliest
possible termination of the war.[16]

The American Communist Party received its directions from Moscow by radio. It was an order to oppose the war and to undermine
the efforts of President Roosevelt to alert Americans to the dangers
of Nazi Germany. Two of the radio messages sent from Moscow to
the American Communist Party were provided by Earl Browder to
his friend Philip J. Jaffe, who published them in his book, *The Rise
and Fall of American Communism*.[17]

Responding to its directions, the Communist Party published
pamphlets with titles like *The Yanks Are Not Coming* and *No Gold
Stars for Us, Our Boys Stay Home*.[18] Leaflets were issued by the
party, addressed to different elements of the population. To the
Jews, an English- and Yiddish-language leaflet proclaimed, "Two
Million Jews Saved From the Clutches of Nazism." It said in part:
"One thing should loom big in everybody's mind—a large section
of the Jews in Poland are being liberated by the Red Army! This
should be paramount in everybody's mind when trying to evaluate
the present developments."

This leaflet was issued by the New York State Communist Party.
However, a leaflet issued to Italian-Americans did not have the same
kind of slogans. Also signed by the New York State Communist
Party, it claimed that "American imperialism led by Roosevelt is
also speeding toward war with the same imperialist aims on the side
of English and French imperialism. The American war makers are
leveling the term 'Fifth Columnists' against those who want peace
and security." A leaflet issued in the predominantly German section
of Ridgewood, Queens, by the Communist Party was titled
"German-Americans want peace!" It said in part:

At this very moment a so-called German-American Congress for Democracy has been called to shuttle millions of freedom-loving
German-Americans into support of the war. This congress, initiated

by the Social Democratic leaders, would betray the interest of the American people in favor of British and American imperialism. The fight of the German-Americans must be directed against Roosevelt, Churchill, and Hitler.[19]

The Young Communist League was particularly active in the antiwar movement. At its National Council meeting in New York City May 5-7, 1940, the president of the YCL, Max Weiss, claimed:

The Roosevelt Administration, acting in alliance with the dominant circles of the Republican Party, is dragging America into the war on the side of the Allies. It no longer bothers to make even a pretense at neutrality. It is today acting as the open, non-belligerent ally of British and French imperialism. . . . But America can be kept out of the imperialist war if the people impose their will on Wall Street, if they reject and defeat the war policy of the Roosevelt Administration which is today the aggressive mouth-piece of Wall Street imperialism![20]

A whole series of pamphlets were issued, signed by Congressman Vito Marcantonio, in which he challenged President Roosevelt and accused him of trying to lead us into war. These pamphlets were published by a group called the American Peace Mobilization, which was a front for the Communist Party.[21]

Even the Cultural Section of the Communist Party got into the act. The Almanac Singers, a group of entertainers, most of whom were members of the Communist Party, published a collection of songs that included such lines as "Remember when the AAA killed a million hogs a day, instead of hogs it's men today, plow the fourth one under, plow under, plow under, plow under, every fourth American boy." In another song they sang, "Franklin, oh Franklin, sent Harry over the sea, but Franklin, you can't send me." These anti-Roosevelt songs were used at various Communist and Communist front meetings including those of the American Peace Mobilization.[22]

The Nazi propaganda machine was paying for the publication of books in the United States through a publisher called Flanders Hall. Some of these books were simply reprints of books that appeared in Nazi Germany. For example, *One Hundred Families Rule the British Empire* first appeared in Berlin as part of a series called "Britain Unmasked" from the German Information Service. Flanders Hall published the identical book in the United States with an introduction by the pro-Nazi propagandist, George Sylvester Viereck. Another Flanders Hall book, *Democracy on the Nile, How Britain Has "Protected" Egypt*, was signed with the odd name, Sayid Halassie, D.D. It was a direct translation of a book published in Berlin, *Englands Gewaltpolitik Am Nil*, credited to Paul Schmitz from Cairo. This German-language publication was also part of the "England Ohne Maske" series.

One publication that was not a reprint of a German original, however, was published by Flanders Hall under the title *Seven Periods of Irish History*. This book was edited by Communist poet, Shaemas O'Sheel. O'Sheel was also the compiler of another anti-British Flanders Hall book, *Lothian vs. Lothian*. The foreword to the book, signed James Burr Hamilton, was also written by O'Sheel.

Louis Budenz, former editor of the *Daily Worker*, later charged that during the Soviet-Nazi Pact period, "American Communists were shutting down a considerable portion of American defense production through the Allis-Chalmers, North American Aircraft and other strikes." He stated that these actions were taken on the orders of the leadership of the American Communist Party.[23]

Harvey Klehr, in his history of American communism in the 1930s, argued that these strikes were for "good and sufficient trade union reasons." He nevertheless admitted that the communists were using them as political strikes against the war effort. Klehr identified the strike leaders as members of the Communist Party.[24]

Political strikes, aiding Nazi propaganda against the Allies, and attempting to prevent the United States from arming against the Nazi threat were not the only activities conducted by American Communists against President Roosevelt's attempt to build America's strength. The Soble spy ring also provided information on Jewish anti-Nazi activities to the Soviets. In addition, the Golos spy ring had Albert Kahn spying on Jewish and anti-Nazi organizations during the Soviet-Nazi Pact period, to gather information on anti-Soviet activities in the United States.

A Change of Heart

On June 21, 1941,[25] Nazi Germany broke the Soviet-Nazi Pact and attacked the Soviet Union. The Communist Party USA front, the American Peace Mobilization, changed its name to American Peoples Mobilization. It published a pamphlet signed by Congressman Vito Marcantonio demanding that the United States get into the war. On the back of the pamphlet were the demands: "Join Great Britain in opening a western front against Hitler! Stop the Japanese fascists in their tracks! Increase U.S. production a hundred-fold! Release a torrent of planes, tanks and other war materials to the soldiers of the Soviet Union, Great Britain, and China!" There were no more political strikes.[26] Now American war production was necessary to aid the Soviet Union.

In 1944 Congressman Marcantonio wrote another pamphlet, this time calling for the reelection of President Roosevelt. This was published by the International Workers Order, a Communist front. It had an introduction written by Max Bedacht, who a decade before had been the Soviet Intelligence Service liaison with the American Communists.[27]

Henry Winston reported to a meeting of the National Committee of the Young Communist League on July 19, 1941, how his organization had reacted to the attack on the Soviet Union. He said:

> When the news of the attack came over the air midnight Saturday, many of our young comrades were coming home tired and ready for a good sleep. Yet, these comrades . . . sat up all night eagerly waiting until the headquarters would be open, ready for activity in the fight to crush Hitlerism. . . . They literally stormed the headquarters to engage in the many-sided activities that were bound to develop as a result of this attack, and to help win the people in support of the Soviet Union and Britain in the fight to smash and wipe Hitlerism from the face of the earth.[28]

The Soviets were taken by surprise by the Nazi attack, but they and the communists around the world reacted quickly. Only Stalin did not. Molotov made a radio address on June 22 calling on the people to support the Soviet government's war effort. Stalin did not get around to making his radio address until July 3.[29]

One of the first Soviet pamphlets to come out after the attack made it plain how the Soviets viewed the Nazis, their former friends, who were now the enemy. It said:

> The fascist cutthroats proclaim themselves a "superior race" whose mission it is to rule the world. A "superior race"!—could anything

be more farcical?. . . This hot bed of perversion, of prostitution and homosexualism a "superior race"! These inhuman and bloodthirsty gangsters a "superior race"!

It goes on to refer to the Nazis as "modern cannibals."[30]

Although Stalin was slow to get into action, the Comintern was not. On June 22, 1941, an expanded session of the Secretariat of the Comintern's Executive Committee was held in Moscow. Among those present were Dimitrov, Manuilsky, and the leaders of the Czech, German, and Italian Communist parties. Dimitrov made a report on the tasks of the Communist movement. Orders were issued. The Communist parties were to unleash armed struggle against the Nazis all over Nazi-occupied Europe. As the Central Committee of the Communist party of Germany and most of the leadership of the Communist parties of Bulgaria, Hungary, Poland, Rumania, Czechoslovakia, and other countries were in Moscow, they ordered their members to begin the insurrection.[31] The Bulgarian Communist Party held a meeting two days after the Comintern met, on June 24. They, of course, ordered an armed insurrection. Within a few days, the first troops took to the mountains with their weapons. By June 27 they were in combat.[32]

The Comintern radio began broadcasting into Europe, urging insurrectionary activities against the Nazis. By January 1942, 162 broadcasts in thirteen languages were conducted each week. Soon, more than forty radio stations were broadcasting from Soviet soil on behalf of the Comintern, urging military operations behind the German lines.[33]

Tito's close associate, Edvard Kardelj, described how the radios were set up for Yugoslavia.

> The "Slobodna Jugoslavija" [Free Yugoslavia] Radio Station was set up on December 11, 1941, in Ufa, U.S.S.R. It broadcasted news within the system of the Comintern Radio Station. From April 1942 until it ceased operating in January 1945, the Station broadcasted programmes from Moscow. Its broadcasts were in Serbo-Croatian and Slovene, and from mid-1944, in Macedonian. From 1943, it broadcasted news in different languages for the people in occupied Europe.[34]

Tito had reentered Yugoslavia prior to the Nazi invasion on a false passport supplied by Soviet intelligence. It had been obtained from an International Brigadier fighting in Spain. In 1944, Howard Fast, then an active member of the American Communist Party, boasted that, "An agent of the Joint Anti-Fascist Refugee Committee contacted Tito, and the Committee provided funds and means for Tito's return to Yugoslavia."[35] If in fact this is true, it indicates that this organization, which was a front for the Communist Party USA, was deeply involved with Soviet intelligence false passport operations.

On June 22, 1941, as soon as the Nazi attack on the Soviet Union became known, the Communist Party of Yugoslavia held a Central Committee meeting and issued a proclamation calling for armed insurrection. The party did not do so on April 6, 1941, when German and Italian troops attacked and occupied their country, but only when the Soviet Union was attacked.[36]

Soviet Spying on the Allies

Despite the Soviet need for American and British participation in the war, Soviet intelligence still operated against the Allies. Through such intelligence efforts the secrets of the atom bomb were obtained for the Soviet Union. The postwar Soviet military threat against Western Europe based on Soviet atomic weapons was the result of their successful espionage.

On April 10, 1943, Zubilin, then the NKVD *rezident*, met with Steve Nelson, a member of the CPUSA National Committee.[37] A U.S. government security report, made available to the Senate, revealed:

> At the time of this meeting, Zubilin was working the Comintern apparatus. Nelson advised Zubilin that his work on behalf of the apparatus had been predicated upon a note from Moscow, which had been brought to him by a courier from New York and that Earl Browder was fully cognizant of the fact that he, Nelson, was engaged in secret work for the Soviets.[38]

Nelson had studied at the Lenin School in Moscow, the training school for communist leaders from all over the world. It still exists and is sometimes called the Higher Party School of the CPSU. Nelson had served as a Comintern courier in Nazi Germany and Switzerland. He had also served as the political commissar of the Abraham Lincoln Battalion in Spain.[39]

During Nelson's meeting with Zubilin, he complained that party members had been recruited directly by the Soviets. They were given espionage assignments and instructions not to say anything to their party superiors. Nelson suggested that to avoid complications the Soviets choose a party official in each city or state where such espionage activities were being carried on. This "trustworthy contact" would be able to deal with both the Communist Party apparatus and the Soviets and could "handle direct contact with the Communist members" who would be involved in espionage.[40]

The previous month, a person identifying himself as "Joe" met with Nelson at his home. According to a Congressional report, "Joe" "furnished Nelson with some highly confidential data regarding the nuclear experiments then in progress at the radiation laboratories at the University of California at Berkeley. The experiments at the University of California had then reached the experimental stage of the atom bomb." "Joe" was identified as Joseph W. Weinberg.

Several days after this meeting Nelson arranged through the Soviet Consulate in San Francisco to meet with Peter Ivanov, a vice consul. When Nelson suggested that the meeting be at a place where they could not be observed, Ivanov responded that the "usual place" would be safe enough. Government agents observed the meeting, which took place in an open park on the grounds of St. Francis Hospital in San Francisco. Nelson was observed passing an envelope or package to Ivanov.[41]

An intelligence report made available to Congress in 1949 contained more details of Nelson's relationship with Weinberg. It said:

> A very reliable and highly confidential informant advised that certain instructions had been given by Steve Nelson, who was at the time a member of the national committee of the Communist Party of the United States, to the scientist identified herein as Joseph W. Weinberg, a research physicist connected with the atomic bomb at the University of California, at Berkeley, Calif. The instructions were that Weinberg should furnish Nelson with information concerning the atomic bomb project so that Nelson could, in turn, deliver it to the proper officials of the Soviet Government. Nelson advised Weinberg to furnish him any information which he might obtain from trustworthy Communists working on the atomic project; he, Nelson, being of the belief that collectively the Communist scientists working on the project could assemble all the information regarding the man-

ufacture of the atomic bomb. Nelson told Weinberg that all Communists engaged on the atomic bomb project should destroy their Communist Party membership books, refrain from using liquor, and use every precaution regarding their espionage activities.

The congressional committee reported that during Nelson's meeting with Zubilin, Nelson was given "10 bills of unknown denominations."[42]

In testimony before the committee, Weinberg denied having ever met Nelson or having provided him with any information regarding the atomic bomb. Nelson invoked the Fifth Amendment on whether he knew Weinberg. A former U.S. Army Counter-Intelligence Corps officer, James Sterling Murray, testified before the committee that on August 12, 1943, he conducted a physical surveillance of Weinberg and observed Steve Nelson enter Weinberg's home, and that he could see them together through a window.[43]

Although Nelson would not answer questions before a congressional committee, he argued in his autobiography that the charges against him were untrue. While admitting that "there may have been a Soviet espionage network operating in this country," he argued that "common sense would dictate against recruiting prominent Party officials."[44] Despite Nelson's denials, the evidence is overwhelming that the activity took place, that Communist Party officials were involved in Soviet espionage—starting in the 1920s—and that Nelson was one of those involved. His meetings with Zubilin and Ivanov were observed by the FBI. Zubilin was the NKVD *rezident* in the United States. He was not wasting his time on casual meetings.

Ivanov also used another contact to obtain atomic information. In late 1942, Ivanov contacted George Charles Eltenton and requested that he obtain information concerning some highly secret experiments on the atomic bomb that were being carried out at the Radiation Laboratory of the University of California, Berkeley. A congressional report revealed:

After this contact by Ivanov, Eltenton in turn approached Haakon Chevalier and requested him to assist in obtaining the desired information. Eltenton explained that he had a direct contact with an official of the Soviet government and that this official had explained that since Russia and the United States were allies, the Soviet government was entitled to any technical data that might be of assistance to that country. Chevalier following this approach of Eltenton, contacted J. Robert Oppenheimer, the director of the atomic bomb project, and told him of the conversation he had with Eltenton. Oppenheimer told Chevalier that he considered such acts or such attempts to obtain information on this project as constituting treason against the United States.[45]

Coincidentally, Steve Nelson also knew Oppenheimer. The wife of Oppenheimer had been a member of the Communist Party and had previously been married to Joe Dallet, an American volunteer killed in Spain. Nelson published the letters written from Spain by Dallet, whom he referred to as "my closest friend and comrade."[46] He obtained the letters from Kitty, who later became Mrs. Oppenheimer.

Oppenheimer testified at a hearing of the Personnel Security Board of the Atomic Energy Commission in 1954. He indicated that he had met Nelson for the first time in 1939 and that during 1941 and 1942 Nelson had visited his home on various occasions. He denied that Nelson asked him questions about his work on atomic energy.[47]

The development of the atomic bomb by the United States also attracted the attention of a veteran Soviet intelligence officer, Arthur Adams. The first Soviet intelligence officer to operate in the United States, Adams left in 1921 after the closing of the Soviet pseudo embassy in New York. He returned for various assignments in 1927, 1932, and 1936. In 1938 he returned with a fraudulent Canadian birth certificate. He became a permanent resident in the U.S. with the help of Samuel Novick. During World War II Novick became president of the Electronics Corporation of America, which held six million dollars worth of government contracts to produce highly secret items related to radar installations. As part of Adams's cover, he used the offices of ECA as well as those of Keynote Recordings, a firm that manufactured phonograph records.

On April 28, 1944, Adams visited Chicago and met Clarence Hiskey, a scientist at the University of Chicago. Congressional investigators concluded:

It became obvious that Hiskey had for some time been supplying Adams with secret information regarding atomic research. Immediately after seeing Adams, Hiskey flew to Cleveland, Ohio, where he

contacted John Hitchcock Chapin. Chapin, through the urging of
Clarence Hiskey, agreed to take over Hiskey's contacts with Adams.[48]

Chapin testified before a congressional committee in 1948 and
admitted that Hiskey had put him in touch with Arthur Adams, who
was identified by Hiskey as "a Russian agent." While Chapin met
with Adams a few times, he denied providing him with any classified
information.[49]

When questioned by congressional investigators, Samuel Novick
claimed that he met Adams for the first time in 1938. When confronted with a statement that he had made to the Immigration and
Naturalization Service on December 19, 1937, that Arthur Adams
had been employed by him in Canada for ten years, Novick claimed
that he could not recall whether his statement had been correct or
when he actually met Adams.

Eric Bernay, the head of Keynote Recordings, claimed that he
met Adams in 1941 or 1942 and hired him as an engineer. He claimed
that he never suspected Adams of being a Soviet agent but did know
that he was under constant surveillance by the U.S. government.
In February 1945, Adams decided to return to the Soviet Union.
He borrowed money from Bernay and went to Portland, Oregon,
where he attempted to board a Soviet vessel. FBI agents prevented
him from going aboard. He then returned to New York and vanished
before he could be arrested.[50]

The real break in the U.S. government investigation of atomic
espionage came when a Soviet code clerk, Igor Gouzenko, defected
in Canada in September 1945. He exposed a substantial network of
people working for Soviet Military Intelligence. Gouzenko told the
Canadian Royal Commission on Espionage that before leaving Moscow he was supplied with a "legend," as were all Soviet intelligence
personnel. When asked what this term meant he answered:

> This legend consists of a fictitious biography of the individual, showing
> that he was born at a certain place, that he received a certain edu-
> cation, that he received certain training, all with the object of covering
> up the fact that he is engaged in intelligence work. Another object
> of compiling this legend is so as to make it impossible for the rep-
> resentatives of foreign powers in Moscow to check up on the data
> given about the individual.[51]

Gouzenko removed a number of significant documents from the
embassy safe when he defected. One of them indicated that a sci-

entist at McGill University in Montreal had supplied information
on the RDX explosive formula. In testimony before the Royal Commission on March 7, 1946, Dr. Raymond Boyer admitted that he
had supplied the information on RDX to Fred Rose, an official of
the Canadian Communist Party.[52]

Documents provided by Gouzenko became the string that unrav-
eled more atomic spying. Telegram 244 was in the handwriting of
the Soviet Military Intelligence chief in Canada, Colonel Zabotin.
It referred to an agent using the code name Alek and provided a
plan to meet Alek in London giving passwords and identification
signs. Moscow's response to the telegram provided new passwords
and a meeting in front of the British Museum. Canadian intelligence
identified Alek as Dr. Allan Nunn May, a reader in physics at London
University and a member of the British government organization
working on the atom bomb. He was in Canada at the time, but the
Canadian government decided to allow May to return to London so
that his meeting with the Soviets could be observed and thus provide
leads for British intelligence. The meeting did not take place.[53]

A report to Moscow dated August 9, 1945, advised the "Director"
about the latest information provided by May (Alek). It was signed
"Grant," Zabotin's code name:

To the Director,
　　Facts given by Alek: (1) The test of the atomic bomb was conducted
in New Mexico, (with "49", "94-239"). The bomb dropped on Japan
was made of uranium 235. It is known that the output of uranium
235 amounts to 400 grams daily at the magnetic separation plant at
Clinton. The output of "49" is likely two times greater (some graphite
units are planned for 250 mega watts, i.e. 250 grams each day). The
scientific research work in this field is scheduled to be published,
but without the technical details. The Americans already have a published book on this subject.
　　(2) Alek handed over to us a platinum with 162 micrograms of
uranium 233 in the form of oxide in a thin lamina. We have had no
news about the mail.

Grant[54]

May was arrested and pleaded guilty to espionage. He was sentenced to ten years in jail. May made a remarkable confession, and
described his motives for spying for the Soviets. He said:

About a year ago whilst in Canada, I was contacted by an individual whose identity I decline to divulge. He called on me at my private apartment in Swail Avenue, Montreal. He apparently knew I was employed by the Montreal laboratory and he sought information from me concerning atomic research.

I gave and had given very careful consideration to correctness of making sure that development of atomic energy was not confined to U.S.A. I took the very painful decision that it was necessary to convey general information on atomic energy and make sure it was taken seriously. For this reason I decided to entertain proposition made to me by the individual who called on me.

After this preliminary meeting I met the individual on several subsequent occasions whilst in Canada. He made specific requests for information, which were just nonsense to me—I mean by this that they were difficult for me to comprehend. But he did request samples of uranium from me and information generally on atomic energy.

At one meeting I gave the man microscopic amounts of U.233 and U.235 (one of each). The U.235 was a slightly enriched sample and was in a small glass tube and consisted of about a milliogram [*sic*] of oxide. The U.233 was about a tenth of a milliogram and was a very thin deposit on a platinum oil and was wrapped in a piece of paper.

I also gave the man a written report on atomic research as known to me. This information was mostly of a character which has since been published or is about to be published.

The man also asked me for information about the U.S. electronically controlled A.A. shells. I knew very little about these and so could give only very little information. . . .

The man gave me . . . some dollars (I forget how many) in a bottle of whiskey and I accepted these against my will.

Before I left Canada it was arranged that on my return to London I was to keep an appointment with somebody I did not know. I was given precise details as to making contact but I forget them now. I did not keep the appointment because I had decided that this clandestine procedure was no longer appropriate in view of the official release of information and the possibility of satisfactory international control of atomic energy."[55]

German-born Klaus Fuchs was one of the scientists sent from Britain to assist in the development of atomic weapons. Based on leads provided by U.S. authorities, the British arrested Fuchs. He also confessed to atomic espionage and said:

When I learned about the purpose of the work I decided to inform Russia and I established contact through a member of the Communist Party. Since that time I have had continual contacts with persons completely unknown to me, except that they would give information to the Russians. At this time I had complete confidence in Russian policy and I had no hesitation in giving all the information I had.

Fuchs was sentenced to fourteen years in jail.[56]

Klaus Fuchs died in 1988. He was a member of the Central Committee of the Socialist Unity Party (SED), the Communist Party of East Germany. The biographical sketch attached to a 1984 article by him in an East German magazine says:

In 1950 he was imprisoned in England on account of his persistent opposition to the U.S.A.'s atom bomb monopoly. Since 1959 he has played a leading part in GDR nuclear research, and since their creation in 1973 and 1979 he has been chairman of the scientific councils of the Academy of Sciences for problems of basic research in energetics and microelectronics.[57]

The British allowed the FBI to interview Fuchs. He led them to Harry Gold, the courier used by the Soviets to maintain contact with Fuchs while he was in the United States. Harry Gold led the FBI to the Rosenbergs.

Gold had served the Soviets for many years. His job was to contact individuals who were supplying the Soviets with information and to carry that information back to Soviet intelligence officers. He confessed, and led the FBI first to David Greenglass, and through him to Greenglass's sister and brother-in-law, Ethel and Julius Rosenberg. When Ronald Radosh and Joyce Milton began their research on the Rosenberg case, they were convinced that the Rosenbergs were innocent. The research proved the opposite, however. Their classic book, *The Rosenberg File*, published in 1983, stands out as an example of intellectual honesty and careful research.

The Rosenbergs were convicted, sentenced to death and, in 1953, executed. The recruiter for their spy ring, Morton Sobell, was sentenced to thirty years. The judge pointed out that since the evidence did not show any direct involvement in atom espionage, but only with espionage activity generally, he could not sentence Sobell to death.[58]

A major campaign was conducted on behalf of the Rosenbergs. Some who believed them guilty asked for clemency rather than the death penalty. As late as 1970 a sympathetic play titled *Inquest*, written by Donald Freed, opened on Broadway, with such well-known actors as George Grizzard, playing Julius Rosenberg, Anne Jackson, playing his wife Ethel, and James Whitmore as their attorney.[59]

Rabbi S. Andhil Fineberg in an early book on the case made it very clear that he believed the Rosenbergs guilty. He accused the defenders of the Rosenbergs of engaging in the "Big Lie." Rabbi Fineberg pointed out that the Rosenbergs were being pressed by the government to reveal what they knew about Soviet espionage in return for a lighter sentence. He quoted their response in a statement read to a March 1952 rally to free the Rosenbergs: "But we will not pay the price that is asked of us to betray our hopes for the peaceful, neighborly, democratic world which our children and all children need if they are to carry on the human race."[60]

Rabbi Fineberg also pointed to a rather bizarre incident, where files had been stolen from the office of the attorney for David Greenglass. Greenglass had turned state's evidence and testified against his sister and brother-in-law. The stolen documents did not prove that Greenglass had not told the truth, but the Rosenberg supporters pretended that they did. In order to explain how they had obtained the stolen documents, the Rosenberg Defense Committee in the United States claimed that they had received them from the Rosenberg Committee in France. But the documents had been stolen in New York.[61]

Former FBI official Robert Lamphere, in a 1986 book, revealed that information obtained through breaking a Soviet code had provided corroboration of the Rosenbergs' espionage activity but could not be used in court to prevent the Soviets from knowing that the code had been broken. He further revealed that in 1957 the FBI found a piece of microfilm in an old wallet owned by the Soviet "illegal," Rudolf Abel, which instructed him to provide money to the "wife of Stone." Stone was the code name for Morton Sobell. The money was to be given to her by Reino Hayhanen, a Soviet officer working for Abel. Hayhanen kept the money, but after his arrest advised the FBI that he knew that Helen Sobell was an agent herself.[62]

During the trial of Abel, Hayhanen testified that he and Abel took a trip to Bear Mountain Park, north of New York City, where he buried five thousand dollars. That money was to be given to Helen Sobell. He was supposed to bring her to the park to give her the money. Abel told him that these were the instructions from Moscow. However, Hayhanen dug up the money, kept it, and told Abel that he had given it to Mrs. Sobell. [63]

Conventional, non-atomic espionage also continued. One such case in 1945 was "fixed" on a very high level. In early 1945, the OSS was concerned that a secret report it had supplied to the State Department had appeared in a pro-communist magazine in New York called *Amerasia*. The OSS decided that a surreptitious entry into the office of *Amerasia* would lead them to the culprits. At midnight on March 11, 1945, five OSS officers, one a locksmith, broke into the *Amerasia* offices. They found stacks of classified documents, including five OSS reports that no one knew were missing, such classified information as "the bombing program for Japan," and other military secrets. They also found sophisticated photostating equipment. It was difficult to explain this, since *Amerasia* was printed on cheap paper and carried no pictures. The explanation appeared to be that this equipment was used to photostat classified documents.

On June 6, 1945, six persons were arrested on espionage charges. They were John S. Service and Emmanuel Larsen, both of the State Department; Andrew Roth, a reserve lieutenant in Naval Intelligence; Mark Gayn, a journalist; Philip J. Jaffe (a close friend of Communist Party leader, Earl Browder) and Kate Mitchell, the coeditors of *Amerasia*. Jaffe, a wealthy man, was the financial backer of the magazine. For a few months there was much delay. The case was removed from one grand jury and given to another. Mitchell, Gayn, and Service had their cases dropped. The three remaining were charged only with conspiracy to steal government property. The charge against Roth was then dropped by the government. Larson was fined five hundred dollars. During Jaffe's trial the prosecutor claimed that Jaffe only wanted the documents for "background material" for articles in his magazine. Jaffe was fined two thousand five hundred dollars. He boasted in a pamphlet published in 1979 that he was carrying five thousand dollars to pay the fine he expected. [64]

An explanation of the light sentences and lack of interest in the case became apparent when the FBI released under the Freedom of Information Act information based on wiretap records. These records revealed that Thomas Corcoran, a well-known wheeler-dealer during the Roosevelt and Truman administrations, had taken a hand in the matter. Corcoran spoke with Lauchlin Currie at the White House about the case. Two years later Currie was publicly accused by Elizabeth Bentley of being a member of a Soviet ring. Currie denied the accusation but left the country rather than face charges.

Currie encouraged Corcoran to defend the *Amerasia* defendants. Corcoran said that he was particularly interested in protecting Service. The FBI log of the telephone conversation reveals that "Currie then made inquiry as to whether Corcoran thought he could possibly do something on the side, to which Corcoran said that he could and mentioned that if he has to, he may even come out in front, but he would rather not have to do this." A meeting was held with Corcoran, Currie, and Service at Currie's office at the White House to discuss the case.

On July 24, 1945, Corcoran contacted the U.S. attorney for the District of Columbia, Edward M. Curran. They discussed whether the grand jury could just drop the case so that the government could "get off the hook." Corcoran said, that they ought to just let the "damn thing drop" or they would have another one of those sedition cases on their hands.

Corcoran made many other telephone calls to Justice Department officials pressing that the case be dropped.[65] As a result, what started as an espionage case dwindled away. The image of a high-ranking White House official, Currie, later accused of Soviet connections, suggesting that a "fixer," Corcoran, "do something on the side," does little for our respect for the criminal justice system. It explains why there was no espionage case against the *Amerasia* group.

While actively spying on the United States, the Soviet Union also spied on Great Britain, its other wartime ally. The famous cases of Kim Philby, Guy Burgess, Donald Maclean, and Anthony Blunt have filled many books. But there are some interesting sidelights to the cases that have not been explored. One of the Soviets who recruited many of these people to communism when they were students at prestigious British universities has been identified as Semyon N. Rostovsky. He is better known under his pen name, Ernst Henry (or Henri).[66] He also uses the name A. Leonidov when writing for *New Times*, a Soviet magazine closely connected with the KGB. His biographical sketch appeared in *New Times* on April 3, 1963:

> A. Leonidov is the pen name of the well-known Soviet journalist Semyon N. Rostovsky. Born in 1904, he has been active in journalism since the twenties and has been widely published in the Soviet Union and Western Europe. Two of his better known books, *Hitler Over Europe?* and *Hitler Over Russia?* were published in the thirties under the pen name Ernst Henri. A masterly exposure of Nazi aggressive plans, they had a wide readership in many parts of the world.

Hitler Over Europe? was published in the United States in 1934 by Simon and Schuster. Henry is also noted for writing Soviet pamphlets attacking the People's Republic of China and the United States. He is a specialist in anti-Semitic and anti-Catholic polemics. In 1963, using the Leonidov name, he wrote an article about Spain, claiming, in a tone reminiscent of Nazi propaganda, that the Rothschilds dominated that country.[67]

In May 1962, under the name Ernst Henry, he represented the Communist Party of the Soviet Union at a conference organized by the editorial board of *World Marxist Review*, the international Communist theoretical organ. The conference was entitled, "Anti-Communism, Enemy of Mankind." Henry told the conference that there was great danger because a Catholic was the president of the United States and that clericalism controlled the country.[68]

Ivan Maisky was the wartime Soviet ambassador to Great Britain. In his officially authorized biography he revealed that the embassy's publication *Soviet War News Weekly* was edited by S. N. Rostovsky. Maisky pointed out that in the prewar years Rostovsky operated as a journalist in Europe under the name Ernst Henry.[69] The ubiquitous Henry was a Soviet diplomat, a journalist and a communist recruiter.

A Soviet magazine recently interviewed Henry. He revealed that he was an old apparatchik of the Comintern, serving in Poland in the 1920s and in Germany until Hitler took power. After a short imprisonment in Germany he escaped to England. Assigned to write an anti-Nazi book, he signed it Ernst Henry, which he described as an "enigmatic name that could belong equally to an Englishman or a German or an American."[70] He still lives in Moscow, and still serves the Soviet regime, although he is now very critical of Stalin.

One young British intellectual who served the Communist cause well was James Klugmann. In the postwar period, as he served as a member of the Executive Committee of the British Communist Party and lectured on behalf of the party's Central Education Department on the subject of Socialist realism.[71] Klugmann, as a British intelligence officer in Cairo during World War II, served the Soviet cause by suppressing messages from Yugoslavia showing the anti-Nazi fighting by the non-Communist Mihailovich, and promoting Tito as the only anti-Nazi force.[72]

Creating a Soviet-controlled Eastern Europe

Not only Yugoslavia, but Poland, too, was destined to have a communist government. A carefully orchestrated plan was used by the Soviets to ensure that non-Communists would not rule postwar Poland. The first indication came when the NKVD rearrested Henryk Erlich and Victor Alter, the leaders of the Jewish-Socialist Bund. As active anti-fascists, the two had escaped the Nazi army and found themselves in Soviet hands. As the Soviet-Nazi Pact was in force, the two Jewish Socialists were arrested by the NKVD in September 1939.

After the Nazi attack on Russia they were released, after spending two years in Soviet prisons. Shortly after the release Colonel Aron Volkovisky of the NKVD suggested that they help form a worldwide Jewish anti-fascist committee. Despite their critical attitude toward the Soviet Union, they agreed. They drew up plans to organize the committee and wrote manifestos to be dropped by Soviet planes behind German lines, urging the Jews in Nazi-occupied Poland to resist the Nazi Army. They said, "The German beast will receive a knock-out . . . . We call upon you to fight. Be brave in battle. May your fight today be your pride tomorrow." Despite this work, in December 1941 they were rearrested.

In January 1943, a group of distinguished Americans, including leaders of the American labor movement, sent a cable to Molotov asking for the release of Erlich and Alter. The signers included William Green, president, American Federation of Labor; Philip Murray, president, Congress of Industrial Organizations; and Albert Einstein. Molotov sent his answer on February 23, 1943, addressed to William Green. The answer was delivered by the Soviet ambassador to the United States, Maxim Litvinov, who was highly regarded among both American Jews and the labor movement. The answer, however, was as brutal as it was false in its accusations against the two victims. Molotov said:

> For active subversive work against the Soviet Union and assistance to Polish intelligence organs in armed activities, Erlich and Alter were sentenced to capital punishment in August 1941. At the request of the Polish government, Erlich and Alter were released in September 1941. However, after they were set free, at the time of the most desperate battles of the Soviet troops against the advancing Hitler army, they resumed their hostile activities including appeals to the Soviet troops to stop bloodshed and immediately to conclude peace with Germany. For this they were rearrested and, in December 1942, sentenced once more to capital punishment by the Military Collegium of the Supreme Court. This sentence has been carried out in regard to both of them.[73]

The Soviet disregard for world public opinion was soon repeated. In April 1943 the Nazis discovered the bodies of more than four thousand Polish officers who had been massacred and buried in the Katyn Forest; actually eleven thousand had been killed. The Nazis, who murdered millions in the same way, saw this as an opportunity to tar the Soviets with the same brush. The evidence was quite clear: the Polish officers had been murdered while the Soviets controlled the burial area, which was near Smolensk in the Soviet Union. American and British doctors who were prisoners of war were brought to the scene to help with the examination of the bodies and to verify the dates of death.

In 1952 a congressional committee reinvestigated the crime and concluded:

> This committee believes the tragic concessions at Yalta might not have taken place if the Polish officer corps. had not been violated by the Soviets at Katyn. With proper leadership, the Polish army could have relieved a great deal of the early reverses suffered by the Allies.[74]

In addition to the extensive documentation and testimony that proved the Soviet culpability for the massacre, the committee also learned that the U.S. Office of War Information had attempted to intimidate Polish-language radio stations in the United States, which had attributed the crime to the Soviets. The man named as the OWI official responsible for the intimidation was Alan Cranston, now a United States senator. In testimony before the committee, Cranston argued that he was only making suggestions, not attempting to intimidate, when he said that the Polish broadcasters were "going haywire" when they discussed the Katyn massacre.[75] However, in 1943, Joseph Lang, the general manager of radio station WHOM in New York, had testified before a congressional committee that Cranston felt "the Polish news commentators had taken a rather antagonistic attitude toward Russian in this matter" and Cranston wanted the situation "straightened out."[76] It is hard to tell whether this was overzealous patriotism, but it served a Soviet purpose in covering up a Soviet atrocity. Cranston admitted that he had hired David Karr, although he knew Karr had written articles for the *Daily Worker*. Cranston claimed he did not know that Karr was a member of the Communist Party.[77]

After the Soviets retook the Katyn area they held their own special commission and revealed that they had found eleven thousand bodies. The Soviets, of course, concluded that the Nazis had committed the crime. Among the witnesses heard by the Soviet commission was the NKVD officer Major Vetoshnikov, who insisted that when the advancing Nazi army arrived the Polish prisoners were still in the camp. He claimed that since there was no transport available he had tried to get in touch with Moscow to get permission to evacuate the Polish officers on foot. He failed to get the permission. Why he needed it, in view of the imminent arrival of the Germans, is unclear.[78]

Polish protests about the Soviet atrocity were used by Stalin as an excuse to break relations with the Polish exile government in London. In a letter addressed to President Roosevelt, Stalin explained:

> The behavior of the Polish government towards the U.S.S.R. of late is, in the view of the Soviet government, completely abnormal and contrary to all the rules and standards governing relations between two allied states.
> The anti-Soviet slander campaign launched by the German fascists in connection with the Polish officers whom they themselves mur-

dered in the Smolensk area, in German-occupied territory, was immediately seized upon by the Sikorski Government and is being fanned in every way by the Polish official press.

These circumstances compel the Soviet government to consider that the present Polish government, having descended to collusion with the Hitler government, has, in practice, severed its relations of alliance with the U.S.S.R. and adopted a hostile attitude to the Soviet Union.

For those reasons the Soviet government has decided to interrupt relations with that Government.

I think it necessary to inform you of the foregoing, and I trust that the U.S. government will appreciate the motives that necessitated this forced step on the part of the Soviet Government.[79]

A pamphlet published by the American Communists to explain the break in relations carried an introduction by the noted apologist for the Soviet Union, Corliss Lamont. He wrote:

Soviet Russia's severance of relations with the Polish government-in-exile, over the Nazi-inspired charge that the Russians murdered 10,000 Polish army officers, shows clearly the danger to the United Nations of the splitting tactics engineered by Hitler and definitely helped along by the general campaign of anti-Soviet propaganda carried on during recent months in Britain and America. According to the London Bureau of the *New York Herald Tribune*, "It is a safe assumption that the Poles would not have taken so tough an attitude toward the Soviet Government if it had not been for the widespread support Americans have been giving them in the cases of Henry Ehrlich and Victor Alter."[80]

The Polish government-in-exile had also protested the executions of Erlich and Alter. A curt note from the Soviet government had rejected that protest:

In reply to your Note of March 8, 1943, I have the honor to inform you that the Soviet government rejects the entirely unfounded protest of the Polish Government concerning the execution of Erlich and Alter, sentenced on account of their activities directed against the U.S.S.R. at the end of the year 1941, which went so far as to appeal to the Soviet armies to cease this bloodshed and to conclude an immediate peace with Germany; this at the time of the hardest struggle of the Soviet armies against the advancing armies of Hitler.[81]

The Polish Home Army was the underground movement that fought against the Nazis throughout the war. In August 1944, as the Red Army approached Warsaw, the Poles rose in revolt to tie down the Nazi troops and facilitate the liberation of their capital. President Roosevelt and Prime Minister Churchill sent an urgent, and most secret, message to Stalin suggesting that the Soviets, "drop immediate supplies and munitions to the patriot Poles of Warsaw, or will you agree to help our planes in doing it very quickly?" Stalin responded, "Sooner or later the truth about the handful of power-seeking criminals who launched the Warsaw adventure will out. Those elements playing on the credulity of the inhabitants of Warsaw, exposed practically unarmed people to German guns, armour, and aircraft." Stalin refused to drop supplies or allow the Allies to do so. But he told the Allied leaders, "I can assure you that the Red Army will stint no effort to crush the Germans at Warsaw and liberate it for the Poles. That will be the best, really effective, help to the anti-Nazi Poles."[82]

The Polish officers, the Jewish Socialists, and the heroic insurgents in Warsaw would have interfered with the Soviet takeover of Poland. Their elimination, at the hands of Hitler and Stalin, ensured the Soviets of a subservient Poland.

The Soviet Intelligence Service found the willing tools. Some were the remnants of the Polish Communist Party. These individuals had spent the war years in Moscow and unlike most of the Polish Communists in Moscow exile, had survived Stalin's purges. The other Soviet tools were a motley crew of collaborators and anti-Semites, such as Boleslaw Piasecki, who in postwar Poland led a Soviet-directed movement called PAX, which attempted to undermine the Catholic Church.

Jakub Berman was one of the Polish Communists who spent the war years in the Soviet Union and was imposed on the Polish people as a Communist Party Politburo member after the war. He was interviewed by a non-Communist researcher during the early 1980s. When asked about PAX, he said that Piasecki had been arrested by the NKVD and was brought to General Ivan Serov, NKVD chief in Poland and later head of the KGB. Serov liked Piasecki and agreed that he would be permitted his freedom to set up the organization, PAX, which would serve as a counterweight to the Catholic Church. Berman admitted that the Soviet embassy supervised the work of PAX.[83]

The Jewish Socialist, Lucjan Blit, knew Piasecki in prewar Poland. He described the 1937 Socialist May Day demonstration in Warsaw, when the marchers were fired upon and a number were killed. Some of the killers were arrested by the Polish police. They turned out to be members of Piasecki's organization, Falanga. One of them, Zygmunt Przetakiewicz, served during the postwar years as a member of the National Executive Committee of PAX. An internal publication of Piasecki's prewar organization boasted of the "deadly attack on the red Jews."[84]

The Soviet Intelligence Service also provided some of the rulers for postwar East Germany. In the pattern established by Dzerzhinsky in 1920, the NKVD organized German prisoners of war into two groups, the National Committee for a Free Germany and the Union of German Officers. They were useful in wartime propaganda, but a number of them, including former Nazi war criminals, were given key jobs in East Germany. Among them were Heinrich Homann, a Nazi party member since 1933 who was the postwar deputy president of the East German Parliament; Guenter Kertzscher, a former Nazi storm trooper and party member who explained that he had joined the storm troopers "with the best of intentions," who, in postwar years, was deputy editor-in-chief of the East German Communist Party newspaper, *Neues Deutschland;* and Major General Arno von Lenski, who served Hitler as a judge in trials against members of the anti-Nazi resistance, and after the war resumed his rank of major general of the Communist East German Army.[85] The Soviet Intelligence Service played a major role in assisting the Red Army in establishing Soviet domination of Eastern Europe.

Although the Comintern had been dissolved in 1943, supposedly to ensure Allied unity, it continued to function. George Dimitrov of Bulgaria and Dimitri Manuilsky directed a section of the Central Committee of the Communist Party of the Soviet Union which was in charge of control of foreign communist parties, the same jobs they held in the Comintern.[86] Dimitrov became the postwar Communist dictator of Bulgaria, while Manuilsky became the Soviet delegate to the United Nations. The section of the Central Committee of the Soviet Communist Party they headed is now called the International Department.

Idealistic young Americans, like their British counterparts, were vulnerable to Soviet recruitment. Michael Straight, a young American, was recruited by Soviet intelligence when he went to school in England. He described his experiences in his book, *After Long Silence*. Straight denied that he had served the Soviets after he came back to the United States. It is interesting to note that he identified two men in his book as his brothers-in-law. Both had significant involvement with the Soviets. One was Louis Dolivet, who had been a member of the Muenzenberg apparatus, working for the Comintern in Europe in the 1930s.[87] After the war he edited the magazine, *United Nations World*, in New York.

Straight's other brother-in-law was Gustavo Duran. Born in Spain in 1906, Duran had lived in the United States since the early 1930s. When the Spanish Civil War broke out, he returned to Spain to fight against Franco. The Spanish Socialist minister of defense, Indalcio Prieto, complained that the Soviets had forced him to appoint a Communist, Duran, as the chief of Spanish Military Intelligence. He claimed that Duran, "of his own accord, and without power to do so, appointed the agents who are under his orders, which to the number of some hundreds were Communists, and only four or five were Socialists." When Prieto fired Duran, the Soviets came to him to protest. After the war Duran was employed by the U.S. State Department. When Congressman J. Parnell Thomas protested to Assistant Secretary of State Spruille Braden that Duran was a Communist, Duran denied that he was the same Gustavo Duran who had run Spanish Military Intelligence. Braden believed his denial.[88] That he was the same Duran was proved when his picture was found in the official newspaper of the International Brigades. He is shown wearing his uniform as head of Spanish Military Intelligence.[89] By the time of this revelation, he had transferred his employment to the U.N.

Jorge Semprun, who served in the Spanish Communist underground from 1956 to 1964 under the name Frederico Sanchez, revealed that it was reported to him by other Spanish communists that Duran had broken with communism by that time and was "a renegade, an agent of the Americans."[90] There is no public record that Duran ever told the truth to the American government about his role in Spain and his connection with the Soviets.

Winston Burdett was a young journalist on the staff of the *Brooklyn Eagle* when he joined the Communist Party in 1937. In 1940 he was put in touch with Joe North, a prominent communist journalist, who also recruited William Remington for Soviet espionage. North told

Burdett that he was to be given an assignment to go to Finland, with whom the Soviet Union was at war, where he would be "useful to the party." North took Burdett to meet Jacob Golos, who instructed him to convince his newspaper to send him abroad as a roving correspondent on his own finances. The *Brooklyn Eagle* accepted his offer. With money supplied by Golos, Burdett set out for Finland. He was in contact with Soviet agents in Stockholm, but the war ended too soon for him to obtain much significant information. Burdett served the Soviets in the Balkans and Turkey prior to the German invasion of Russia. When his wife was killed in Iran in 1942 in an area controlled by Soviet troops, Burdett broke with the Soviets.[91]

An indication of the mind-set that encouraged Soviet espionage against the Western Allies was shown by the attitude of the former United States ambassador to the Soviet Union, Joseph E. Davies. When the revelations of Soviet atomic espionage surfaced in 1946, Davies told the *New York Times*, "Russia in self-defense has every moral right to seek atomic-bomb secrets through military espionage, if excluded from such information by her former fighting allies."[92] Davies, in his wartime book, *Mission To Moscow*, defended the Soviet purge trials and claimed that they were justified. He also wrote a jacket blurb for the notorious *The Great Conspiracy against Russia* by Sayers and Kahn (see chapter 7). Davies wrote of this Stalinist diatribe, "I hope that every American will read this book. It is a very valuable contribution as the background for an understanding of one of the most serious situations which probably has ever confronted us, namely, the preservation of good relations with the Soviet Union."[93]

The wartime opportunities to spy on the United States provided a basis for spying during the early postwar years. A pro-Soviet atmosphere immediately following the war, combined with aggressive Soviet recruitment, left a significant number of agents in place when the atmosphere later changed and the cold war began.

12

The Cold War Period

As the Soviet Union took control of Eastern Europe, "liberated" by the Red Army, the friendly attitude of the American people toward the Soviet Union during World War II became more and more difficult to maintain. As an actual war between the United States and the Soviet Union was unthinkable because of atomic weapons, an atmosphere of relatively nonviolent conflict developed that came to be called the cold war. The period of friendship preceding the cold war had been used to good advantage by the Soviet Intelligence Service.

The tip-off that the Soviet line had changed, and the cold war begun, came when new orders were given to the American Communists in April 1945. Just as Stalin had supposedly dissolved the Comintern in the interests of unity against fascism, the Communist Party USA had dissolved itself at a convention in May 1944, and reappeared as the Communist Political Association. The new CPA, like its predecessor, the Communist Party, was led by Earl Browder, who no longer used the foreign-sounding title "general secretary," but now had the American title, "president." Stalin was collaborating with the American and British capitalists to defeat Hitler, while Earl Browder announced a "camp of national unity" whereby the American Communists could cooperate with the capitalists for "orderly progress in the post-war."[1]

The April 1945 issue of the French Communist Party theoretical organ, *Cahiers du Communisme*, carried an article by Jacques Duclos criticizing the line of the American Communists. Duclos had been a member of the Executive Committee of the now supposedly nonexistent Comintern. He spoke for Moscow. The article sent shock waves through the leadership of the American Communist Party. Browder was ousted from the leadership and soon expelled from the party. In July 1945 the CPA held a convention and changed its name back to Communist Party USA.[2]

Browder later explained that he allowed himself to be pushed out of the party leadership because if he had fought back:

> It would have involved the whole international leadership of Communism, with whose knowledge, consent, and support I had developed all my policies until 1945. . . . I believed (mistakenly, as it turned out) that, by permitting myself to be removed from the scene, I would hasten the reconsolidation of the American Communist Party on a sound basis, with a new leadership, if necessary by means of help from the international movement.

He went on to say in an odd third-person style:

> During the 15 years of the Browder leadership in the CP USA, all major policies put into effect had the previous knowledge, consent, and active support of the decisive international Communist leadership, which thereby fully shared responsibility for those policies, including those of 1944, later challenged. When that support was declared withdrawn, through the Duclos article and the absence of any other intervention, Browder was removed from leadership.[3]

During this period Soviet intelligence officers were also receiving new instructions.

Yuri Rastvorov was an MVD[4] intelligence officer until his defection in Tokyo in 1954. His cover was second secretary in the Soviet mission.[5] In congressional testimony he identified Anatole Gromov as the MVD *rezident* in the United States for the first year after the war. Gromov, who replaced Zubilin, then returned to Moscow to become chief of the American section at MVD headquarters.

Rastvorov had gone to Japan in January 1946 after a briefing from MVD lieutenant general Fitin, who told him that he needed to concentrate on the recruitment of Americans and British. Fitin said, "with collapse of Hitlerite Germany, our principal enemies remain the United States and Great Britain. This is the direction of the main Soviet effort, and within it the principal place is assigned to the Soviet Intelligence Service operations."[6]

The Communist Information Bureau, or Cominform, was established at a meeting in Poland in September 1947. Soviet Politburo member, Andrei Zhdanov, spelled out the Soviet concept of the cold war. He explained that the world was divided into two camps, and the "principal driving force of the imperialist camp is the U.S.A. Allied with it are Great Britain and France." He claimed that "the anti-imperialists and anti-fascist forces comprise the second camp. This camp is based on the U.S.S.R. and the new democracies."[7] The "new democracies" were the countries forcibly incorporated into the Soviet bloc and were not democracies at all.

Gerhart Eisler

The changed atmosphere led the American government to begin taking action against the Soviet apparatus functioning in the United States. Louis Budenz had been the editor of the *Daily Worker*, the Communist Party's newspaper. He left the party in 1945 to rejoin the Catholic church. On November 22, 1946, Budenz testified before Congress. He revealed that in 1942, Eugene Dennis, who directed the activities of the *Daily Worker* as a representative of the Communist Party leadership, had advised him that in Dennis's absence Budenz would get instructions from Hans Berger. Dennis told Budenz that Berger's real name was Gerhart Eisler and that he was "equivalent to a representative of the Communist International." Dennis said that Eisler had previously functioned "in China, Spain, and here in America." Eisler wrote articles for the Communist Party theoretical organ, *The Communist*, that provided direction to the American Communists. These articles were signed Hans Berger and were written in collaboration with Joseph Starobin.[8] Starobin will be remembered as the author of an article threatening the life of Soviet defector, Victor Kravchenko.

Eisler had entered the United States on June 14, 1941, with a woman he identified as his fiancée, Brunhilda Rotstein. He was interviewed by the Immigration and Naturalization Service at Ellis Island and denied that he had ever been a member of any communist organization or was sympathetic to the communist cause. He claimed he intended to transit the United States on his way to Mexico and would remain in the U.S. for only eight days. Eisler admitted that he had "no legal right to stay in the U.S." He claimed that he was going to Mexico to stay with a friend, Otto Katz. This was, of course, the Otto Katz of the Muenzenberg apparatus. Eisler revealed that he had received money for travel and expenses from the "Spanish Refugee Aid Society." This was a name used by the Joint Anti-Fascist Refugee Committee, the Communist front that boasted of providing the money to send Tito into Yugoslavia. The immigration authorities released him but ordered that Eisler leave the country within sixty days. He failed to do so.[9]

The FBI reported on October 16, 1946:

Almost immediately after his release by the Immigration and Naturalization Service in 1941, Gerhart Eisler became active in the American Communist movement and in recent years he has been a figure of considerable importance in connection with the policies and operations of the Communist Party, U.S.A. It is of particular significance to note that through the investigation of Gerhart Eisler, it has been ascertained that he is identical with an individual previously known as "Edwards" who, from approximately 1933 until approximately 1938, was the representative of the Communist International to the Communist Party, U.S.A., by virtue of which position he was responsible for and instrumental in the determination of American Communist policy and the control and the direction of American Communist operations. During the period he served in the capacity of Comitern [*sic*] representative in the United States under the name "Edwards" he was recognized by Party leaders as a figure of primary importance and also unlimited authority. A number of individuals who knew "Edwards" have definitely identified Gerhart Eisler as "Edwards." In addition, persons who have been acquainted with Eisler for a number of years have reported that he has served as a Comintern representative and a Soviet agent in other parts of the world also.

The FBI also reported:

For the past several years Eisler has made regular daily visits to the offices of the Joint Anti-Fascist Refugee Committee, a well-known Communist front organization in New York City, and it is indicated that Eisler may have been regularly employed by this organization, although he has frequently described himself as unemployed. Contacts with Eisler have been made by numerous individuals, including important Communist Party functionaries, through officials of the Joint Anti-Fascist Refugee Committee, and on many occasions at the offices of the Joint Anti-Fascist Refugee Committee. In this connection, it appears that Eisler has been extremely careful about any visits to Communist Party headquarters. Through the investigation of Eisler, the possibility was developed that Eisler is identical with one Julius Eisman who is known to have been receiving for a considerable period of time, regular monthly checks from the Joint Anti-Fascist Refugee Committee in New York City, in the amount of $150. Subsequent investigation has identified Julius Eisman as Gerhart Eisler. . . . All of these checks which were from the funds of the Joint Anti-Fascist Refugee Committee and were made payable to Julius Eisman were endorsed by Gerhart Eisler.[10]

The FBI was keeping a careful watch on Eisler. He did not like this. On October 29, 1946, his attorney, Carol King, wrote a complaint to the FBI:

When Mr. Eisler came to my office to retain me, three agents of the Federal Bureau of Investigation were stationed in the hall during the entire interview. When he came to my home for a conference, three agents of your Bureau stood outside my house during the entire time and an automobile containing an uncertain number of further agents was parked across the street, shortly after my interview with my client began. He informs me that about eight agents are continually watching him and making a normal private life impossible. I will take upon myself, personal responsibility to guarantee that Mr. Eisler will appear before any agency of the government seeking his presence. . . . I trust that this constant surveillance may be brought to a prompt termination.[11]

On February 6, 1947, Eisler appeared at a congressional hearing. During that hearing it was revealed that while he was in the United States during the 1930s, he traveled on a passport in the name of Samuel Liptzen. The real Liptzen was a Communist Party functionary, but the photograph on the passport application, printed in the hearing record, was that of Eisler. Also printed in the record was a photostat of a letter, dated June 17, 1935, to a Mr. Zolotarev, a Soviet official with Intourist in Paris. The letter was signed by J. N. Golos, manager of World Tourists, Inc. The U.S. government had found the letter during its investigation of World Tourists. Golos, as discussed in chapter 7, was the head of the spy ring exposed by Elizabeth Bentley.

The letter read:

> Dear Mr. Zolotarev:
>
> This will introduce to you, Mr. Samuel Liptzen, a good friend of mine, who will ask you to arrange a trip for him to the Soviet Union via the Soviet steamer from Dunkirk, France, to Leningrad.
>
> Will you kindly use your influence to secure the best accommodations for him and give him your best attention.
>
> With personal best wishes, I remain,
>
> > Very truly yours,
> > WORLD   TOURISTS,
> > INC.
> > J. N. Golos, Manager[12]

The same day Eisler testified, Ruth Fischer appeared before the committee. She was a former member of the Executive Committee of the Communist International and had been a top official of the German Communist Party. She had been expelled from both in 1926 because of her opposition to Stalin. Ruth Fischer revealed that her true name was Elfriede Eisler and that she was the sister of Gerhart Eisler. In explaining to the committee "why, I, a sister by blood, and having been very near to my brother in our childhood, why I am forced to testify before a House Committee of the United States against my own brother," she testified:

> I consider Eisler the perfect terrorist type, most dangerous for the people of both America and Germany. The fact that this man is my brother has only given me a deeper insight in the technique of Stalin's NKVD and the terror system it imposes on the peoples of Europe. In a totalitarian party, all human relations are deteriorated; a man who serves Stalin is conditioned to hand over to the GPU, his child, his sister, his closest friend. Since I learned that Eisler was in this country I have been exposing him. He has used the sympathy of the American people for the suffering and tortured victims of Nazism, to mask his dirty work. I consider him particularly dangerous for the German workers, whom he now pretends to love so much. For years he relentlessly demanded the purge of the German people. That is, decided the slaughter and enslavement of millions on the arbitrary decision of the GPU. In the inner circles of the Comintern, it is well

known that Eisler has denounced to the GPU many [anti-] Nazi refugees living in Moscow. He is particularly responsible for the death of the German Communist Hugo Eberlein, the leader of Eisler's own caucus, and of Nikolai Bukharin, the great Russian theorist, his one-time friend and protector. Eisler's presence in Germany will help to build up another Nazi system which will differ from the old one only by the fact that the Fuehrer's name will be Stalin.[13]

Although he refused to answer the questions of the committee, Eisler made public statements denying the charges against him. On December 11, 1946, he made a speech at the Fraternal Clubhouse in New York City. It was a clever and amusing speech, but Eisler avoided discussing any of the real issues. Referring to his address in Queens, he said:

Apparently, the FBI made a big mistake during the war. They should not have watched "the house on 92nd Street," but the house on 47th Street in Queens. Hollywood should remake the picture. I know everything is big in your country, apparently also the stupidity of your agent-provocateurs and of people who believe them. Idiots' delights do not know any limitations.

After his speech an Eisler Defense Committee was announced. One of the first joiners was Max Bedacht,[14] who fifteen years earlier had recruited Whittaker Chambers for Soviet espionage.

Protests against the investigation of Eisler were organized by the Communist Party and its fronts. Albert Kahn, who had been identified to the FBI as a member of the Golos spy ring, sent a message to the congressional committee, saying, "As an American and a Jew I feel a profound debt to Gerhart Eisler for his heroic, self-sacrificing struggle against fascism, and I cannot witness in silence your indescribably shameful persecution of this outstanding German anti-fascist." Kahn described himself as "co-author of the best selling books, *Sabotage, The Plot Against the Peace,* and *The Great Conspiracy.*"[15]

The Civil Rights Congress, a communist front, published the statement that Eisler claimed he would have made before the committee had he not refused to testify.[16] The organization also published a petition to raise funds for Eisler and to protest the investigation. The petition said:

TARGET FOR TODAY . . . GERHART EISLER

The red scare hysteria fomented by the Un-American
Activities Committee sets the stage for an all-out
attack on organized labor, the educational system
and the entire progressive movement in America.

TARGET FOR TOMORROW . . . MAY BE YOU

PROTECT PROGRESSIVE THOUGHT
ABOLISH THE UN-AMERICAN ACTIVITIES COMMITTEE

DEFEND GERHART EISLER

GIVE TO WIN THE RELEASE OF GERHART EISLER
TO HELP ABOLISH THE UN-AMERICAN ACTIVITIES
COMMITTEE

Eisler was convicted of contempt of Congress in 1948, and faced
false passport charges.

Despite Eisler's earlier protests, the FBI continued to watch him.
However, he outwitted them. On May 13, 1949, while free on bail
furnished by the Civil Rights Congress, Eisler was smuggled aboard
the Polish ship, *Batory,* and succeeded in getting to East Germany
where he became an important functionary.[17] As part of the successful deception of FBI surveillance, Eisler had written an article
under his own name in the May 8, 1949, issue of the Communist
Party newspaper the *Daily Worker,* leaving the impression that he
intended to continue his work in the United States.

Defectors and Others

As FBI surveillance of suspected Soviet intelligence officers increased, more Americans working for Soviet intelligence were identified. One of these identifications was a shocker. FBI agents observed
a clandestine meeting on March 4, 1949, between Judith Coplon,
an employee of the United States Department of Justice, and Valentine A. Gubitchev, a Soviet citizen employed by the United Nations. They were arrested and searched. Coplon had in her purse
summaries of confidential FBI reports on Soviet espionage.

Coplon claimed that the pair were lovers. She said she was only trying to help her boyfriend, and her actions were not prompted by her own left-wing background. The pair were convicted of espionage and sentenced to fifteen years in prison. Gubitchev had his sentence suspended as part of an agreement that he would leave the United States and never return. Coplon's conviction was overturned on technical grounds. She was freed and never retried.[18]

When Gubitchev was arrested he had in his possession the address of Dr. Robert Soblen.[19] It is not known how the Soble spy ring was related to that of which Gubitchev was a part.

During the postwar period the Soviets encountered great difficulties in using the members of local communist parties for espionage. The U.S. government investigations, as well as the declining membership of the American Communist Party, severely hampered the Soviets because few American communists now had access to classified materials. In 1952 instructions were issued from Moscow to the Soviet and bloc intelligence services advising them not to use members of the local communist parties. The intelligence services could use locals only when it was safe and necessary, and with special permission of the Moscow Centre. This was reported by Wladyslaw Tykocinski, a top-level intelligence officer who was head of the Polish Military Mission in Berlin when he defected on May 16, 1965, and asked for political asylum in the United States.[20]

In 1959, Pawel Monat, who had served as Polish military attaché in Washington from 1955 to 1958, defected and asked for political asylum in the United States. He was a high-ranking Polish military intelligence officer. Monat was asked whether the Polish Intelligence Service used members of the American Communist Party as agents. He answered that generally they did not, but

> in a particular instance, if Polish intelligence knew of a CP member who would make a good agent, worth the risk involved, efforts would probably be made to recruit him—but only after the Warsaw authorities had cleared their intention with the appropriate authorities in Moscow. This would not be done though just in order to use a person at the level of a mere informant.

Monat suggested that among the problems inherent in using CP members were that it could compromise the party, in addition there was concern that many CP members were really working for the FBI, and that others were already being used by the Soviets and there, "might be a danger of compromising a Russian operation."[21]

Frantisek Tisler was the chief of Czechoslovakia Military Intelligence in the United States when he defected in July 1959. He served in the United States from August 1955 until his defection. He identified Antonin Krchmarek as an official of the Communist Party USA who worked very closely with the Czech embassy. According to Tisler, Krchmarek was provided with money by the Czech government to defend himself during his 1955–1956 trial for violation of the Smith Act. The funds were provided through intermediaries. In 1956 the Czech ambassador had requested Prague's permission to pay Krchmarek three thousand dollars to cover living expenses and activities.

In August 1958 the ambassador reported to the International Section of the Central Committee of the Communist Party of Czechoslovakia that Krchmarek had been made a member of the Executive Committee of the CPUSA. That same month the ambassador had met with Krchmarek in New York, but during an earlier period the contact had been maintained through an intermediary, as the Soviets had advised the Czechs to be careful in their contacts with the members of the CPUSA. Also in 1958 the Czech ambassador submitted a report to Prague on the American elections that had been prepared with the help of Krchmarek.[22]

These defectors had been from the military intelligence services of Poland and Czechoslovakia. Their interest was collecting military and technological information. Political intelligence was the job of the bloc versions of the KGB.

In 1969 a high-ranking defector appeared from the Czechoslovak Intelligence Service. He was Frantisek August. He described how in 1964, Czech intelligence was ordered by Moscow to use members of the Communist Party of Iraq as agents. The Czechs arranged for a member of the Iraqi Communist Party to be sent to England to serve as a secretary to the philosopher, Bertrand Russell. The Iraqi's control officer in London was Jan Koska of Czech Intelligence. August revealed:

> Every Communist Party has within its organizational structure a committee of party control that is concerned, among other things, with

preventing the penetration of police agents into the party. It is specifically these committees, or rather small groups within these committees, whose members are recruited by KGB agents and who then operate, under the guise of the committee, almost entirely in behalf of the KGB, in the interest of the Soviet Union.

In the American Communist Party this committee has been called the Control Commission and the Cadre and Review Commission. In 1946, David Carpenter, who had served the Hiss-Chambers ring, and Charles Krumbein, of the 1930s spy ring in China, were on the commission.[23]

August also revealed that when he was stationed in Beirut from 1966 to 1969, he ran an agent in the American embassy. This man was a local Lebanese employee who did not have access to classified information. However, he was able to supply copies of an unclassified internal embassy publication. This revealed that a particular American was coming to live in Beirut. The Czechs had identified this individual as a CIA officer as a result of his attempting to recruit someone during an assignment in another country, and they organized a surveillance of him. This CIA officer was under deep cover and the surveillance allowed the Czechs to identify some of his contacts. August was asked if the Czechs had been able to neutralize this CIA man. He answered, "No, I would say not. As a professional, I had a high regard for him. He behaved very well professionally. He was a good officer who knew how to control himself. And it was a hard job for us just to run the surveillance on him."[24]

In 1958, when the Israeli authorities arrested a ring of thirteen persons who were spying for the Syrian Intelligence Service, which was closely connected to Soviet intelligence, at least three of the spies were Arab members of the Israeli Communist Party. One was secretary of a Communist Party branch.[25]

Local communists and sympathizers continue to be used for influence operations, or "active measures." In 1959, Aleksandr Kasnacheyev, a Soviet intelligence officer in Burma, defected to the United States. He described his work using the press in Burma and neighboring countries to place forgeries and disinformation stories. Kasnacheyev testified to a congressional committee:

One of my assignments with the Intelligence Service was the work with usage of Burmese press for Communist aims. Soviet Intelligence regularly published in different Burmese publications, provocative, anti-American and anti-West articles. These articles were fabricated in Moscow, in KGB headquarters, sent to Burma on microfilms, then developed in Soviet Embassy. One intelligence officer was translating the text from Russian into English. Another officer was planting this material in Burmese press. . . . I know directly that Soviet intelligence manipulated such newspapers as the *Mirror*, the *Vanguard*, the *New Path, People's Journal*, and Dagon Publishing House.

Kasnacheyev identified two newspapers in neighboring India that were used by the Soviet Intelligence Service for "active measures." These were *Blitz* and the *New Delhi Times*.[26]

Émigré Organizations

The Trotskyites had been successfully liquidated, and the United States was now the "main enemy" of Soviet intelligence, but the Soviets had not forgotten their émigré enemies. They were particularly concerned about defectors from the KGB. But leaders of anti-Soviet émigré organizations, which the Soviets claimed were involved with Western intelligence, also continued to receive a great deal of attention. Sometimes the attention was fatal.

Petr Deriabin defected from the Soviet Intelligence Service in Vienna in 1954. He had worked in both intelligence collection and counterintelligence. In 1965 he revealed to a Senate committee:

The State Security office responsible for kidnapping and murder and assassination until Stalin's death was known as Spetsburo No. 1. It was organized with the approval of the Central Committee of the Soviet Communist Party. At that time the Chief of the Spetsburo No. 1 was Lieutenant General Sudoplatov. And his deputy was Major General Eitingon. After Stalin's death, the Buro was reorganized. Before, it was strictly under the Chairman of State Security; and then it was put under the Foreign Intelligence Directorate of State Security and known as the Ninth Department—Otdel—and the boss in 1953 and 1954 was Colonel Studnikov. And, as I said before, nowadays this Department is known as No. 13, under the Foreign Intelligence Directorate of Soviet State Security.[27]

Eitingon was involved in the murder of Trotsky (see chapter 9).

In October 1953 the Soviet intelligence officer, Nikolai Khokhlov, was given an assignment to murder Georgi Okolovich, a leader of the Russian anti-communist émigré organization, NTS (National Alliance of Russian Solidarists), headquartered in Frankfurt, West Germany. NTS, an effective opponent of the Soviet regime, has long been the target of Soviet intelligence. The assignment had been given to Khokhlov by his superior, Colonel Lev Studnikov, whose superior was Panyushkin, former ambassador to the United States. Studnikov instructed Khokhlov not to carry out the assassination himself but to use two East Germans who were working for the Soviets. Khokhlov requested permission to use poison bullets that he knew were in preparation in the Soviet Intelligence Service laboratory. He made that request directly to Panyushkin in a personal meeting. Panyushkin granted the request.

However, instead of murdering Okolovich, Khokhlov identified himself to the victim and asked for his help in obtaining political asylum.[28] Khokhlov used the cover name Yegorov and identified the two East Germans as Hans Kukowitsch and Kurt Weber. Khokhlov convinced the two Germans to surrender themselves to the Americans. U.S. authorities found their weapons where they had been checked at the Frankfurt railroad station.[29]

On September 15, 1957, Khokhlov attended a conference in Frankfurt, sponsored by the NTS newspaper *Possev*. He fell ill and was taken to the hospital. It took a few days before the German doctors realized that the symptoms indicated poisoning. He was transferred to a U.S. Army hospital, where his illness was diagnosed as acute and critical with "marked bone marrow depression, high fever, and . . . hemorrhagic skin eruption" and loss of hair. U.S. Army doctors concluded that his illness had been "due to poisoning, probably by thallium and/or other chemical agents."[30] Khokhlov recovered, and at a press conference in New York, October 14, 1957, he declared, "I am here alive today because humanitarian American medical science triumphed over destructive Soviet chemical science."

The Organization of Ukrainian Nationalists, which fights for Ukrainian independence, has also been a major target of the KGB. In 1951 Bogdan Stashynsky was planted by the KGB as an informer in an underground group of the OUN in the Soviet Union. After serving for a few months he was pulled out of the group and transferred to Kiev, where he received two years training by the Soviet Intelligence Service. One of the subjects he was taught was German, indicating that he would be used as an agent in West Germany. In

January 1956 he traveled to Munich on a Soviet zone travel permit made out to the false name Lehmann. In Munich he met with a Soviet agent named Bisaha, who, under the alias Nadytshyn, was working on the staff of the Ukrainian Nationalist newspaper *Ukrainski Samostinik*. Stashynsky provided Bisaha with money and received his reports. He traveled to Munich at least five times on this assignment. Finally he provided Bisaha with a travel permit from the KGB authorizing his return to the Soviet Union.

Subsequently Stashynsky served as a courier for other agents, as well as servicing "dead drops," or secret hiding places in Munich. In the spring of 1957 he received orders to watch the movements of one of the Ukrainian Nationalist leaders, Lev Rebet. In September 1957 Stashynsky met with his control officer, whom he knew by the name Sergei Alexandrovitch. Alexandrovitch introduced Stashynsky to another Soviet officer who demonstrated a weapon, a metal tube about seven inches long and consisting of three sections. A firing pin in the bottom section ignited a small percussion cap, causing a metal lever in the middle section to move and crush a glass ampoule. This released a poison that escaped out of the front of the tube in the form of a gas. The weapon was to be fired into the face of a person a foot and a half away, who would die upon inhaling the fumes. The attacker carried an antidote to be inhaled within a few minutes. Stashynsky was ordered to use this weapon to kill Rebet.

On October 12 he carried out the murder, traveling from Munich to Frankfurt and back to East Berlin the next day. An examination of the victim showed no signs of poison, just as Stashynsky had been advised by his control officer.

In January 1959 Stashynsky was sent again to Munich, this time to watch Stefan Bandera, the head of the OUN. In April 1959 Stashynsky was recalled to Moscow. Here he met a high-ranking KGB officer who identified himself as Georgi Aksentevitch. Aksentevitch informed Stashynsky that a decision had been reached by "the highest authority" that he must liquidate Bandera in the same way he had murdered Rebet.

He made the attempt in May but reported failure to Moscow. In October he was ordered to try again. On October 15, 1959, he succeeded, but this time he had stood too close to the victim and the autopsy revealed glass splinters in the victim's face and poisoning as the cause of death.

In December 1959 Stashynsky, back in Moscow, was brought in to meet Aleksandr Shelepin, the head of the KGB. Also present were the two KGB officers he knew as Sergei Alexandrovitch and Georgi Aksentevitch. Shelepin read a document to them, stating that Stashynsky was awarded the Order of the Red Banner, by decree of the Presidium of the Supreme Soviet of November 6, 1959. He had been given this award for carrying out an "important government commission."

In August 1961 Stashynsky and his German wife, while on a visit to East Berlin, escaped across the border into West Berlin and asked to be put in touch with U.S. government officials. He gave them a full account of what he had done and was placed in the custody of German officials.

Stashynsky was tried in a German court for his crimes. Because he confessed, his sentence was relatively light: eight years at hard labor for the two murders. When the president of the German court sentenced him on October 19, 1962, he said, "this murder trial has, unfortunately, definitely proved that so-called coexistence and so-called Socialist lawfulness by no means exclude so-called individual terrorism—all of them terms used in the Communist vocabulary."[31]

Vladimir Petrov

Western intelligence services were still in the process of trying to obtain a clear picture of the Soviet Intelligence Service when on April 3, 1954, a windfall fell into their laps. Vladimir Petrov, the MVD *rezident* in Australia, defected. He and the documents he provided gave Western intelligence experts significant insights into Soviet espionage methods against the democratic countries. On April 20, Petrov's wife, Evdokia, asked for, and was given, protection by the government of Australia. She was the MVD cipher clerk, and the Soviets had been trying to take her back to Moscow.

Petrov was born in 1907 to a peasant family. His real name was Shorokhov. In 1923 he joined the Komsomol, and in 1927 the Communist Party. In 1929 he took the name Proletarsky to show his loyalty to Communism. In 1933 he joined the OGPU. He served as a cipher clerk in Moscow until September 1937, when he was sent to China. In 1938 he was appointed to the cipher section of the NKVD, which had changed its name from Ogpu in 1934. He later became head of that section, with a rank of Major. In 1942 he was posted to the Soviet Embassy in Stockholm as cipher clerk for the *rezident* and for counterintelligence duties. It was then that he received the name Petrov, which sounded better for use in Sweden than Proletarsky. In 1945 he was promoted to lieutenant colonel.

After a tour of duty in Moscow, he was assigned to Australia in January 1951. At the end of that year he was named temporary *rezident,* a post he held until his defection.

When Petrov left the embassy, he took with him a collection of documents that were to stun the Australian government and public. Some of the documents were published by an Australian Royal Commission on Espionage in 1955, but the two most significant were only quoted. The full texts were not released for three decades.

The two sensitive documents were marked by the commission Exhibit H and Exhibit J. Exhibit H was written by Fergan O'Sullivan in 1951, when he was an employee of the *Sydney Morning Herald,* for which he covered the Parliament at Canberra. He wrote the document at the request of I. M. Pakhomov, who was at that time the temporary MVD *rezident* (later replaced by Petrov). Pakhomov was undercover as a journalist for the Soviet news agency, TASS. The document was photographed and the undeveloped negative sent by courier to the Moscow Centre. The original was kept in the MVD safe until Petrov brought it to the Australian authorities.[32]

Exhibit H is now available for public examination. It is a collection of capsule reports on Australian journalists, evaluating them by religion, political persuasion, sexual proclivities, and susceptibility to liquor. This was exactly what the Soviets needed to know for recruitment, or for a campaign to discredit an enemy. O'Sullivan testified before the Royal Commission on July 14, 1954, and admitted that he wrote the document late in 1951, at the request of Pakhomov.[33]

Exhibit J was the same, only more damaging to Australian security. In addition to revealing the personal lives of fellow journalists and other Australians, this document also reported the location of airfields and identified persons the author thought were members of the Australian Intelligence Service. The author of Exhibit J was a communist journalist named Rupert Lockwood, who actually spent three days in the Soviet embassy in May 1953 typing it.

One journalist Lockwood described in Exhibit J had once been a member of the Communist Party and shortly after World War II had agreed to smuggle messages between Australian Communists and the Japanese Communist Party. Lockwood reported to the Soviets that, as the journalist had not been trusted by the Japanese Communists, he was given only innocuous material to smuggle. Lockwood wrote of him, "In spite of his drunkenness, he has many contacts in Parliament House, among Ministers, Members, and staff." This is the kind of information needed by the Soviets in assessing a possible recruit.

Lockwood also reported to the Russians information obtained from a woman who was spying on her American employer, a businessman. She did this on behalf of a friend, who was a member of the Communist Party.

Much of Lockwood's report was so vile and slanderous that the Australian government kept it under seal for thirty years.[34]

Lockwood, the author of a Communist Party pamphlet titled *Wall Street Attacks Australia*, testified before the Royal Commission a number of times. He answered "yes" to the question, "Have you communicated to any Russian the names of persons whom you believe to be connected with the Australian Security Service?" He also admitted communicating to the Russians the location of Australian airfields, but claimed that this was public information. After much evasion he finally admitted authorship of Exhibit J, but claimed that he was not responsible for some parts. After more evasion he admitted that he had typed Exhibit J at the Soviet embassy and that it took him three days. He admitted that he provided Exhibit J to a Soviet official named Antonov. This was an MVD officer who had taken over the TASS cover from Pakhomov when Petrov took over Pakhomov's job as *rezident*.

Some of the information provided by Lockwood to the Russians had been described by members of the commission as filth. Lockwood responded that the document "was stolen by Petrov and handed around by the Security police, and I believe that was filth to do it." He was asked by a commission member, "But not filth to write it?" He answered, "To warn Mr. Antonov against provocations which would lead to disruption with the Soviet Union, I believe is a duty and not filth."

Lockwood was asked about a hypothetical case, "Suppose a Soviet citizen told the Australian embassy (in Moscow) the names of persons whom he believed to be in the Soviet security police; what do you think would happen to him?" Lockwood answered, very frankly:

> The Australian Embassy represents the Commonwealth of Australia under the Menzies Government, which is in alliance with people who have threatened to drop atom bombs on the Soviet Union. Therefore, in those circumstances, I believe that anyone who assisted a government that was in alliance with people who threatened to use atom bombs would be punished, and rightly so.[35]

Petrov also turned over to the Australians copies of letters that had been received from the Centre in Moscow. Each letter was photographed on 35mm film and the undeveloped film sent to the embassy by diplomatic pouch. The film was given to the *rezident* and developed by his technical assistant. After one copy was printed the negative was destroyed. The letters were encrypted, and key words were in code. Some frequently used code words were actual words. Others were numbers, which changed with each transmission.[36] This is similar to the method described in the Comintern instructions for underground work (see chapter 2), written in 1931.

One collection of documents made available by Petrov concerned the attempted recruitment of an Israeli diplomat. Those documents are particularly valuable for understanding Soviet intelligence work against the United States and other Western countries. The collection was sealed by the commission in 1955 and released thirty years later. The documents provide insights into both code procedures and the extraordinary methods the Soviets used in attempted recruitment.

Following are portions of the Moscow letters, with the code words in all capitals. Below each letter is its decoded version.

Code Message

As enclosure No. 3 to this letter we send you particulars concerning an employee of the BERABIAN Department in IZMIR NO. 14 (In future referred to as ARAB). According to VALENTIN's data, ARAB is sociable and talkative, and has made wide connections. He speaks favourably about SPARTA's culture, but comes out with slanderous statements about SPARTA. Thus, at a reception for businessmen he dwelt on the "dreadfully high prices" in SPARTA.

We ask you to assign to IGNAT the study of ARAB with a view to determining the feasibility and expediency of his CREDIT. When deciding this question it is essential to give consideration to the possibilities of exploiting the material available concerning him, which is set out in the enclosure, as well as the presence of relatives of his in SPARTA.

For the purpose of effecting IGNAT's acquaintance with ARAB we think it would be most expedient to make use of an invitation of the latter, among other departmental workers, to NO. 50 in the DIRECTORATE. If for some reason he should not put in an appearance at the NO. 50, then arrange a luncheon for this purpose, during one of your visits to IZMIR, exploiting the circumstance that you are already acquainted with him.

Keep us informed about progress in the supervision of ARAB.

Decoded Message

As enclosure no. 3 to this letter we send you particulars concerning an employee of the *Israeli Consulate* in *Sydney: Arie Gamlielievich Lapid (also known as Lubich)* (in future referred to as Arab). According to *Pakhomov's* data, *Lapid* is sociable and talkative, and has made wide connections. He speaks favourably about *Soviet* culture, but comes out with slanderous statements about the *Soviet*. Thus, at a reception for businessmen he dwelt on the "dreadfully high prices" in the *Soviet*.

We ask you to assign to *Antonov* the study of *Lapid* with a view to determining the feasibility and expediency of his *recruitment*. When deciding this question it is essential to give consideration to the possibilities of exploiting the material available concerning him, which is set out in the enclosure, as well as the presence of relatives of his in the *Soviet*.

For the purpose of effecting *Antonov's* acquaintance with *Lapid* we think it would be most expedient to make use of an invitation of the latter, among other consular representatives, to the *November Reception* in the *Embassy*. If for some reason he should not put in an appearance at the *November Reception*, then arrange a luncheon for this purpose, during one of your visits to *Sydney*, exploiting the circumstances that you are already acquainted with him.

Keep us informed about progress in the study of *Lapid*.

Code Message

NO. 14, born in 1916, in the city of Grodno, NO.15, BERABIAN citizen, in 1948–1950 was 2nd Secretary of the BERABIAN DIRECTORATE in OLYMPUS.

NO.14 comes of an artisan family. Formerly he was a member of the Zionist youth organization "Hashomer Hatzair." In 1937–38 he left ASCANIA for Palestine, where he graduated from Jerusalem University, and subsequently from the higher diplomatic school in ARABAT.

During the war he served for several years with the rank of captain as a commissariat officer of the IRANIAN Army, and then for a long time served in the ranks of the Jewish Military Organization "Haganah."

Following the creation of BERABIA, NO.14 worked in the general staff of the BERABIAN Army with rank of major.

He has a command of the language of SPARTA, GRAN, UMBIA, NO.17 and of BERABIA.

N0. 14's parents perished during the war. Among his close relatives there are his two brothers, one of whom, NO.17, born in 1906, is situated in the BRUMIAN zone of occupation in UMBIA; the other NO.18, born in 1903, a citizen of SPARTA, engineer, candidate of technical science.

In 1937, NO. 18 was sentenced to 5 years in a corrective Labour Camp for anti-SPARTAN agitation and was later ACCREDITED to the SUPERVISION of former prisoners. In 1949, NO.18 was moved to OLYMPUS, where NO.14 established AGREEMENT with him, and, despite prohibition by the MANAGEMENT OF THE DIRECTORATE, he SETTLED ACCOUNTS with him regularly.

Besides this, there lives in the town of Lvov a distant relative of No.14-No.19 Blanka Yakovlevna, born in 1924, who is under SUPERVISION under suspicion of NO.20.

In January, 1950 one of our PLANNERS was sent to NO.14 in the guise of a close friend of NO.18. In this connection NO.18, acting on our instructions, informed his brother that he was under a great obligation to this friend since the latter had, by making use of his connections, arranged the transfer of NO.18 to OLYMPUS at the risk of his own safety, and so NO.18 looked upon him as his best friend.

Our PLANNER succeeded in gaining the confidence of NO.14 and in the course of six months he used to meet him periodically in a family circle.

In June 1950, our PLANNER, who assumed the role of a journalist vis a vis NO. 14, received from NO.14 an article written by the latter in his own hand concerning the influence of SPARTA on the development of culture in BERABIA. NO.14 was handed 475 roubles as a fee for the article. In accepting the money NO.14 remarked that he was committing an offence because a NO.11 worker was not permitted to do such things.

NO.14 also concealed his SETTLEMENTS with our PLANNER from fellow workers in the DIRECTORATE. The last SETTLEMENT of NO.14 with our PLANNER was documented with a PROFITABLE REPRINTING.

In the DIRECTORATE NO.14 carried out all the clerical work and performed the duties of MANAGER. The leading employees of the DIRECTORATE looked upon NO.14 as a thoughtless person and adopted a somewhat disdainful attitude towards him.

At the beginning of 1950 NO. 14 married the daughter of one of the employees of the BERABIAN DIRECTORATE in BRUMIA - NO.21, and in August 1950, he left SPARTA and on account of this it was impossible to effect his CREDIT.

During the time of his stay in SPARTA, several of NO.14's accounts with SPARTAN citizens were noted, some of which were exploited by him for the purpose of obtaining slanderous ASSERTMENT concerning the situation of NO.15 in SPARTA.

Decoded Message

Arie Gamlielievich Lapid (also known as Lubich), born in 1916, in the city of Grodno, *Jew, Israeli* citizen, in 1948-1950 was 2nd Secretary of the *Israeli Embassy* in *Moscow*.

Lapid comes of an artisan family. Formerly he was a member of the Zionist youth organization "Hashomer Hatzair." In 1937–38 he left *Poland* for Palestine, where he graduated from Jerusalem University, and subsequently from the higher diplomatic school in *Arabat*(?).

During the war he served for several years with the rank of captain as a commissariat officer of the *British* Army, and then for a long time served in the ranks of the Jewish Military Organization "Haganah."

Following the creation of *Israel*, *Lapid* worked in the general staff of the *Israeli* Army with the rank of major.

He has a command of the *Russian, English, German, Arabian*, and *Hebrew* languages.

His parents perished during the war. Among his close relatives there are his two brothers, one of whom *S. G. Lubich*, born in 1906, is situated in the *American* zone of occupation in *Germany;* the other *M. G. Lubich*, born in 1903, a *Soviet* citizen, engineer, candidate of technical science.

In 1937, *M. G. Lubich* was sentenced to 5 years in a corrective Labour Camp for anti-*Soviet* agitation and was *recruited* for *surveillance* of former prisoners. In 1949, he moved to *Moscow*, where *A. G. Lapid* established *contact* with him, and, despite prohibition by the *Embassy*, he *met* him regularly.

Besides this, there lives in the town of Lvov a distant relative of *A. G. Lapid*—one Blanka Yakovlevna *Shohet*, born in 1924, who is under *surveillance* under suspicion of *espionage*.

In January 1950, one of our *cadre workers* was sent to *A. G. Lapid* in the guise of a close friend of *M. G. Lubich*. In this connection *M. G. Lubich*, acting on our instructions, informed his brother that he was under a great obligation to this friend since the latter had, by making use of his connections, arranged the transfer of *M. G. Lubich* to *Moscow* at the risk of his own safety, and so *M. G. Lubich* looked upon him as his best friend.

Our *cadre worker* succeeded in gaining the confidence of *A. G. Lapid* and in the course of six months he used to meet him periodically in a family circle.

In June 1950, our *cadre worker*, who assumed the role of a journalist vis-a-vis *A. G. Lapid*, received from him an article written by the latter in his own hand concerning the influence of the *Soviet* on the development of culture in *Israel. A. G. Lapid* was handed 475 roubles as a fee for the article. In accepting the money he remarked that he was committing an offence, because a *diplomatic* worker was not permitted to do such things.

A. G. Lapid also concealed his *meetings* with our *cadre worker* from fellow workers in the *Embassy*. The last *meeting* of *A. G. Lapid* with our *cadre worker* was documented with a *valuable photograph*.

In the *Embassy A. G. Lapid* carried out all the clerical work and performed the duties of *commercial attaché*. The leading employees of the *Embassy* looked upon him as a thoughtless person, and adopted a somewhat disdainful attitude towards him.

At the beginning of 1950 *A. G. Lapid* married the daughter of one of the employees of the *Israeli Embassy* in *America—Eleonora Gold-*

berg, and in August 1950 he left the *Soviet* and on account of this it was impossible to effect his *recruitment.*

During the time of his stay in the *Soviet Union,* several of *A. G. Lapid's* meetings with *Soviet* citizens were noted, some of which were exploited by him for the purpose of obtaining slanderous *information* concerning the situation of *Jews* in the *Soviet Union.*[37]

The attempted recruitment of Lapid failed. The Australian government advised the Israelis of both the attempt and the failure. It is possible that the Israeli diplomat was working for his own country's intelligence service and was gathering information on Soviet intelligence methods.

The methods used by the MVD are instructive. The Soviets used the target's brother to put him in contact with a Soviet intelligence officer. The target was paid money to write an unimportant article. The Soviets used normal diplomatic contact at a reception and they planned to exploit his unhappiness at his job. These are all classic methods of Soviet recruitment.

The Petrovs wrote a book about their experiences. They pointed out that Moscow required that every conversation of any significance with a foreigner be reported. Embassy receptions "were fishing grounds for useful contacts, which might ultimately produce recruits for our espionage networks."[38]

Among the Moscow letters provided by Petrov was one dated November 15, 1952, which described the procedures for sending operational letters. Each section or "Line" of the *Rezidentura* would send separate reports to the Centre. The section responsible for intelligence collection was called Line O, counterintelligence was K, scientific and technical was X, illegal was NL, émigrés was EM, Soviet colony was SK, Soviet seamen was M, and visiting delegations D.

The main function of Line O was the collection of political intelligence. It is now called Line PR. Counterintelligence, or Line K, is responsible for protecting the KGB against hostile intelligence services. It still has the same designation but it now has subsections to surveil Soviet seamen and delegations visiting the target countries as well as the Soviet personnel, or Soviet colony, residing in the target country. Line X still has the function of stealing scientific and technical information. We will say more about the current apparatus of the *Rezidentura* in the final chapter.

The illegal line, NL, is responsible for providing support to Soviet intelligence officers operating without official cover. Official cover is provided by the embassy, and semiofficial cover is provided by entities such as TASS. The illegals often pretend to be natives of a country other than the Soviet Union. If they can speak the local language without an accent, they pretend to be natives of the target country. A Moscow letter of June 6, 1952, ordered the creation of an illegal apparatus in Australia as "one of the top-priority tasks . . . of the Australian MVD section."[39]

In 1948 a very experienced Soviet intelligence officer entered the United States as an illegal. He called himself Emil Goldfus and was sometimes known as Martin Collins. When he was arrested by the FBI in June 1957, he gave his name as Colonel Rudolf Ivanovich Abel. The FBI had found him as a result of leads provided by a Soviet defector who had worked for Abel, Reino Hayhanen. The defector had walked into the American embassy in Paris in 1957 and asked for political asylum rather than return to Moscow. Although he had worked for Abel for five years, he knew neither his name nor address. Nevertheless, the FBI was able to trace Abel based on the bits and pieces of information provided by Hayhanen. Abel was convicted of espionage in November 1957 and was sentenced to thirty years in jail.[40] In February 1962, Abel was exchanged for Gary Powers, the U2 pilot who had been shot down over the Soviet Union.[41]

It was reliably reported that upon returning to the Soviet Union, Abel protested to the authorities about the imprisonment of two of his old close associates, Leonid Eitingon, the mastermind of the murder of Trotsky, and Pavel Sudoplatov, who headed Spetsburo No. 1, the unit charged with kidnapping and assassinations abroad during Stalin's latter days. Eitingon had served as Sudoplatov's deputy. The two had been arrested as the result of the downfall of Beria after Stalin's death.[42]

Abel died in 1971. An article eulogizing him appeared in the Red Army newspaper, *Krasnaya Zvezda (Red Star)*, on November 17, 1971. Signed a "Group of Comrades," it revealed that Abel had become an officer of the OGPU in 1927, and a member of the Communist Party of the Soviet Union in 1931. In the forty-five years of his work for Soviet intelligence his comrades declared him to be a, "daring, experienced, intelligence officer and capable leader." What they did not reveal, however, was that even Abel, the name he gave the FBI, was not his true name. In 1972 American reporters in Moscow discovered his gravestone in a cemetery, which read "Fisher, William Genrykovich" and in smaller letters, "Abel, Rudolf Ivanovich." It gave his date of birth as July 11, 1903. The name Fisher confirmed a story that had been heard in Moscow, that Abel actually was born in England the son of a radical activist. A check of the Soviet encyclopedia revealed that Genrykh Fisher was living in England at the time of his son's birth. Genrykh had been an associate of Lenin and emigrated to England in 1901. He returned to Russia in 1921 and became active in the Bolshevik Party.[43]

13

The Lean Years

THE 1960s were not good years for Soviet intelligence operations against the United States. The loyal, dedicated Soviet patriots in the Communist Party USA were no longer of much use. Party membership declined to a few thousand, while government surveillance made it almost impossible for these few to gain access to government secrets. They were still useful for "active measures," but classical espionage was almost impossible.

The party had been severely damaged by FBI penetration and criminal trials for Smith Act violations. But the most damage was done by Khrushchev's 1956 revelations about the crimes of Stalin. The rock upon which the American Communists had built their faith was smashed with one blow. The Soviet invasion of Hungary later that year did additional damage. In February 1957 the American Communist Party held its national convention. The boiled up anger spilled forth as delegates expressed their horror at what they now knew. One delegate, identified as Al in the official transcript (probably Albert Lannon), explained, "after spending a couple of years in jail, I don't think we have much democracy as personified in China, the Soviet Union, and the People's Democracies."[1] Another delegate, identified as Olga (probably Olga Agosto), complained: "In the thirties, in Lower Harlem we had as many as a fourteen hundred members. As late as 1954, we had four hundred members. Today, we have dwindled to less than a hundred, of which only about a third are active."[2]

The heart had gone out of the Communist movement worldwide. In the United States, American communism was a battered remnant of its heyday of the 1930s. The communists lost their intellectuals and most of the middle generation. What was left, very old diehards and young inexperienced fanatics, provided little opportunity for espionage recruiting.

Mercenary Spies

The typical spy of the 1960s was the mercenary, although even then a few new political opportunities began to develop. The Soviets were able to use the disaffected, those who no longer felt a loyalty to the United States. One such case was a twenty-two-year-old U.S. Air Force enlisted man named Robert Glenn Thompson. In June 1957, while stationed in West Berlin, he walked across the sector border one Saturday morning and volunteered himself to the East German Secret Police. Because he was attached to the Air Force Office of Special Investigation, he was able to supply the East Germans with interesting information about American intelligence activities in West Berlin.

Thompson would meet his East German contacts by taking the S-Bahn, elevated train, into East Berlin. From the Russian War Memorial, he would walk a few blocks so that his East German handlers could watch for surveillance. They would then pick him up and take him to a safe house. At his fourth meeting the East Germans provided him with a Minox camera to photograph documents, and the sum of fifty West German marks, then worth about $12.50.

Thompson supplied the East Germans with a list of air force intelligence safe houses in West Berlin and helped them try to identify army and CIA safe houses. Why did he do this? Because he was unhappy with the treatment he was receiving in the air force. As he explained it later in a *Saturday Evening Post* article, "I was doing it just for my own personal satisfaction, getting back at the people who had given me so much hell."

The East Germans handed Thompson over to the Russians, who trained him in secret communications and other intelligence trade craft, both in East Berlin and on a secret trip to the Soviet Union.

In early 1958 Thompson rotated back to the United States. He had one thousand dollars, which the Soviets had given him to buy a shortwave radio and a camera. He used the shortwave radio to receive communications from somewhere in Russia. The first message was that someone would contact him soon. The contact was a woman he had met in the Soviet Union during his training. Thompson claimed that he tried to break contact with the Soviets. However, after his discharge from the air force in December 1958, he was contacted at his Detroit home by a man who gave his name as John Kurlinsky.[3] The FBI was later able to identify the man as Boris V. Karpovich, whose cover was counselor of the Soviet embassy in Washington. When he first contacted Thompson, Karpovich was listed as a translator at the United Nations. He left that post in 1961 and then reappeared at the Soviet embassy.[4]

Thompson was arrested on January 7, 1965, and Karpovich was ordered to leave the United States. The day after his arrest Thompson spoke to the press in the office of his lawyer. He denied that he had spied for the Soviet Union and said, "The charges against me are fantastic and absolutely untrue. I am 100 percent American and I am shattered because I can't believe this could happen to me."[5] However, on January 18 he admitted in an interview with a *New York Times* reporter that he was in fact a spy for the Soviet Union. The *Times* withheld the story until March 9, when Thompson pleaded guilty in court.[6] He was sentenced to thirty years' imprisonment.[7]

A valuable, well-documented study on "Air Force Traitors," written by Special Agent David J. Cranford of Air Force Special Investigations, reveals that Thompson, while in prison, claimed to be a German-born Soviet illegal, ten years older than his official age. Lending credibility to the claim was the fact that in 1978 the East Germans traded him for an Israeli pilot held in Mozambique.[8] The Soviet bloc does nothing for its recruited agents who are captured, but it does try to exchange its own citizens who are captured while on intelligence assignments.

A few months after Thompson's arrest the FBI captured two other mercenary spies, Corporal Robert Lee Johnson and James Allen Mintkenbaugh. Both were forty-six years old. Johnson, a former Pentagon courier, had been recruited in 1953 in Berlin. He in turn introduced Mintkenbaugh to the Soviets. After the latter's discharge in 1956, he was brought to Moscow where he was trained in codes, secret writing, microdots, and photography. He later served as a courier, transmitting information stolen by Johnson.[9] They pleaded guilty to spying for pay, and each was sentenced to twenty-five years in jail.[10]

The penetration of a hostile intelligence service has always been a high priority for the KGB. In late 1955 a Soviet "illegal" operating in Canada returned to Moscow for debriefing. The plan was for him to resume his work in Canada after the Moscow trip. Using the name David Soboloff, the Soviet "illegal" had operated in Canada since 1952. However, he had been turned and was working as a double agent for the Royal Canadian Mounted Police, which at that time was responsible for Canadian counterintelligence. His Soviet control officer, working under embassy cover, was Vladimir Bourdine. What Soboloff did not know was that Bourdine had purchased the services of a Mounty working on Soviet espionage cases.

Although not involved in the double-agent case, the mounty, Corporal James Morrison, had once been asked to drive Soboloff to Montreal after a meeting. He had been ordered never to reveal the identity of the agent, but for less than five thousand dollars he sold the information to Bourdine's successor, Nikolai Ostrovsky. Morrison was desperately in need of money and sold secrets to the Soviets from April 1955 to January 1958. Soboloff never returned to Canada, and Canadian authorities believe that he was executed when he arrived in Moscow.

In 1957 Morrison confessed his relationship with the Soviets to his superiors. He was not arrested for espionage but only demoted and dismissed from the RCMP in 1958. In 1983 Morrison appeared on a Canadian television program wearing a disguise. He confessed that he had turned over the name of the double agent to the KGB. He claimed that he had not sold out his country but had only sold one Russian "down the drain." In January 1986, Morrison pleaded guilty to unlawfully communicating secret information to the KGB.[11]

During the lean years the Soviets also made extensive use of "illegals" who could operate where KGB officers under official cover would have no access. The placing of an "illegal" officer in the government of a target country was a major triumph for the Soviets. Richard Sorge, the Soviet agent who became the confidant of the German ambassador to Japan and the de facto embassy press officer, was such a master spy. Another operated in Israel during the 1950s and early 1960s. Using the name Yisrael Beer, he became the personal secretary of then prime minister David Ben-Gurion. He was also a lieutenant colonel in the reserves. The Israelis who arrested him during the 1960s have never revealed his true name or how he was caught. However, he is known to have inflicted substantial damage through his spying.

One possible explanation of the Israeli capture of Beer, who later died in prison, was provided by Professor John P. Roche, who served as dean of the Fletcher School at Tufts University in Massachusetts. Roche was in Israel in 1960 to evaluate that country's social science programs. While Roche was having dinner at a restaurant, an American approached him and asked if he were John Roche. The American, who was of Italian descent, reminded him that they had met previously in socialist and anti-fascist activities in New York during the 1930s. At that time the Italian-American had gone to Spain to fight in the communist-led International Brigades. In 1960 he was in Israel to attend his daughter's wedding to a young Israeli.

While he and Roche were speaking, the Italian-American said, "Don't move abruptly, but next time you look around the room focus on that Israeli colonel two tables over." When Roche looked around he saw a man in uniform with dried, sunken features. Roche's companion told him about the colonel: "The last time I saw him, he was my GPU interrogator at their prison in Alcara de Henares, outside Madrid. He accused me of being a Trotskyist-fascist spy—only my American passport saved me." Roche believed that the colonel was Beer and that the Italian-American informed the Israelis about him. Beer was arrested as an East German spy. He claimed to have survived a World War II Nazi concentration camp and had been smuggled into Palestine shortly after the war.[12] It is unknown whether Beer was even Jewish, as so few Jewish officers of the service had survived Stalin's purges. Here again, Soviet intelligence operations from Spain reached into the postwar period.

The Soviets have a continuing interest in obtaining U.S. passports for use by their agents. In February 1963, Paul Carl Meyer, then twenty-three years old, provided fifteen American passports to Soviet intelligence officers at a meeting in East Berlin. He was indicted on February 2, 1965.[13] He pleaded guilty the next day and admitted that he had advertised for people to be employed abroad and chosen fifteen of the applicants. He asked the fifteen to obtain passports, which he took, supposedly to make arrangements for their employment.[14] He took the passports to the Soviet embassy in East Berlin.

The Soviets took the passports and suggested that Meyer work for them to obtain "political secrets." He agreed to do so. He was given training in an East Berlin apartment and supplied with a camera disguised as a portable radio. The Soviets ordered him to strike up a relationship with a woman working in the U.S. mission in Berlin so that he could gain access to the premises and photograph documents. He was unsuccessful. He was also ordered to blackmail a West German woman employed at the British mission to supply him with documents. She agreed to do so but never supplied them. He came back to the United States and spoke to U.S. authorities, who were already investigating him. Meyer was sentenced to two years in prison.[15]

Another example of mercenary spying during the lean years was retired Lieutenant Colonel William Henry Whalen of Alexandria, Virginia. Between 1959 and 1961 he received fifty-five hundred dollars for information in a variety of areas, including atomic weaponry, missiles, intelligence reports, and plans of the Strategic Air Command. His Soviet contacts were Colonel Serge Edemski and Mikhail A. Shumaev, both of the Soviet embassy. They left the country before Whalen's arrest in 1966.[16] Whalen pleaded guilty to conspiracy to commit espionage and was sentenced to fifteen years in jail.[17]

Other mercenaries included twenty-three-year-old Sergeant Herbert William Boeckenhaupt, who received a thirty-year sentence after being convicted of supplying information to a KGB officer under diplomatic cover, Aleksey R. Malinin; and Sergeant First Class Jack Dunlap, a clerk messenger at the National Security Agency, the U.S. code-breaking department. Dunlap, who was accused of selling information to the Soviets, committed suicide in 1963.[18]

Even during the lean years, not all who spied for the Soviets did so for money. It was still possible, at least in some countries, to get Communist Party members to spy for ideological reasons. Two interesting incidents surfaced in 1962. The Japanese Communist Party, then still allied with the Soviet Union, provided details in its newspaper of American, South Korean and other Allied planes taking off and landing at Itazuke Air Base in Japan. The information was supplied by people observing the base and collecting information.[19] On April 5, 1962, the Japanese Communist Party daily reported on information gathered at the American Itami Air Base. It reported that 688 military planes had landed in August 1961, 565 in September, 188 in October, 186 in November, and 213 in December.[20] Since that time the Japanese Communist Party has become very critical of Moscow, and except for those of its members secretly recruited by KGB unbeknownst to the leaders, the Japanese Communist Party no longer spies for the Soviet Union.

Technology Theft and Forgeries

The theft of technology is of major interest to Soviet intelligence. It remained so during the late 1950s and 1960s. As most Communist Party members no longer had access to such information, the Soviets were reduced to buying it from mercenaries. Sometimes this worked, sometimes it didn't. When Boris Gladkov tried to buy information on atomic submarines from an American citizen he succeeded only in being thrown out of the country. Until his expulsion on July 12, 1956, Gladkov was an adviser to the military staff of the United Nations in New York.

Equally unsuccessful was his colleague, Vadim Isakov. He tried to obtain classified equipment from a Paterson, New Jersey, machinery corporation. The company immediately contacted the FBI. Isakov's conduct "unbecoming a UN official" was reported to his employer, UNICEF, where he served as a procurement officer.

An American engineer, John Butenko, employed by an ITT subsidiary that did classified work for the Strategic Air Command, agreed to sell classified information to the Soviets. On October 29, 1963, he was arrested, and on December 2, 1964, convicted and sentenced to thirty years in prison. One of the Soviet officers, Igor Ivanov, undercover as a chauffeur for Amtorg, was sentenced to twenty years in jail, and three Soviet diplomats were expelled from the country.[21]

In addition to the theft of technology, Soviet influence operations (active measures) are a major function of the KGB. In 1961 the CIA reported, "During the past four years we have discovered no fewer than thirty-two forged documents designed to look as though they had been written by or to officials of the American government." These forgeries, like the forged Tanaka Memorial, created by the

Soviets in 1929, were designed to discredit an enemy, in this case the United States. Richard Helms, then the assistant director of the CIA, revealed to Congress that of the thirty-two documents packaged to look like communications to or from American officials, twenty-two were meant to demonstrate "imperialist" American plans and ambitions. Seventeen of them "showed" U.S. interference in the affairs of free world countries. The charge of imperialism was the first of the two major canards spread by the Soviet bloc in Asia, the Middle East, Africa, Europe, and wherever else they commanded suitable outlets.

Eleven of the Soviet forgeries charged U.S. intervention in the private business of Asian nations. One was a faked secret agreement between the U.S. secretary of state and Japanese premier Kishi "to permit use of Japanese troops anywhere in Asia." Another alleged that U.S. policy in southeast Asia called for U.S. control of the armed forces of all SEATO nations. Four more were supposed to make the Indonesian government view the United States as a dangerous enemy. Two of these offered forged proof that the Americans were plotting the overthrow of President Sukarno. The other two were supposed to demonstrate that the U.S. government, despite official disclaimers, was secretly supplying the anti-Sukarno rebels with military aid.

Of the remaining five Asian affairs forgeries, two claimed that the Americans were plotting to assassinate Chiang Kai-shek. Another had the American embassy in Phnom Penh deeply involved in a conspiracy with a Cambodian dissident, Sam Sary, to overthrow the government of Prince Sihanouk. The fourth was a State Department order that U.S. intelligence agencies were to "screen the loyalty" of the king of Thailand and the members of his government. The fifth "revealed" that the U.S. Information Service was directing the press of one Asian country in attacks upon another.[22]

A CIA report on *The Soviet and Communist Bloc Defamation Campaign* was put in the *Congressional Record* on September 28, 1965, by Congressman Melvin Price of Illinois. The report revealed that the KGB section responsible for forgeries and disinformation was called Department D. It was headed by General Ivan Agayants and "makes use of local Communist and pro-Communist propagandists and of cooperating Communists bloc intelligence and security services." The CIA identified Agayants as "a senior professional intelligence officer with long experience and well-developed agent and political contacts in Western Europe, especially in France, where he served under the name Ivan Ivanovich Avalov." One of his assignments in France was controlling the spy Georges Pasques, who was sentenced to life imprisonment on July 7, 1964. Department D was staffed by forty to fifty specialists in Moscow and a substantial amount of manpower abroad.[23]

On May 15, 1968, the Soviet press reported the death of KGB major general Ivan Ivanovich Agayants. He had served in the Soviet Intelligence Service since 1930, when he was nineteen years old, and the Communist Party of the Soviet Union since 1936.[24]

Under KGB Control

The intelligence services in the Soviet bloc are completely under the control of the KGB. This has been reported by defectors from those services in the last few decades. This is seldom admitted by the Communists themselves, but in 1968 there was such an admission. During the "Prague Spring" when Czechoslovakia attempted to democratize, information began to leak out. Before the Soviet and Warsaw Pact forces suppressed Czech democracy, participants in the dreadful Stalinist purges publicly admitted their roles. Karol Bacilek, the former Czech minister of national security was interviewed by the press. He was responsible for the persecutions during the early 1950s. He disclaimed culpability and explained, "Soviet advisors worked in every department of the Ministry. There were about twenty six of them." He claimed that the tortures of the victims were done by the Soviet advisers.[25]

Ladislav Bittman, a senior officer in the Czech Intelligence Service who defected in 1968, revealed that the Soviets controlled the external intelligence operations just as they did the internal. Bittman testified:

> The role of the Soviet advisors is very important . . . [T]hey were in the Czechoslovak service even during the political spring in 1968 during the democratization process. . . . There is a special school in Moscow educating Czechoslovak intelligence officers. A similar school there is training Hungarian officers, another school Polish officers or East German officers. It is not one school training all

satellite intelligence officers because of the secrecy. Anyhow, anyone who wants to achieve an important position within the Czechoslovak service has to have attended a Soviet intelligence school.[26]

The Polish Intelligence Service also operates under the direction of the Soviets. In May 1958, Anczel Grau, a Polish Jew, arrived in New York. He was no communist; indeed he had spent a year in a Soviet slave labor camp during the era of the Soviet-Nazi Pact, when the area where he lived in Poland had been overrun by the Soviets. He had tried, unsuccessfully, a number of times to get permission to leave Poland. In 1955 he was visited by a representative of the Polish Intelligence Service. Grau was told that he would be allowed to leave if he agreed to perform some services for the intelligence service. He agreed.

Between January and September 1956, he was given training in intelligence trade craft. Although he did not meet with other students, four instructors participated in his training. Grau described his courses:

> Surveillance—Here I was instructed in the methods of how to avoid being followed and how to follow someone if necessary; Locating and Clearing Mail Drops—I was taught how to determine whether I was to place or pick up material from mail drops and how to clear mail drops; Cypher—I was instructed in the use of codes, and taught one code whose key was a line in any book chosen by the parties involved; Microphotography—I was taught how to take microfilm, develop same, and how to conceal the film.[27]

When Grau arrived in the United States, he revealed to the American government the story of his training. One of the authors of this book met him during the 1960s and heard the story of how a man who hated communism was pressured into serving a Soviet bloc intelligence organization. The Soviets apparently believed that they had so terrified him that he would be reluctant to contact the American authorities. They were wrong. During the 1960s Anczel Grau was living quietly with his family in New York City and enjoying American freedom.

Laszlo Szabo was an "active measures" specialist for the Hungarian Intelligence Service, the AVH. After his defection in 1965, he de-

scribed the Soviet control of Hungarian intelligence. He told a 1966
Senate committee:

> The AVH works closely with the Soviets. Since the Hungarian Rev-
> olution of 1956, however, the Soviets have relaxed their hold on the
> Hungarian government somewhat, and the number of advisors has
> been cut down. Soviet cooperation with the AVH is carried out by
> advisors who are assigned to that service. There is a chief advisor.
> The other advisors are assigned to the Counterintelligence Depart-
> ment, and to the Intelligence Department. According to the general
> agreement between the two services, the Soviet advisors can see all
> the important AVH papers, including the annual report of the service.
> The Information Department selects the most valuable intelligence
> information to send to Moscow. Hungary has no secrets from the
> Soviet Union. Officials of the AVH run to the Soviet advisors with
> any information they think is important. They are happy to be of
> service to the Soviet State Security—the KGB. When the Soviets
> need it, they can get the operational assistance of the AVH.

Szabo had defected while he was serving as second secretary in
the Hungarian embassy in London, as a cover for his intelligence
activities. Among his assignments were disinformation operations.
He was instructed to try to cause friction between the United States
and the United Kingdom. Szabo revealed that, "All disinformation
activities must have the approval of the Central Committee of the
Hungarian Communist Party before they can be carried out. I know
that Hungarian disinformation work is discussed with the Soviets."[28]
    One of the vicious "active measures" campaigns, done on behalf
of the Soviets by a surrogate intelligence service, was the book,
Who's Who in the CIA. The book was published in 1968 in East
Germany and signed with the name Julius Mader. Ladislav Bittman
testified in 1980 before Congress:

> I am very familiar with the book, because I am very sorry to admit
> that I am one of the coauthors of the book. The book *Who's Who in
> the CIA* was prepared by the Czechoslovak Intelligence Service and
> the East German Intelligence Service in the mid Sixties. It took a
> few years to put it together. About half of the names listed in the
> book are real CIA operatives. The other half are people who were
> just American diplomats or various officials; and it was prepared with
> the expectation that naturally many, many Americans operating abroad,

diplomats and so on, would be hurt because their names were exposed as CIA officials. It was published under the name of Julius Mader. Many people here in this country, including many journalists, don't know that Julius Mader is actually an East German intelligence officer and author of several books dealing specifically with intelligence and propaganda.[29]

Who's Who in the CIA appeared in English. Other books signed by Mader appeared in German. One, *Nicht Laenger Geheim (No Longer Secret),* also an attack on the CIA, revealed Mader's affiliation. It was published in 1969 by Deutscher Militaerverlag, the East German military publishing house. Another Mader book, an attack on former CIA chief Allen Dulles, was titled *Allens Gangster in Aktion (Allen's Gangsters in Action).* This was published in East Berlin in 1959. Two years later the Soviets wrote a similar attack, this time in English, called *A Study of a Master Spy (Allen Dulles).* Signed by a British Labour M.P., Bob Edwards, and Kenneth Dunne, it was actually written in Moscow by Colonel Vassily Sitnikov, a veteran KGB disinformation officer.[30]

The damage done by Mader's *Who's Who* was illustrated by the murder of an American falsely identified as a CIA officer. In 1970, Dan Mitrione, an officer of the Agency for International Development, was kidnapped by the Cuban-sponsored Tuparmaros terrorists in Uruguay. On August 9, 1970, he was murdered. On August 30, 1970, the Cuban Communist Party newspaper, *Granma,* justified the murder by reproducing the page of Mader's book that identified the victim as a CIA officer. Two weeks later, *Granma* published the transcript of the interrogation of Mitrione by the terrorists.[31]

Active Measures

"Active measures" have been used to interfere in the American electoral process. Ladislav Bittman testified before the United States Senate in 1971 using the name Lawrence Britt. He revealed that during the 1964 American election, when he was deputy chief of the Disinformation Section of Czech intelligence, a disinformation campaign was carried out against the Republican presidential candidate, Barry Goldwater. He testified:

I think that it was a leaflet of several pages attacking Mr. Goldwater as a racist. Some facts in this leaflet about Mr. Goldwater were picked up from American books and newspapers and they were mixed with sensational ingredients attacking Mr. Goldwater as a racist. . . . They were distributed anonymously. I think that these letters were sent to the United States in diplomatic bags and mailed by the members of the Czechoslovakian intelligence station in the United States.[32]

The false charge that Goldwater was a racist was only one of the smear campaigns used against his candidacy by the Soviets and their surrogates. The American Communists covertly assisted in this "active measures" campaign. A 1963 booklet claimed that Goldwater was conspiring with the John Birch Society to organize a "putsch," or violent insurrection, to take over the United States in 1964. The booklet, *Birch Putsch Plans for 1964*, contained no address for the publisher, Domino Publications. The author used the not-very-imaginative pseudonym, "John Smith, as told to Stanhope T. McReady." There was nothing to tie this publication to the communists until an ad for the book in the pro-communist *National Guardian* for April 25, 1963, listed the publisher as "Domino Publications, Suite 900, 22 West Madison Street, Chicago, Illinois." This was in fact the address of Translation World Publishers, which was registered under the Foreign Agents Registration Act as an agent of the Soviet Union. The co-owners, LeRoy Wolins and David S. Canter, were identified by the House Committee on Un-American Activities as members of the Communist Party USA. In 1965 Domino Publications of Chicago published a pamphlet attacking the NATO multilateral nuclear force (MLF). The pamphlet, by David S. Canter, was titled *MLF—Force or Farce?* It presented the Soviet arguments against the NATO nuclear defense.[33]

By the 1960s the American Communist Party was weak. It had few members and little influence. Its ability to assist the Soviets in intelligence collection was severely limited. Nevertheless, it did its best to assist the Soviet cause through such "active measures."

During the 1960s a climate had developed in the United States in which a radicalized, violence-prone, minority of young people made their voices heard far beyond their numbers. Some met with Vietnamese intelligence officers in Hanoi, Paris, and Prague to plan actions against the U.S. involvement in Vietnam. The American

Communists tried to take advantage of this situation. The party played an active role in organizing the anti-Vietnam movement.[34] Although they constituted a small minority of the participants, they were able to influence the direction of the movement, both because they were organized and because they could provide practical support to the activity. One example was the violent demonstrations against the Democratic Party Convention held in Chicago during the week of August 25, 1968. The majority of the demonstration leaders were not under Soviet control, but the Communist Party was able to contribute to the disorder. An FBI report in March 1968 about the planned demonstrations revealed that a member of the National Committee of the Communist Party USA had been assigned to coordinate activity between the party and the New Left. The FBI reported, "He is to assist in setting up a coordinating office to be financed in part by the party and to recruit full-time personnel to man it."[35]

An official publication of the demonstration organizers listed the names of those in attendance at a February 11, 1968, meeting. A number of Communist Party members participated, but they constituted less than 20 percent of the attendees. Only one party member identified himself as such, but Charlene Mitchell, a National Committee member of the Communist Party, identified herself only as representing the "black caucus." Jack Spiegel, who had been a member of the Communist Party for decades and who had run for public office on the party ticket, identified himself only as representing The Chicago Peace Council. Spiegel predicted violence at the demonstrations, saying, "We can't call 200,000 people to Chicago and then disassociate ourselves from violence. Disruption and violence will occur."[36]

Not a single Communist Party member was arrested or injured during the violent demonstrations. They helped set in motion others who would suffer the consequences. Rennie Davis and Tom Hayden, both non-Communists, were among the demonstration organizers. Davis was in charge of the demonstration headquarters, which the Communist Party helped to finance. In a document written by Davis and Hayden, they expressed their purpose:

> The Democratic Party is not "the party of the people." It is an instrument for the use of corporation executives and their lawyers, the

military brass, segregationists, machine politicians, and the old narrow-minded preservers of an "American way of life." . . . Our goal should be to brand the U.S. an outlaw power in the international community as long as it continues its racist and imperialist policies.

Hayden admitted in congressional testimony that he and Davis wrote the document.[37]

The young people injured or arrested during the violence had no idea these things would happen to them. The organizers did. In January 1968 legal and medical facilities were being organized to take care of those arrested and injured. Hayden admitted in congressional testimony that "we had to have legal and medical committees far in advance."[38]

The Communist Party did not have the ability to organize the violent demonstrations by themselves. They could and did provide encouragement and practical support to those who did organize the demonstrations. The Communist Party used a lesson taught by Lenin in 1905: get someone else to do the violence for you. As violence was developing in Russia in October 1905, Lenin wrote to his Bolshevik supporters:

You must proceed to propaganda on a wide scale. Let five or ten people make the round of *hundreds* of workers' and students' study circles in a week, penetrate wherever they can, and everywhere propose a clear, brief, direct, and simple plan: organise combat groups immediately, arm yourselves as best you can, and work with all your might; we will help you in every way we can, but *do not wait for our help;* act for yourselves.[39] [emphasis in original]

That is the essence of Soviet "active measures," influencing someone else to take the action, not having to do it themselves.

The climate of disaffection and violence attracted a minority of Americans. It was useful for the Soviets in anti-American propaganda campaigns worldwide. In the 1970s and 1980s it provided the opportunity for the Soviets to use anti-American attitudes of Americans in recruiting for espionage.

14

The KGB Today
and Tomorrow

T HE Soviet intelligence threat at this time is a sophisticated,
multifaceted data collection and influence machine. The First
Chief Directorate of the KGB is responsible for foreign intelligence.
It is divided into geographical departments, Directorates, and Services, which are responsible for specific activities. The First Chief
Directorate, called the Centre by KGB officers, operates through
branch offices, called *Rezidenturas*, in target countries. Wherever
possible, the *Rezidentura* is based in a Soviet embassy. While many
of the KGB officers work under diplomatic cover, some are ostensibly
journalists, trade mission officials, or connected with Aeroflot, the
Soviet airline, and other Soviet organizations. A few KGB officers
are "illegals," led by a KGB "illegal" *rezident*. These are KGB officers who do not appear to be Soviets. They are supplied with
"legends," or totally fictitious identities. The *Rezidentura* in each
country is responsible for all collection and influence operations.
The tasking of collection of technology and military information is
coordinated with the GRU, Soviet Military Intelligence.

The *Rezidentura*

The KGB *Rezidentura* is headed by a chief, called the *rezident*, and
is divided into four lines, each with a specific function. Line PR, or
Political Intelligence, collects both classified and unclassified information about political developments in the target country. It is also
responsible for conducting influence operations, or "active meas-

ures." Line PR recruits its agents from among government officials, politicians, and journalists, as well as people with access to one of these classes. Almost half of the KGB officers serve in Line PR.

Line PR's collection of intelligence activities is directed by the appropriate geographical desk. "Active measures" are coordinated by Service A, formerly Department D, of the First Chief Directorate. There are four components of Line PR in addition to intelligence collection against the host country. These are: the "main enemy" group, which is targeted against the United States and its citizens, regardless of the country in which it operates (this component does not appear in the U.S.); the People's Republic of China group, targeted against the Chinese and their activities in the host country; the émigré group, targeted on former Soviet citizens (Line KR also assists with this work); and the "active measures" group, which is responsible for disinformation, including forgeries, and other operations designed to influence a target audience.

Line X, or technical intelligence, collects high-tech data and is responsible to Directorate T in the Centre. Line X, like Line PR, has a large number of officers. Between the two, they constitute most of the officers of a *Rezidentura*.

Line KR is counterintelligence. Its job is to protect the Soviet colony in the host country from hostile intelligence activity. It is also responsible for recruiting agents in the host country's intelligence service, and particularly the penetration of the American intelligence community. Although only a relatively small number of KGB officers serve in this line, it is divided into components responsible for watching Soviet defectors and émigrés, Soviet diplomats, students, visiting delegations, seamen and others present in the host country. In the 1950s each of these functions was a separate line, but they are now part of Line KR, which reports to Directorate K at the Centre.

Line N, which is directed by the Illegal Service at the Centre, is responsible for providing support to KGB officers serving as "illegals." It is a very small unit. But it is particularly highly skilled. This enables them to guard against the surveillance techniques of the opponent intelligence services.

The work of the KGB *Rezidentura* in the United States can best be understood by examining some of the recent cases. In many of these cases, techniques developed decades ago appear in their modern context.

A dramatic example of the work of Line N was revealed by the FBI in March 1980. Colonel Rudolph Albert Herrmann was surfaced at a press conference at FBI headquarters. Colonel Herrmann had served the KGB for twenty-five years. Although he is of Czech origin and received his intelligence training in East Germany, he was commissioned an officer in the Soviet Intelligence Service. In 1962 Herrmann emigrated to Canada, where he spent six years before moving to the United States.

The entire Herrmann family was part of the operation. His wife and older son were KGB co-optees, Soviets who while not trained officers, carry out KGB tasks. His other son was too young to participate. Herrmann periodically returned to the Soviet Union for debriefing and retraining, the last time in 1977.

The FBI has never revealed how and when it identified Herrmann as a Soviet "illegal." When confronted, however, he agreed to work as a double agent, and convinced his wife, Inga, and his son also to cooperate. The decision to surface Herrmann came when the KGB insisted that the older son return to Moscow for advance training, with no guarantee that he would be reassigned to the United States.

Herrmann was a "sleeper." The work he did in the U.S. was routine. He identified sites for dead drops and tracked down agents with whom the Centre had lost contact. His major responsibility, however, was to be prepared to take control of a variety of Soviet espionage networks in the event that a deterioration of American-Soviet relations would cause the KGB officers under embassy cover to return home.

The Soviets had a special plan for Herrmann's son, Peter, whom they ordered to enroll in Georgetown University. His political science training would enable him to infiltrate the U.S. State Department. Peter graduated from Georgetown, where he served as photography editor of the school newspaper, *The Georgetown Voice*.

Colonel Herrmann was not an ideological defector. In 1986 he revealed to the *Los Angeles Times* that he cooperated with the FBI to avoid jail for himself and his family. As an "illegal" he did not have diplomatic immunity. Herrmann provided the FBI with considerable information on KGB methods of communication, cipher systems, secret writing, and accommodation addresses. He also identified and provided information about the many Line N, KGB officers with whom he had worked in the United States and Canada. These included several officials of the Soviet U.N. mission and employees of the U.N. Secretariat.

By 1986 Herrmann had built a business and amassed $300,000 in savings. At that point he decided to return to Czechoslovakia. But he underestimated the Czech Communist bureaucracy. Gabriel Brenka, the consul at the Czech embassy in Washington, told him that he had been stripped of his Czech citizenship "because of collaboration with anti-socialist activities." Brenka told the *Los Angeles Times* that Herrmann, whom he identified as Valousek, could not return because he is no longer a Czech citizen.[1]

During Herrmann's 1980 press conference the FBI revealed that he had identified a number of Soviet agents, including a Canadian university professor, Hugh George Hambleton. The FBI had made the information available to Canadian authorities months earlier. The Royal Canadian Mounted Police had then interrogated Hambleton, an economics professor at Laval University in Quebec. He admitted that he had been a Soviet spy for thirty years. His spy missions included travels in the summer of 1979 to Israel and Saudi Arabia under the guise of studying economic conditions. He had also spied in Latin America, and against NATO, by which he had previously been employed. Before confronting Hambleton the RCMP surveillance team watched him walk into a bookstore in Ottawa, take a magazine off the rack, look at it, and place it back on the rack, while the KGB *rezident* stood behind him. Hambleton never revealed what the signal was designed to convey.

When he admitted working for the Soviets, he allowed the mounties to search his home. They found a basement filled with shortwave radio equipment, code books, and decoding devices. Hambleton admitted meeting Vladimir Borodin, a KGB officer assigned to the Soviet embassy in Ottawa during the late 1940s. He had agreed then to provide information for Soviet intelligence, but he claimed that he was not formally recruited by Soviet intelligence until 1963 in Paris.

In May 1980 Canadian justice minister Jean Chretien announced that no charges were being filed, as Hambleton had not broken any Canadian law. Hambleton had claimed that all of his spying took place abroad, which didn't explain the communications paraphernalia and Soviet contacts in Canada. Critics complained that he had gotten away with spying because the then Canadian government did not wish to offend the Soviets.

In July 1982 Hambleton took a trip to Britain where he was arrested for violating the Official Secrets Act. He held both Canadian and British citizenship and thus could be tried in a British court. Hambleton was convicted and sentenced to ten years in prison.[2]

The Soviet intelligence tradition of using "illegals" in the United States is a long one. The earliest Soviet intelligence officers were all "illegals," attached to the Soviet pseudo embassy in New York. Arthur Adams, who started his career at that time, served as an "illegal" every time he worked in the United States over a period of at least twenty-five years. Rudolf Abel, the legendary Soviet spy, was here as an "illegal." Zubilin, the Soviet *rezident* during the war, spent his first U.S. tour during the 1930s as an "illegal."

The Herrmann case adds a new dimension to American counterintelligence concerns about "illegal" KGB officers. The training of Herrmann's son to penetrate the U.S. government raises the question of whether other Herrmann juniors are not in place even now, and whether others are being trained for such assignments.

One of the KGB's other units in Washington, Line KR, attracted some attention when the FBI arrested a former CIA officer, David H. Barnett, as a Soviet spy. His assignment, to repenetrate the American intelligence community, was intended to assist a major Line KR responsibility.

Barnett had been recruited by the KGB in 1976 in Indonesia, where he had previously served as a CIA officer. He provided the Soviets with details of CIA operations in Indonesia and identified to them thirty CIA officers and a number of local agents.

Under Soviet instructions, Barnett attempted to secure employment with the House and Senate Intelligence Committees and with the Intelligence Oversight Board. Any one of these jobs would have provided the spy with access to a variety of intelligence information. As a result of the compartmentation of intelligence information, there is no position in the intelligence community that can provide a spy with as much access to a variety of highly classified information as a staff position on one of the two intelligence committees. Barnett did not succeed in getting those jobs, although the Soviets had offered as much as $100,000 if he had succeeded. His previous work for the Soviets had netted him $92,000. Barnett pleaded guilty at his trial and on January 8, 1981, was sentenced to eighteen years in prison.[3]

One of Line KR's most successful recruitments was of CIA employee William Kampiles. For a mere three thousand dollars he supplied the Soviets with the technical manual for the KH-11 Reconnaissance Satellite, one of the most advanced pieces of American technology. Kampiles, a low-level CIA employee, had been employed as a watch officer at the Operations Center of the CIA's directorate responsible for intelligence analysis. Dissatisfied with his low-grade and boring job, Kampiles asked for a transfer to the Directorate of Operations, where he could become a case officer. When this request was turned down because of his poor work performance, he contacted the Soviets.

For some reason Kampiles confessed his crime to a colleague. When this was reported, Kampiles was arrested. On December 22, 1978, he was sentenced to forty years in prison. The damage that he did to the U.S. ability to monitor Soviet compliance with arms control treaties cannot be calculated in dollars. For three thousand dollars the Soviets obtained enough information about American technical surveillance to substantially enhance the possibility of cheating.[4]

Defections and Recruitments

The United States government obtained significant insight into the operations of Line KR in July 1985, when Vitaly Yurchenko defected in Rome. From 1975 to 1980 Yurchenko was the principal security officer at the Soviet embassy in Washington.

Yurchenko was born in 1936, in a village near Smolensk. Commissioned in the Soviet navy, he was later transferred to the KGB and was trained at the school of the Third Chief Directorate, which is responsible for counterintelligence in the Soviet armed forces. He served in the Third Chief Directorate until 1975, when he was assigned to the First Chief Directorate and sent to the United States.

During his service as chief security officer in Washington, he directed the agents assigned to watch other Soviet officials in the

United States and handled some of the Americans who volunteered to serve Soviet intelligence. He was also in charge of liaison with U.S. officials concerning embassy security.

After returning to the Soviet Union, Yurchenko worked in the First Chief Directorate, which is in charge of foreign intelligence. From September 1980 to March 1985 he was chief of the Fifth Department (internal security) of Directorate K (counterintelligence) of the First Chief Directorate. The Fifth Department is responsible for investigations of KGB officers, to prevent defections or double agents.

From April to July 1985, Yurchenko was deputy chief of the First, or North American, Department, responsible for supervising the KGB *Rezidentura* in the U.S. and Canada, as well as for coordinating the work of other components of operations against the United States and its citizens abroad. This coordination is handled through Group NORD (North), which was established in the 1970s by General Vladimir Kryuchkov, then head of the First Chief Directorate, to improve operations against the American target. Kryuchkov headed Group NORD (North), and the North American Department provided the staffing. One of Yurchenko's responsibilities was supervising the handling of important cases in the United States. Shortly before his defection Yurchenko was awarded the title "Distinguished Officer of the Organs of State Security," the KGB's highest honor.[5]

On August 9, 1985, the Milan, Italy, newspaper, *Corriere Della Sera,* revealed that the "Soviet diplomat" Yurchenko had disappeared while on temporary duty in Rome. The Soviets had requested Italian government assistance in locating him. Yurchenko had slipped away from his bodyguard while on a visit to the Vatican Museum and had defected to the United States. Yurchenko revealed a considerable amount of information to the American authorities and identified both KGB officers and Americans who had been recruited as Soviet spies.

On November 4, 1985, Yurchenko shocked the world by redefecting. On the evening of November 2, he slipped away from a young CIA officer with whom he was having dinner and made his way to the Soviet embassy. Less than forty-eight hours later he was participating in a press conference at the Soviet embassy, where he claimed that he had been kidnapped in Rome, brought to the United

States, and fed powerful drugs. He claimed that he was offered "financial security" by one of the closest aides to CIA director William Casey.[6]

The short time between Yurchenko's redefection and the press conference forced the KGB to concoct quickly his "legend" of kidnapping and drugging. They simply reused a legend that had been created to explain a previous redefection, that of Oleg Bitov, a correspondent of the Soviet newspaper, *Literaturnaya Gazeta*. Bitov had defected in 1983 while attending the International Film Festival in Venice. Although Bitov was not a KGB officer, he knew a great deal about the service because his newspaper had a close relationship with it. He was smuggled from Italy to England, where he provided a considerable amount of information to the authorities.[7] Bitov was soon a public figure. He granted interviews to the press and even made a broadcast over Radio Liberty, on March 13, 1984.[8]

On September 18, 1984, Bitov turned up in Moscow, claiming that he had been kidnapped in Venice and treated with "mind altering drugs." He said that he escaped from his captors and flew back to Moscow. Bitov was introduced at the press conference by S. S. Ivanko, the deputy chairman of the Novosti Press Agency.[9]

Bitov was certainly not held prisoner. During his defection he visited the United States and met many Americans. One of those with whom he had an hour-long conversation was one of the authors of this book (Romerstein). The two were alone, and Bitov could have left and gone to the Soviet embassy at any time. One of the things Bitov told Romerstein was that a colleague of his on *Literaturnaya Gazeta*, Yona Andronov, had boasted of being a high-ranking official of the KGB. Andronov is now stationed in New York as the newspaper's correspondent.

Levchenko, coauthor of this book, noted at the time of Yurchenko's press conference that Yurchenko's case provided the Soviets with a dilemma. If they punished him, they proved his press conference story to be false. If they did not punish him, they encouraged others to try defection. Their only solution, Levchenko felt, would be to confine Yurchenko to a mental institution.

Levchenko's prediction soon proved correct. On November 14, 1985, Yurchenko was presented at a press conference in Moscow. After he finished his presentation, a Soviet doctor, Nikolay Zharikov, spoke. He claimed that Yurchenko exhibited "neurological disorders" and "psychotic states." The doctor also diagnosed "acute organic damage to the brain" and said that Yurchenko displayed "emotional instability."[10] The KGB had solved its dilemma.

Some months later, when the Western press speculated that Yurchenko had been killed, he suddenly reappeared. A West German television correspondent, Lutz Lehmann, "accidentally ran into Yurchenko in the bar of the Soviet press center in Moscow." The press center, which is part of the Novosti Press Agency building, can be entered only by persons possessing a special card and is guarded by uniformed police. Yurchenko volunteered to be interviewed and claimed that he was working in his office in Moscow and had no difficulty with the Soviet authorities.[11]

Yurchenko has not been seen since, but on August 9, 1986, *Moskovskaya Pravda* carried what was supposed to be an interview with him. The main theme was that the Bulgarians and Soviets had nothing to do with the attempted assassination of the Pope, a matter which was then before the Italian courts.[12]

One of the important items of information provided to U.S. authorities by Yurchenko helped identify a former CIA officer who was selling secrets to the KGB. Yurchenko reported that in the fall of 1984 senior KGB officials had met in Austria with the former officer, who was paid money in exchange for classified information relating to U.S. intelligence operations in the Soviet Union. An investigation identified the former CIA employee as Edward Lee Howard of Santa Fe, New Mexico. He had been employed by the CIA from January 1981 until June 1983. The *Wall Street Journal* reported that Howard provided the KGB with information that identified a valuable Soviet CIA agent, who is believed to have been executed.

Although a polygraph test taken before Howard joined the CIA indicated that he was an occasional drug user, Howard was hired when he promised not to use drugs in the future. He entered a training program to become a CIA case officer in Moscow and to run CIA agents in that dangerous environment. Howard took another polygraph examination before being sent to Moscow, which indicated that he had continued his drug use. He was dismissed by the agency.

On September 20, 1985, Howard was interviewed by the FBI. The next evening he slipped away from his residence and disappeared. On September 14, 1986, he showed up in Moscow and appeared on a television program where he was interviewed by Genrikh Borovik, the brother-in-law of Vladimir Kryuchkov, then head of the First Chief Directorate of the KGB.[13] Borovik read to the television audience a decree of the Presidium of the Supreme Soviet:

> The U.S.S.R. Supreme Soviet Presidium received a request from U.S. citizen Edward Lee Howard, former CIA employee, to grant him political asylum in the U.S.S.R. He explained that the reason for his request was the need to hide from the U.S. special services which were groundlessly persecuting him. Proceeding from human-itarian considerations, the U.S.S.R. Supreme Soviet Presidium granted Edward Lee Howard's request. He was given leave to reside in the U.S.S.R. for political reason.

Borovik boasted that Howard "is the first former employee of the CIA to seek political asylum in our country." Howard, during the interview, claimed that his escape was accomplished with Soviet help. He described those CIA workers who work on Soviet cases as follows: "[M]any of these people have Slavonic roots. Either they themselves emigrated in their time, or their ancestors emigrated. They have Slavonic names, and their attitude toward the Soviet Union is the same as that of the old émigrés." He said that there were also others, "who escaped from the Soviet Union comparatively recently." Borovik's response revealed the anti-Semitic attitude the Soviets have toward Jews who leave the country. He was asked, "Are you talking about Soviet citizens of Jewish nationality?" Howard answered, "Well, for example, my Russian teacher left the Soviet Union in 1979, and she was Jewish."[14]

The recruitment of a CIA case officer, even a failed, short-term employee such as Howard, provides valuable information for Line KR in its work against the United States. Howard was paid, but money appears to have been only part of his motivation. Another factor was his resentment of the United States government for interfering with his drug use. The disaffection of members of the "me first" product of the 1960s and 1970s can provide a valuable tool for KGB recruitment.

Another recent Line KR success was the recruitment of FBI special agent Richard W. Miller. In an affidavit in that case, Bryce

Christensen, head of the Los Angeles office of the FBI, identified one of the methods used by the KGB to recruit Americans:

> One technique used by the Soviet Intelligence Service (SIS) to obtain information is to identify a flaw or weakness in a target person and, through a variety of means, exploit this weakness in order to ultimately convince the target to cooperate with the SIS. Some of the weaknesses successfully exploited in the past by the SIS include money, ideological persuasion, personal rapport with an SIS officer, coercion, flattery, and material assistance.

The recruiter of FBI agent Miller was not an experienced KGB officer, but a mere agent. She was Svetlana Ogorodnikova, who, with her husband, Nikolay, had emigrated from the Soviet Union in 1973. Svetlana performed a number of chores for the KGB. In 1979 a Soviet citizen who was seeking political asylum in the United States reported to the FBI that two women had confronted her and urged her to return to the Soviet Union. The women later brought to her apartment two men, identified as officials of the Soviet consulate in San Francisco, to continue the pressure. The Soviet citizen identified Svetlana Ogorodnikova as one of the two women. When the FBI interviewed Ogorodnikova in 1982 she admitted that, on one occasion, acting on instructions of the Soviet consulate, she located the former Soviet citizen and brought two consulate officials to her apartment to pressure her to return. She admitted also that she had a close relationship with the Soviet consul general in San Francisco, Aleksandr Chikvaidze, and Vice Consul Victor Zonov. She also identified other Soviet officials with whom she was acquainted.

At various meetings with the FBI, Ogorodnikova admitted that in June 1982 she visited the Soviet embassy in Washington, where an official requested that she work for the Soviet government in the Los Angeles area. In August 1982, she revealed, Boris Belyakov, a vice consul of the Soviet Consulate in San Francisco, urged her to maintain contact with special agents of the FBI "in order to assist the Soviet government."

Special Agent Miller became Svetlana's lover and began to supply her with documents. In September 1984 Miller was confronted by his FBI colleagues. He admitted that on August 12, 1984, Svetlana had asked him if he would be willing to work for the KGB and provide FBI documents, for which he would be well paid. She claimed, falsely as it turned out, that she was a major in the KGB. Miller provided Svetlana with a copy of an FBI document, classified secret, that, according to the FBI, "would give the KGB a detailed picture of FBI and U.S. intelligence activities, techniques and requirements." Svetlana also introduced Miller to a man she called Nikolay Wolfson, whom she described as having thirty years' experience in handling financial matters for the KGB. This person was actually her husband, Nikolay Ogorodnikov.

At the request of Svetlana, Miller attempted to use his FBI contacts to learn the address of former KGB officer Stanislav Levchenko, one of the authors of this book. Svetlana also attempted to get the same information through an attorney. Both failed. When Svetlana tried to arrange for Miller and herself to go abroad to meet with an officer of the Soviet GRU in Vienna, they were arrested.

The Ogorodnikovs pleaded guilty. Nikolay was sentenced to eight years in prison. Svetlana got eighteen years. Nikolay claimed that his only involvement was to help his wife, who he said had been "a drunk all her life." He was particularly bitter about Miller's love affair with Svetlana. He said that Miller, "took my wife and used her like a prostitute. I was left outside like a dog." Miller was tried and convicted and was given two concurrent life sentences plus fifty years. The judge made clear that he felt Miller should never be paroled from prison.[15] Miller's weaknesses, money and sex, enabled the KGB to use him. The availability of Svetlana and her husband facilitated the operation, even though the FBI was aware of their relationships with the Soviet consulate.

Line X = Technology

One of the largest and most significant of the KGB functions is the collection of technology. This work is performed by Line X of the KGB *Rezidentura* and is directed by Directorate T of the KGB's First Chief Directorate. An evaluation of this activity was provided by the U.S. government to Congress in 1982. The unclassified report revealed:

The United States and its Allies traditionally have relied on the technological superiority of their weapons to preserve a credible counterforce to the quantitative superiority of the Warsaw Pact. But that technical superiority is eroding as the Soviet Union and its Allies introduce more and more sophisticated weaponry—weapons that all too often are manufactured with the direct help of Western technology. . . .

Since at least the 1930s, the Soviet Union has devoted vast amounts of its financial and manpower resources to the acquisition of Western technology that would enhance its military power and improve the efficiency of its military manufacturing technology. Today this Soviet effort is massive, well planned, and well managed—a national-level program approved at the highest party and governmental levels. This program accords top priority to the military and military-related industry, and major attention is also given to the civilian sectors of Soviet industry that support military production.

The Soviets and their Warsaw Pact allies have obtained vast amounts of militarily significant Western technology and equipment through legal and illegal means. They have succeeded in acquiring the most advanced Western technology by using, in part, their scientific and technological agreements with the West to facilitate access to the new technologies that are emerging from the Free World's applied scientific research efforts; by spending their scarce hard currency to illegally purchase controlled equipment, as well as to legally purchase uncontrolled advanced Western technologies that have military-industrial applications; and by tasking their intelligence services to acquire illegally those US and Western technologies that are classified and export controlled.[16]

The Military Industrial Commission of the Soviet Presidium of the Council of Ministers (VPK) coordinates the development of both Soviet weapons and the program to acquire Western technology for those weapon systems. KGB Directorate T and the GRU provide much of this information.

The U.S. government estimates that in the early 1980s approximately five thousand Soviet military research projects per year benefited from Western hardware and technical documents. During that time more than thirty-five hundred instructions were sent to the KGB to acquire specific Western hardware and documents. The KGB was successful in roughly one-third of the cases. This saved the Soviets approximately a half a billion rubles a year in research costs. Most of these savings were realized by the Ministry of the Defense Industry, responsible for armor and electro-optics, and the Ministry of the Aviation Industry.

Based on KGB documents the U.S. government revealed in an other unclassified study:

> The Soviets estimate that by using documentation on the US F-18 fighter their aviation and radar industries saved some five years of development time and 35 million rubles (the 1980 dollar cost of equivalent research activity would be $55 million) in project manpower and other developmental costs. The manpower portion of these savings probably represents over a thousand man-years of scientific research effort and one of the most successful individual exploitations ever of Western technology.
>
> The documentation of the F-18 fire-control radar served as the technical basis for new lookdown/shootdown engagement radars for the latest generation of Soviet fighters. US methods of component design, fast-Fourier-transform algorithms, terrain mapping functions, and real-time resolution-enhancement techniques were cited as key elements incorporated into the Soviet counterpart.
>
> Moreover, F-18 and F-14 documentation served as the impetus for two long-term research projects to design from scratch a new radar-guided air-to-air missile system. The documentation also was instrumental in formulating concrete specifications to develop new Soviet airborne radar countermeasures equipment against the F-18 and F-14.[17]

The same U.S. government report estimates that Directorate T has approximately one thousand officers, with three hundred of them stationed abroad as part of Line X. The estimate for GRU officers with similar assignments was approximately fifteen hundred serving outside the U.S.S.R.

Some Western technology is not stolen by spies. It is openly sold to the Soviet Union by businessmen and governments who do not understand the military use of the technology. One of the instruments for overt technology transfer is the U.S.S.R. Chamber of Commerce and Industry. Until recently its chairman was Yevgenyi Petrovich Pitovranov, who is a reserve lieutenant general in the KGB. From 1962 to 1964 he was the director of the KGB training school. Of the 140 officials of the Chamber of Commerce identified by the U.S. government, about one-third are known or suspected intelligence officers. A few are GRU, but most are KGB.[18]

Americans willing to spy for the KGB also have played a major role in the transfer of classified technology information to the Soviet Union. Agents recruited in American corporations have done substantial damage to U.S. security. One shocking case came to light when a U.S. embassy official was leaving the Soviet embassy in Mexico City on January 6, 1977. He found a young American being questioned by the police after throwing an object on the Soviet embassy grounds. The young American, Andrew Daulton Lee, asked the official for help in explaining himself to the police. A second U.S. official was called and accompanied Lee to the police station, where it was discovered that Lee had in his possession an envelope containing a number of filmstrips. They turned out to be documents marked "Top Secret," relating to a U.S. government project at the California-based space and defense communication company, TRW, Inc. When questioned by Mexican authorities and the FBI, Lee identified his accomplice, Christopher John Boyce, an employee of TRW. When questioned, Boyce admitted providing Lee with the documents, which he claimed were outdated and valueless, but for which the Soviets had paid approximately $70,000.

Lee needed the money to finance his drug habit and business ventures. Money was not the only motive, however. Boyce, who was radicalized during the 1970s, was an active opponent of the war in Vietnam and hated the U.S. government. Interviewed on the television news program, "Nightline," in June 1985, Boyce explained, "I was so foolish I thought that the CIA was the enemy, and I thought that I would be able to manipulate the KGB into punishing what I thought was the enemy, the CIA." Boyce and Lee were convicted and sentenced to life in prison for espionage.[19]

The Walker Spy Ring

Substantial damage was done to the United States by the spy ring headed by John Anthony Walker, Jr. Walker was born in 1937, served in the U.S. Navy from 1955 to 1976, and retired with the rank of chief warrant officer. During his navy career he held clearances that gave him access to the most highly sensitive top secret cryptographic communication information. This related to communication between navy ships and submarines and would be enormously important to an enemy of the United States.

In November 1984 Walker's estranged wife told the FBI that her husband was a Soviet spy and that twice—in 1968 and 1974—she had accompanied him when he placed secret information in dead drops for the Soviets to pick up. The FBI placed a court-authorized wiretap on Walker's phone. When his phone conversations indicated that he had something to do on the weekend of May 18 and 19, 1985, the FBI surveillance team knew to be particularly alert. Although Walker had told people he intended to go to North Carolina, the FBI watchers followed him to the Washington metropolitan area. Near Potomac, Maryland, Walker began making U-turns, driving circuitous routes and stopping at the side of the road, in an attempt to detect possible surveillance. At one point, he succeeded in evading the watchers for over an hour and a half. When they observed him again, Walker was still engaging in countersurveillance techniques. Soon he left his vehicle near a tree marked with a "No Hunting" sign. When Walker left the area, an FBI agent later found a brown shopping bag containing trash and a manila envelope sealed with masking tape left behind.

While observing Walker, the FBI team spotted Aleksey G. Tkachenko, a known KGB officer assigned to the Soviet embassy. Tkachenko apparently sensed that something was wrong and did not attempt to pick up Walker's package. Shortly after Walker's arrest, Tkachenko's tour of duty was cut short and he left the country. He was a highly experienced KGB officer, formerly attached to the Seventh Directorate in Moscow, which is responsible for surveillance. As far as could be learned, his only KGB assignment in the United States was to clear Walker's dead drops two or three times a year.

When FBI investigators examined Walker's envelope, they found 120 U.S. Navy communications documents marked "secret" and "confidential." Some of the documents appeared to have come from the USS *Nimitz*. Walker's son, Michael Lance Walker, was a navy yeoman 3d class then assigned to the *Nimitz*. With the documents was a letter, which said, in part:

> This delivery consists of material from "S" and is similar to the previously supplied material. The quantity is limited, unfortunately, due

to his operating schedule and the increased security prior to deployment. His ship departed in early March and they operated extensively just prior to deployment. . . . Since "S" is providing a large quantity of material, the quantity of film to shoot is all *[sic]* is also becoming large. I have been trying to figure out an alternative method that will decrease the size of the packages to deliver. I have a Super 8mm movie camera, which is capable of single frame shots . . . . I have enclosed a short sample of a document shot with a camera using different focusing methods . . . they don't look very good to me, but I thought you may have an idea on how we could make this method work.

The designation "S" referred to John's son, Michael, who was arrested on board the *Nimitz*. John's brother, Arthur, was also arrested. All of them confessed their activity. John Walker received a life sentence as did his brother, Arthur. Michael got twenty-five years.

Walker's brother, Arthur, complained to the *Washington Post* that his sentence was too harsh: "There is no fairness anymore. I used to go to the movies and you would see John Wayne and there was a sense of fair play, okay? I mean, if you made a mistake and you were sorry and you tried to make up for it, everything would be okay in the end, right? What ever happened to fair play?"

In 1981 John Walker had become a partner in a private detective business. It is interesting that ten years earlier the London *Sunday Telegraph*, May 16, 1971, revealed that foreign embassies in London were using British private detectives to gather information that could be used for blackmail and corruption in espionage.

The Walker case revealed how carefully the Soviets handle an important agent. Most of his meetings with the Soviets were in Vienna, Austria, a typical "third-country" operation. During these meetings Walker and his KGB contact would walk the streets, even in very cold weather. Even when Walker complained about the cold they would not obtain a safe house to meet in, as his contact had come directly from Moscow and the Vienna *Rezidentura* was unaware of the operation. Thus the representative of the Centre could not use the *Rezidentura* to obtain a safe indoor location. Walker's information was kept closely held to avoid letting too many Soviet officials know of his existence. In that way KGB hoped the Americans would not learn that their highly sensitive communications systems had been compromised.

Walker identified his old friend, Jerry Alfred Whitworth, as a member of his ring. Whitworth served in the navy from 1956 to 1983. Sometime in the 1970s he began to supply John Walker with highly classified information to be given to the Soviets. He supplied documents, cryptographic keylists, and keycards, which could be used by the Soviets to break American codes.

Before Vitaly Yurchenko redefected, he revealed to the FBI that he had received a briefing in Moscow on the Walker/Whitworth case. Yurchenko learned that the KGB regarded the work of this spy ring to be "the most important operation in the KGB's history." The material turned over by Walker and Whitworth enabled the KGB to decipher over one million sensitive American military communications.

Early in the Walker operation the KGB transferred the case to Department 16, which is responsible for the most sensitive and important KGB clandestine operations around the world. A number of KGB officers received high awards for their work in this case. Tkachenko was assigned to Department 16 when he worked in the United States handling Walker's dead drops. Yurchenko was informed by a high-ranking KGB official that the information obtained from the Walker/Whitworth spy ring would be "devastating" to the United States in case of war.

Whitworth received more than $300,000 from the KGB. After his conviction the judge ensured that he would spend the rest of his life in prison.

Walker, on the other hand, appears not to have been a purely mercenary spy. He had an ideology, based on an arrogant belief that he did not need to be loyal to the United States. Although Walker's political views have been described as right wing, they did not include patriotism. While not radicalized like Boyce, Walker, too, felt no loyalty to his country.[20]

Another Soviet spy who did extensive damage to American security was Ronald William Pelton. He did it for the money. Pelton was an employee of the highly sensitive National Security Agency from November 1965 to July 1979. NSA is the code-breaking organization of the U.S. intelligence community.

Based on information provided by Yurchenko, the FBI interviewed Pelton. He admitted that in January 1980, six months after leaving government service, he had visited the Soviet embassy in Washington and agreed to provide sensitive information in exchange for cash. During this first meeting he told the KGB the details of a highly sensitive U.S. collection system, which gathered information about the Soviet Union. Pelton identified Anatoly Slavnov, a KGB officer, as the man who debriefed him on American secrets.

On two occasions the Soviets used a third-country operation. In October 1980, and in January 1983, Pelton traveled to Vienna, Austria. Each time he was housed in the apartment of the Soviet ambassador, which is within the Soviet embassy compound, for three to four days of debriefings. He provided Slavnov with written answers to written questions. The Soviets attempted to organize a third trip to Vienna in 1985, but Pelton failed to make the meeting.

During Pelton's trial the government presented evidence that he had provided the Soviets with detailed information about six separate top secret NSA projects aimed at intercepting and analyzing Soviet communications signals. Pelton also provided the Soviets with "an encyclopedia" that he had developed for NSA on Soviet communications. This told the Soviets which of their signals were being intercepted and could be analyzed. The encyclopedia allowed the Soviets to develop security procedures to deny the United States this information.

Pelton took the stand in his own defense and admitted receiving $35,000 from the Soviets for the highly classified information. He was convicted of espionage.[21]

The Polish Intelligence Service, which is controlled by the KGB, assists in the collection of high technology. The Polonia Society for Liaison with Poles Abroad is a front for contact with Poles in the West who might have access to high tech. In a recent interview with a Polish journal, Jozef Klasa, the secretary general of the society, admitted, "The Society desires to gain entry to the scientific and technical groups in which émigrés participate." The society is planning a Congress of Scientists of Polish Origin, to take place in Poland in 1989, to facilitate the contacts.[22]

Line X and GRU officers also do overt collection of intelligence when possible. On September 2, 1981, Yuri Petrovich Leonov, a

GRU officer serving as assistant military air attaché at the Soviet embassy in Washington, visited the office of Representative David F. Emery (R–Maine). He asked John Rabb, Congressman Emery's aide, for a copy of a plan the congressman had developed for basing the MX missile. Rabb called the FBI as soon as the Soviet left the office. He reported that Leonov had a heavy Russian accent and spoke poor English. In response to Rabb's question, Leonov identified himself and said he was from the Soviet embassy. Rabb immediately ordered him to leave.

Congressman Emery wrote a letter to the FBI requesting that members and employees of Congress be briefed about the Soviet intelligence threat. He wrote that he has become "increasingly alarmed at what appears to be a heightened intelligence effort on Capitol Hill on the part of the Soviet Embassy personnel. . . ." His aide, John Rabb, told the press, "These [Soviet] agents operate with impunity on Capitol Hill. They try to monitor hearings, get copies of testimony, copies of things that interest them like the MX plan and various proposals disseminated by Congress." He said the Soviets, "have a large contingent of agents available" to do this kind of intelligence collection.[23]

This case recalled an earlier example of an attempt at overt collection of sensitive information by Soviet intelligence. On January 19, 1979, Vladimir Kvasov, who identified himself as a Soviet embassy official, visited the distribution center of the U.S. government's General Accounting Office in Washington, D.C. He had made a number of previous visits, but this time he requested several GAO reports. He asked for them by number, indicating a knowledge of the specific subjects of the reports. Some that he requested had not yet been issued, two were classified (the distribution center has available only unclassified reports). The matter was reported to the FBI. Their investigation determined that the Soviets had not been able to secure classified information in this manner.[24] In an open society, a considerable amount of information is available to anyone who wants it. The Soviets take advantage of this openness.

Soviet intelligence uses a method called the "mosaic concept" in analyzing overt information. The Soviets have concluded, quite correctly, that if enough unclassified information is collected about a subject and carefully analyzed, it can reveal the classified or protected data. If enough pieces of the "mosaic" can be gathered, it is possible to discern the picture.

In 1967, in an article in *Sovetskaya Rossia* celebrating the fiftieth anniversary of the KGB, V. Petrov provided an illustration of how the "mosaic concept" works:

> On 20 March, 1935, the affair of the writer Berthold Jacob, kidnapped from Switzerland by agents of the Hitlerite Secret Service, resounded throughout the world.
>
> Jacob at that time was writing much on the German Army, in a state of rearmament. He was able to reveal all the organizational details of the fascist army in a small book. The book gave short biographic information on the 168 Hitlerite generals, the disposition of many divisions was revealed, and so on.
>
> When the kidnapped Jacob was brought for interrogation to Walter Nikolay, the Chief of the fascist secret service, he proved that he had borrowed all his information for this book from the open German press, from journals, and papers. So, for example, the basis of the assertion that General Haase commands the 17th Division billeted at Nuremburg was taken from an obituary notice in a Nuremburg paper which said that the commander of the 17th Division, recently transferred to Nuremburg was present at the funeral. In an Ulm paper he turned attention to the description of the marriage ceremony of a Major Stemmermann at which Colonel Virov, Commander of the 36th Regiment of the 25th Division was present. Evidently, in order to give the wedding a more solemn character, the local journalists had mentioned that the Commander of this Division himself, General Shaller, was at the wedding. For what sort of wedding is it without a General! And so, patiently, Jacob had collected information on 168 Generals and on what they are doing.[25]

The Soviet writer, interested only in describing what has become a standard Soviet intelligence method, did not reveal the rest of the Berthold Jacob story. As a result of mass protests in Switzerland and elsewhere, the Nazis were forced to free Jacob. They did not allow the matter to rest, however. In 1941 they discovered that he was in Portugal, a neutral country. The Gestapo kidnapped him again, and in 1944 he died in a Nazi prison.[26]

Early in 1987 three Soviet diplomats working in Tokyo returned home after Japanese authorities charged that they were part of a spy network seeking information about the U.S. F-16 and AWACS (Airborne Warning and Control System) aircraft. On August 20, 1987, the Japanese expelled Yuri Pokrovsky, a Soviet deputy trade representative. He was caught illegally trying to purchase documents relating to military aircraft. In January 1987 a Soviet embassy official in Bonn was expelled for attempting to recruit German citizens for intelligence gathering.

The government of Norway expelled three Soviet officials for illegally gathering high-tech industrial intelligence. They were Valentin V. Korpusov and Valeriy I. Reschetnikov, of the Soviet embassy, and Aleksandr I. Sergienko, of the Soviet trade mission. A fourth Soviet accused in the case, Vladimir M. Vetrov, of the Soviet trade delegation, had departed earlier.[27]

Line PR

The largest KGB component in the *Rezidentura* is Line PR. It often accounts for half of the KGB officers in a given country. Its function is the collection of political information and the execution of "active measures" (influence operations). In most countries Line PR has four components: the main enemy group, targeted against the United States, American installations, and Americans abroad; the PRC group targeted against facilities and personnel of the People's Republic of China; the émigré group targeted against former Soviet citizens; and the "active measures" group. While the appropriate country desk at the Centre directs the collection activities of Line PR, Service A directs the "active measures" group. Service A was originally established as Department D for Disinformation, but in the early 1970s it was upgraded to Service A.[28]

In 1976 the FBI nipped in the bud a potentially dangerous Line PR initiative. James Frederick Sattler applied for a job as a minority staff consultant to a subcommittee of the House International Relations Committee. He had been recommended for the job by Congressman Paul Findley. The FBI warned Findley that Sattler had been recruited by the East German intelligence service and was being run as an agent on behalf of the Soviets. Sattler was denied the job but somehow learned of the FBI interest. In the hope that he could protect himself from criminal charges, he filed a foreign agent's registration statement with the Department of Justice.

Sattler admitted in the statement:

> In 1967, I was recruited by an individual named "Rolf" who identified himself as a member of the "Coordinating Staff of the Countries of the Warsaw Treaty Association." Since then, I have learned that "Rolf" is connected with the section for Strategy and Tactics, Institute for Marxism and Leninism, which is connected with the Central Committee of the SED of the German Democratic Republic (GDR). I drafted and signed a statement indicating my willingness to cooperate with the "Coordinating Staff of the Countries of the Warsaw Treaty Organization" and have received approximately $15,000 for my services. I have also received an "honor decoration" for my services issued to me by the Ministry for State Security of the GDR.
>
> Since 1967, I have transmitted to my principals in Berlin, GDR, information and documents which I received from the North Atlantic Treaty Organization and from individuals in institutions and government agencies in the Federal Republic of Germany, United States, Great Britain, Canada, and France.
>
> I photographed a portion of this information with a microdisc camera and placed the microdiscs in packages which I mailed to West Germany which I know were subsequently received by my principals in Berlin, GDR. Other documents and information I photographed with a Minox camera and personally carried the film to my principals in Berlin or handed them to a courier. The microdisc camera was given to me by my principal.

Sattler admitted that he was working on behalf of the Combined Intelligence Services of the Warsaw Treaty Organization, headquartered in East Berlin. He also admitted receiving training in "codes and ciphers, microphotography, radio and mail communications, clandestine meetings, [and] concealment devices" from several East Germans, whom he knew as Rolf Winzer, Hans, Horst, Juergen, and Gunther. During his last visit to East Germany, in November 1975, he was instructed to obtain a position in the United States government with access to classified information. He was not to attempt to make contact with his handlers in East Germany until after he succeeded in gaining that employment. The plan was that he was to return to East Germany clandestinely, while a U.S. government employee, to be debriefed.[29]

Sattler disappeared immediately after filing the statement in 1976. He has not been seen since. Had he succeeded in obtaining the employment he sought, he would have had access to a substantial amount of classified information relating to the foreign policy of the United States, our relationship with our Allies, and our concerns about our adversaries.

The KGB has a program of recruiting students who may in later life have access to classified information. An example of this was revealed in 1975, when a young American journalist who had been targeted by the KGB revealed his story. Paul J. Browne had been cooperating with the FBI, who used the double-agent case to identify Soviet recruitment methods.

Browne was a journalism student at Columbia University in September 1973 when he first met Alex Yakovlev, a Soviet employed by the United Nations to broadcast news to Eastern Europe. Yakovlev was charming and frequently took the young American out for drinks and dinner. But Browne became concerned when the Russian kept asking him questions about Jewish professors and students at Columbia. He was also bothered by Yakovlev's clandestine behavior. Browne asked the FBI for advice.

Soon Yakovlev suggested that the young American write freelance articles for the Soviet press, for which he would be paid thirty to fifty dollars each. The offer of payment for something that the Soviets did not need revealed to the FBI that this was not mere socializing but a recruitment. His FBI contact suggested to Browne that Yakovlev was serving as a recruiter and that he would soon be introduced to another Soviet who would be the real agent handler. This evaluation was correct. Yakovlev introduced Browne to Boris Mikhailov, a translator at the U.N. Mikhailov suggested that Browne spy on and prepare reports on a Jewish student organization on campus. Spying on his fellow students was more than the young American was willing to do. He broke the contact and wrote an account of his experiences in the *Washington Post*.[30]

The use of the access agent and the hand-over to a case officer is classic KGB recruitment technique. The desire to recruit a bright young journalism student who might one day have access to significant information is also a time-worn KGB objective.

A U.S. Information Agency officer was arrested in 1978 for turning classified cables over to Vietnamese intelligence officers. The Vietnamese Intelligence Service is directed by the KGB. Ronald Louis Humphrey, the USIA officer, was neither a mercenary nor an ideological spy. The Vietnamese recruited him by threatening the family of his Vietnamese common-law wife, who were still in Vietnam. Humphrey's wife revealed to the press, after his arrest, that her sixteen-year-old son was a hostage in Vietnam.

Humphrey turned the classified documents over to David Truong, a Vietnamese resident in the United States who had been active in the anti-Vietnam War movement. He in turn gave the information to a courier who took it to Vietnamese officials at the U.N. and in Paris. What the conspirators did not know was that the courier, Mrs. Dung Krall, was a double agent for the FBI. The defenders of Humphrey and Truong complained that "everything Truong sent to Paris by her was first turned over to the FBI and CIA for examination."

The secret and confidential documents turned over contained information on United States political, military, and diplomatic relations, and intelligence assessments. Humphrey and Truong were convicted and each was sentenced to fifteen years in prison.[31]

During his appeal David Truong had the active support of an organization called the National Alliance Against Racist and Political Repression. This group filed an amicus curiae brief with the Supreme Court in 1981. The executive secretary of the organization was Charlene Mitchell, a high-ranking functionary of the Communist Party USA. A cochairperson was another national leader of the Communist Party, Angela Davis. In 1973 the House Committee on Internal Security, after public hearings, offered the characterization of this organization:

> Based on the evidence presented in the hearings . . . the committee concludes that the National Alliance Against Racist and Political repression is completely controlled by the Communist Party USA, and represents one of the most ambitious attempts ever mounted by the party to establish a "defense" apparatus for the purpose of duping the unwary into supporting CP USA aims under the guise of appearing to support humanitarian or reform objectives.[32]

The public support of a convicted spy by the Communist Party USA is not a usual phenomenon. While the communists mounted a major campaign for the Rosenbergs in the early 1950s, the party usually tries to disassociate itself from identification with Soviet and bloc espionage.

One of Line PR's most effective spies against NATO was the Norwegian, Arne Treholt. Treholt, who assisted the Soviets both in "active measures" and in classical espionage, was not a mercenary. He spied for ideological reasons. Although not a member of the Communist Party, Treholt was active in the extreme left wing of the Norwegian Labor Party and was vehemently anti-NATO and anti-U.S. He masked these attitudes when he worked for the Norwegian U.N. delegation in New York from 1980 to 1982.

When he was arrested in January 1984 he was head of the press and information office of the Norwegian foreign ministry. A Norwegian government press release of January 21, 1984, revealed that Treholt had been arrested while attempting to travel abroad "to a meeting with representatives of the KGB." Treholt was on his way to meet his case officer, Gennadi Fedorovich Titov, in Vienna. Titov, who had been the *rezident* in Oslo until he was expelled in 1972, handled Treholt in a typical third-country operation, meeting him in Vienna and Helsinki.

Treholt admitted spying for the Soviets but insisted that the only money he received was actual payment for his expenses, such as travel to make the meetings with KGB. His first contact with the Soviets was in 1967, when he was a young journalist and political activist. He was activated as an agent in 1974, when he became secretary to the Norwegian minister for trade and shipping. In that capacity he played an important role in undermining the Norwegian bargaining position during fishery negotiations with the Soviets. He also promoted, through the minister, propaganda in support of a "Nordic Nuclear Weapons Free Zone." This, of course, is a favorite Soviet theme. Treholt used his government positions to influence policy and to manipulate the press. Two Norwegian journalists, Thorleif Andreassen and Gunnar Moe, writing about the case, pointed out that there was "nothing illegal in Arne Treholt's clever manipulation of the Norwegian press. It was more a case of his utilizing what many saw as a lack of professionalism among journalists."

When Treholt was arrested he was carrying classified documents. In addition to Titov, KGB officer Alexsandr Lopatin met with Treholt in Vienna, and Vladimir Zhizhin handled him from 1980 to 1982 at the U.N. Treholt was convicted of espionage and sentenced to twenty years in prison.[33]

Arne Treholt served as both a spy and an agent of influence. Both KGB or GRU officers handle agents engaged only in classical espionage, but agents of influence, while usually handled by KGB officers, can also be controlled by Soviet journalists, academicians, or other officials on behalf of the KGB. In 1986 the U.S. government released details of Soviet methodology in their control of agents involved in influence operations. According to the U.S. government analysis:

> The KGB uses several terms to characterize different types of Soviet relationships with foreigners used in influence operations. These terms reportedly are used loosely, and the relationships vary from case to case in the extent of cooperation involved, the degree of leverage or control the Soviets are able to exert, the frequency of contact, and the type of reward received by the foreigner. Rewards range from financial payments to such intangible benefits as publicity of the collaborator's accomplishments or the promise of special channels of communication to the Kremlin.
>
> Three of the terms used by the KGB in reference to agents of influence are:
>
> - A *trusted relationship* is one between a foreigner in a high position and a Soviet who may or may not be an intelligence officer. The extent to which the foreigner—called a trusted contact—cooperates with the Soviets ranges from very limited to complete cooperation.
> - A *controlled agent of influence* is a foreigner who has actually been recruited by the KGB. Often these individuals are developed as agents in their youth and later achieve prominence. The KGB often, but not always, provides financial assistance. Once the individual has been recruited, he may not be contacted again until he has reached a position of importance.
> - A *special contact* is an individual who maintains a relationship with the KGB in a country that has close relations with the USSR, and where active KGB recruitment of agents is constrained by political considerations. Although the special contact does not receive a regular salary from the KGB, the relationship is often reinforced by gifts and other forms of attention.

The motivations of foreigners whom Moscow regards as agents of influence or special contacts can vary widely. Some individuals cooperate with the Soviets basically because they are flattered by Soviet attention and favors. Others cooperate out of fear; a time-honored KGB practice is to compromise foreigners visiting the U.S.S.R. so as to make them vulnerable to blackmail later. Still other individuals cooperate largely because of ideological compatibility or because their own tactical political objectives coincide with those of the Soviets. In addition, some foreign leaders may find it convenient to maintain a tie to the KGB in the belief that it serves as an effective channel for expressing views to Moscow.[34]

The targets of agents of influence are usually government officials or journalists. One particularly effective Soviet agent of influence against Western journalists was the famous Victor Louis. According to the U.S. government report:

> The USSR also uses Soviet citizens as unofficial sources to leak information to foreign journalists and to spread disinformation that Moscow does not want attributed directly. One of the most prolific of these individuals is Vitality Yevgeniyevich Lui—better known as Victor Louis—a Soviet journalist who several KGB defectors have independently identified as a KGB agent. In addition to his leaking such newsworthy items as Khrushchev's ouster, the imminent Soviet invasion of Czechoslovakia, and the reassignment of Marshall Ogarkov, he has been used to try to discredit the memoirs of Stalin's daughter Svetlana and, more recently, to surface a videotape on the physical condition of Soviet dissident Andrei Sakharov. After the Chernobyl accident, Victor Louis was the vehicle for publicizing distorted statements of Sakharov that implied he was supportive of the Soviet handling of the accident and critical of the Western reaction to it.[35]

While it is now difficult for Moscow to use members of the American Communist Party in classical espionage, they frequently use them for active measures. Testifying before the House Intelligence Committee in 1982, Edward O'Malley, then assistant director of the FBI and head of the Intelligence Division, was asked by Congressman Bill Young (R–Florida) whether the Communist Party USA was still the main recruiting ground for Soviet espionage. O'Malley responded:

No, it's not. The Soviets, as a result of the Smith Act trials in the 1950s, no longer have the degree of trust that they once had that the activities of the CP USA membership will be unknown to us. The Soviets are well aware that the CP USA is highly vulnerable to penetration, and I believe that with this in mind they would prefer to go elsewhere to recruit their agents. Marxist ideology as a motivation is not what it once was, although it is not totally useless. Many of the people that the Soviets are recruiting today are not affiliated with a leftist movement in the United States or any part of the Communist Party, and the motivation more often than not today is money. I am not saying that they do not use and recruit in the CP USA, but they do it for reasons other than classical espionage. They do it for active measures, encouraging people who may be members of the Communist Party or their front groups to conduct certain activities or engage in certain activities which would be of benefit to the Soviet Union. So I would have to say, summing up, that the Soviet use of the CP USA and its front groups today is primarily in the area of active measures. We are aware of the Soviets' contacts with second-generation individuals who may be the sons and daughters of CP USA members and with former members of the CP USA. I do not rule out the use of these people in classical espionage operations as well as active measures.[36]

O'Malley revealed during this testimony that, "the KGB has clandestinely transferred funds to the CP USA on behalf of the CP Soviet Union." KGB officers both in Washington and at the U.N. in New York are in regular contact with members of the American Communist Party and its front groups. They monitor party activities and transmit guidance to CP officials. O'Malley reported that KGB officers under diplomatic cover carry cash to fund the activities of the American Communist Party. In addition, O'Malley revealed that in the United States the KGB has developed a few "trusted contacts" in the local press. These contacts accept guidance and in some cases direction from the KGB. While these journalists are apparently not prominent, O'Malley suggested that the Soviets are also, "interested in developing contacts and cultivating prominent journalists."[37]

The Communist Party USA is tiny. Its few members are not likely to have access to classified information. The FBI is alert to preventing them from gaining such access. The limited influence of the American Communist Party restricts its capability even in active measures. Nevertheless the party sometimes achieves significant gains. According to an FBI report, printed in the *Congressional Record* by Congressman Bill Young, the U.N. Special Session on Disarmament in June 1982 was a principal target of Soviet active measures. The Soviets found particularly useful the mass peace demonstration that took place in New York on June 12, 1982. Although approximately 500,000 people participated in the march, few of them knew of the Soviet manipulation. Of the twenty-eight members of the steering committee for the march, only five were controlled by the CP USA. The five convinced the other twenty-three that signs carried in the march should reflect only those views on which everyone agreed. Since everyone agreed that U.S. nuclear weapons were a threat to peace, that should be reflected in the signs. Since there was disagreement concerning Soviet nuclear weapons, they should not be mentioned. Most of the demonstrators did not make their own signs. They carried signs that were handed to them. A *Pravda* correspondent boasted that during the demonstration, "I did not see a single anti-Soviet placard."[38] A Soviet propaganda film found in Grenada after the liberation showed pictures of the march, while the Soviet narrator said in English that the American people courageously understood that it was their country's nuclear weapons that threatened world peace, not the Soviet Union's.

A handful of people were able to manipulate a situation to make it look as if hundreds of thousands of Americans were condemning their own government and supporting Soviet policies. This, of course, was not true. Almost all of the Americans who participated in the march were there to express a desire for peace, not anti-Americanism. The target audience of the Soviet propaganda film in Grenada and elsewhere was in no position to know that. A relatively small effort succeeded in creating a false impression in the interest of the Soviet Union. This concept was explained by Boris Ponomarev, a former top Soviet official with long Comintern experience. He referred to "the conscious choice of tools of struggle capable of yielding the biggest and most solid results with the least expenditure of efforts."[39]

The Communist Party USA had decided in April that it would actively participate in the June 12 march. Michael Myerson, a member of the Communist Party National Council and head of the party's front, the U.S. Peace Council, reported to a party conference in Milwaukee on April 23–25, 1982, that the party had decided:

That there be a strong Party presence on June 12th, with banners and literature in addition to the Party press. That we help develop a national trade union peace network out of the local union activity on behalf of the Freeze and in support of June 12. That where the U.S. Peace Council (USPC) exists, we work with others to aid its participation for June 12; where it doesn't exist we work with others to try to launch local Peace Council participation with buses and banners; that we undertake to help distribute a half-million USPC special leaflets for June 12th.[40]

A few weeks after the march, the Communist Party sent a secret communication to its members boasting, "The Party was extremely active in working to make the June 12th Demonstration an outstanding success." The party members were instructed to utilize the contacts that they had made in the peace movement to organize opposition to the Israeli invasion of Lebanon.[41]

In 1987 the FBI revealed how one front organization for the Communist Party USA assists Soviet intelligence operations. In an FBI report placed in the *Congressional Record* by Congressman Bill Young, the activities of the National Council of American-Soviet Friendship was exposed. The FBI reported that the NCASF was formed by the Communist Party in 1943. According to the FBI, "the Soviet Union provides funding for NCASF operations." An important function of the organization is to provide the opportunity for Soviet groups to visit areas of the United States "where they previously had limited access or to travel to areas closed to Soviet diplomats assigned in the United States. The Soviet officials who are visiting the United States under NCASF assistance are also in a position to provide assessments of Americans for possible targeting and recruitment by the KGB."[42]

The KGB has even been able to use Israeli Communists to spy for their client states in the Arab world. In 1972 four Israeli Jews and an Arab were arrested for spying for Syria. The authorities indicated that these were leftists. Most were members of the Israeli Communist Party. The party responded that one of the accused was a dissident Communist who had left the party some years earlier.[43] The use of dissident Communists and other leftists by Soviet intelligence is a long-standing practice.

In 1966 a Soviet agent who had penetrated British intelligence, George Blake, escaped from prison. He had been serving a forty-two-year sentence for espionage. He had served only five years of his sentence. Blake succeeded in getting to the Soviet Union. In 1970 he wrote a series of articles for IZVESTIA about his experiences. The editors wrote, "we introduce him to our readers: George Blake, Soviet intelligence agent."[44] Blake boasted of the significance of the information he had been able to supply the KGB. The Soviets revealed that Blake had been awarded the Order of Lenin, the second highest Soviet medal.[45]

Blake's escape baffled the British for many years. In 1970 a former convict, Sean Bourke, wrote a book in which he revealed that he had organized Blake's escape. Bourke went with Blake to Moscow where he was quite well treated, but he longed to return to the West. The KGB had confiscated Bourke's manuscript describing the prison break. He received it by mail from Moscow, heavily corrected in a hand he believed was George Blake's.[46]

Bourke was careful in his book not to identify his accomplices. They were finally identified in 1987, when it became apparent that they were ideological, not mercenary, accomplices. Three founders of Britain's Campaign for Nuclear Disarmament raised seven hundred pounds to cover the cost of transportation, food, lodging, and a walkie-talkie set for the escape. They also arranged for a CND doctor to treat the injuries Blake sustained when he fell from the prison wall. The three were Michael Randle, who now heads Bradford University's peace studies department, his wife, Anne, and Pat Pottle, now an antique dealer. When their names were discovered by the *London Sunday Times,* Randle and Pottle conceded that they were "undoubtedly" the two men involved in the incident. Randle suggested that the government would have to prove that he was guilty and that he would refuse to say anything. Nevertheless, he told the *Times* that while he disapproved of Blake's communism, he supported freeing him on "morale" grounds since both East and West employed spies.[47]

Target: Émigrés

The KGB, in the tradition of its predecessor, the GPU, continues to target Soviet émigrés. On April 12, 1986, a press conference in Moscow heard Oleg Tumanov, a former senior editor of the Russian service of Radio Liberty, denounce the radio, the United States, and his fellow émigrés. The émigrés were all CIA agents, he claimed.[48]

Radio Liberty, with headquarters in Munich, is funded by the United States government to provide a forum for the views of the Soviet people and an alternative to the controlled Soviet media. Most of the staff are former Soviet citizens. In the 1950s the CIA ran the radio. That is no longer true, and Radio Liberty now is overtly funded by the United States Congress.

Tumanov had become unhappy in the West. He decided to return to the Soviet Union and do whatever was needed to ingratiate himself with the Soviet authorities. He ended up assisting in the smear campaign against Anatoly Shcharansky.

Shcharansky, a leader of the Soviet Jewish dissidents, was finally released by the Soviet Union in 1986. When he arrived in Israel, rather than retiring in silence, Shcharansky continued to speak out for the right of the Soviet Jews to emigrate. The Soviet government, which had long falsely accused Shcharansky of being a CIA agent, needed to damage his image.

On May 19, 1986, Tumanov met with a group of Soviet journalists in Moscow to announce that Shcharansky was a "decoy duck" for the CIA. He claimed that 80 percent of the employees of the Russian service of Radio Liberty "are connected with Zionist organizations." The Soviets use the term Zionist as a synonym for Jew. As part of their campaign against the émigrés, the Soviets claim that those who speak out against the Soviet Union must be Jews, as real Russians would support the Soviet regime. Anti-Semitism appears frequently in Soviet anti-émigré propaganda. Consistent with Soviet propaganda, Tumanov claimed that Western concern about the treatment of Soviet Jews was just a "fuss started by the U.S. Administration and Zionists."[49]

Soviet concern about Western understanding of the plight of Soviet Jews was illustrated by a 1979 book, published in Moscow, attacking those who raise the issue. Particular targets were Jewish groups in the United States that visit the Soviet Union to assist the Soviet Jews. The book also zeroed in on Avraham Shifrin, who had spent ten years in a Soviet slave labor camp. Shifrin now heads an institute in Israel that interviews Jewish former inmates of the Soviet camps.[50]

A whole series of Soviet pamphlets and books attacking the émigré organizations have been printed in the Soviet Union and distributed in the West. Occasionally one of those books provides information that contradicts the Soviet propaganda line. One book, *Anatomy of Treason,* an attack on the Ukrainian Nationalists, admitted that during World War II the leaders of the group, Bandera and Stetsko, whom the Soviets accuse of being Nazi collaborators, had been imprisoned by the Nazis in the Sachsenhausen concentration camp. This was not a normal habitat for Nazi collaborators. Even more significant, the book revealed a wartime collaboration between the Ukrainian Nationalists and the Jewish victims of the Nazis. Although written in the usual incredible Soviet style, the information is clear:

> During the Great Patriotic War 1941-1945, many Zionists were members of the Ukrainian Insurgent Army (UPA) and the Ukrainian People's Revolutionary Army (UPRA). For example, the Zionist Haim Sigal, alias Sigalenko, was a chieftain and "Bulba's" right-hand man. He was a participant of many bloody massacres of the Ukrainian, the Polish, and the Jewish population. A number of Zionists such as Margosh, Maximovich, "Kun" and others were the "Ukrainian Insurgent Army" officers. According to a report by a Nazi Einsatzcommando, Zionists closely cooperated with the Bandera ringleaders. The latter provided them with the forged German documents. The contacts with Zionists were also maintained through Metropolitan Andrei Sheptitski.[51]

The Ukrainian-Jewish connection and anti-Nazi activities of the Organization of Ukrainian Nationalists (OUN) and the Ukrainian Insurgent Army (UPA) are shown in a Nazi proclamation posted in the Ukraine, January 21, 1944. It listed the death penalty for twenty Ukrainians: six for membership in the OUN, thirteen for participation in the UPA (described by the Nazis as a bandit group), and one for hiding Jews.[52]

That Soviet Jews participated in Ukrainian combat units that fought against both the Nazis and Soviets, and that Ukrainian Nationalists saved the lives of Jews by providing forged identity papers, shows a common interest going back many decades. That common interest troubles the Soviet leaders. The KGB has taken advantage of the legitimate concern in the West that Nazi war criminals be punished in order to divide the Jews from their East European allies in the struggle for human rights in the Soviet Union.

The late congressman John Ashbrook wrote in the *Congressional Record* that he disagreed with the U.S. government taking Soviet-produced evidence that any particular individual was a war criminal. Ashbrook wrote:

> We cannot condemn anyone based on Soviet evidence but we must make sure that no Nazi or Communist criminal should receive sanctuary here. We can be sure of this by using our basic American laws of evidence. Soviet evidence is tainted and should not be utilized in American courts. We will not forgive Nazi Germany or Soviet Russia for their crimes. The policy of our government must be based on this moral principle.[53]

An American scholar, expressing his personal view at a U.S. government-sponsored conference, also criticized the use of Soviet-provided documents in American cases against alleged war criminals. He pointed out that the Soviets have succeeded in their campaign to divide the natural allies:

> The most important gain for the Soviets in this regard is the almost certain prevention of a political alliance between American Jews, on the one hand, and the Baltic-Ukrainian communities, on the other. The 1970s had seen some significant efforts both in the Ukrainian and Baltic communities to build bridges toward the Jewish communities to forge a common anti-Soviet front. The chasm may have now become too deep and too wide to be bridged effectively in the near future.[54]

On September 14, 1988, the KGB held a press conference in the Ukrainian city of Kiev. KGB colonel Konstantin Vysotsky claimed to have neutralized the operations of the Organization of Ukrainian Nationalists in the Ukraine by placing two agents inside the group. The two KGB agents, Lvov physician Syvatoslav Panchishin, and Kiev journalist Yuri Ivanchenko, claimed to be the "virtual leaders" of the underground group's center. They were assisted by Aleksander Minkowicz, a major in the Polish Intelligence Service.

If the KGB claim is true, this operation would be a repeat of the 1920s *TRUST* operation. However, the leadership of the OUN outside of the Ukraine says it never heard of the two agents, and that there is no "center" of the OUN in the Ukraine, as the underground groups in different cities are kept apart for security reasons. The documents of the 1987 OUN 7th Grand Assembly, which were shown at the press conference to prove the story, have been distributed in large numbers in the Ukraine through the underground. The authors have a copy of the documents of the 5th Grand Assembly of OUN, disguised as the materials of the 25th Congress of the Communist Party of the Ukraine, for underground distribution.

In a peculiar error, the KGB claimed that the "neutralized" group in the Ukraine was "the Foreign-Based Units of the Organization of Ukrainian Nationalists." This is actually the name used by the OUN outside the Ukraine, not inside.

The KGB claimed to have seized "large sums of money in Soviet and foreign currencies, photo cameras, radio systems, and copying equipment meant for espionage and ideological provocations," and accused the OUN of gathering intelligence on missiles and military units. The OUN denies this and says it is engaged only in political activity. The KGB also accused the OUN of having close connections with "reactionary groups" such as "Afghan antigovernment forces, Zionists, and Vietnamese and Laotian counterrevolutionaries, as well as the backing given them by the U.S. administration."[55]

There is no documented case of the KGB committing a murder outside of the Soviet Union since the killing of the Ukrainian leader, Bandera, in 1959. Other bloc intelligence services have certainly done so, and the Soviet Union retains the capability.[56] The head of the Bulgarian Secret Police, Dimitur Stoyanov, declared on Bulgarian television September 15, 1978, "Our enemies are not safe from us anywhere. The counterrevolution must realize that it has no safe places of asylum." One month earlier a Bulgarian émigré, Georgi Markov, was murdered by a stab from a poison umbrella in London. The stab left a tiny poison pellet in his body. When analyzed, the pellet, the size of a pinpoint, was discovered to contain a microscopic hole filled with a deadly poison. A week later Markov's compatriot, Vladimir Kostov, barely survived an attack by the same method in Paris.[57]

Kim Philby, the Soviet master spy who penetrated British intelligence, hinted in his autobiography that he was responsible for the failure of an attempt of British and American intelligence to send a group into Albania to overthrow that communist government in 1949.[58] Philby, who served as the British liaison with the CIA, warned the Soviets that the émigrés would invade. They were massacred when they arrived.

In 1982 the Albanian émigrés tried again. They landed on the Albanian coast and were wiped out. This time the landing was betrayed by an Albanian intelligence officer who penetrated the exile movement pretending he was Xhevdet Mustafa, a hero of the postwar Albanian fight against the Communists. The real Mustafa had died in the United States a few years earlier.[59]

The Russian émigré organization, NTS (National Alliance of Russian Solidarists), has long been a target of the KGB. In the 1950s, kidnappings and attempted murder were commonplace in the anti-NTS campaign. In 1969 the KGB tried a new—actually very old—tactic, *TRUST*. That year a man using the cryptonym Peter made contact with the NTS. He identified himself as Constantin S. Malyshev. He was actually Vladimir N. Lopukhov, a KGB officer. An unusual Soviet, with opportunities to travel to the West, Peter brought a letter back from a group of his friends in the Soviet Union. They were supposedly members of an underground group operating against the Soviet government, similar to the 1920s *TRUST*. After exchanging some letters, the leader of the supposed group asked for a meeting with the NTS in Helsinki. He used the cryptonym Yuri and claimed his name to be Andrei N. Rodionov. In reality he was the senior KGB officer, Valery V. Karpinsky. The first meeting with him took place in 1970. Other meetings followed. He sometimes brought his assistants, Igor and Gleb. Their real names were given as Pyotr K. Didko (in reality, Yuri F. Baryshev) and Vladimir Lesnitsky (in reality, Anatoly Burlov). They, too, were KGB officers.

One of the insistent demands of the KGB officers was that NTS officials go to Moscow to meet with their group. NTS, remembering Savinkov and Reilly and the experience with *TRUST*, never made the trip. The KGB officers also wanted to identify members of the NTS operating in the Soviet Union. Because the NTS instructs its members to operate in small groups and not to contact each other, in order to prevent the KGB from identifying them, the names were not provided. In 1982 the NTS exposed the operation as a KGB provocation. The NTS concluded that its purpose was to capture NTS leaders, to break down the small cell structure of the organization in the Soviet Union, to interfere with the ability of the NTS to smuggle out documents of the internal opposition and to smuggle in NTS literature, and to discourage Soviet citizens from contact with NTS.

Once again the KGB had used methodology developed decades earlier to carry out its work. It counted on no one remembering the *TRUST* operation, but NTS's recollection of history interfered with this KGB operation.[60]

One of the most important functions of Line PR is the creation of forgeries. In the post-World War II period, hundreds of forgeries aimed at discrediting the United States and its allies were created by the KGB. Some forgeries are created at the Centre in Service A. These are sent via diplomatic pouch to the *Rezidentura*. The chief of the Active Measures group of Line PR receives the envelope containing the forgery. He is instructed to open the envelope while wearing gloves, so that the forgery, when mailed, will contain no fingerprints of KGB officers. Other forgeries are created within the active measures group in the *Rezidentura*.

One Soviet forgery that has been used many times in the last dozen years is a supposed U.S. Army field manual, marked "Top Secret," which claims that the United States creates terrorist groups in friendly countries to force those countries to go along with U.S. policies. This bizarre document first appeared in Bangkok, Thailand, in September 1976. It was left on the bulletin board of the Philippines embassy. In 1978 it reappeared in two Spanish-language publications, where it had been placed by a Spanish communist and a Cuban intelligence officer. In 1979 the KGB prepared a Portuguese-language version of the forgery and covertly circulated it among military officers in Lisbon.[61]

In 1981 a scandal broke in Rome concerning the political influence of a Masonic Lodge called P-2. The Soviets took advantage of the scandal by claiming that a copy of the "field manual" had turned up in the P-2 files. The purpose, of course, was to authenticate the old forgery, which had been exposed many times in the past and to link the United States to the P-2 scandal. In 1983, two Soviet books repeated the false story linking the forgery to the actual P-2 scandal.[62]

In 1981 the Soviets forged a letter signed with the name of President Reagan to the king of Spain. The purpose of the forgery was to complicate U.S.-Spanish relations and to interfere with Spain's plan to enter NATO.[63]

A forgery appeared during the Carter administration that purported to be a presidential review memorandum in which the administration supposedly supported South Africa and was planning to persecute American blacks. This forgery, which got some play in the black American press, was first surfaced in the San Francisco *Sun Reporter* dated September 18, 1980, but distributed a few days earlier. The newspaper was published by Carlton Goodlett, at that time a member of the Presidential Committee of the international Soviet front, the World Peace Council.[64]

In congressional testimony in 1982, FBI official Edward J. O'Malley revealed that "the KGB officers abroad have obtained stationery, letterheads, and signatures of high-ranking American officials, presumably to use in additional forgery 'active measures' operations."[65]

In 1986 a West German journalist obtained a copy of a document that purported to be a 1983 confidential speech of U.S. secretary of defense Caspar Weinberger. The journalist requested that the U.S. government verify its authenticity. In recent years, due to an active campaign by the U.S. government, most serious journalists check on questioned documents before they publish them. This document, like so many others, turned out to be a forgery. It was related to the Strategic Defense Initiative (SDI) and said exactly the opposite of what Weinberger would have. It claimed that SDI was an offensive rather than a defensive system, that it would be used to control the NATO allies, that it would enable the United States to maintain a technological lead over its allies, and—the biggest lie of all—that the Soviets do not have their own SDI program.

The forgery was exposed in the West German daily, *Bild Zeitung*, of July 29, 1986.[66]

One of the authors of this book (Levchenko) served as chief of the active measures group in the Tokyo *Rezidentura*. He had considerable experience with Soviet forgery operations. In 1986 coauthor Romerstein had his own experience.

In August 1986 the *Washington Post* and *U.S. News and World Report* received through the mail in plain white envelopes photocopies of a letter on the letterhead of the United States Information Agency, signed Herbert Romerstein. The letter was supposedly sent to Senator David F. Durenberger, former chairman of the Senate Intelligence Committee, and appeared to spell out a program to make the Soviets look bad in connection with the Chernobyl disaster. No such letter was ever sent, nor was there any such program. Both publications contacted USIA for verification and were told that the letter was a forgery. Both carried stories exposing the Soviet forgery.

The FBI report on Soviet active measures in the United States, 1986-1987, contained more detail concerning this forgery. The FBI described this forgery as

an especially interesting example of Eastern-Bloc support of a Soviet active measures operation. The USIA letterhead and the signature block on the forgery were taken from a genuine letter Romerstein had previously written to Lieutenant General Robert Schweitzer concerning the analysis of another Soviet forgery allegedly written by Schweitzer. During September 1985, Romerstein testified before the Senate Foreign Relations Committee on Soviet forgeries and offered to provide them with a copy of his letter to Schweitzer for congressional publication. Subsequently, the Press Attaché of the Czechoslovakian Embassy, Vaclav Zluva, requested a copy of Romerstein's unclassified letter to Schweitzer. Romerstein provided him with a copy, but uniquely marked the one copy he gave Zluva. When the forgery bearing Romerstein's name surfaced in the United States, it was obvious, because of the unique markings Romerstein had put on the Schweitzer letter, that it had been used as the exemplar to fabricate the Chernobyl forgery. When Romerstein confronted Zluva with the forgery, Zluva denied being involved in its preparation but admitted sending a copy of the Schweitzer letter supplied by Romerstein to Prague. Romerstein, who is an expert on active measures operations, believes Prague officials sent the Schweitzer letter to Moscow where it was used as the exemplar for the Chernobyl forgery. This forgery technique of photocopying a genuine letterhead and signature onto a document that contains a bogus text is common among Soviet forgeries. It facilitates preparation of the forged document and generally makes the task of analysis more difficult.[67]

Alert journalists exposed this forgery in time, and it backfired on the Soviet perpetrators. However, anti-American forgeries continue to be produced by the KGB. There are gullible people in the world who will believe some of the forgeries even after they are exposed.

It might be supposed that KGB forgeries and disinformation would cease during periods of friendly relations between the United States and the Soviet Union. Unfortunately, this does not happen. KGB Line PR officers continue their forgeries and disinformation, and the friendlier relationship enables them to contact a wider range of Westerners for spotting and assessment for recruitment.

Three Line PR officers were expelled from Zaire on July 31, 1987. They were Embassy First Secretary Yuri D. Churyanov and two technical personnel, V. M. Zotov and I. A. Ivanov. Churyanov had been expelled from France in April 1983. The government of Zaire accused them of involvement in "infiltration and disinformation activities."

New Zealand in 1987 expelled Sergey Budnik, a KGB officer involved in operations with members of the Socialist Unity Party, a pro-Moscow communist organization. In 1980 then Soviet ambassador Vsevolod Sofinsky was expelled for passing money to this organization.[68]

Regardless of what else happens in the world, the KGB officers, who call themselves "fighters of the invisible front,"[69] will continue their work. Their quality has improved over the years. The heavy-handed Stalinists, who replaced the early idealist Chekists, have given way to the highly professional KGB officers of today. In an interview with *Pravda* September 2, 1988, then KGB chief V. M. Chebrikov revealed that twenty thousand Soviet intelligence personnel fell victim to Stalin's purge. That wiped out an entire generation of the early idealists. Among the victims Chebrikov listed were Artuzov, the godfather of *TRUST*, Berzin, and Unschlicht. They were followed by a generation of heavy-handed Stalinists.

The KGB officers of recent decades have been of a higher caliber. They are better educated and more cosmopolitan than their immediate predecessors. This has been a mixed blessing for the KGB bosses. It has resulted in significant defections of KGB officers to the West. Chebrikov admitted in his *Pravda* interview that KGB employees have been among those who have cooperated with Western intelligence services. This is the price the KGB has paid for an improvement in quality.

Americans who have had recent contact with Soviets with known KGB connections have reported an even greater improvement in their quality. Many speak excellent English. They show a broader knowledge of the United States and the world than would have been permitted before the era of *glasnost*. Some have exhibited a sense of humor, even joking about the KGB at times. However, the United States remains the main enemy. KGB officers will make a significant effort to recruit Americans both at home and abroad. They have been taught that Americans are vulnerable to recruitment. Some can be bought with money, others with flattery. Some Americans, the KGB believes, because they are alienated from their own country, will be willing to spy for its enemies. And there are always those who, through ego or vulnerability to blackmail, can be used by the KGB.

During the December 1987 summit in Washington, longtime observers of the KGB were shocked when one of the members of the Soviet delegation was identified as Vladimir Kryuchkov. He was the head of the First Chief Directorate of the KGB, the man in charge of foreign intelligence operations. There was considerable speculation as to why such a high-ranking intelligence officer would visit "the main enemy." One explanation seems logical. Kryuchkov was taking advantage of the opportunity to see the target close up. Instead of sitting at his desk and reading reports about the United States, its people, and its leaders, he saw for himself. This innovative approach indicates that the KGB of the future will be an even more effective weapon in the hands of the Soviet Communist Party leaders than it has been in the past.

Kryuchkov, although a protégé of the late Yuri Andropov, is regarded as a representative of the "new political thinking" personified by Mikhail Gorbachev. After serving as a diplomat in Hungary under Ambassador Andropov during the 1956 uprising, Kryuchkov followed him back to Moscow. When Andropov assumed leadership in 1957 of the Central Committee department responsible for bloc relationships, Kryuchkov assisted him. When Andropov became head of the KGB in 1967, Kryuchkov went with him and later headed the First Chief Directorate, which is charged with overseas intelligence gathering and active measures.[70]

"Group NORD"

One of Kryuchkov's important duties as head of the First Chief Directorate of the KGB was to chair "Group NORD," which since the 1970s has been responsible for recruiting Americans as KGB agents. This unit was created on Kryuchkov's initiative. He has argued within the KGB that during periods of friendlier relations with the United States, Americans become more vulnerable to KGB recruitment.

Speaking at a conference at the Soviet Foreign Ministry in July 1988, Kryuchkov made some significant comments. These were published in the open Soviet press. He criticized the "old thinking":

> We poorly study and know people; we pay too little attention to the development of contacts with foreign political and public figures, and we are too sluggish and inconsistent in fighting for their hearts and minds. It is evidently easier to create enemies than to win supporters. . . .
>
> Without an objective vision of the world, a vision of it without embellishments, cliches and stereotypes, all talk about the effectiveness of our foreign policy actions is mere phrase-mongering.

Speaking of the innovations developed by the KGB during the Gorbachev period, Kryuchkov said:

> The changes taking place in the country today and their impact on the international situation have posed the issue of a revamping and further improvement of the performance of the security organs, specifically, the external service. Its range of tasks is being clarified and expanded. A deeper and more sober approach to assessing the work of the special services is being elaborated, and work forms and methods are being reviewed where necessary. . . .
>
> The Soviet security service is waging a stubborn and complicated struggle. We attach great importance to the human factor, to teaching staff members to think in new political categories.[71]

In October 1988, V. M. Chebrikov was replaced as head of the KGB by Vladimir Kryuchkov.[72]

Notes

Full citations (with the exception of newspapers) may be found in the bibliography.

Introduction

1. Lenin wrote in his 1918 "Letter to American Workers": "America has taken first place among the free and educated nations in level of development of the productive forces of collective human endeavor, in the utilisation of machinery, and of all the wonders of modern engineering." Nevertheless, he accused "The American people" of being "hired thugs" of the "wealthy scoundrels." But he concluded: "The American workers will not follow the bourgeoisie. They will be with us, for civil war against the bourgeoisie." (Lenin, *Collected Works*, Vol. 28, 62–3, 70).
   In 1929 Lenin's successor, Stalin, said: "[T]he American Communist Party is one of those few communist parties in the world upon which history has laid tasks of a decisive movement. . . . I think the moment is not far off when a revolutionary crisis will develop in America, that will be the beginning of the end of world capitalism as a whole." (Speech delivered in the American Commission of the Presidium of the Executive Committee, *Communist International*, May 6, 1929, 19–20).
2. Ponomarev et al., *The International Working Class Movement*, Vol. 4, 87–88.
3. Serov, TASS, December 23, 1957, in Russian, translated in *FBIS Daily Report*, December 24, 1957, CC1–2.
4. On July 25, 1988, Foreign Minister Shevardnadze spoke at an extraordinary conference for the employees of the Ministry of Foreign Affairs. It lasted three days, and more than three hundred people spoke during the discussion, which was divided into eight panels. An abridged version of the Shevardnadze speech and reports from the panels were published in *International Affairs*, Moscow, October and November 1988.
5. Andropov, *Pravda*, December 21, 1967, in Russian, translated in Novosti Press Agency, *Daily Review*, December 21, 1967.
6. Dzerzhinsky, *Prison Diary and Letters*, 290–291.
7. Ibid., 293.

8. Lenin, *Collected Works*, Vol. 30, 503.
9. Dzerzhinsky, op. cit., 178.
10. Ibid., 297–298.
11. Ibid., 299.
12. Lenin, op. cit., Vol. 31, 444.
13. U.S. House of Representatives, Committee on Un-American Activities, 1952, *The Shameful Years*, 5.
14. Lenin, op. cit., Vol. 33, 358–359.
15. Smirnov, *Sovetskaya Kultura*, From the Biography of a Chekist, December 10, 1983 (in Russian).

1. Early Days

1. United States Senate, Committee on Foreign Relations, *Russian Propaganda*, 7, 11, 14, 33.
2. Ibid., 44, 76f.
3. Ibid., 125.
4. Ibid., 127.
5. See chapter 11.
6. U. S. Senate, op. cit., 42.
7. Ibid., 41; and Nuorteva, *An Open Letter to American Liberals*.
8. U.S. Senate, op. cit., 420–421.
9. Gitlow, *I Confess*, 28.
10. New York State, Joint Legislative Committee Investigating Seditious Activities, *Revolutionary Radicalism*, Vol. 1, 678.
11. Ibid., 681.
12. People's Commissariat for Foreign Affairs, *The Foreign Policy of Soviet Russia*, 15–16.
13. U.S. House of Representatives, Special Committee to Investigate Communist Activities in the United States (Fish Committee), *Investigation of Communist Propaganda*, Part 2, Vol. 1: Testimony of J. Edgar Hoover, 16–22.
14. Lenin, *Collected Works*, Vol. 21, 342.
15. United States Senate, Committee on the Judiciary, *Brewing and Liquor Interests and German and Bolshevik Propaganda*, Vol. 3, 1185.
16. Communist Party of America, *Manifesto and Program, Constitution, Report to the Communist International*, 40.
17. *The Communist*, June 12, 1920, 3.
18. *Communist Labor*, February 25, 1920, 5.
19. *The 4th National Convention, Workers (Communist) Party of America*, 37.
20. Foster and Gitlow, *Acceptance Speeches*, 12.
21. U.S. House of Representatives, Special Committee on Un-American Activities (Dies Committee), *Investigation of Un-American Propaganda Activities in the United States*, Vol. 13, 8137–138, 8141–142.
22. *The American Labor Who's Who*, 62.
23. Dies Committee, op. cit., 8160–161.
24. Dies Committee, Executive Hearing, Vol. 2, 564.

25. Workers (Communist) Party, *Minutes of the Political Committee, January 14, 1927* (mimeographed and marked "Read and Destroy") 4.

26. Dies Committee, Executive Hearing, op. cit., 564.

27. Workers (Communist) Party, *Minutes,* op. cit., 1.

28. Dies Committee, op. cit., Vol. 7, 4675–676.

29. *International Press Correspondence,* May 6, 1925, 535–540. The identification of "Powers" as Lovestone may be found in Draper, *American Communism and Soviet Russia,* 134.

30. U.S. House of Representatives, Committee on Un-American Activities, *Hearings Regarding Communist Espionage,* 3540–542.

31. Gitlow, *The "Red Ruby";* and *Gitlow vs. New York,* 268 U.S. 652 (1925).

32. *International Press Correspondence,* December 12, 1928, 1676.

33. Stalin, *Speeches on the American Communist Party,* 37–38.

34. Ibid., 17.

35. Communist Party USA, *On the Road to Bolshevization,* 43–44.

36. Lovestone, et al., *Appeal to the Comintern,* 4.

37. Lovestone was interviewed by Theodore Draper. See Draper, *American Communism and Soviet Russia,* 428.

38. Dies Committee, Executive Hearing, op. cit., Vol. 2, 568.

39. U.S. House, *Hearings Regarding Communist Espionage,* op. cit., 3556; and Dies Committee, op. cit., Vol. 7, 4684.

40. U.S. House, *Hearings Regarding Communist Espionage,* op. cit., 3558.

41. Dies Committee, op. cit., Vol. 10, 5875.

42. Gitlow, *I Confess,* 569.

43. Bedacht, et al., *Five Years International Workers Order,* 5.

44. *Towards Socialism,* (newsletter), New York, May 1, 1949.

45. Gitlow, *Some Plain Words On Communist Unity,* 10–11.

46. Dies Committee, op. cit., Vol. 11, 7100–101.

47. *International Press Correspondence,* December 19, 1936, 1498–499.

48. Dies Committee, op. cit., Vol. 11, 7100–101.

49. Szinda, *Die XI Brigade.*

50. Stern, *Spaniens Himmel,* 34.

51. U.S.S.R. Institute of the International Working-class Movement, *International Solidarity With the Spanish Republic,* 46.

52. U.S. House Committee on Un-American Activities, *The Shameful Years,* 8–9.

53. Ibid., 11; and U.S. House of Representatives, *Hearings Regarding Communist Espionage,* op. cit., 3564–569.

54. *Shameful Years,* 1952, 12–13.

55. Agabekov, OGPU, *The Russian Secret Terror,* 195–196, 198.

56. Ibid., 12.

57. Ibid., 44–45.

58. Ibid., 54–55.

59. Ibid., 272.

60. *International Press Correspondence,* June 18, 1924, 343, and Apr. 4, 1925, 350.

61. Lazitch, *Biographical Dictionary of the Comintern*, 312, 412; and *The Communist International*, September 20, 1935, 1363–364; and Sobolev, et al., *Outline History of the Communist International*, 39.
62. Dzhirkvelov, *Secret Servant*, 52–55.
63. U.S. House of Representatives, Special Committee to Investigate Communist Activities in the United States (Fish Committee), *Investigation of Communist Propaganda*, Part 2, Vol. 1: 46.
64. Ibid., Part 1, Vol 4, 211–14.
65. Ibid., 217–18.

2. Influence Operations

1. A fingerprint record in the files of the New York State correction authorities shows Julius Hammer, prisoner #71516, white male, 5 ft. 10-1/2 in., born 1874, was convicted of first-degree manslaughter and confined to Sing Sing Prison, Ossining, New York. The fingerprint record was taken 7/19/20.
2. Lenin, *Collected Works*, Vol. 45, 337.
3. Ibid., 346–347.
4. Ibid., Vol. 33, 291.
5. Ibid., Vol. 45, 355.
6. Ibid., 362–363.
7. Ibid., 542–544.
8. Ibid., 559.
9. Lenin, *Sochineniva*, Vol. 40, 152 (Russian Fifth Edition). This interview does not appear in the English-language *Collected Works*, which are based on the Russian Fourth Edition. The interview was published in *The World*, February 21, 1920.
10. A number of books provide extensive information on the TRUST, including Blackstock, *The Secret Road to World War Two;* Bailey, *The Conspirators;* Reilly, *Britain's Master Spy;* Nikulin, *Mertvaya Zyb' (The Swell of the Sea);* Ardamatsky, *Vozmezdiye (Revenge);* and Wraga, *The Trust* (unpublished manuscript).
11. *Sovetskaya Kultura*, Moscow, December 10, 1983.
12. The Soviet version of the Savinkov Case appears in Ardamatsky, *Vozmezdiye*. The Soviet version of the Reilly Case appears in the magazine *Nedelya*, Moscow, No. 44, 1982.
13. Reilly, *Britain's Master Spy*, 45.
14. Ibid., 199; and *Nedelya No. 44*, 1982.
15. *International Press Correspondence*, June 23, 1927, 755–756.
16. *Pravda*, April 29, 1988.
17. *International Press Correspondence*, April 15, 1926, 429.
18. Zetrin, et al., *They Knew Lenin, Reminiscences of Foreign Contemporaries*, 79–86.
19. Adler, *The Anglo-Russian Report*, 47. The authenticity of the quotation from Muenzenberg was admitted by his widow, Babette Gross, in her biography *Willi Muenzenberg*, 121, 133.

20. Workers (Communist) Party USA, *Minutes of Political Committee*, June 15, 1928, 1.
21. Muenzenberg, *Erobert den Film! Winke aus der Praxis fuer die Praxis proletarischer Filmpropaganda* (in German).
22. *Communist International*, April 1939, 381–383.
23. Schleimann, *The Life and Work of Willi Muenzenberg*, in *Survey*, No. 55, 1965, 86–90.

3. Forgeries

1. Cohn, *Warrant for Genocide*.
2. Alimov and Lynev, *Where "Pamyat" is Heading*, in *Izvestia*, June 3, 1987, 3 (in Russian); Cherkizov, *On Genuine Values and Imaginary Enemies*, in *Sovetskaya Kultura*, June 18, 1987, 3 (in Russian); and Laqueur, *Glosnost's Ghosts*, in *The New Republic*, August 3, 1987, 13–14.
3. Francis, *Russia From the American Embassy*, 214, 302.
4. Mock and Larson, *Words that Won the War*, 314–316.
5. The Committee on Public Information, *The German-Bolshevik Conspiracy*, October 1918.
6. Schuman, *American Policy Toward Russia Since 1917*, 152.
7. Kerensky, *The Catastrophe*, 229.
8. Printed in full in Katkov, *German Foreign Office Documents on the Financial Support to the Bolsheviks in 1917*, in *International Affairs*, April 1956, 189.
9. Kennan, George, *The Sisson Documents* in Blackstock, *Agents of Deceit*, 247–248.
10. Chester, Faye and Young, *The Zinoviev Letter*, photo after page 108.
11. Ibid., pp 545–6.
12. U.S. National Archives file 861.00B/259, cable to State Department from Paris, November 28, 1924.
13. *International Press Correspondence*, November 6, 1924, 859–860.
14. USSR Peoples Commissariat of International Affairs, *Anti-Soviet Forgeries*, 36–37. This book, published by the British Communists in 1927, is a direct translation of *Antisovietskie Podlogi*, published by the Soviet Union in 1926.
15. Lazitch and Drachkovitch, *Biographical Dictionary of the Comintern*, 102.
16. Fischer, *Stalin and German Communism*, 463.
17. Kuusinen, *The Rings of Destiny*, 50–52.
18. *Anti-Soviet Forgeries*, op. cit., 7.
19. *International Press Correspondence*, April 23, 1925, 475–476.
20. *Data for a Report on the Life and Work of Georgi Dimitrov*, 10–12.
21. Otto Katz, *The Reichstag Fire Trial*, 227–228. This book, subtitled *The Second Brown Book of the Hitler Terror*, was prepared by Willi Muenzenberg's apparatus.
22. Dimitrov, *Political Report v. Congress of the Bulgarian Communist Party*, 21–22.
23. *Izvestia*, Moscow, July 3, 12, and 13, 1927.
24. Seldes, *You Can't Print That!* 336.

4. The Whalen and Tanaka Forgeries

1. A collection of photostats of five of the six Whalen Documents is in the possession of the authors.
2. Fish Committee, Part 3, Vol. 3, 23f.
3. Government of the United Kingdom, *Communist Papers*, opposite 48.
4. Ibid., opposite 29, opposite 51.
5. Spivak, *A Man In His Time*, 139.
6. Ibid., 143.
7. Ibid., 146.
8. *Congressional Record*, May 12, 1930, 8769–770.
9. Fish Committee, op. cit., 287.
10. Ibid., 20.
11. Bentley, Statement to the FBI, November 30, 1945, 26, 29, 67 (released under the Freedom of Information Act).
12. Spivak, op. cit., 161.
13. *Official Report of Proceedings Before the Subversive Activities Control Board, Attorney General v. The Communist Party of the United States of America, Docket No. 51–101*, February 11, 1952, transcript 10009–10 (mimeographed).
14. U.S. House of Representatives, Special Committee on Un-American Activities, Vol. 17, 10287.
15. Browder, *War Against Workers' Russia*, Communist Party USA, New York, 1931, 13.
16. Fish Committee, op. cit., 281, 283, 304.
17. U.S. House of Representatives, Committee on Rules, *Investigation Into the Activities of Communists in the United States;* and Fish Committee Report, January 17, 1931, 50.
18. *Congressional Record*, May 22, 1930, 9396.
19. *The Communist*, October 1930, 881.
20. *International Press Correspondence*, May 8, 1930, 399.
21. *Revolutionary Age*, May 21, 1930, 3.
22. *Communist International*, December 30, 1931, 731–732; Tanaka, *Japanese Imperialism Stripped, The Secret Memorandum of Tanaka, Premier of Japan;* Crow, *Japanese Dream of World Empire, The Tanaka Memorial.*
23. Tanaka, *Japanese Imperialism Exposed, The Secret Tanaka Documents*, 5–6.
24. Mao Zedong, et al., *China: The March Toward Unity.*
25. *Japanese Imperialism Exposed*, op. cit., 6.
26. Tanin and Yohan, *Miltarism and Fascism in Japan*, 129.
27. The Negro Commission, National Committee Communist Party U.S.A., *Is Japan The Champion of the Colored Races?*, 7–8.
28. *Fourth International*, June 1941, 131–135.
29. *Mikhail Abramovitch Trilisser*, the first chief of the Foreign Section of the Soviet Intelligence Service. Under the name Moskvin, he became a member of the Executive Committee of the Communist International in 1935. He disappeared in the purges of 1937–1938. *Jan Berzin*, the first chief of Soviet military intelligence, was executed during the purges. *Efraim Sklyansky*, Soviet

military intelligence chief in the United States, died in an accident in 1925. *Jozef Unschlicht* served as deputy directory of the GPU and as an official of the Communist International, was killed in the Purges in 1938. *Arkady Rosengoltz*, an official of the Communist Party of the Soviet Union for many years, was executed after the 1938 purge trial.

30. Tanaka did not become prime minister of Japan until 1927. Why he should have drafted such a document in 1925 is unexplainable.

31. A valuable contribution to the literature on the history of Soviet disinformation and forgeries was provided by Natalie Grant in her 1987 brochure, *Deception, Tool of Soviet Foreign Policy*.

5. On-the-Job Training for Spies

1. Manuilsky, et al., *Le Parti Communiste Francais Devant L'International*.

2. U.S. House Committee on Un-American Activities (HCUAA), hearing, August 9, 1949, 563.

3. HCUAA, hearing, March 17, 1955, 279–280.

4. Vassiliev, *How The Communist International Formulates at Present the Problem of Organization*, 19–20. (A copy of this mimeographed document was seized by Canadian authorities in Toronto on August 11, 1931. A small part of the pamphlet was reprinted in the CP USA's internal magazine, *Party Organizer*, March 1931. Pages 31 and 32 of the magazine reproduced a section from pages 9 and 10 of the mimeographed pamphlet.)

5. Haessler, *Shop Paper Manual*.

6. Peters, "Strengthen the Fighting Ability of the Party," in *Party Organizer*, September 1934, 26.

7. Central Committee CP USA, *Recognition and the Tasks of the Communists*, December 12, 1933.

8. Workers (Communist) Party, *Minutes of the Secretariat*, September 21, 1927, 4. A set of Workers (Communist) Party minutes, some marked "read and destroy," are in the possession of the authors.

9. Workers (Communist) Party, *Minutes of the Political Committee*, November 2, 1927, 4.

10. Ibid., October 12, 1927, 4.

11. HCUAA, 1941, *Testimony of Paul Crouch*, 184, 186–188, 211.

12. Dennis, *The Autobiography of an American Communist*.

13. Due to its great success recruiting a number of capable agents in the United States, most of whom were intellectuals, the Soviet Intelligence Service used them for both information collection and influence operations in other parts of the world.

14. Mader, *Dr. Sorge Report*, 41 (in German).

15. Sorge, *Sorge's Own Story*, 4.

16. Sorge, op. cit., 24.

17. Werner, *Sonjas Rapport* (in German).

18. Ibid; and Willoughby, *A Partial Documentation of the Sorge Espionage Case*.

19. Dennis, op. cit., 39.

20. Willoughby, *Partial Documentation*, op. cit.
21. Communist International, *VII Congress of the Communist International*, 295.
22. *Commemorative Folder of Stamps in Honor of the Victims of Ravensbrueck Concentration Camp*, September 1959.
23. *International Press Correspondence*, 1936, especially issues February 15, 29; March 21, 28; April 4, 11; May 2; June 6; November 7, 28; December 19.
24. Luis Carlos Prestes, *The Struggle for Liberation in Brazil*; and George, *The Crisis in CP USA*.
25. Sorge, op. cit., Part 2, 24.
26. *New Times, No. 43*, 1964, 19–20.
27. USSR, Ministry of Foreign Affairs, *Soviet Peace Efforts on the Eve of World War II*, 60, 104, 137, 256, 270, 271, 310, 394–395.
28. Mader, op. cit., 175.
29. U.S. Senate, Committee on the Judiciary, Subcommittee on Internal Security (SISS), *Scope of Soviet Activity in the United States*, Part 23A, A80, A89–90, A109–110.
30. Ibid., Part 23A, A100–101.
31. Ibid., A128–129; and Government of the United Kingdom, *Documents Illustrating the Hostile Activities of the Soviet Government and Third International Against Great Britain*, 20, 25.
32. Ibid., SISS, A22.
33. Ibid., A5.
34. Browder, *Socialism in America*, 101.

6. The 1930s: Heyday for Soviet Espionage
Part 1: Whittaker Chambers

1. Chambers, *Statements to the Federal Bureau of Investigation*, January–April 1949, 26–27 (released under the Freedom of Information Act).
2. Ibid., 60.
3. Ibid., 12.
4. Bedacht, *The Menace of Opportunism*, 1.
5. Gitlow, *The Whole of Their Lives*, 336–337.
6. U.S. House of Representatives, Committee on Un-American Activities (HCUAA), *Hearings Regarding Communist Espionage in the United States Government*, 1948.
7. "Karl" (Chambers), "The Faking of Americans," Part 1: "The Soviet Passport Racket," (manuscript), 21–22; Solow Papers, Hoover Institute.
8. U.S. Senate Judiciary Committee, Subcommittee on Internal Security, *Scope*, Part 27, 185–186.
9. HCUAA, 1948, op. cit., 569.
10. Ibid., 1283.
11. SSIS, op. cit., Part 27, 1487.
12. Ibid., 1490–493.
13. Ibid., 1514.
14. Solow, undated letter to Lovestone, *Solow Papers*, Hoover Institution.

15. "Karl," op. cit.
16. Solow, "Stalin's American Passport Mill" in *American Mercury,* July 1939.
17. "Karl," op. cit., Part 1, 3.
18. The full text of the memo may be found in SISS, *Interlocking Subversion in Government Departments,* Part 6, 329–330.
19. See Weinstein, *Perjury,* 245–246 for an interesting account of Alger Hiss and this document.
20. "Karl," op. cit., Part 1, 9–10.
21. Ibid., 18.
22. Ibid., Part 2, 1–2.
23. Ibid., 16–19.
24. Chambers, op. cit., 14.
25. Ibid., 29.
26. Ibid., 30–32.
27. Weinstein, *Encounter,* June 1977.
28. Ulanovskaya, *Istoriya Odnoi Semyi (History of One Family),* (in Russian).
29. Willoughby, *Partial Documentation,* 36 (reproduction of card from Shanghai Police file).
30. Chambers, op. cit., 39.
31. Ibid., 58–59.
32. Ibid., 40–44.
33. Ibid., 53–54.
34. Ella Reeve Bloor.
35. Chambers, op. cit., 72–73.
36. Harris, *Harold M. Ware (1890–1935) Agricultural Pioneer, U.S.A. and U.S.S.R.,* 3–4, 17–18, 59.
37. See chapter 5.
38. Testimony of Benjamin Gitlow in U.S. House of Representatives, Special Committee on Un-American Activities, Part 7, 4594–595.
39. Ads in series of pamphlets issued by International Publishers, New York, during 1931 and 1932.
40. Chambers, op. cit., 75.
41. Ibid., 86–87.
42. Ibid., 91–98.
43. Ibid., 99.
44. Ibid., 100–101.
45. U.S. House of Representatives, Committee on Internal Security (HCIS), *Theory and Practice of Communism,* 2757.
46. HCUAA, *Hearings Regarding Communist Espionage in the United States Government,* 1020–1021.
47. U.S. Senate, Committee on Government Operations, *Subversion and Espionage in Defense Establishments and Industry,* 97–98, for the testimony of Felix Inslerman.
48. Chambers, op. cit., 101–102.
49. Ibid., 102, 106–109.
50. Ibid., 147–148.

51. Massing, *This Deception*, 164–165.
52. Lewis, *The Man Who Disappeared*, 141–142.
53. Field, "Hitching Our Wagon to a Star," in *Mainstream*, January 1961, 4–6.
54. SISS, *Activities of United States Citizens Employed by the United Nations*, Part 1, 154, 1952.
55. HCUAA, op. cit., 566–567.
56. Ibid., 1351.
57. Ibid., 2855.
58. HCUAA, *Hearings Regarding Communism in the United States Government (Part 2)*, 1948, 2844.
59. HCUAA, *Hearings Regarding Communist Espionage*, 1948, 565.
60. Chambers "Meet the Press" transcript in *American Mercury*, New York, February 1949, 153–160.
61. "Hiss's Latest Appeal Denied by Federal Judge," *New York Times*, July 18, 1982, 35.
62. Weinstein, *Perjury*.

7. The 1930s: Heyday for Soviet Espionage
Part 2: Elizabeth Bentley

1. Bentley, *Statement to the Federal Bureau of Investigation, November 30, 1945*, 1–4, 6–9 (released under the Freedom of Information Act).
2. U.S. Senate, Committee on the Judiciary (SISS), *Scope of Soviet Activity in the United States*, Part 13A.
3. Bentley, op. cit., 14.
4. U.S. House of Representatives, Committee on Un-American Activities (HCUAA), *Hearings Regarding Communist Espionage in the United States Government*, 1349–350.
5. Ibid., 1360–361; letter from Bernard S. Redmont.
6. Bentley, op. cit., 49–51.
7. SISS, *Exposé of Soviet Espionage* (FBI report), 1960, 15–16.
8. SISS, *Morgenthau Diary (Germany)*. Introduction by Anthony Kubek, 2–5.
9. SISS, *Scope*, Part 30, 2637ff.
10. U.S. Senate, Committee on Government Operations (McCarthy Committee), *Transfer of Occupation Currency Plates—Espionage Phase*, 45, 47, 48, 52, 53, and appendix.
11. Toy, *World War II, Allied Military Currency*, 20.
12. McCarthy Committee, op. cit., 9.
13. SISS, *Institute of Pacific Relations*, Vol. 2, 419.
14. Bentley, op. cit., 25, 44.
15. HCUAA, *Hearings Regarding Communist Espionage*, op. cit., 553.
16. Ibid., 541, 857–858.
17. Lamphere, *The FBI–KGB War*, 84.
18. HCUAA, op. cit., 557–558.
19. Ibid., 864–865.
20. West, *A Thread of Deceit*, 130.

21. Troy, *Donovan and the CIA*, 82.
22. Bentley, op. cit., 43–44.
23. Belfrage, *Seeds of Destruction*.
24. Belfrage, *The American Inquisition*, 240.
25. Belfrage, "After McCarthy," *New Times*, August 1, 1957, 13.
26. Bentley, op. cit., 28.
27. *Sabotage! The Secret War Against America* (1942) was endorsed by Carl Van Doren and received favorable mention in the *New York Herald Tribune, Chicago Daily News, Reader's Digest*, etc. The *Great Conspiracy Against Russia* (1946) had an introduction by Senator Claude Pepper and endorsements by former vice president Henry Wallace and former ambassador to Russia Joseph E. Davies. It received favorable reviews in *Newsweek, Chicago Daily News*, and *New York Herald Tribune* (taken from the dust jackets).
28. Sayers and Kahn, *Sabotage! The Secret War Against America*, 256–257.
29. Sayers and Kahn, *The Plot Against the Peace*.
30. Sayers and Kahn, *The Great Conspiracy Against Russia*.
31. SISS, *Institute of Pacific Relations*, Vol. 13, 4514.
32. SISS, *Communist Activity in Mass Communications*, 58, 112.
33. Collection of Communist Party documents on the promotion of Sayers and Kahn's book, *The Great Conspiracy*, in the possession of the authors.
34. Copy of letter from Robins to a friend, in possession of the authors.
35. *Die Wahrheit Ueber Den Weltfriedensrat* (in German), 52.
36. News story in *Independent-Journal*, Marin County, California, September 17, 1979.
37. U.S. House of Representatives, Special Committee on Un-American Activities (Dies Committee), Executive Hearings, Vol. 7, 3383 ff.
38. "David Karr's Soviet Connection" in *Business Week*, May 19, 1975, 2.
39. *Fortune*, December 3, 1979, 94ff.

8. The Spanish Civil War

1. *International Press Correspondence*, May 17, 1938, 519.
2. *Communist International*, May 1, 1938, 445.
3. Browder, *The People's Front*, 182.
4. Krivitsky, *I Was Stalin's Agent*, 100–101.
5. Ibid., 116.
6. Cornford, *Communism Was My Waking Time*, 87.
7. U.S. House of Representatives, Special Committee on Un-American Activities (Dies Committee), Vol. 13, 7811ff.
8. Ibid., 7826f.
9. Ibid., 7730f.
10. Ibid., 7795.
11. Subversive Activities Control Board, *Attorney General v. Veterans of the Abraham Lincoln Brigade, Recommended Decision*, 38–39.
12. King et al., *We Accuse*, 14.
13. Dies Committee, op. cit., Vol. 11, 6548f.

14. HCUAA, *Hearings Regarding Leon Josephson and Samuel Liptzen*, 37–38.
15. *United States of America v. Judith Coplon, Transcript* (typescript), 5542–547, 5570.
16. Dies Committee, op. cit., Vol 11, 7147.
17. HCUAA, *Hearing Regarding Leon Josephson*, op. cit., 69–74.
18. Oak, "I Am Exposed as a Spy," *Socialist Call*, December 18, 1937.
19. For an account of the uprising see Souchy, *The Tragic Week in May*.
20. Dies Committee, op. cit., Vol. 14, 1941, 8512–520.
21. U.S. Justice Department press release, November 24, 1942.
22. Whaley, *Guerrillas in the Spanish Civil War*, 117, 124–125.
23. *Soviet Russia Today*, October 1941.
24. Vidali, *Diary of the Twentieth Congress of the Communist Party of the Soviet Union*, Introduction, 35, 39, 44, 65.
25. Tresca Memorial Committee, *Who Killed Carlo Tresca?* 10, 11, 14.
26. U.S. Senate, Subcommittee on Internal Security, *Scope of Soviet Activities in the United States*, 1122–123.
27. National Control Commission, CP USA, *On Guard Notice* (typescript), updated to March 23, 1939, in the possession of the authors.
28. Otto Katz, *Brown Book of The Hitler Terror*.
29. For information on this trial see the American Jewish Committee, *The Anti-Semitic Nature of the Czechoslovak Trial*.
30. Otto Katz, *The Brown Network*.
31. Koestler, *Invisible Writing*, 328.
32. Ibid., 333.
33. Cockburn, *A Discord of Trumpets;* and Pitcairn (Cockburn), *Reporter in Spain*.
34. Ibid., *Discord*, 306–309.

9. The Murder of Leon Trotsky

1. Lazitch and Drachkovitch, *Biographical Dictionary of the Comintern*, 413, 414.
2. Trotsky, *Germany: The Key to The International Situation*, 27.
3. Lenin, *Die Wahlen zur Konstituierenden Versammlung und die Diktatur des Proletariats*, 4, 5. See also Lenin, *Collected Works*, Volume 30, 254.
4. Lenin, *Speech At the Third All-Russia Trade Union Congress*, 4. See also Lenin, *Collected Works*, Volume 30, 503.
5. Kolontay, *The Workers Opposition in Russia*, 42.
6. Lenin, *Collected Works*, Volume 32, 248.
7. Ibid., 244.
8. Berkman, *The Kronstadt Rebellion*, 10.
9. Translation of footnote from Volume 17, Book 2, of Trotsky's *Sochineniya (Works)*, in Lenin and Trotsky, *Kronstadt*, 6–8.
10. Lenin, *Collected Works*, Volume 30, 233.
11. Trotsky, *Dictatorship vs. Democracy*, 58–59.
12. Trotsky, *Documents of the 1923 Opposition*, 2.
13. Lenin, *Letter to the Congress*, 11, 12.

14. *The Workers Monthly,* September 1925, 516.
15. Eastman, "The Character and Fate of Leon Trotsky," in *Foreign Affairs,* January 1941, 340.
16. *International Press Correspondence,* September 3, 1925, 1005.
17. Trotsky, *The Real Situation in Russia;* and Trotsky, *The Suppressed Testament of Lenin.*
18. U.S. Department of State press releases, June 4 and June 30, 1956 (mimeo.).
19. Adler et al., *The Moscow Trial and the Labour and Socialist International,* front cover (picture), 22–32.
20. Trotsky, *The Kirov Assassination,* 3, 4.
21. Stalin, *Works,* Volume 10, 193.
22. Orlov, *The Secret History of Stalin's Crimes,* 311–312.
23. *FBI report, NY 65–14702,* April 1, 1952, 8–13 (released under Freedom of Information Act).
24. Soble, Jack, and Lotto, Jack, "How I Spied on U.S. for the Reds," in *The New York Journal-American,* November 10–20, 1957.
25. See *International Bulletin of the Communist Left Opposition,* May 1931, No. 3, 6; June 1931, No. 6, 9, and undated No. 7, 5 (mimeo.).
26. Sedov, *The Red Book,* 80–81.
27. Communist League of America, *Internal Bulletin,* No. 6, January 15, 1933, 4–5 (mimeo.).
28. Katz, *The Assassination of Kirov,* 4–5.
29. Trotsky, *The Kirov Assassination,* 3, 26, 28, 29.
30. Stalin, *Works,* Volume 2, 51–52.
31. Khrushchev, *Secret Speech,* 13 (released by U.S. Department of State, mimeo.).
32. Stalin, *Defects in Party Work and Measures for Liquidating Trotskyite and Other Double-Dealers,* 20–21.
33. *Pravda,* September 2, 1988.
34. USSR Commissariat of Justice, *Report of Court Proceedings—The Case of the Trotskyite-Zinovievite Terrorist Centre,* 100.
35. Adler, *The Witchcraft Trial in Moscow,* 11–14.
36. Trotsky, *I Stake My Life!* 5.
37. Dewey Commission, *The Case of Leon Trotsky* (hearings) and *Not Guilty* (report of the commission).
38. Dewey Commission, *The Case of Leon Trotsky,* 551.
39. Marley, "The Real Trygve Lie, Stalin's Tool in the U.N.?" *Plain Talk,* October 1947, 4–5.
40. Dewey Commission, *The Case of,* op. cit., 38.
41. Photostatic copies of the Western Union telegrams were provided to the authors by the widow of J. B. Matthews, Ruth Matthews.
42. Goldman, *The Assassination of Leon Trotsky,* 65–67.
43. Committee for the Release of Siqueiros, *Siqueiros in Jail* (leaflet published in London), 4.
44. Trotsky, "Trotsky Letter Exposes Stalin Role in Recent Assassination Attempt," *Socialist Appeal,* June 15, 1940, 4.

45. Trotsky, *The Comintern and the GPU*, in *Fourth International*, November 1940, 157–158.
46. Ibid., 163.
47. Goldman, op. cit., 11–12.
48. Levine, *The Mind of an Assassin*, 18, 32–34.
49. Agabekov, *OGPU*, 180, 207–208.
50. Dziak, *Chekisty*, 141.
51. Goldman, op. cit., 36–37.
52. The passport used by Tito was reproduced in Stevenson, *A Man Called Intrepid*. It had been altered by placing Tito's picture in place of that of the real Canadian passport holder, Spiridon Mekas.
53. U.S. Senate Judiciary Committee, Subcommittee on Internal Security, *Scope of Soviet Activity in the United States*, Part 23, 1221.
54. U.S. House of Representatives, Committee on Un-American Activities, *American Aspects of Assassination of Leon Trotsky*, v–viii.
55. Ibid., 3401–406.
56. Ibid., 3409–414.

10. The Classic Soviet Espionage Ring

1. House Committee on Un-American Activities (HCUAA), *American Aspects of Assassination of Leon Trotsky*, viii–ix.
2. Caldwell, *Confession of a GPU Spy* (grand jury transcripts).
3. Hanson, *Healy's Big Lie*, 9.
4. Cannon, *The History of American Trotskyism*, 252.
5. Cannon, *The First Ten Years of American Communism*, 205–206.
6. Tank, *Inside Job!* 45. A 1946 pamphlet by Tank titled "Communists on the Waterfront" identified the author as "a member of the Communist Party and also of the National Maritime Union, C.I.O.," 2.
7. U.S. Senate, Judiciary Committee, Subcommittee on Internal Security (SISS), *Strategy and Tactics of World Communism*, Part 7, 645.
8. HCUAA, *The Shameful Years*, 13–19.
9. SISS, *Scope of Soviet Activities in the United States*, Part 21, 1113–124.
10. SISS, *Exposé of Soviet Espionage* (FBI report), 37.
11. FBI Report, *NY 65-14702*, 1b, 2–4.
12. HCUAA, *International Communism (Espionage)*, 8.
13. FBI Report, *NY 65-14702*, 196b.
14. SISS, *Exposé*, op. cit., 37.
15. Morros, *My Ten Years as a Counterspy*, 26–34.
16. FBI Report, *NY 65–14702*, 196c.
17. HCUAA, *International Communism*, op. cit., 8.
18. FBI Report, *NY 65–14702*, 197a.
19. SISS, *Exposé*, op. cit., 37–38.
20. Typescript of statement made by Zborowski to Mrs. Lilia Dallin, on October 3, 1955, and typed notes by Ben Mandel, of the Senate Subcommittee on

Internal Security, of a telephone conversation with David J. Dallin, September 27, 1955, provided to the authors by the late Ben Mandel.

21. SISS, *Scope*, Part 4, 89–92.
22. Trotsky, *Leon Sedoff*, 23–24, 26.
23. SISS, *The Legacy of Alexander Orlov*, 1973, 3–8.
24. SISS, *Testimony of Alexander Orlov*, 2–4. *See also* SISS, *The Legacy of Alexander Orlov*, 16–18.
25. SISS, *Scope*, op. cit., Part 51, 3425–426. *See also* U.S. Senate *Legacy*, op. cit., 6–7, 37–38.
26. SISS, *Testimony of Alexander Orlov*, 6–7. *See also* SISS *Legacy*, op. cit., 20–21.
27. SISS, *Scope*, op. cit., Part 4, 80–101, Part 5, 103–109.
28. The Soviet Intelligence Service has been called KGB since 1954.
29. International Committee of the Fourth International, *How the GPU Murdered Trotsky*, 209–210.
30. Ibid., 211; and SISS *Exposé* op. cit., 37–38, 41.
31. International Committee of the 4th International, op. cit., 182–187.
32. Ibid., 179–181.
33. Kravchenko, *I Chose Justice*, 8, 9, 13.
34. U.S. Department of State, *Foreign Relations of the United States, 1944*, Vol. 4, 1226–227.
35. Soble, "How I Spied on U.S. for the Reds," *New York Journal-American*, November 10–20, 1957.
36. *U.S. v. Soblen* (typescript), 672.
37. FBI Report, *NY65-14702*, 19, 20, 29.
38. Ibid., 30.
39. Ibid., 257, 260.
40. Soble and Lotto, op. cit.
41. U.S. State Department files on Alfred K. and Martha Dodd Stern (released under Freedom of Information Act [FOIA]).
42. *New York Times*, August 21, 1957.
43. Cable from U.S. embassy Prague to secretary of state, September 7, 1957 (released under FOIA).
44. Cable from U.S. embassy Asuncion, Paraguay, to Department of State, September 24, 1957 (released under FOIA).
45. SISS, *Scope*, op. cit., 4938–939.
46. Correspondence made available to the press by the office of Congressman Don Edwards.
47. "Alfred Stern: Accused of Spying for Soviets," *Los Angeles Times*, June 24, 1986.
48. FBI Report, *NY65-14702*, 32–33, 42.
49. FBI Report, *100-91470*, 2, 8, 9, 22.
50. SISS, *Scope*, op. cit., Part 72, 4379–381.
51. SISS, *Exposé*, op. cit., 39–40.
52. U.S. Department of State cable 3651, January 29, 1957, Paris to State Department, confidential (released under FOIA).

53. Counter Intelligence Corps, report September 5, 1957 from 66th CIC Group to G2 Heidelberg, Germany, 1, 2; (released under FOIA).
54. William A. Reuben, "Soblen Defense Asks New Trial, Says U.S. Hid Vital Evidence," in *National Guardian*, October 30, 1961, 1, 4.
55. State Department cables Berlin to State Department, November 4, 1959, #437, secret; November 28, 1959, #476, secret; December 2, 1959, #491, secret; December 9, 1959, #506, limited official use (released under FOIA).
56. FBI Report, *NY65-14702*, 13–14.
57. House of Representatives, Committee on Un-American Activities, *Annual Report for the Year 1962*, 131.
58. U.S. Department of State cables, Embassy Tel Aviv to State Department, June 30, 1962, #967, secret; and Embassy London to State, July 1, 1962, #1, limited official use (released under FOIA).
59. U.S. Department of State cables #463, August 2, 1962, embassy London to State Department, unclassified.
60. U.S. Department of State cables, embassy London to State Department, September 11, 1962, #1002, unclassified; embassy Moscow to State Department, September 14, 1962, #682, limited official use (released under FOIA).
61. FBI Report, *NY65-14702*, 238.
62. Ibid., 43–45.
63. Morros, op. cit., 35–36.
64. Agabekov used the term *Section of Foreign Affairs* to mean the Foreign Department of the OGPU, rather than the People's Commissariat of Foreign Affairs. He used the term *collaborator* to mean officer of the intelligence service.
65. Agabekov, OGPU, 216–223.
66. SISS, *Scope*, op. cit., Part 51, 3466–7. The story is also told in Orlov, *The Secret History of Stalin's Crimes*, 192–194.
67. Massing, *This Deception*, 224–299.
68. FBI Report, *NY65-14702*, 48.
69. Dzhirkvelov, *Secret Servant*, 62.

11. World War II: Spying on the Allies

1. U.S. Department of State, *Nazi-Soviet Relations, 1939–1941*, 76–78, 105–108.
2. Molotov, *The Meaning of the Soviet-German Non-Aggression Pact*, 12–13.
3. Hitler, *Speech Delivered in the Reichstag on September 1, 1939*, 7–9.
4. *Nazi-Soviet Relations*, op. cit., 86.
5. Ibid., 87.
6. Ibid., 91.
7. Ibid., 92–93.
8. Hitler, *Speech at the Langer Markt in Danzig, September 19, 1939*, 10.
9. Molotov, *Report to the Supreme Soviet, October 31, 1939*, 4, 6.

10. Attfield & Williams, *1939: The Communist Party of Great Britain and the War*, 147.
11. War Cabinet (Great Britain), *Communist Party of Great Britain, Memorandum by the Home Secretary, March 13, 1943*, Appendix 1, 7. The text may also be found in Attfield & Williams, op. cit., 160–168.
12. Marty, *The Trial of the French Communist Deputies*, 113.
13. *Communist International*, July 1940, 474.
14. Bullitt, *Report to the American People*, 23–25.
15. *Communist International*, February 1940, 88.
16. Ross, *A History of Soviet Foreign Policy*, 44–45.
17. Jaffe, *The Rise and Fall of American Communism*, 44–47.
18. Quin, *The Yanks Are Not Coming*; and Rivington, *No Gold Stars for Us, Our Boys Stay Home*.
19. Copies of these leaflets are in the possession of the authors.
20. Weiss, et al., *Youth Fights for Peace, Jobs, Civil Rights*, 6, 8.
21. Marcantonio, *Congressman Vito Marcantonio Speaks Out Against This War; Marcantonio Answers FDR!* A reprint of this same speech published in California was titled *Marcantonio's Reply to F.R.* (Franklin Roosevelt).
22. Almanac Singers, *Sign of the Times* (original copy in the possession of the authors).
23. Budenz, *Men Without Faces*, 141, 178–179.
24. Klehr, *The Heyday of American Communism*, 404–405.
25. While in the West it was still June 21, in the Soviet Union the attack started in the early morning of June 22. Soviet sources always use the June 22 date.
26. Marcantonio, *Should America Go To War?*
27. Marcantonio, *Security with FDR*.
28. Winston, "Our Tasks Today," *Clarity*, Summer 1941, 30.
29. Molotov et al., *The German Attack on the USSR*, 3–10.
30. Alexandrov, *Fascism the Diabolical Enemy of Mankind*, 7.
31. Skorodenko, *Vo Glave Boyevogo Soyuza* (At the Head of the Combat Alliance), chapter 1.
32. Gramenov, "In the Partisan Detachment," in *Kommunist*, October 1985, 57ff (in Russian).
33. Skorodenko, op. cit.
34. Kardelj, "The Struggle for Recognition of the National Liberation Movement of Yugoslavia," in *Macedonian Review*, Vol. 11, No. 2, 1981, 201.
35. Fast, *The Incredible Tito, Man of the Hour*, 14.
36. Tito, *Political Report*, 49, 51.
37. U.S. House of Representatives, Committee on Un-American Activities (HCUAA), *The Shameful Years*, 30.
38. U.S. Senate, Committee on the Judiciary, Subcommittee on Internal Security (SISS), *Scope of Soviet Activity in the United States*, Part 1, 1956, 7.
39. Nelson et. al., *Steve Nelson, American Radical*, 125, 136f, chapter 7.
40. HCUAA, op. cit., 30–31.

41. Ibid., 31.
42. HCUAA, *Report on Atomic Espionage*, 5.
43. Ibid., 6ff; and HCUAA, *Hearings Regarding Communist Infiltration of Radiation Laboratory and Atomic Bomb Project at the University of California, Berkeley, Calif.*, Vol 2, 799–806, 831–832.
44. Nelson et. al., op. cit., 294.
45. HCUAA, op. cit., 41.
46. Dallet, *Letters From Spain*, 6.
47. U.S. Atomic Energy Commission, *In the Matter of J. Robert Oppenheimer*, 194–195.
48. HCUAA, *The Shameful Years*, op. cit., 34.
49. HCUAA, *Excerpts from Hearings Regarding Investigation of Communist Activities in Connection with the Atom Bomb*, 54f.
50. HCUAA, op. cit., 36–38.
51. Bothwell and Granatstein, eds., *The Gouzenko Transcripts*, 28.
52. Ibid., 103, 252–254.
53. Ibid., 74, 97.
54. Canada Royal Commission on Espionage, *The Report of the Royal Commission* (Canada), 450.
55. U.S. Joint Committee on Atomic Energy, *Soviet Atomic Espionage*, 58.
56. Ibid., 16, 34.
57. "Obituaries: Klaus Fuchs Gave Secrets to Soviets," *Chicago Sun-Times*, January 29, 1988, Fuchs, in *Prisma* (East Berlin), No. 2, 1984, 10; and Ibid., 35.
58. *U.S. v. Julius Rosenberg et al.*, transcript, 1620 (reprint, National Committee to Secure Justice in Rosenberg Case).
59. Freed, *Inquest;* and *Playbill*, April 1970.
60. Fineberg, *The Rosenberg Case*, 45–46.
61. Ibid., 87–94.
62. Lamphere, *The FBI–KGB War*, 275; and *Exposé of Soviet Espionage*, 43–44.
63. Donovan, *Strangers on a Bridge*, 154–157.
64. Woltman, *The Shocking Story of the* Amerasia *Case;* and Jaffe, *The Amerasia Case*, 32–34.
65. FBI Summary, May 31, 1950, *File 100 267360, 1516*, page 3 of report and page 10 of wiretap log (released under FOIA).
66. "Head of Blunt Spy Ring Named by London Paper," *New York Times*, December 3, 1979, 17.
67. Leonidov, "The Shadows in the Santa Cruz Palace," *New Times*, May 22, 1963, 9.
68. Rumjanzew, *Antikommunismus, Feind der Menschheit*, 254.
69. Maisky, *Memoirs of a Soviet Ambassador*, 206–207.
70. "Against One's Conscience," *Literaturnyy Kirgizstan*, No. 3, March 1988 (in Russian).
71. *Resolutions and Proceedings, 24th National Congress of the Communist Party, 1956*, 19; Communist Party of Great Britain, *Communist Party 26th Congress Report*, 1959, 70; and Klugman, *Essays on Socialist Realism and the British Cultural Tradition*, 15ff.

72. Martin, *Patriot or Traitor, The Case of General Mihailovich*, 118–121.
73. "Bund," *The Case of Henryk Erlich and Victor Alter*, 4–14.
74. U.S. House of Representatives, Select Committee [on the] Katyn Forest Massacre, *Final Report*, 5.
75. Ibid., *The Katyn Forest Massacre*, transcript, Part 7, 2174–195; 2272–293.
76. U.S. House of Representatives, Select Committee to Investigate the Federal Communications Commission, *Study and Investigation of the Federal Communications Commission*, Vol. 1, 388.
77. Select Committee on Katyn Forest Massacre, op. cit., transcript, Part 7, 2186–189, 2278–279.
78. Special (Soviet) Commission, *The Truth About Katyn*, 2–4.
79. USSR Ministry of Foreign Officers, *Correspondence between the Chairman of the Council of Ministers of the U.S.S.R. and the Presidents of the U.S.A. and the Prime Ministers of Great Britain During the Great Patriotic War of 1941–1945*, 60–61.
80. Brody, *Behind the Polish-Soviet Break*, 2.
81. Government of Poland, *Polish-Soviet Relations, 1918–1943, Official Documents*, 180.
82. USSR Ministry of Foreign Affairs, op. cit., 156–157.
83. Toranska, *"Them,"* 270.
84. Blit, *The Eastern Pretender, Boleslaw Piasecki: His Life and Times*, 18–19, 55.
85. Bundes Deutscher Offiziere, *Deutsche Offiziere Haben Das Wort*, 5–7 (in German); Merker and Von Golssenan, *Deutsche, Wohin?* 13 (in German); *Freies Deutschland*, December 1944 (in German); *Ehemalige Nationalsozialisten In Pankows Diensten*, 44, 49, 62–63 (in German); *Treffpunkt Berlin*, 8 (in German).
86. Djilas, *Conversations with Stalin*, 24.
87. Lewis, *The Man Who Disappeared*, 132.
88. HCUAA, *Staff Report, Investigation of Un-American Activities and Propaganda*, 10–18.
89. *The Volunteer for Liberty*, September 6, 1937, 5.
90. Semprun, *The Autobiography of Frederico Sanchez and the Communist Underground in Spain*, 76.
91. SISS, *Strategy and Tactics of World Communism, Recruiting for Espionage*, Part 14, 1328–342, 1347–358.
92. "Davies Says Soviet Has Right To Spy," *New York Times*, February 19, 1946.
93. Sayers and Kahn, *The Great Conspiracy Against Russia* (pbk. ed.), inside back cover.

12. The Cold War Period

1. Communist Political Association, *The Path to Peace, Progress and Prosperity; Proceedings of the Constitutional Convention of the Communist Political Association, New York, May 20–22, 1944*, 3, 11, 42.
2. Communist Party USA, *On the Struggle Against Revisionism*, 19ff, 44ff.

3. Browder, *Modern Resurrections and Miracles,* 49–50.
4. In the postwar years the Soviet people's commissariats became ministries, so the NKVD became the MVD. In 1954 its name was changed to KGB.
5. U.S. Senate, Committee on the Judiciary, Subcommittee on Internal Security (SISS), *Scope of Soviet Activity in the United States,* Parts 1, 2.
6. Ibid., Part 14, 779, 802–803.
7. Zhdanov, *The International Situation,* 17–18.
8. U.S. House of Representatives, Committee on Un-American Activities (HCUAA), *Investigation of Un-American Propaganda Activities in the United States: Louis F. Budenz,* 12, 20.
9. HCUAA, *Hearings on Gerhart Eisler,* 4–10.
10. Ibid., 11–12.
11. United States District Court, Southern District of New York, *Eisler v. Immigration and Naturalization of the Port of New York, Memorandum for Relator,* Appendix F, 20–21.
12. HCUAA, *Hearings on Gerhart Eisler,* op. cit., 18.
13. Ibid., 31.
14. Eisler, *Eisler Hits Back,* 10, 15.
15. *Message of Albert E. Kahn to the House Un-American Activities Committee,* press release (mimeo.).
16. Eisler, *My Side of the Story.*
17. HCUAA, *The Shameful Years,* 45.
18. SISS, *Expos⁺ of Soviet Espionage* (FBI report), 17–18.
19. FBI Report, *NY 65-14702,* op. cit., 208.
20. HCUAA, *Testimony of Wladyslaw Tykocinski,* 1966, 873.
21. SISS, *Soviet Espionage Through Poland,* 22–23.
22. HCUAA, *Communist Espionage in the United States,* 8, 31–32, 1723.
23. Communist Party USA, op. cit., 2.
24. SISS, *Communist Bloc Intelligence Activities in the United States,* 77–78, 99–101, 106.
25. Foreign Broadcast Information Service, August 18, 1958, *Tel Aviv (Radio) in Arabic,* (translation) *August 17, 1958,* H1.
26. SISS, *Soviet Intelligence in Asia,* 14, 15, 17.
27. SISS, *Murder International Inc.,* 19.
28. SISS, *Activities of Soviet Secret Service,* 5–6, 32–34.
29. Russian Press Agency (NTS), press release, September 30, 1957.
30. Col. F. Y. Leaver, *Memorandum, Subject: Hospitalization of Mr. Khokhlov,* 9, October 1957.
31. SISS, *Murder International,* op. cit., Introduction, 81–168; *Ukrainian Quarterly,* Winter 1962, 293. For a detailed account, see Anders, *Mord Auf Befehl (Murder on Order)* (in German).
32. Royal Commission on Espionage (Australia), *Report,* 3, 20–22, 35.
33. Royal Commission on Espionage (Australia), *Transcript,* 284; and Australian Archives: *CA1882, CRS A6202.*
34. Australian Archives, op. cit., and Royal Commission, *Report,* 38.

35. Royal Commission, *Report,* 38, 91; and *Transcript,* 475–478, 496–499, 523–524, 547.
36. Royal Commission, *Report,* 41.
37. Australian Archives *CA1882, CRS A6219, Annexure to the Report,* 5–8; and Royal Commission, *Transcript,* in *Camera, October 18, 1954,* 4689–96 (Sealed, released in 1985).
38. Petrov, *Empire of Fear,* 241.
39. Royal Commission *Report,* op. cit., 330ff, 349ff.
40. SISS, *Scope,* op. cit., Part 72, 4407–412; and SISS, *Exposé,* op. cit., 43–44.
41. Copp, *Famous Soviet Spies,* 138.
42. "Abel Bid to Aid 2 In Jail Reported," *New York Times,* November 21, 1971.
43. Soviet Spy Born, Bred In England, *Washington Post,* August 22, 1972.

13. The Lean Years

1. Communist Party USA, *Proceedings 16th National Convention Communist Party, U.S.A.,* February 9–12, 1957, 121.
2. Ibid., 154–155.
3. Thompson, "I Spied for the Russians," in *Saturday Evening Post,* May 22, 1965, and June 5, 1965.
4. "L.I. Man Who Served in Berlin Indicted as a Spy," *New York Times,* January 8, 1965.
5. "Thompson Denies Spy Charge and Says He's '100% American'," *New York Times,* January 9, 1965.
6. "L.I. Man Tells of Serving Soviet," *New York Times,* March 9, 1965.
7. "Ex-Airman Given 30 Years as a Spy," *New York Times,* May 14, 1965.
8. Cranford, *Volunteers, The Betrayal of National Defense Secrets by Air Force Traitors,* 157–161.
9. "Ex-Pentagon Aide and Ex-G.I. Held as Red Spies," *New York Times,* April 6, 1965.
10. "Two Get 25 Years as Soviet Agents," *New York Times,* July 31, 1965.
11. Sawatsky, *For Services Rendered,* 34–35, 43, 59, 67, 71; and "Ex-Mountie Admits Spying for Soviet," *International Herald Tribune,* January 25, 26, 1986.
12. Blitzer, "Fear of Spying," *Jerusalem Post International Edition,* September 21, 1985.
13. U.S. Department of Justice press release, February 2, 1965; and "U.S. Says Man Gave Soviet 15 Passports," *New York Times,* February 3, 1965.
14. "Chicagoan Admits Passport Frauds," *New York Times,* February 4, 1965.
15. "Agent of Soviets is Given 2 Years," *New York Times,* February 27, 1965.
16. "Retired Pentagon Officer is Seized as Spy for Soviet," *New York Times,* July 13, 1966.
17. "Ex-Officer Given 15-Year Term for Supplying Secrets to Soviet," *New York Times,* March 2, 1967.
18. *New York Times,* "U.S. Airman Accused of Plot to Spy for Soviet," November 1, 1966; "Air Force Sergeant Convicted of Conspiring With Soviet Aide," May

26, 1967; "Air Sergeant Gets 30 Years for Plot to Spy for Soviet," June 8, 1967; and "Airman Arrested for Having Secret Data," October 22, 1971.

19. *Akahata,* February 21, 1962 (in Japanese).
20. *Akahata,* April 5, 1962 (in Japanese).
21. Ligue de la Liberte, *Soviet Spies in the Scientific and Technical Fields,* 23, 27–32.
22. U.S. Senate, Judiciary Committee, Subcommittee on Internal Security (SISS), *Communist Forgeries,* 1961, 6, 18.
23. Government Printing Office, *Congressional Record,* September 28, 1965, H2447ff.
24. *Izvestiya* and *Krasnaya Zvezda,* May 15, 1968 (in Russian).
25. *Smena,* Bratislava, April 28, 1968 (in Slovak), translated in *FBIS Daily Report,* supplement, June 14, 1968, 78ff.
26. U.S. House of Representatives, Committee on Intelligence (HPSCI), *Soviet Covert Action,* 42–43.
27. U.S. Department of Justice, *Registration Statement of Anczel Grau,* March 19, 1962.
28. U.S. House of Representatives, Armed Services Committee, *Statement of Laszlo Szabo,* 5332, 5339, 5348.
29. HPSCI, *Soviet Covert Action,* op. cit., 58.
30. Mader, *Who's Who in CIA;* Mader, *Allens Gangster in Aktion;* and Charisius and Mader, *Nicht Laenger Geheim;* Edwards and Dunne, *A Study of a Master Spy (Allen Dulles);* and CIA Report "The Soviet and Communist Bloc Defamation Campaign," placed in the *Congressional Record* by Congressman Melvin Price in September 1965.
31. *Granma,* August 30, 1970, 7; and September 13, 1970, 11 (English-language editions published in Havana).
32. SISS, *Testimony of Lawrence Britt* (Ladislav Bittman) 4–5.
33. Smith, *Birch Putsch Plans for 1964;* U.S. House of Representatives, Committee on Un-American Activities (hereafter HCUAA), *1962 Annual Report,* 17–18; Canter, *MLF-Force or Farce?*
34. For details on Communist Party involvement in anti-Vietnam War movement, see HCUAA, *Communist Origin and Manipulation of Vietnam Week (April 8–15, 1967).*
35. U.S. Senate, Intelligence Committee (Church Committee), *Volume 6, Federal Bureau of Investigation,* 740–741. The FBI report dated March 8, 1968, was censored by the Intelligence Committee, and the name of the Communist organizer was deleted.
36. *Convention Notes, February 17, 1968,* published in full, with identifications from the committee files, in HCUAA, *Subversive Involvement in Disruption of the 1968 Democratic Party National Convention,* Part 1, 1968, 2293–2301.
37. HCUAA, *Subversive Involvement,* op. cit., Part 2, 2519, 2563–568.
38. Ibid., 2615.
39. Lenin, *Collected Works,* Vol. 9, 345.

14. The KGB Today and Tomorrow

1. Federal Bureau of Investigation, *Press Briefing, March 3, 1980;* "FBI Tells How Soviet Spy Became a U.S. 'Double Agent'," *Washington Post,* March 4, 1980; "G.U.–KGB Connection," *Georgetown Voice,* April 1, 1980, 6; and "Former KGB Agent Wants to Go Home with His Cash," *Los Angeles Times,* November 2, 1986.

2. FBI, *Press Briefing,* op. cit.; "Jailed Canadian Admits Soviet Links," *Toronto Star,* July 6, 1982; and *Los Angeles Times,* November 2, 1986, op. cit.

3. "Alleged Spy Reportedly Sought a 2d Sensitive Post," *New York Times,* October 23, 1980; and U.S. Senate, Committee on Governmental Affairs, *Federal Government Security Clearance Programs,* FBI prepared statement, 174.

4. U.S. Senate, *Federal Government Security,* op. cit., 178–179.

5. U.S. District Court, Northern District of California, *U.S. v. Whitworth,* Declaration of John L. Martin, U.S. Department of Justice, August 26, 1987.

6. TASS *International Service,* November 5, 1985 (in Russian), translated in *Foreign Broadcast Information Service (FBIS), III,* November 5, 1985, A22–A23.

7. "A Soviet Defector is Granted Permission to Stay in Britain," *New York Times,* October 26, 1983.

8. Radio Liberty, *Radio Liberty Background Report,* Munich, March 30, 1984.

9. *Literaturnaya Gazeta,* September 19, 1984 (in Russian), translated in *FBIS, III,* 20 September 1984, R1f.

10. Moscow Television Service, November 14, 1985, press conference (in Russian), translated in *FBIS, III,* November 15, 1985, A3f.

11. *DPA* (German Press Agency), Hamburg, March 14, 1986 (in German), translated in *FBIS III,* March 19, 1986, G3–G4.

12. *Moskovskaya Pravda,* August 9, 1986 (in Russian), translated in *FBIS, III,* 18 August, 1986, A1–A3.

13. U.S. Department of State, *Soviet Influence Activities, A Report on Active Measures and Propaganda,* 1986–87, 23.

14. United States District Court, New Mexico, *United States of America v. Edward L. Howard,* affidavits of FBI Special Agents Martin R. Schwarz and Gerald B. Brown, October 2, 1985; "FBI Says Ex-C.I.A. Agent Went to Austria in '84 to Betray Secrets," *New York Times,* October 5, 1985; "KGB Defector Confirms U.S. Intelligence Fiasco," *Wall Street Journal,* October 17, 1985; and Moscow Television Service, September 14, 1986 (in Russian), translated in *FBIS, III,* 16, September, 1986, A1f.

15. United States District Court, Central District of California, *United States v. Svetlana Ogorodnikova,* affidavit of P. Bryce Christensen, 1, 3–6, 8, 10–13, 21, 24; Verbitzky and Adler, *Sleeping with Moscow,* 52, 54; "Two Russians Plead Guilty In Spy Case," *Washington Post,* June 27, 1985; and "Miller Gets 2 Life Terms and 50 Years for Spying," *Los Angeles Times,* July 15, 1986.

16. U.S. Senate, Committee on Governmental Affairs, hearings May 4, 5, 6, 11, and 12, 1982, Exhibit 1, *Soviet Acquisition of Western Technology.*

17. U.S. Department of Defense, *Soviet Acquisition of Militarily Significant Western Technology: An Update,* September 1985, 2, 3, 6, 8, 16.

18. U.S. Department of State, *Intelligence Collection in the USSR Chamber of Commerce and Industry*, 2.
19. Senate Committee on Governmental Affairs, *Federal Government Security*, op. cit., 181–182; and "Nightline Transcript" in *The Washington Times*, June 10, 1985, D1.
20. Federal Bureau of Investigation, *The Sentinels of Freedom, The American People and the Defense of the Nation's Secret*, April 1987, 1–4; United States District Court, Eastern District of Virginia, *U.S. v. John Anthony Walker, Jr., Affidavit of Joseph R. Wolfinger, FBI*, and *Affidavit of Unidentified Special Agent* (these two affidavits were related to search warrants of John Walker's property); "Accused Spy's Son Arrested, Held Aboard USS *Nimitz*," *Washington Post*, May 23, 1985; "Foreign Spies Using our 'Private Eyes'," London *Sunday Telegraph*, May 16, 1971; "A Firsthand Look at a Spy's World," *Washington Post*, May 4, 1986; "Spy's Ex-Wife Takes Stand," *San Francisco Chronicle*, May 13, 1986; "Confessions of a Spy," *The Washington Post Magazine*, September 15, 1985; U.S. District Court, Northern District of California, *U.S. v. Jerry Alfred Whitworth, Second Superseding Indictment*, and *Affidavit of Rear Admiral William O. Studeman, U.S. Navy*, and *Affidavit of John L. Martin U.S. Department of Justice*; and Barron, *Breaking the Ring, The Bizarre Case of the Walker Family Spy Ring*, 153, 207. This book, by one of America's leading journalists, is the most comprehensive account of the Walker case available.
21. United States District Court, Maryland, *U.S. v. Ronald William Pelton, Criminal Complaint, Affidavit of Unidentified FBI Special Agent*; FBI *The Sentinels of Freedom*, op. cit., 6; "Sentencing Is Delayed In Pelton Espionage Case," *Washington Post*, November 11, 1986; and "Pelton Guilty of Selling Secrets to Soviet Union," *Chicago Tribune*, June 6, 1986.
22. *Przeglad Techniczny*, Warsaw, September 27, 1987, 22 (in Polish).
23. "Soviet Agent Visits Hill Office to Ask for MX Missile Plans," *Washington Post*, September 11, 1981.
24. Letter made available to the press from the comptroller general of the United States to Congressman Jack Brooks, chairman of the House Committee on Government Operations, January 27, 1982.
25. Petrov, in *Sovetskaya Rossia* (in Russian), December 19, 1967.
26. Eschwege, "Resistance of German Jews against the Nazi Regime," in *Leo Baeck Institute Year Book, 1970*, 163–164.
27. U.S. Department of State, *Foreign Affairs Note, Expulsions of Soviet Officials*, 1987, 2.
28. U.S. House of Representatives, Intelligence Committee (HPSCI), *Soviet Covert Action*, 1980, 61–62.
29. U.S. Department of Justice, *Registration Statement of James Frederick Sattler*, March 23, 1976.
30. Browne, "A Tale of Rendezvous and Rubles," in *Washington Post*, February 9, 1975.
31. "2 Charged Here as Spies for Hanoi," *Washington Star*, January 31, 1978; "USIA Aide, Vietnamese Held in Theft," *Washington Post*, February 1, 1978;

"Accused Man's Spouse Says Vietnam Holds Son Hostage," *Washington Post*, February 3, 1978; Vietnam Trial Support Committee, Circular Letter, June 8, 1978, 3; and U.S. Senate, *Federal Government Security Clearance Programs*, op. cit., 186.

32. Senate Committee on Governmental Affairs, National Alliance Against Racist & Political Repression, Circular Letter and Brief, October 30, 1981; and U.S. HISC, *Report on Revolutionary Target: The American Penal System*, 1973, 96, 99.

33. Andreassen and Moe, *Spies and Spies' Objectives in Norway* (in Norwegian); and U.S. Department of State, *Active Measures: A Report on the Substance and Process of Anti-U.S. Disinformation and Propaganda Campaigns*, August 1986, 82.

34. U.S. Department of State, *Active Measures*, op. cit., 81.

35. Ibid., 83.

36. HPSCI, *Soviet Active Measures*, op. cit., 209–210.

37. Ibid., 203, 223.

38. Young, "Young Releases FBI Report," in *Congressional Record*, March 24, 1983, H1791f.

39. Ponomarev, Boris, "CPSU History: The Leninist Traditions and Contemporaneity," in *CPSU: Documents and Analysis*, May 22, 1986, 29. This publication is distributed to foreign Communist Parties by Novosti, Moscow.

40. *Party Organizer*, Vol. XVI, No. 4, 5, 6 (1982), 48. This is an internal Communist Party magazine meant for members only. A copy of this issue is in the possession of the authors.

41. Communist Party USA, Organization Department and National Peace and Solidarity Committee, *Memo to All Districts*, June 30, 1982. This is an internal document meant for Communist Party members only. A copy is in the possession of the authors.

42. Young, "Soviet Active Measures in the United States—an Updated Report by the FBI," in *Congressional Record*, December 9, 1987, E4717f.

43. Communist Party of Israel, Foreign Relations Department, *Information Bulletin*, Tel Aviv, December 1972.

44. "Soviet Introduces Its Spy in Izvestia," *New York Times*, February 15, 1970.

45. "Spy in Berlin Given 2 Top Soviet Medals," *Washington Post*, February 17, 1970.

46. Bourke, *The Springing of George Blake*.

47. *London Sunday Times*, October 4, 1987 and October 11, 1987.

48. TASS, Moscow, April 28, 1986 (in English), in *FBIS, III*, 29 April, 1986, A1f.

49. TASS, Moscow, May 19, 1986, International Service (in Russian), translated in *FBIS, III*, 20 May, 1986, A1–A2.

50. Smirnov et al., *The White Book: Evidence, Facts, Documents*, 147f, 199f.

51. Cherechnychenko, *Anatomy of Treason*, 8fl, 244.

52. Reproduced in *The Restoration of the Ukrainian State in World War II*, 14.

53. Ashbrook, "Soviet Evidence Has Always Been Fraudulent and Should Not Be Used in American Courts," in *Congressional Record*, May 28, 1981.

54. Parming, "The Soviet Union and the Émigré Communities: A Case Study in Active Measures and Disinformation," in U.S. Department of State and Central Intelligence Agency, *Contemporary Soviet Propaganda and Disinformation, A Conference Report*, 328.
55. *Pravda*, September 12, 1988; TASS, September 14, 1988; and discussion of Romerstein with OUN official, October 7, 1988.
56. Dziak, *Chekisty*, 162–163.
57. *Der Spiegel*, October 9, 1978, 152f.
58. Philby, *My Silent War*, 194–199.
59. Visnar, "Death in the Albanian Bay of Pigs," in *Start*, January 15, 1983, 29–31 (in Serbo-Croatian).
60. *Possev*, No. 11, 1982 (in Russian), also published as a four-page pamphlet in Russian, *Novoye Ruskoye Slovo*, January 16, 1983; "Cat and Mouse with the KGB," *London Times*, April 27, 1983.
61. HPSCI, *Soviet Covert Action*, op. cit., 86f.
62. Pankov (ed.), *Political Terrorism—an Indictment of Imperialism*, 213, 262; and Svetov, et al., *International Terrorism and the CIA*, 225–227.
63. HPSCI, *Soviet Active Measures*, op. cit., 95–102.
64. Ibid., 111f, 216.
65. Ibid., 202.
66. U.S. Department of State, *Soviet Influence Activities*, op. cit., 30; U.S. Information Agency, *Soviet Active Measures In the Era of Glasnost*, 52, and reproduction of forgery.
67. Young, "Soviet Active Measures," op. cit., E4718.
68. U.S. Department of State, *Expulsions of Soviet Officials 1987*, op. cit., 1, 3.
69. Tsinev, "Fighters of the Invisible Front," in *Sovetskaya Rossia*, December 20, 1967 (in Russian).
70. "K.G.B.'s New Chief 'Spymaster' Up From Ranks," *New York Times*, October 3, 1988, 12.
71. Kyruchkov, "Viewing The World Objectively," *International Affairs*, Moscow, November 1988, 34–36.
72. *New York Times*, October 3, 1988, op. cit.

Bibliography

Adler, Friedrich. *The Anglo-Russian Report*. London: P. S. King & Son, Ltd., 1925.

————. *The Witchcraft Trial in Moscow*. New York: Pioneer Publishers, 1937.

Adler, Friedrich; Abramovitch, R.; Blum, Leon; and Vandervelde, Emile. *The Moscow Trial and the Labour and Socialist International*. London: Labour Party, 1931.

Agabekov, Georges. *OGPU, The Russian Secret Terror*. New York: Brentano's, 1931.

Alexandrov, G. *Fascism, The Diabolical Enemy of Mankind*. Moscow: Foreign Languages Publishing House, 1941.

American Jewish Committee. *The Anti-Semitic Nature of the Czechoslovak Trial (Nov.–Dec. 1952)*. New York: Library of Jewish Information, American Jewish Committee, 1952.

Anders, Karl. *Mord auf Befehl: Der Fall Staschynskij: Eine Documentation Aus Den Akten*, Tubingen Am Neckar: Verlag Fritz Schlichtenmayer, 1963.

Andreassen, Thorleif, and Moe, Gunnar. *Spioner Og Spionmal I Norge* (Spies and Spies Objectives in Norway). Oslo: Atheneum, 1984.

Anstrom, George [Harold Ware]. *The American Farmer*. New York: International Pamphlets, 1932.

Ardamatsky, V. I. *Vozmezdiya*. Moscow: Molodaya Gvardiya, 1968.

Ashbrook, John. "One Man's Soviet Trade." *Congressional Record*, October 17, 1973 (unbound).

————. "Soviet Evidence Has Always Been Fraudulent and Should Not Be Used in American Courts." *Congressional Record*, May 28, 1981 (unbound).

Attfield, John, and Williams, Stephen, eds. *1939: The Communist Party of Great Britain and the War: Proceedings of a Conference Held on April 21, 1979, Organized by the Communist Party History Group*. London: Lawrence and Wishart, 1984.

Australia, Commonwealth of. *Report of the Royal Commission on Espionage*. Sydney: Government Printer, 1955.

————. *Royal Commission on Espionage, Official Transcript of Proceedings*, Sydney: Government Printer, 1985.

————. *Royal Commission on Espionage*. Sealed files CA1882 CRSA6202 released by Australian Archives in 1985.

Bailey, Geoffrey. *The Conspirators*. New York: Harper & Brothers, 1960.

Barron, John. *Breaking the Ring*. Boston: Houghton Mifflin, 1987.

Bedacht, Max. *Anti-Soviet Lies and the Five-year Plan*. New York: Workers Library Publishers for Daily Worker, 1931.

————. *The Menace of Opportunism*. Chicago: Daily Worker Publishing Co., circa 1926.

Bedacht, Max, et al. *Five Years of International Workers Order*. New York: International Workers Order, 1935.

Belfrage, Cedric. *The American Inquisition 1945–1960*. Indianapolis/New York: Bobbs-Merrill, 1973.

————. *Seeds of Destruction: The Truth About the U.S. Occupation of Germany*. New York: Cameron & Kahn, 1954.

Bentley, Elizabeth. *Out of Bondage*. New York: The Devin-Adair Company, 1951.

Bergmeister, Karl. *The Jewish World Conspiracy: The Protocols of the Elders of Zion before the Court in Berne*. Erfurt, Germany: U. Bodung-Verlag, 1938.

Berkman, Alexander. *The Kronstadt Rebellion*. Berlin: Der Syndikalist, 1922.

Bernstein, Herman. *The Truth About "The Protocols of Zion."* New York: Ktav Publishing House, 1971.

Bittman, Ladislav. *The Deception Game: Czechoslovak Intelligence in Soviet Political Warfare*. Syracuse, New York: Syracuse University Research Corporation, 1972.

Blackstock, Paul W. *Agents of Deceit, Frauds, Forgers and Political Intrigue Among Nations*. Chicago: Quadrangle Books, 1966.

————. *The Secret Road to World War II*. Chicago: Quadrangle Books, 1969.

Blit, Lucjan. *The Eastern Pretender Boleslaw Piasecki; His Life and Times*. London: Hutchinson & Co., 1965.

Bothwell, Robert, and Granatstein, J. L. *The Gouzenko Transcripts: The Evidence Presented to the Kellock-Taschereau Royal Commission, 1946*, Ottawa: Deneau Publishers, n.d., circa 1983.

Bourke, Sean. *The Springing of George Blake*. New York: The Viking Press, 1970.

Brody, Alter. *Behind The Polish-Soviet Break*. (Introduction by Corliss Lamont.) New York: Soviet Russia Today, circa 1943.

Browder, Earl. *Modern Resurrections and Miracles*. Yonkers, New York: Earl Browder (privately printed), 1950.

————. *The People's Front*. New York: International Publishers, 1938.

————. "Socialism in America" in *International Communism*. (Ed. David Footman.) Carbondale, Illinois: Southern Illinois University Press, 1960.

————. *War Against Workers' Russia*. New York: Communist Party USA, 1931.

Budenz, Louis Francis. *Men Without Faces*. New York: Harper & Brothers, 1950.

————. *This Is My Story*. New York: McGraw-Hill, 1947.

Bullitt, William C. *Report to the American People*. Boston: Houghton Mifflin, 1940.

"Bund" (General Jewish Worker's Union of Poland). *The Case of Henryk Erlich and Victor Alter*. (Foreword by Camille Huysmans.) London: Liberty Publications, 1943.

Bundes Deutschen Offiziere (Union of German Officers). *Deutsche Offiziere Haben Das Wort*. Stockholm: Magnus Ekenberg, 1943.

Caldwell, Sylvia. *Confession of a GPU Spy*. London: New Park Publications, 1983.

Canada, Royal Commission on Espionage. *Report of the Royal Commission*. Ottawa: Controller of Stationery, 1946.

Cannon, James P. *The First Ten Years of American Communism*. New York: Lyle B. Stuart, 1962.

————. *The History of American Trotskyism*. New York: Pioneer Publishers, 1944.

Canter, David S. *MLF—Force or Farce?* Chicago: Domino Publications, 1965.

Chambers, Whittaker. *Can You Hear Their Voices?: A Short Story*. New York: International Pamphlets, 1932.

————. "Meets the Press." *The American Mercury*, New York: February 1949, 153–60.

————. *Witness*. New York: Random House, 1952.

Cherednychenko, V. *Anatomy of Treason*. Kiev: Politvidav Ukraini Publishers, 1984.

Chester, Lewis; Fay, Stephen; and Young, Hugo. *The Zinoviev Letter*. Philadelphia/New York: J. B. Lippincott, 1968.

Clubb, O. Edmund. *The Witness and I*. New York/London: Columbia University Press, 1975.

Cockburn, Claude. *Cockburn in Spain*. London: Lawrence and Wishart, 1986.

————. *A Discord of Trumpets*. New York: Simon and Schuster, 1956.

Cohn, Norman. *Warrant for Genocide*. New York: Harper & Row, 1966.

Committee on Public Information. *The German-Bolshevik Conspiracy*. Washington, D.C.: Committee on Public Information, 1918.

Communist International. *VII Congress of the Communist International, July–August, 1935* (abridged stenographic report). Moscow: Foreign Language Publishing House, 1939.

Communist Party of America. *Manifesto, Program, Report to the Communist International*. Chicago: Communist Party of America, circa 1920.

Communist Party of Great Britain. *Communist Party, 26th Congress Report*, London: Communist Party, 1956.

————. *Resolution and Proceedings, 24th National Congress of the Communist Party, 1956*. London: Communist Party, 1956.

Communist Party USA. "On Going to the Soviet Union" in *Party Organizer*. New York: Central Committee Communist Party USA, August 1931.

————. *Proceedings 16th National Convention Communist Party, USA February 9–12, 1957*. New York: New Century Publishers, 1957.

Communist Party USA, Central Committee. *On the Road to Bolshevization*. New York: Workers Library Publishers, 1929.

————. *Recognition and the Tasks of the Communists*. New York: Communist Party, USA, 1933 (mimeo.).

Communist Party USA, National Committee, Negro Commission. *Is Japan the Champion of the Colored Races?* New York: Workers Library Publishers, 1938.

Communist Party USA, National Veterans Committee. *On the Struggle against Revisionism*. New York: Communist Party USA, 1946.

Communist Party USA, New York State Committee. *Attack Hitler Now!: A May Day Call*. New York: Communist Party, New York State Committee, circa 1942.

Communist Political Association. *The Path to Peace, Progress and Prosperity; Proceedings of the Constitutional Convention of the Communist Political Association, New York, May 20–22, 1944*. New York: Communist Political Association, 1944.

Copp, Dewitt. *Famous Soviet Spies, The Kremlin's Secret Weapon*. Washington D.C.: U.S. News & World Report, Inc., 1973.

Cornford, John. *Communism Was My Waking Time*. Moscow: Foreign Languages Publishing House, 1958.

Cowl, Margaret. *The Soviet Union, Your Questions Answered*. New York: Workers Library Publishers, 1934.

Cranford, David J. *Volunteers: The Betrayal of National Defense Secrets by Air Force Traitors*. Washington: Government Printing Office, 1988.

Crow, Carl, ed. *Japan's Dream of World Empire, The Tanaka Memorial*. New York: Harper & Brothers, 1942.

Dallet, Joe. *Letters from Spain*. New York: Workers Library Publishers, 1938.

Data for a Report on the Life and Work of Georgi Dimitrov. Sofia, Bulgaria: Sofia Press, 1972.

De Leon, Solon. *The American Labor Who's Who*. New York: Hanford Press, 1925.

de Toledano, Ralph, and Lasky, Victor. *Seeds of Treason: The True Story of the Hiss-Chambers Tragedy*. New York: Funk & Wagnalls Co., 1950.

Dennis, Peggy. *The Autobiography of an American Communist*. Westport, Conn:/ Berkeley, Calif.: Lawrence Hill & Co./Creative Arts Book Co., 1977.

Deriabin, Peter; and Gibney, Frank. *The Secret World*. New York: Doubleday & Company, 1959.

Dewey Commission. (Commission of Inquiry into the Charges Made against Leon Trotsky in the Moscow Trial). *Not Guilty*. New York: Harper & Brothers, 1938.

———. (Preliminary Commission of Inquiry). *The Case of Leon Trotsky Report of Hearing on the Charges Made against Him in the Moscow Trial*. New York: Harper & Brothers, 1937.

Dimitroff, Georgi. *Letters from Prison*. New York: International Publishers, 1935.

———. *Political Report: V Congress of the Bulgarian Communist Party*. Sofia, Bulgaria: Press Department, Ministry of Foreign Affairs, 1949.

Djilas, Milovan. *Conversations with Stalin*. New York: Harcourt, Brace & World, 1962.

Dodd, William, Jr., and Dodd, Martha. *Ambassador Dodd's Diary, 1933–1938*. New York: Harcourt, Brace, 1941.

Dodd, Martha. *Aus dem Fenster der Botschaft* (Through the Window of the Embassy) Berlin: Publishing House of the Soviet Military Government, 1947.

———. *Through Embassy Eyes*. New York: Harcourt, Brace, 1939.

Donovan, James B. *Strangers on a Bridge, The Case of Colonel Abel*. New York: Atheneum, 1964.

Draper, Theodore. *American Communism and Soviet Russia*. New York: Viking Press, 1960.

Dzerzhinsky, Felix. *Prison Diary and Letters*. Moscow: Foreign Languages Publishing House, 1959.

Dzhirkvelov, Ilia. *Secret Servant, My Life with the KGB and the Soviet Elite*. New York: Harper & Row, 1987.

Dziak, John J. *Chekisty*. Lexington, Massachusetts: Lexington Books, 1988.

Eastman, Max. "The Character and Fate of Leon Trotsky," *Foreign Affairs*, January 1941, 332–342.

Edwards, Bob, and Dunne, Kenneth. *A Study of a Master Spy (Allan Dulles)*. London: Chemical Workers Union, 1961.

Eisler, Gerhart. *Eisler Hits Back*. New York: The German American, n.d. (1947).

———. *My Side of the Story*. New York: Civil Rights Congress, 1947.

Eisler, Gerhart, et al. *Treff-punkt Berlin*. (Obtained at information kiosk in East Berlin, 1959.)

Eschwege, Helmut. "Resistance of German Jews Against the Nazi Regime." In *Year Book XV*, from Leo Baeck Institute. London: East and West Library, 1970.

Fast, Howard. *The Incredible Tito, Man of the Hour*. New York: Lev Gleason Publishers, 1944.

Field, Noel. "Hitching Our Wagon To A Star," *Mainstream*, January 1961, 3–17.

Fineberg, S. Andhil. *The Rosenberg Case*. New York: Oceana, 1953.

Fischer, Ruth. *Stalin and German Communism*. Cambridge: Harvard University Press, 1948.

Foote, Alexander. *Handbook for Spies*. Garden City, New York: Doubleday & Company, 1949.

Foster, William Z. *For Speedy Victory The Second Front NOW*. New York: Workers Library Publishers, 1943.

Foster, William Z., and Gitlow, Benjamin. *Acceptance Speeches*. New York: Workers Library Publishers, 1928.

Francis, David R. *Russia from the American Embassy, April 1916–November, 1918*. New York: Charles Scribner's Sons, 1921.

Freed, Donald. *Inquest*. New York: Hill and Wang, 1969.

Fuchs, Klaus. "Nuclear Power: Blessing or Nemesis," *Prisma*, East Berlin, No. 2, 1984.

George, Harrison. *The Crisis in the C.P.U.S.A.* Los Angeles: privately printed, 1947.

———. *Luis Carlos Prestes: The Struggle for Liberation in Brazil*. New York: Workers Library Publishers Inc., 1936.

Gitlow, Benjamin. *I Confess: The Truth About American Communism*. New York: E. P. Dutton & Company, 1939.

———. *The Red Ruby*. New York: Communist Labor Party, circa 1920.

———. *Some Plain Words on Communist Unity*. New York: Workers Age Publishing Assn., circa 1932.

———. *The Whole of Their Lives*. New York: Charles Scribner's Sons, 1948.

Gladkov, Theodore, and Zaitsev, Nikolai. "And I Cannot But Believe Him," *Nedelya*, Moscow, No. 44, 1982.

Goldman, Albert. *The Assassination of Leon Trotsky, the Proofs of Stalin's Guilt*. New York: Pioneer Publishers, 1940.

Grant, Natalie. *Deception, A Tool of Soviet Foreign Policy*. Washington: The Nathan Hale Institute, 1987.

[Graves, Philip]. *The Truth About "The Protocols:" A Literary Forgery*. London: Reprinted from *The Times*, August 16–18, 1921.

Haessler, Gertrude. *Shop Paper Manual: A Handbook for Comrades Active in Shop Paper Work*. New York: Central Committee, Communist Party USA, 1930.

Halassie, Sayid. *Democracy on The Nile, How Britain has "Protected" Egypt*. Scotch Plains, N.J.: Flanders Hall.

Hanson, Joseph, et al. *Healy's Big Lie*. New York: Socialist Workers Party, 1976.

Harris, Lement. *Harold M. Ware (1890–1935) Agricultural Pioneer, U.S.A. and U.S.S.R.* New York: American Institute of Marxist Studies, 1978.

Henry, Ernst. *Can Socialists and Communists Co-Operate?* Moscow: Progress Publishers, 1972.

———. *China Swallow Asia?* Moscow: Novosti Press Agency, 1979.

———. *Hitler Over Europe*. New York: Simon and Schuster, 1934.

———. *Stop Terrorism!* Moscow: Novosti Press Agency, 1982.

———. *The Strategy of Revenge*. New York: New Century Publishers, 1961.

———. *What Are They After in Peking*. Moscow: Progress Publishers, 1979.

Herbst, Josephine. *Behind the Swastika*. New York: The Anti-Nazi Federation, 1936.

Hitler, Adolf. *Speech Delivered in the Reichstag on September 1, 1939*. Berlin: M. Mueller & Sohn, 1939.

———. *Speech by the Fuhrer and Reich Chancellor Adolf Hitler on the Langer Market in Danzig*. Germany: publisher unknown, September 19, 1939 (mailed in packet of propaganda literature from Germany in 1939).

International Brigades. *The Volunteer for Liberty* (official organ of the English-speaking brigade in Spain). Madrid: 1937–1938.

———. Commissariat of War XV Brigade. *The Book of the XV Brigade: Records of British, American, Canadian and Irish Volunteers in Spain*. Reprint. New Castle upon Tyne, England: Frank Graham, 1975 (original 1938).

International Committee of the 4th International. *How the GPU Murdered Trotsky*. London: New Park Publications, 1981.

Jaffe, Philip. *The Amerasia Case from 1945 to the Present*. New York: Philip J. Jaffe, 1979.

———. *The Rise and Fall of American Communism*. (Introduction by Bertram D. Wolfe.) New York: Horizon Press, 1975.

Joliot-Curie, Frederic. *Die Wahrheit uber den Weltfriedensrat*. (The Truth about the World Peace Council.) Berlin: Herausgegeben vom Deutschen Friedensrat.

Kardelj, Edward. "The Struggle for Recognition of the National Liberation Movement in Yugoslavia." *Macedonian Review*, Vol. II, No. 2, 1981.

Katkov, George. "German Foreign Office Documents on the Financial Support to the Bolsheviks in 1917." *International Affairs*, April 1956, 181–189.

Katz, M. *The Assassination of Kirov, Proletarian Justice vs. White Guard Terror*. New York: Workers Library Publishers, 1935.

[Katz, Otto]. *The Brown Book of the Hitler Terror and the Burning of the Reichstag*. (Introduction by Lord Marley.) New York: Alfred A. Knopf, 1933.

————. *The Brown Network: The Activities of the Nazis Foreign Countries*. (Introduction by William Francis Hare, Earl of Listowel.) New York: Knight Publications, 1936.

————. *Das Braune Netz* (The Brown Network). Paris: Editions du Carrefour, 1935.

————. *The Nazi Conspiracy in Spain*. London: Victor Gollancz, Ltd., 1937.

————. *The Reichstag Fire Trial: The Second Brown Book of the Hitler Terror*. London: John Lane the Bodley Head, Ltd., 1934.

Kaznacheev, Aleksandr. *Inside a Soviet Embassy, Experiences of a Russian Diplomat in Burma*. Philadelphia/New York: J. B. Lippincott, 1962.

Kerensky, Alexander. *The Catastrophe*. New York: D. Appleton and Company, 1927.

King, Jerry, et al. *We Accuse* (From the Record). New York: privately printed, 1940.

Klehr, Harvey. *The Heyday of American Communism: The Depression Decade*. New York: Basic Books, Inc., 1984.

Klugman, James. "Basis and Superstructure." In *Essays on Socialist Realism and the British Cultural Tradition*. London: Arena Publication, no date.

Koestler, Arthur. *The Invisible Writing*. London: Collins with Hamish Hamilton, Ltd., 1954.

Kolontay, A. *The Workers Opposition in Russia*. Chicago: Industrial Workers of the World, circa 1921.

Kravchenko, Victor. *I Chose Freedom*. New York: Charles Scribner's Sons, 1946.

————. *I Chose Justice*. New York: Charles Scribner's Sons, 1950.

Kravchenko versus Moscow. (Introduction by Sir Travers Humphries.) London/New York: Wingate, 1950.

Krivitsky, W. G. *I Was Stalin's Agent*. Great Britain: Hamish Hamilton, 1939.

Khrushchev, Nikita. *Secret Speech at 20th Congress of the Communist Party of the Soviet Union*. Washington: Department of State 1956 (mimeo.).

Kuusinen, Aino. *The Rings of Destiny: Inside Soviet Russia From Lenin to Brezhnev*. New York: William Morrow and Company, 1974.

Lamphere, Robert J.; and Shachtman, Tom. *The FBI–KGB War*. New York: Random House, 1986.

Langer, Elinor. *Josephine Herbst: The Story She Could Never Tell*. Boston: Little, Brown, 1984.

Lazitch, Branko, and Drachkovitch, Milorad M. *Biographical Dictionary of the Comintern*. Stanford, Calif.: Hoover Institution Press, 1973.

Ligue de la Liberte. *Soviet Spies in the Scientific and Technical Fields*. Mavre, Belgium: Ligue de la Liberte, 1968.

Lenin, N. (V. I.) *Die Wahlen zur Konstituierenden Versammlung und die Diktatur des Proletariat*. (The Elections to the Constituent Assembly and the Dictatorship of the Proletairiat.) Petrograd: Verlag Der Kommunistischen Internationale, 1920.

Lenin, V. I. *Collected Works* (45 volumes). Moscow: Progress Publishers, various dates.

————. *Letter to the Congress—The Question of Nationalities or of "Autonomization."* Moscow: Foreign Language Publishing House, no date (after 1956).

————. *Problems of Building Socialism and Communism in the U.S.S.R.* Moscow: Foreign Languages Publishing House, no date (after 1956).

————. *Sochineniya.* (Works.) 5th ed. Moscow: Izdatelstvo Politicheskoi Literatur, various dates.

————. *Speech At The Third All-Russia Trade Union Congress.* Moscow: All-Russian Central Council of Trade Unions, 1920.

————. *The Suppressed Testament of Lenin* (with 2 articles by Leon Trotsky). New York: Pioneer Publishers, 1935.

Lenin, V. I., and Trotsky, Leon. *Kronstadt.* New York: Monad Press, 1979.

Levchenko, Stanislav. *On the Wrong Side: My Life in the KGB.* Washington: Pergamon-Brassey's, 1988.

Levine, Isaac Don. *The Mind of an Assassin.* New York: Farrar, Straus & Cudahy, 1959.

Lewis, Flora. *The Man Who Disappeared: The Strange History of Noel Field.* London: Arthur Baker, Ltd., 1965.

Lord Marley. "Introduction." In *The Brown Book of Hitler Terror and the Burning of the Reichstag,* by Otto Katz. New York: Alfred A. Knopf, 1933.

Lovestone, Jay, et al. *Appeal to the Comintern.* (Four newspaper-size printed pages issued by the Lovestone group in New York), 1929.

Mader, Julius. *Allens Gangster in Aktion.* (Allen's Gangsters in Action). East Berlin: Kongress Verlag, 1959.

————. *Dr. Sorge—Report.* East Berlin: Deutscher Militaerverlag, 1984.

————. *Who's Who in CIA.* East Berlin: Julius Mader, 1968.

Mader, Julius, and Charisius, Albrecht. *Nicht Laenger Geheim* (No Longer Secret). East Berlin: Deutscher Militaerverlag, 1959.

Maisky, Ivan. *Memoirs of a Soviet Ambassador The War: 1939–43.* New York: Charles Scribner's Sons, 1967.

Manne, Robert. *The Petrov Affair Politics and Espionage.* New York: Pergamon, 1987.

Manuilsky, Dimitry, et al. *Le Parti Communiste Francais Devant L'International* (The French Communist Party at the International). Paris: Bureau d'Editions, 1931.

Mao Tse-Tung, et al. *The March Toward Unity.* New York: Workers Library Publishers, 1937.

Marcantonio, Vito. *Marcantonio Answers F.D.R.!* New York: American Peace Mobilization, May 1941.

————. *Marcantonio's Reply to F.R.: 'Save Your Peace, Save Your Sons, Save Your Liberties.'* San Francisco: American Peace Mobilization, May or June 1941.

————. *Security with FDR.* New York: National Fraternal Committee for Re-election of FDR, 1944.

————. *Should America Go to War.* New York: American People's Mobilization, circa 1941.

————. *Vito Marcantonio Speaks Out Against This War.* New York: American Peace Mobilization, February 1941.

Marley, Sheppard. "The Real Trygve Lie: Stalin's Tool in the U.N.?" *Plain Talk*, October 1947, 3–9.

Martin, David. *Patriot or Traitor: The Case of General Mihailovich*. Stanford, Calif.: Hoover Institution Press, 1978.

Marty, Andre. *The Trial of the French Communist Deputies*. London: Lawrence and Wishart, 1941.

Massing, Hede. *This Deception*. New York: Duell, Sloan and Pearce, 1951.

Merker, Paul, and Von Golssenau, Arnold Vieth. *Deutsche, Wohin*. Mexico City: Latein-Amerikanisches Komitee, Freres Deutchland, 1944.

Mock, James R, and Larson, Cedric. *Words That Won the War*. Princeton: Princeton University Press, 1939.

Molotov, V., et al. *The German Attack on the U.S.S.R*. London: The Anglo-Russian Parliamentary Committee, 1941.

Molotov, V. M. *The Meaning of the Soviet-German Non-Aggression Pact*. New York: Workers Library Publishers, 1939.

———. *Molotov's Report to the Supreme Soviet, October 31, 1939*. New York: Workers Library Publishers, no date (1939).

Morros, Boris. *My Ten Years as a Counterspy*. New York: Viking Press, 1959.

Muenzenberg, Willi. *Erobert den Film! Winke aus der Praxis fuer die Praxis proletarischer Filmpropaganda*. (Capture the Film! Suggestions from the Practice for the Practice of Proletarian Film Propaganda.) Berlin: Neuer Deutscher Verlag, 1925.

Murphy, Thomas F. (Prosecutor). "Summation to the Alger Hiss Jury," *Plain Talk*, August 1949, 1–13.

National Komitees Freies Deutschland. *Freies Deutschland* (magazine). Soviet Union (?): 1944.

Nelson, Steve; Barrett, James R., and Ruck, Rob. *Steve Nelson: American Radical*. Pittsburgh: University of Pittsburgh Press, 1981.

Neuberg, A. [pseud.] et al. *Armed Insurrection*. London: N.L.B., 1970.

Nikulin, Lev. *Mertvaya Zub'*. Moscow: Voyenizdat, 1965.

Nuorteva, Santeri. *An Open Letter to American Liberals*. New York: Socialist Publication Society, 1918.

O'Sheel, Shaemas. *Seven Periods of Irish History*. Scotch Plains, N.J.: Flanders Hall, 1940.

[O'Sheel, Shaemas]. *Lord Lothian vs. Lord Lothian*. Scotch Plains, N.J.: Flanders Hall, 1940.

Orlov, Alexander. *The Secret History of Stalin's Crimes*. New York: Random House, 1953.

Pankov, Yu., ed. *Political Terrorism—An Indictment of Imperialism*. Moscow: Progress Publishers, 1983.

Pepper, John. *"Underground Radicalism:" An Open Letter to Eugene V. Debs and to All Honest Workers*. New York: Workers Party of America, circa 1923.

Peters, J. *The Communist Party—A Manual on Organization*. New York: Workers Library Publishers, 1935.

———. "Strengthen the Fighting Ability of the Party." *Party Organizer* (New York: Central Committee, Communist Party USA), September 1934, 24–8.

————. "Mass Defense Is the Only Answer to Terror." *Party Organizer* (New York: Central Committee, Communist Party USA), July 1934 26–31.

Petrov, Vladimir and Evdokia. *Empire of Fear*. New York: Frederick A. Praeger, 1956.

Philby, Kim. *My Silent War*. New York: Grove Press, 1968.

Pitcairn, Frank [Claude Cockburn]. *Reporter in Spain*. Moscow: Co-operative Publishing Society of Foreign Workers in the U.S.S.R., 1937.

Playbill. *Inquest*. New York: Playbill, 1970.

Poland, Government of. *Polish-Soviet Relations 1918–1943*. Washington: Polish Embassy, circa 1943.

Ponomarev, B. N., et al. *The International Working Class Movement*. Vol. 4. Moscow: Progress Publishers, 1984.

Price, Melvin. "The Soviet and Communist Bloc Defamation Compaign." *Congressional Record*, September 28, 1965 (unbound).

Quin, Mike. *The Yanks are Not Coming*. San Francisco: The Yanks Are Not Coming Committee, 1940.

Radosh, Ronald, and Milton, Joyce. *The Rosenberg File*. New York: Holt, Rinehart & Winston, 1983.

Rees, David. *Harry Dexter White: A Study in Paradox*. New York: Coward, McCann & Geoghegan, 1973.

Reilly, Sidney. *Britain's Master Spy: The Adventures of Sidney Reilly*. U.S.A.: Dorset Press, 1985.

Reilly, Sidney and Mme P. *La vie aventureuse de Sidney Reilly*. Paris: Editions de la Nouvelle Revue Critique, 1931.

The Restoration of the Ukrainian State in World War II. London: Ukrainian Central Information Service, 1987.

Rivington, Ann. *No Gold Stars for Us—Our Boys Stay Home!* New York: Workers Library Publishers, 1940.

Ross, M. *A History of Soviet Foreign Policy*. New York: Workers Library Publishers, 1940.

Rumjanzew, A.M., et al. *Antikommunismus—Feind der Menschheit*. (Anti-Communism Enemy of Mankind). Berlin: Dietz Verlag, 1963.

Sawatsky, John. *For Services Rendered: Leslie James Bennett and the RCMP Security Service*. New York: Doubleday & Company, 1982.

Sayers, Michael, and Kahn, Albert. *The Great Conspiracy*. Boston: Little, Brown, 1946.

————. *The Great Conspiracy*. New York: Boni & Gaer, 1947.

————. *The Great Conspiracy Against Russia*. New York: Boni & Gaer, 1946.

————. *The Plot Against the Peace*. New York: Book Find Club, 1945.

————. *Sabotage! The Secret War Against America*. New York: Harper & Brothers, 1942.

Scheer, Maximilian. *Ethel und Julius Roman eines Prozesses* (Ethel and Julius: A Novel about a Trial). East Berlin: Aufbau-Verlag, 1959.

Schleimann, Jorgen. "The Organization Man—The Life and Work of Willi Muenzenberg," *Survey*, No. 55, 1965.

Schmitz, Paul. *Englands Gewaltpolitik am Nil*. (England's Power Politics on the Nile.) Berlin: Umschlagentwurf Horst Michel, 1940.

Schuman, Frederick Lewis. *American Policy Toward Russia Since 1917*. New York: International Publishers, 1928.

Sedov, Leon. *The Red Book on The Moscow Trial*. London: New Park Publications, 1980.

Seldes, George. *You Can't Print That!: The Truth Behind the News 1918–1928*. Garden City, New York: Garden City Publishing, 1929.

Semprun, Jorge. *The Autobiography of Federico Sanchez and the Communist Underground in Spain*. New York: Karz Publishers, 1979.

Skorodenko, P. O. *Vo Glave Boyerogo Soyuza*. (At the Head of the Combat Alliance.) Moscow: Voyenizdat, 1985.

Smirnov, L., et al. *The White Book: Evidence, Facts, Documents*. Moscow: Progress Publishers, 1981.

Smith, John. *Birch Putsch Plans for 1964*. [Chicago]: Domino Publications, 1963.

Sorge, Richard. *Sorge's Own Story*. Translated from Japanese by Military Intelligence Section Far East Command, privately printed, circa 1950.

Souchy, Augustin. *The Tragic Week in May*. Barcelona: C.N.T./F.A.I., 1937.

Spain, Government of. *The International Brigades, Foreign Assistants of the Spanish Reds*. Madrid: Spanish Office of Information, 1948.

Spivak, John L. *A Man in His Time*. New York: Horizon Press, 1967.

———. *Pattern for American Fascism*. New York: New Century Publishers, 1947.

———. *Plotting America's Pogroms*. New York: New Masses, 1934.

———. *The "Save The Country" Racket*. New York: New Century Publishers, 1948.

———. *Secret Armies*. New York: Modern Age Books, 1939.

Stalin, J. *Defects in Party Work and Measures for Liquidating Trotskyite and other Double-Dealers*. Moscow: Co-operative Publishing Society of Foreign Workers in the U.S.S.R., 1937.

Stalin, J. V. *Works*. 13 Vols. Moscow: Foreign Languages Publishing House, various dates.

Stalin, Joseph. *Speeches on the American Communist Party*. New York: Central Committee, Communist Party USA, circa 1931.

Stern, Max. *Spaniens Himmel, Die Oesterreicher in den Internationalen Brigaden*. (Spanish Heavens, The Austrians in the International Brigades.) Vienna: Schoenbrunn-Verlag, 1966.

Stevenson, William. *A Man Called Intrepid*. New York: Harcourt Brace Jovanovich, 1976.

Straight, Michael. *After Long Silence*. New York/London: W. W. Norton, 1983.

Strasser, Otto. (pub.) *Die Deutsche Revolution* (The German Revolution) magazine in German. Prague: Schwarzen Front, 1937.

———. *Free Germany Against Hitler*. Brooklyn, New York: printed privately, circa 1941.

———. *The Gangsters Around Hitler*. London: W. H. Allen & Company, circa 1942.

Strong, Anna Louise. *Modern Farming—Soviet Style*. New York: International Pamphlets, circa 1930.

Szetov, Boris, et al. *International Terrorism and the CIA*. Moscow: Progress Publishers, 1983.

Szinda, Gustav. *Die XI Brigade* (The 11th Brigade). East Berlin: Ministeriums fuer Nationale Verteidigung, 1956.

Tanaka [Forgery]. *Japanese Imperialism Exposed: The Secret Tanaka Document*. New York: International Publishers, 1942.

———. *Japanese Imperialism Stripped, The Secret Memorandum of Tanaka, Premier of Japan*. London: Modern Books, Ltd., circa 1932.

Tanin, O., and Yohan, E. *Militarism and Fascism in Japan*. New York: International Publishers, 1934.

Tank, Herb. *Communists on the Waterfront*. New York: New Century Publishers, 1946.

———. *Inside Job!: The Story of Trotskyite Intrigue in the Labor Movement*. New York: New Century Publishers, 1947.

Thompson, Robert G. "I Spied for the Russians," *Saturday Evening Post*, May 22, 23–29 and June 5, 1965, 38–49.

Tito, Josip Broz. *Political Report of the Central Committee of the Communist Party of Yugoslavia*. Belgrade: 1948.

Toranska, Teresa. *"Them": Stalin's Polish Puppets*. New York: Harper & Row, 1987.

Toy, Raymond S. *World War II Allied Military Currency*. Tucson: privately published, n.d.

Tresca Memorial Committee. *Who Killed Carlo Tresca?* New York: Tresca Memorial Committee, 1945.

Trotsky, Leon. *Dictatorship vs. Democracy (Terrorism and Communism)*. (Foreword by Max Bedact [sic].) New York: Workers Party of America, 1922.

Trotsky, Leon, et al. *Documents of the 1923 Opposition*. London: New Park Publications, 1975.

Trotsky, Leon. "The Comintern and the G.P.U." *Fourth International*, November 1940.

———. *Germany: The Key to the International Situation*. London: Revolutionary Communist Party, 1944, 148–63.

———. *I Stake My Life!* New York: Pioneer Publishers, 1937.

———. *The Kirov Assassination*. New York: Pioneer Publishers, 1935.

———. *Leon Sedoff: Son—Friend—Fighter*. New York: Young People's Socialist League (4th International), 1938.

———. *The Real Situation in Russia*. New York: Harcourt, Brace, 1928.

———. "The Tanaka Memorial." *Fourth International*, June 1941, 131–5.

———. *Writings of Leon Trotsky (1939–40)*. New York: Pathfinder Press, 1969.

Troy, Thomas F. *Donovan and the CIA*. [Langley, Virginia]: Central Intelligence Agency, 1981.

Trumbull, Walter. *Life in the U.S. Army*. New York: Workers Library Publishers, circa 1931.

Uhse, Bodo. *Die Erste Schlacht*. (The First Battle). Strasbourg: Editions Prome-
thee, 1938.

Ulanovskaya, Nadezhda and Maya. *Istoriya Odnoi Semyi*. (History of One Family).
New York: Chalidze Publications, 1982.

United Kingdom, Government of. *Communist Papers*. London: His Majesty's Stationery Office, 1926.

———. *Documents Illustrating the Hostile Activities of the Soviet Government and
the Third International Against Great Britain*. London: His Majesty's Stationery
Office, 1927.

———. *Communist Party of Great Britain, Memorandum by the Home Secretary*.
(Most Secret, declassified). London: War Cabinet, 1943.

United States Atomic Energy Commission. *In the Matter of J. Robert Oppenheimer,
Texts of Principal Documents and Letters*. Washington: Government Printing
Office, 1954.

———. *In the Matter of J. Robert Oppenheimer, Transcript of Hearing before
Personnel Security Board*. Washington: Government Printing Office, 1954.

[United States Department of Defense]. *Soviet Acquisition of Militarily Significant
Western Technology: An Update*. Washington: released by Defense Department,
1985.

United States Department of State. *Active Measures: A Report on the Substance
and Process of Anti-U.S. Disinformation and Propaganda Campaigns*. Washington: Department of State, 1986.

———. *Foreign Affairs Note: Expulsions of Soviet Officials*. Washington: Department of State, 1987.

———. *Foreign Relations of the United States Diplomatic Papers 1944, Volume
IV: Europe*. Washington: Government Printing Office, 1966.

———. *Intelligence Collection in the U.S.S.R. Chamber of Commerce and Industry*. Washington: Department of State, circa 1987.

———. *Nazi-Soviet Relations 1939–1941*. Washington: Department of State, 1948.

———. *Soviet Influence Activities: A Report on Active Measures and Propaganda,
1986–87*. Washington: Department of State, 1987.

United States Department of State, and Central Intelligence Agency. *Contemporary Soviet Propaganda and Disinformation, A Conference Report*, Washington:
Department of State, 1987.

United States House of Representatives, Committee on Internal Security. Washington: Government Printing Office, 1969–1974.

United States House of Representatives, Committee on Un-American Activities.
Washington: Government Printing Office, 1945–1968.

United States House of Representatives, Permanent Select Committee on Intelligence. *Soviet Covert Action*, 1980; *Soviet Active Measures*, 1982. Washington:
Government Printing Office.

United States House of Representatives, Select Committee to Investigate Katyn
Forest Massacre. *The Katyn Forest Massacre*, Washington: Government Printing
Office, 1952.

United States House of Representatives, Select Committee to Investigate the Federal Communications Commission. *Study and Investigation of the Federal Communications Commission.* Washington: Government Printing Office, 1943.

United States House of Representatives, Special Committee to Investigate Communist Activities in the United States (Fish Committee). *Investigation of Communist Propaganda.* Washington: Government Printing Office, 1930.

United States House of Representatives, Special Committee on Un-American Activities. *Investigation of Un-American Propaganda Activities in the United States.* Washington: Government Printing Office, 1938–1944.

United States House of Representatives, Special Committee on Un-American Activities, Executive Hearings. *Investigation of Un-American Propaganda Activities in the United States.* Washington: Government Printing Office, 1939–1943, released in 1951.

United States Information Agency. *Soviet Active Measures in the Era of Glasnost.* Washington: USIA, 1988.

United States Senate, Committee on Governmental Affairs. *Federal Government Security Clearance Programs.* Washington: Government Printing Office, 1982.

United States Senate, Committee on Foreign Relations. *Russian Propaganda.* Washington: Government Printing Office, 1920.

United States Senate, Committee on Judiciary. *Brewing and Liquor Interests and German and Bolshevik Propaganda.* Washington: Government Printing Office, 1919.

United States Senate, Intelligence Committee. Washington: Government Printing Office, 1976 to date. (libraries bind by year)

United States Senate, Judiciary Committee, Sub-Committee on Internal Security. Washington: Government Printing Office, 1951 to 1976. (libraries bind by year)

United States Subversive Activities Control Board. *Attorney General v. The Communist Party of the United States of America.* Washington: SACB (mimeographed transcript), 1952.

———. *Attorney General v. Veterans of the Abraham Lincoln Brigade, Recommended Decision.* Washington: SACB, 1955.

Untersuchungsausschuss Freiheitlicker Juristen. *Ehemalige Nationalsozialisten in Pankows Diensten.* (Former National Socialists in the Service of Pankow [East Germany].) 5th ed. West Berlin: Investigating Committee of Free Jurists, 1965.

U.S. v. Julius Rosenberg et al. : Transcript of Record on Appeal. Washington: Supreme Court of the United States, October 1951, reprint by National Committee to Secure Justice in Rosenberg Case, New York, circa 1953.

U.S.S.R. Institute of the International Working-Class Movement. *International Solidarity with the Spanish Republic: 1936–1939.* Moscow: Progress Publishers, 1975.

U.S.S.R. Ministry of Foreign Affairs. *Soviet Peace Efforts on the Eve of WWII.* Moscow: Progress Publishers, 1973.

U.S.S.R. Ministry of Foreign Affairs. *Correspondence Between the Chairman of the Council of Ministers of the U.S.S.R. and the Presidents of the U.S.A. and the Prime Ministers of Great Britain During the Great Patriotic War of 1941–1945*. 2 vols. Moscow: Foreign Languages Publishing House, 1957.

U.S.S.R. People's Commissariat for Foreign Affairs. *Antisovetskie Podlogi* (Anti-Soviet Forgeries). Moscow: Izdanie Litizdata N.K.I.D., 1926.

———. *Anti-Soviet Forgeries* (translation of above). London: Worker's Publications, Ltd., 1927.

———. *The Foreign Policy of Russia: Report to 7th All-Russian Congress of Soviets—Nov. 1918*. London: B.S.P. (British Socialist Party), circa 1920.

U.S.S.R. People's Commissariat of Justice. *Report of Court Proceedings: The Case of the Trotskyite-Zinovievite Terrorist Centre*. Moscow: People's Commissariat of Justice of the USSR, 1936.

U.S.S.R. Special Commission. *The Truth About Katyn*. London: Soviet War News, 1944.

Valtin, Jan [Richard Krebs]. *Out of the Night*. New York: Alliance Book Corporation, 1941.

Vassiliev, B. *How the Communist International Formulates the Problem of Organization*. circa 1931 (mimeo.).

———. "Some Problems of Organization" *Party Organizer*. New York: Central Committee, Communist Party USA, March 1931, 31–32.

Verbitzky, Anatole; and Adler, Dick. *Sleeping with Moscow*. New York: Shapolsky Publishers, 1987.

Vereeken, Georges. *The GPU in the Trotskyist Movement*. London: New Park Publications, 1976.

Vidali, Vittorio. *Diary of the 20th Congress of the Communist Party of the Soviet Union*. Westport Conn./London: Lawrence Hill & Co./The Journeyman Press, 1974.

Voroshilov, K.; Mekhlis, L.; Budyonny, S.; Stern, G. *The Red Army Today: Speeches at the 18th Congress of the C.P.S.U.(B.) March 10–21, 1939*. Moscow: Foreign Languages Publishing House, 1939.

Wakefield, Lowell. *Hitler's Spy Plot in the U.S.A.* New York: Workers Library Publishers, 1939.

Wang Ming. *The Revolutionary Movement in the Colonial Countries* (Speech at 7th Cong. Comintern). New York: Workers Library Publishers, 1935.

Weinstein, Allen. *Perjury: The Hiss-Chambers Case*. New York: Alfred A. Knopf, 1978.

Weiss, Max, et al. *Youth Fights for Peace, Jobs, Civil Rights*. New York: New Age Publishers, May 1940.

Werner, Ruth. *Sonjas Rapport*. East Berlin: Verlag Neus Leben, 1977.

West, Nigel. *A Thread of Deceit: Espionage Myths of World War II*. New York: Random House, 1985.

Whaley, Barton. *Guerrillas in the Spanish Civil War*. Cambridge: Massachusetts Institute of Technology, 1969.

White, Nathan I. *Harry Dexter White: Loyal American*. Waban, Massachusetts: Bessie (White) Bloom Independent Press, Inc., 1956.

Willoughby, General Charles A. *A Partial Documentation of the Sorge Espionage Case*. Tokyo: privately published, 1950.

Winston, Henry. "Our Tasks Today: Report to National Committee Young Communist League July 19, 1941," *Clarity* (theoretical organ of the YCL USA), Summer 1941, 30–40.

Wirsing, Giselher. *One Hundred Families Rule the British Empire*. Berlin: Deutscher Verlag, 1940.

Wolfe, Bertram D. *The Trotsky Opposition: Its Significance for American Workers*. New York: Workers Library Publishers, 1928.

Woltman, Frederick. *The Shocking Story of The Amerasia Case*. New York: New York World-Telegram Corporation, 1950.

Workers (Communist) Party of America. *The 4th National Convention*. Chicago: Daily Worker Publishing, 1925.

Workers Party USA (CP USA). *Report of the Central Executive Committee to the 3rd National Convention The Second Year of the Workers Party of America*. Chicago: Literature Department, Workers Party of America, 1924.

Wraga, Richard. *The TRUST*. Unpublished manuscript, 1955.

Young, C. W. Bill. "Soviet Active Measures in the United States—An Updated Report by the FBI," *Congressional Record*, December 9, 1987 (unbound).

———. "Young Releases FBI Report," in *Congressional Record*, March 24, 1983 (unbound).

Zborowski, Mark. *People in Pain*. San Francisco: Jossey-Bass, 1969.

Zborowski, Mark, and Herzog, Elizabeth. *Life is With People: The Jewish Little-Town of Eastern Europe*. New York: International Universities Press, Inc., 1952.

Zetkin, Klara, et al. *They Knew Lenin, Reminiscences of Foreign Contemporaries*. Moscow: Progress Publishers, 1968.

Zhdanov, A. *The International Situation*. Moscow: Foreign Languages Publishing House, 1947.

Index

About the Authors

Herbert Romerstein investigated Soviet espionage and influence operations for eighteen years as a professional staff member of the U.S. House of Representatives. From 1983 to 1989 he was a senior policy officer for the United States Information Agency, where he was director of the Office to Counter Soviet Active Measures and Disinformation. Romerstein has lectured and written extensively on Soviet espionage, active measures, and international terrorism.

Stanislav Levchenko came to the United States in 1979. He had served the KGB for eight years, reaching the rank of major. His last assignment was as head of the Active Measures section of the KGB in Tokyo, Japan. That unit ran a network of agents assigned to influence the political life of Japan. Levchenko's insights into KGB operations played a major role in alerting the U.S. government to Soviet active measures. He now lectures about KGB operations. Levchenko's autobiography was published in 1988.